# Better Homes and Gardens.

## ANNUAL
## Recipes
### 2004

**Veggie Jumble Stew**
(page 12)

Meredith. Books
Des Moines, Iowa

**Grape Pie**
(page 188)

THIS PAST YEAR, 2004, *BETTER HOMES AND GARDENS®* MAGAZINE FEATURED A SPECIAL SUMMERTIME SERIES ABOUT FAMILY REUNIONS—PLANNING THEM, PUTTING THEM ON, AND PRESERVING THE MEMORIES. As much as we love that kind of reunion—where relatives travel great distances to gather in one spot for days of fun, games, and food—there is another kind of family reunion we celebrate. It happens every evening throughout the country on a much smaller scale: Gathering around the table for a meal shared with those we love. Communing over food is a reunion too. You catch up, laugh, and build connections with each other.

For the 80-plus years of our existence, our mission at *Better Homes and Gardens®* magazine has always been to make people's everyday lives better and more beautiful. That means we want to draw you and yours to the table with recipes you know will work and that will be absolutely delicious—whether you want to get a quick, healthful weeknight dinner on the table any day of the year or you're planning a once-in-a-lifetime party for a special graduate.

Each and every recipe we publish is tested, tasted, and retested in the most trusted kitchen in America—the Better Homes and Gardens® Test Kitchen. We know you have busy lives and want ease and comfort when you walk into the kitchen. We stay on top of trends while always focusing on the kinds of simple, great-tasting, fresh foods you want—and have the time—to make and serve to your friends and family. Only when a recipe meets our editors' and home economists' high standards do we give you our promise of quality.

So you don't have to wait for an invitation to arrive in the mail for your next family reunion. There's a standing invitation at your table every day.

*Karol*

KAROL DEWULF NICKELL, EDITOR IN CHIEF
*Better Homes and Gardens®* magazine

*Better Homes and Gardens® Annual Recipes 2004*
Project Editor: Jan E. Miller
Contributing Editors: Tami Leonard, Joyce Trollope
Contributing Designer: Kimberly B. Zarley
Copy Chief: Terri Fredrickson
Publishing Operations Manager: Karen Schirm
Edit and Design Production Coordinator: Mary Lee Gavin
Editorial Assistants: Cheryl Eckert, Kairee Windsor
Book Production Managers: Pam Kvitne, Marjorie J.
    Schenkelberg, Rick Von Holdt, Mark Weaver
Contributing Copy Editor: Joyce Gemperlein
Contributing Proofreaders: Callie Dunbar, Maria Duryée,
    Gretchen Kauffman, Susan J. Kling
Indexer: Elizabeth Parson
Test Kitchen Director: Lynn Blanchard
Test Kitchen Product Supervisor: Maryellyn Krantz

## Meredith® Books
Editor in Chief: Linda Raglan Cunningham
Design Director: Matt Strelecki
Managing Editor: Gregory H. Kayko
Executive Editor: Jennifer Dorland Darling

Publisher: James D. Blume
Executive Director, Marketing: Jeffrey Myers
Executive Director, New Business Development:
    Todd M. Davis
Executive Director, Sales: Ken Zagor
Director, Operations: George A. Susral
Director, Production: Douglas M. Johnston
Business Director: Jim Leonard

Vice President and General Manager: Douglas J. Guendel

### *Better Homes and Gardens®* Magazine
Vice President/Editor in Chief: Karol DeWulf Nickell
Executive Editor: John Riha
Creative Director: Bradford W.S. Hong
Managing Editor: Lamont D. Olson
Art Director: Michael D. Belknap
Deputy Editor, Food and Entertaining:
    Nancy Wall Hopkins
Editor: Jeanne Ambrose
Associate Editors: Richard Swearinger, Stephen J. Exel
Editorial Assistants: Karen Pollock, Anna Anderson

## Meredith Publishing Group
President, Magazine Group: Jack Griffin
Senior Vice President: Bob Mate
Vice President, Corporate Solutions: Michael Brownstein
Vice President, Creative Services: Ellen de Lathouder
Vice President, Manufacturing: Bruce Heston
Vice President, Consumer Marketing: Karla Jeffries
Vice President, Finance and Administration:
    Max Runciman
Consumer Product Associate Marketing Director:
    Steve Swanson
Business Manager: Darren Tollefson
Database Project Director: Chuck Howell

## Meredith Corporation
Chairman and Chief Executive Officer: William T. Kerr
President and Chief Operating Officer: Stephen M. Lacy

In Memoriam: E.T. Meredith III (1933-2003)

**Pictured on front cover:** Raisin-Apple Cake (see recipe, page 267)

The Recipe Center at www.bhg.com contains more than 10,000 recipes and tips, all tested in the Better Homes and Gardens® Test Kitchen

Our seal assures you that every recipe in *Better Homes and Gardens® Annual Recipes 2004* has been tested in the Better Homes and Gardens® Test Kitchen. This means that each recipe is practical and reliable, and meets our high standards of taste appeal. We guarantee your satisfaction with this book for as long as you own it.

All of us at Meredith® Books are dedicated to providing you with the information and ideas you need to create delicious foods. We welcome your comments and suggestions. Write to us at: Meredith Books, Cookbook Editorial Department, 1716 Locust St., Des Moines, IA 50309-3023.

If you would like to purchase any of our cooking, crafts, gardening, home improvement, or home decorating and design books, check wherever quality books are sold. Or visit us at: bhgbooks.com

# RECIPES FOR BUSY FAMILIES

**Rosy Berries and Melon Salad**
(page 164)

Busy lives and breakneck speeds mean sometimes the best intentions, such as clipping and cooking a delicious-looking recipe from our magazine, go uncompleted. If you missed trying a recipe or two during the past year, here it is—and a whole lot more too! Every recipe that appeared in *Better Homes and Gardens*® magazine during 2004—more than 400 of them—is right here, bound in one handy volume. In addition to the feature stories that appeared in the magazine, there are shorter related stories about ingredients, for quick and easy cooking, and tips for menu planning and entertaining with ease. *Better Homes and Gardens*® *Annual Recipes 2004* is organized by month, so you'll know right where to look for recipes to suit any season or occasion. As a bonus, you also get:

Extra Recipes: A few recipes from two newly revised cookbooks—*Better Homes and Gardens*® *New Grilling Book* and *Better Homes and Gardens*® *New Junior Cook Book*—to whet your appetite for what's new.

Prizewinning Recipes: You'll find the top $400 and $200 blue-ribbon winners from the magazine's monthly Prize-Tested Recipes® contest starting on page 254. You'll also find Honor Roll winners for the monthly contests.

Healthy Recipes and Nutrition Information: Nutrition information is listed with the recipes to help you plan your family's meals. To find out how the nutrition information is calculated for these recipes, turn to page 334. A healthy icon found next to the recipe's nutrition information means that it meets certain calorie, fat, sodium, and cholesterol guidelines.

Fast Recipes and Preparation Times: For recipes that can be prepared in 30 minutes or less, check out the recipes marked with a fast icon next to the prep times. All of the recipes in the book have preparation times that will aid in planning your meal prep schedule. If you can't find some of the basic ingredients on your cupboard shelves while you are cooking, turn to the Emergency Substitutions chart found on page 335.

Kid Friendly: The recipes marked with a special icon next to the title are especially appealing to the younger crowd.

Menu Ideas: Throughout the book you'll find menus that accompany each monthly feature story. You can make every recipe on the menu or just a few to help you create a meal whose elements work beautifully together.

# <sup>2004</sup>contents

124

133

# January

IF SAVING TIME AND MONEY IS ON YOUR NEW YEAR'S RESOLUTION LIST, CHECK OUT THESE FAMILY-PLEASING MEAL SUGGESTIONS.

65 MINUTES

27 MINUTES     20 MINUTES     23 MINUTES

# Fast Dinners Under $15

40 MINUTES

# Fast Dinners Under $15

No-Bake Tuna Noodle Casserole

YOUR NEW YEAR'S SALVATION: HEALTHY FAMILY DINNERS THAT ARE READY IN NO TIME FOR LESS MONEY THAN YOU WOULD SPEND ON TAKEOUT.

## No-Bake Tuna Noodle Casserole

**20 MINUTES**

**$13 TOTAL COST**

Take advantage of the amazing array of flavored cheeses that melt into a creamy sauce when stirred into pasta.

**SHOPPING LIST**
Wagon wheel macaroni
Cucumber-dill light
  semisoft cheese
Solid white tuna in water

**FROM THE PANTRY**
Milk

---

# Meal-planning strategies

With weeknight dinners, the path from fridge to stove to table takes many detours. When your after-work job as parent ranges from trigonometry tutor to marching-band-instrument finder, you need family recipes that are flexible and undemanding.

You can stress or you can strategize. The second option has a much happier ending. Take healthful ingredients, add easy ideas, and build in flavor choices for finicky eaters. Now mealtime becomes manageable, and your kids arrive to 6:30 p.m. choir practice well fed, happy, and on time.

Our form of fast food doesn't mean unhealthy. We've held down the fats and focused on pumping up the nutrition with vegetables and other goodies.

Keeping the cost down is easy: Instead of fancy cuts and expensive add-ons, everyday staples are used in new ways. And, if you don't get to the meal on the night you planned, the ingredients we recommend will be fine in the refrigerator for a few extra days.

Each of these quick-to-serve menus is a complete, hearty meal for four.

---

**Kid Friendly** ## No-Bake Tuna Noodle Casserole

Peas are the traditional side dish with this favorite. Try them in the form of this fresh-tasting pea salad: While the pasta cooks, in a bowl toss together one cup of thawed frozen white whole kernel (shoe peg) corn, one cup of thawed frozen baby peas, a chopped stalk of celery, and one-half of a chopped red sweet pepper. Toss with two tablespoons of vinegar, a teaspoon of brown sugar, and a dash of crushed red pepper. You're finished.

**Fast!** **START TO FINISH:** 20 minutes

| | |
|---|---|
| 8 oz. dried wagon wheel macaroni or medium shell macaroni | 1 12¼-oz. can solid white tuna (water pack), drained and broken into chunks |
| ¼ to ½ cup milk | |
| 1 6½-oz. container light semisoft cheese with cucumber and dill or garlic and herb | |

**1.** Cook pasta in lightly salted water according to package directions. Drain and return to pan.

**2.** To the pasta add ¼ cup of the milk and the cheese. Cook and stir over medium heat until cheese is melted and pasta is coated, adding additional milk as needed to make of creamy consistency. Gently fold in tuna; heat through. Makes 4 servings.

Each serving: 417 cal., 10 g total fat (7 g sat. fat), 66 mg chol., 552 mg sodium, 45 g carbo., 2 g fiber, 33 g pro. Daily Values: 2% vit. A, 7% calcium, 20% iron.

BY RICHARD SWEARINGER PHOTOGRAPHS BY COLLEEN DUFFLEY FOOD STYLING BY ANN DISRUDE PROP STYLING BY JOSEPH BOEHM AND BARB FRITZ

---

## HOW WE ESTIMATED THE COST OF MEALS

Our cost estimates are based on prices of national brands purchased in the Midwest during September 2003. Prices across the country vary widely, according to the USDA, and your final cost will depend on what staples, such as Parmesan cheese, you keep on hand. The estimates include drinks and side dishes. Nutritional analysis will also vary depending on the products you choose.

Using an unsliced loaf allows you to be creative when it comes to cutting the bread slices that go beneath the stew.

# 40
## MINUTES
# $12
## TOTAL COST

## Veggie Jumble Stew

Dinner is quicker and the flavors deeper when you build the dish, layer by layer, all in one pot. Serve the stew over planks of toasty, thick-sliced bread to soak up the savory broth.

**SHOPPING LIST**
New potatoes
Brussels sprouts
Baby carrots
Frozen pearl onions
Celery
Apple
Garlic
Apple cider
White bread
White cheddar cheese

**FROM THE PANTRY**
Olive oil
Flour

## Veggie Jumble Stew

Mix and match the vegetables you and your family like. Keep vegetables small—about thumb size—so that they all reach perfect doneness at the same time. The recipe has been tested both with frozen and fresh vegetables; it's delicious either way. Using fresh, however, adds to the preparation time.

**PREP:** 20 minutes  **COOK:** 20 minutes

| | |
|---|---|
| 2 Tbsp. olive oil | 1 cup frozen pearl onions or purple boiling onions |
| 3 Tbsp. all-purpose flour | |
| ¼ tsp. salt | 2 stalks celery, cut into 1½-inch pieces (1 cup) |
| ¼ tsp. ground black pepper | |
| 1 lb. new potatoes (halve any large potatoes) | 1½ tsp. bottled minced garlic or 3 cloves garlic, minced |
| 1½ cups packaged peeled baby carrots or 3 parsnips, cut into 1½-inch pieces | 1 14-oz. can vegetable broth or chicken broth |
| | 1½ cups apple cider |
| 8 oz. small Brussels sprouts (halve any large sprouts) or one 9-oz. pkg. frozen whole green beans | 1 loaf of unsliced white bread or 6 slices bread |
| | 4 oz. thinly sliced white cheddar cheese or Swiss cheese |
| | Fresh apple wedges |

**1.** In a 4-quart Dutch oven heat oil over medium heat. Stir in flour, salt, and pepper; cook and stir for 2 minutes. Add potatoes, carrots, Brussels sprouts, onions, celery, and garlic. Cook and stir for 5 minutes more.

**2.** Stir in broth and cider. Bring to boiling; reduce heat. Simmer, uncovered, about 20 minutes or until potatoes are tender.

**3.** Meanwhile, cut 6 thick slices lengthwise from loaf of bread (see photo, upper left). If desired, toast bread and halve slices.

**4.** To serve, place bread in 6 shallow bowls or on individual plates. Divide stew among plates, pouring over bread. Top with cheese. Serve with fresh apple wedges. Makes 6 servings.

Each serving: 461 cal., 12 g total fat (4 g sat. fat), 16 mg chol., 818 mg sodium, 72 g carbo., 7 g fiber, 15 g pro. Daily Values: 205% vit. A, 77% vit. C, 25% calcium, 27% iron.

## MIDWEEK SUPPER

Veggie Jumble Stew (above)
served over white bread slices
Fresh fruit salad
Chocolate cake
Iced tea or milk

A DINNER MADE SO LITTLE FINGERS CAN
PICK THE PARTS THEY LOVE.

**Veggie Jumble Stew**

**Turkey Dinner Burgers**

## THE ANSWER TO THE PLEA: "HOW ABOUT A NEW BURGER?"

# 27
**MINUTES**

# $13
**TOTAL COST**

### Turkey Dinner Burgers

This burger couldn't be any meatier, but there's some subtlety here that elevates it to dinner-worthy: a peppery, sweet glaze; a switch to poultry; and the potato roll that brings its own kind of hearty style.

**SHOPPING LIST**

Lean ground turkey
 or chicken
Bread crumbs
Jalapeño jelly
Shredded red cabbage
Red onion
Potato rolls

**FROM THE PANTRY**

Olive oil

Egg

---

**Kid Friendly** **Turkey Dinner Burgers**

For a healthful accompaniment, try a medley of vegetables microwaved and tossed with your favorite salad dressing.

**Fast!** **PREP:** 15 minutes **COOK:** 12 minutes

| | |
|---|---|
| 1 egg, slightly beaten | ¼ cup jalapeño jelly, melted, or barbecue sauce |
| ½ tsp. salt | |
| ¼ tsp. ground black pepper | Packaged shredded red cabbage, thinly sliced red onion, and/or other desired toppings |
| 1 lb. uncooked lean ground turkey or lean ground chicken | |
| ¼ cup fine dry bread crumbs | 4 potato rolls, kaiser rolls, or hamburger buns, split and toasted |
| 1 Tbsp. olive oil | |

**1.** In a bowl combine egg, salt, and pepper. Add turkey and bread crumbs; mix well. Shape the turkey mixture into four ³⁄₄-inch-thick patties.

**2.** In a large nonstick skillet cook patties over medium heat in hot oil for 10 minutes, turning once halfway through cooking, or until an instant-read thermometer inserted into the thickest part of the burgers registers 165° F. Brush patties on each side with jalapeño jelly. Cook 1 minute more on each side.

**3.** To assemble, place cabbage and red onion on bottoms of rolls and top with meat. Makes 4 servings.

**BROILER METHOD:** Place patties on the unheated rack of a broiler pan. Broil 4 to 5 inches from the heat for 10 minutes, turning once halfway through cooking, or until an instant-read thermometer inserted into the thickest part of the burgers registers 165° F. Brush patties on each side with jalapeño jelly. Cook 1 minute more on each side to glaze. Continue with Step 3.

**ELECTRIC TABLETOP GRILL METHOD:** Lightly grease the rack of grill and preheat. Place patties on the grill rack. If using a covered grill, close lid. Grill patties until an instant-read thermometer inserted into the thickest part of the burgers registers 165° F. (For a covered grill, allow 5 to 7 minutes. For an uncovered grill, allow 14 to 18 minutes; turn once halfway through grilling.) Brush patties on each side with jalapeño jelly and cook 1 minute more on each side to glaze. Continue with Step 3.

Each serving: 453 cal., 15 g total fat (3 g sat. fat), 58 mg chol., 835 mg sodium, 48 g carbo., 2 g fiber, 31 g pro. Daily Values: 2% vit. A, 6% vit. C, 12% calcium, 20% iron.

## INSTANT-READ THERMOMETERS

Because it's difficult to know the doneness of a burger just by looking at it, use an instant-read thermometer to check the temperature. For a dial instant-read thermometer, be sure the stem is at least 2 inches into the food. For thin foods, such as burgers, insert it through the side of the burger. When using a digital instant-read thermometer, place the probe at least ¹⁄₂ inch into the food and wait about 10 seconds.

## Smashed Veggie-Cheese Sandwich and Tomato Soup

**Kid Friendly**

**Fast!** **PREP:** 20 minutes **COOK:** 3 or 6 minutes

| | |
|---|---|
| 4 | ½-inch-thick slices country French white bread |
| 4 | ½-inch-thick slices wheat bread |
| 1 | Tbsp. olive oil or cooking oil |
| 2 | Tbsp. honey mustard or bottled ranch salad dressing |
| 3 | to 4 oz. thinly sliced farmer cheese or cheddar cheese |
| ½ | cup thinly sliced cucumber or roma tomatoes |
| ½ | cup fresh spinach leaves or broccoli slaw |
| ¼ | cup thinly sliced red onion or red sweet pepper strips |
| 1 | recipe Tomato Soup (below) |

**1.** Brush 1 side of all 8 bread slices with oil. Brush other side of each bread slice with honey mustard. Lay the French bread slices down with the mustard side facing up. Top French bread with the cheese. Top cheese with cucumber, spinach, and red onion. Top with wheat bread slices, mustard side down.

**2.** Preheat an indoor electric grill or a large skillet over medium heat. Place the sandwiches on the grill rack. If using a covered grill, close lid. Grill sandwiches until bread is golden and cheese is melted. (For a covered grill, allow 3 to 5 minutes. For an uncovered grill or skillet, allow 6 to 8 minutes, turning once halfway through grilling.) Cut each sandwich into 4 slices. Serve Tomato Soup with sandwiches. Makes 4 servings.

**TOMATO SOUP:** In a medium saucepan stir together one 32-ounce container ready-to-serve tomato soup, 1 cup chopped roma tomatoes (about 3), and 1 tablespoon balsamic vinegar. Heat through. Ladle soup into serving bowls. Top each serving with 1 tablespoon plain low-fat yogurt or light dairy sour cream; swirl slightly. Sprinkle soup with 1 tablespoon snipped fresh chives.

Each serving: 365 cal., 10 g total fat (3 g sat. fat), 14 mg chol., 1,200 mg sodium, 58 g carbo., 5 g fiber, 12 g pro. Daily Values: 29% vit. A, 29% vit. C, 18% calcium, 15% iron.

### QUICK DINNER IDEAS **Fast!**

When the day gets out of hand and your three children have to be at three different practices, here are delicious "walking dinner" options.

**CHICKEN PEACH SALAD:** Layer torn salad greens, sliced fresh or canned peaches, baked popcorn chicken, and honey-mustard dressing in a disposable container. Top with baked potato chips or chow mein noodles.

**TUNA-BROCCOLI SALAD:** Toss together packaged shredded broccoli, ready-to-eat tuna from a pouch, almonds, and canned mandarin orange sections, drained. Add a favorite salad dressing.

**RICE-IN-A-CUP:** Toss together leftover cooked rice or packaged cooked rice, frozen peas, and purchased shredded carrot. Cook in the microwave on 100-percent power for 1 to 1½ minutes. Place rice mixture in a reseal-able plastic bag or disposable container. Add a favorite salad dressing.

**Smashed Veggie-Cheese Sandwich and Tomato Soup**

## Smashed Veggie-Cheese Sandwich and Tomato Soup

Sandwiches make satisfying dinners, too, and a tabletop grill makes short work of this crispy, melty farmer cheese version. Layer your family's favorite veggies between the bread slices.

**23 MINUTES**

**$14 TOTAL COST**

**SHOPPING LIST**

Country French and
   whole wheat bread
Farmer cheese
Cucumber
Spinach
Red onion
Canned tomato soup
Roma tomatoes
Plain low-fat yogurt
Chives

**FROM THE PANTRY**

Honey mustard
Balsamic vinegar

AN ENTIRE MEAL
IN ONE PAN, THIS OVEN
MEAL ALLOWS YOU TIME
TO CATCH YOUR BREATH
WHILE IT COOKS.

**Pork Tenderloin with Carrots and Fries**

## Pork Tenderloin with Carrots and Fries

**Kid Friendly**

Find oven cooking bags in the paper products section of your supermarket; find precut vegetables in the produce section.

**PREP:** 15 minutes **ROAST:** 50 minutes

| | |
|---|---|
| 1 Tbsp. all-purpose flour | 2 tsp. dried rosemary, crushed |
| 1 3/4- to 1-lb. pork tenderloin | 1/4 tsp. ground black pepper |
| 1 16-oz. pkg. frozen crinkle-cut sliced carrots, thawed | 1/2 of a 22-oz. pkg. (about 4 cups) frozen french-fried waffle-cut potatoes |
| 1/3 cup pure maple syrup | Salt and ground black pepper |
| 4 Tbsp. olive oil | |

**1.** Preheat oven to 350° F. Shake flour in a large oven cooking bag. Place tenderloin and thawed carrots in bag. In a small bowl combine maple syrup, 2 tablespoons of the oil, 1 teaspoon of the dried rosemary, and the 1/4 teaspoon pepper. Pour into oven bag; close bag using ties provided. Turn bag to coat meat and carrots with maple mixture. Place filled bag on one end of a large roasting pan. Cut six 1/2-inch slits in top of bag.

**2.** In bowl toss potatoes with remaining 2 tablespoons oil and 1 teaspoon rosemary. Transfer to roasting pan next to cooking bag.

**3.** Roast for 30 minutes. Cut open top of bag, being careful to avoid any steam. Roast for 20 to 25 minutes more or until an instant-read thermometer inserted into thickest part of the meat registers 160° F and potatoes are browned and crisp. Carefully remove meat and carrots from oven bag. Season to taste with salt and pepper. Makes 4 servings.

Each serving: 488 cal., 22 g total fat (4 g sat. fat), 50 mg chol., 97 mg sodium, 54 g carbo., 6 g fiber, 20 g pro. Daily Values: 575% vit. A, 27% vit. C, 7% calcium, 17% iron.

## 65 MINUTES

## $10 TOTAL COST

## Pork Tenderloin with Carrots and Fries

The oven cooking bag is a kitchen tool that's underused. It keeps the pork moist while the carrots cook to an ideal state of tenderness.

**SHOPPING LIST**
Pork tenderloin
Crinkle-cut fresh carrots
Maple syrup
Frozen french-fried waffle-cut potatoes

**FROM THE PANTRY**
Rosemary
Black pepper

# QUICK DESSERT IDEAS FOR 4 *Fast!*

**EASY STRAWBERRY SHORTCAKES:** Bake 4 frozen unbaked buttermilk biscuits according to package directions. Cool. Meanwhile, in a small saucepan heat 1/3 cup strawberry jelly just until melted. Slice 1 pint fresh strawberries and place in a bowl; add melted jelly and toss gently to coat. To serve, split the biscuits horizontally. Divide 1/3 cup purchased lemon curd among the 4 biscuit bottoms; replace biscuit tops. Place biscuits on dessert plates. Spoon strawberries over biscuits and top with sweetened whipped cream. *(Start to Finish: 30 minutes)*

**CRUNCHY POUND CAKE SLICES:** Place four 1/2-inch slices purchased pound cake on a baking sheet. Broil 3 to 4 inches from heat for 1 minute on each side or until light brown. Cool slightly. Divide 1/4 cup chocolate-hazelnut spread among the cake slices, spreading on 1 side of each slice. Sprinkle with 1/2 cup coarsely chopped roasted mixed nuts; pat gently to form an even layer. Transfer each slice to a dessert plate and top with a scoop of caramel or vanilla ice cream. Serve immediately. *(Start to Finish: 20 minutes)*

**CREAMY RICE PUDDING:** Prepare one 4-serving-size package instant vanilla pudding mix according to package directions using 2 cups milk; set aside. Meanwhile, heat 1 1/4 cups milk over medium heat just to boiling. Stir in 1 cup quick-cooking rice and 1/4 cup dried tart cherries or snipped dried apricots. Remove from heat; cover and let stand for 5 minutes. Stir in prepared vanilla pudding and 1/4 teaspoon ground cardamom or cinnamon. Serve the pudding warm or cover surface of pudding with plastic wrap and chill. *(Start to Finish: 25 minutes)*

## Stack-It-Up Chicken Salad

**Fast!** **START TO FINISH:** 30 minutes

1 peeled, cored fresh pineapple

1 2- to 2¼-lb. purchased whole roasted chicken

½ head napa cabbage, cut into 1-inch crosswise pieces, or 2 romaine hearts, halved crosswise

1 cup seedless green and/or red grapes, halved

1 Granny Smith apple, cut into chunks

½ cup bottled ginger-sesame stir-fry sauce or 1 recipe Homemade Peanut Dressing (below)

¼ cup creamy peanut butter

¼ tsp. crushed red pepper

Water

**1.** Slice pineapple pieces lengthwise into ½-inch spears. If desired, remove skin from chicken and discard. Remove meat from bones; discard bones. Cut chicken into bite-size pieces. On 4 dinner plates build a stack of alternating layers of cabbage, chicken, grapes, apple chunks, and pineapple.

**2.** In a small bowl whisk together stir-fry sauce, peanut butter, and crushed red pepper until well combined. If necessary, add water, 1 teaspoon at a time, until sauce reaches drizzling consistency. Drizzle sauce over stacked salad. Makes 4 servings.

**HOMEMADE PEANUT DRESSING:** In a small saucepan combine 3 tablespoons rice vinegar, 2 tablespoons reduced-sodium soy sauce, 1 tablespoon peanut butter, 1 tablespoon honey, 1 tablespoon toasted sesame oil, 1 teaspoon minced fresh ginger, 1 teaspoon minced garlic, and ½ teaspoon crushed red pepper. Cook and stir until mixture is combined.

Each serving (skinless chicken): 529 cal., 19 g total fat (5 g sat. fat), 123 mg chol., 998 mg sodium, 44 g carbo., 5 g fiber, 45 g pro. Daily Values: 45% vit. A, 144% vit. C, 7% calcium, 15% iron.

## Stack-It-Up Chicken Salad

**30** MINUTES

**$15** TOTAL COST

**SHOPPING LIST**
Fresh pineapple
Napa cabbage
Deli-rotisseried chicken
Granny Smith apple
Green grapes
Ginger-sesame stir-fry sauce

**FROM THE PANTRY**
Peanut butter
Crushed red pepper

**35** MINUTES

**$10** TOTAL COST

## Pasta with Baby Salisbury Steaks

At last, a sure cure for the kid with a bottomless hunger.

**SHOPPING LIST**
Mafalda pasta
Raisin bread
Ground beef
Zucchini and summer squash
Prepared pasta sauce

**FROM THE PANTRY**
Milk
Onion
Olive oil
Parmesan cheese

**Kid Friendly** **Pasta with Baby Salisbury Steaks**

Here's a bonus recipe for your weeknight repertoire that lets you get reacquainted with that kitchen workhorse, the broiler.

**START TO FINISH:** 35 minutes

Nonstick cooking spray

8 oz. dried mafalda (wide, ripple edge) pasta or spaghetti

2 slices raisin bread or cinnamon-raisin bread, torn into small pieces

¼ cup milk

1 lb. lean ground beef

1 medium onion, finely chopped (½ cup)

1 egg, lightly beaten

½ tsp. dried oregano, crushed

¼ tsp. salt

2 cups sliced zucchini and/or summer squash

1 Tbsp. olive oil

1 26-oz. jar prepared tomato pasta sauce

Finely shredded Parmesan cheese

**1.** Preheat broiler. Lightly coat the rack of a broiler pan with cooking spray; set aside.

**2.** In a large saucepan cook pasta according to package directions. Meanwhile, in a large bowl stir together bread and milk; let stand for 5 minutes. Add ground beef, onion, egg, oregano, and salt. Mix well. Place a piece of waxed paper on a large cutting board. Pat meat mixture into an 8×6-inch rectangle on the waxed paper. Cut the meat mixture in half crosswise and lengthwise to form four 4×3-inch rectangles.

**3.** Using a large spatula, transfer meat to prepared broiler rack. Broil meat 4 to 5 inches from the heat for 12 to 15 minutes, turning once, until an instant-read thermometer inserted into the thickest part of the meat registers 160° F. Cut each rectangle diagonally, forming a total of 8 steaks.

**4.** Drain pasta; set aside. In the same pan cook the zucchini in hot oil for 2 to 3 minutes or until crisp-tender. Stir in pasta sauce and pasta; heat through. Serve steaks with pasta mixture. Sprinkle each serving with cheese. Makes 4 servings.

Each serving: 618 cal., 20 g total fat (7 g sat. fat), 131 mg chol., 1,254 mg sodium, 76 g carbo., 8 g fiber, 37 g pro. Daily Values: 7% vit. A, 33% vit. C, 20% calcium, 35% iron.

**Pasta with Baby Salisbury Steaks**

# STEAK AND PASTA

This steak is the kind the youngsters will like; it's made with seasoned ground beef just like burgers only it's shaped into rectangles. If you prefer, split them in half lengthwise for serving.

# SALAD NIGHT

Some nights you want a dinner that's light and completely no-cook, yet substantial. You can substitute your favorite vegetables, but keep to the specified amounts. If you want to use carrots instead of grapes or add fresh broccoli, no problem! For speed, use the peeled, cored fresh pineapple from the produce section.

**Stack-It-Up Chicken Salad**

# EAT WELL

LET'S FACE IT. FEEDING YOUR FAMILY HEALTHFULLY ISN'T ALWAYS A PIECE OF CAKE. However, it's an achievable goal. Lunch is a good place to begin. A little prep work the night before will launch a lunch that will be the envy of the brown-bag crowd. A flashy tote can make a big difference too.

When packing family-friendly noontime meals, simple is swell. Make a habit of tossing in no-fuss fresh fruit. Here's why:

- Kiwifruit has mega levels of vitamin C and eye-protecting lutein.
- Blueberries contain antioxidants that may enhance memory.
- Purple grapes and purple grape juice can both help maintain a healthy heart.

**▶ A QUICK PICK-ME-UP** The small-fry set will have fun with this finger food. It's fiber-friendly and has calcium-rich cheese—a boon for bones. Wrap cheese sticks and pieces of apple and carrot in a slice of ham. Bundle it up in a lettuce leaf and dunk it into plain yogurt.

**▼ NEED A BURST OF BRAIN POWER?** Test-taking teens might try tuna or salmon salad. The tuna in these mini tacos contains plenty of energy-producing protein, plus omega-3 fatty acids essential for peak brain function.

**▲ BLEARY-EYED?** Those who put in long hours and drive home in the dark will appreciate the addition of carrots and spinach to a favorite sandwich. Carrots are loaded with vitamin A, which helps maintain night vision. Folate-rich spinach may lift harried spirits.

**◀ GOT STRESS?** A natural substance in turkey induces a calm feeling, making it a soothing meal for women on the run. Start the night before by pouring hot broth over couscous. Stir in smoked cooked turkey, dried cranberries, toasted nuts, orange peel, and ground ginger. Refrigerate overnight. Squeeze a fresh orange wedge over it all before eating.

# February

DURING THE HEART OF WINTER THERE'S
GREAT APPEAL IN A WARMING MEAL OR
A DECADENT DESSERT THAT'S
PERFECT FOR SHARING.

# Get Cozy with Lodge Food

Beef Hash with a Spicy Kick

# GET COZY WITH LODGE FOOD

WHEN IT'S BURIED UP TO ITS EAVES IN SNOW, OREGON'S TIMBERLINE LODGE WEATHERPROOFS CHILL-SEEKING VISITORS WITH COMFY-WARM FARE.

## Beef Hash with a Spicy Kick

Canned chipotle peppers often come packed in a tomato-vinegar-chile sauce called adobo. For a hash without as much kick, omit the adobo sauce from the marinade.

**PREP:** 30 minutes **MARINATE:** 30 minutes **COOK:** 15 minutes

| | | | |
|---|---|---|---|
| ½ | cup orange juice | 1 | Tbsp. cooking oil |
| 2 | Tbsp. lime juice | 1½ | lb. Yukon Gold potatoes or |
| 1 | Tbsp. adobo sauce | | red skinned potatoes, |
| | (from canned chipotle | | cooked* and diced |
| | peppers) | 1 | Tbsp. chopped chipotle |
| 1¼ | lb. beef sirloin or top loin | | peppers in adobo sauce |
| | steak, finely chopped | 2 | roma tomatoes, seeded |
| 2 | large onions, diced | | and chopped |
| | (2 cups) | ¼ | cup snipped fresh cilantro |
| 2 | Tbsp. minced garlic or | | Salt and ground black pepper |
| | bottled minced garlic | | Fried eggs (optional) |
| 1 | Tbsp. chili powder | | Fresh cilantro sprig (optional) |

**1.** For marinade, in a large plastic bag set in a bowl combine orange juice, lime juice, and adobo sauce. Add meat, turning the bag to coat the meat. Close bag. Marinate in refrigerator for 30 minutes. Drain and discard marinade. Pat meat dry with clean white paper towels. (Removing as much moisture as possible from the meat makes for a crispy hash.)

**2.** In a 12-inch heavy skillet cook the onion, garlic, and chili powder in hot oil over medium heat for 5 minutes or until onion is tender. Increase heat to medium-high. Add meat to skillet; cook and stir about 2 minutes or until meat is browned. Stir in cooked potatoes and chipotle peppers. Spread in an even layer in the skillet. Cook for 8 minutes more or until potatoes are golden brown, turning occasionally. Stir in tomatoes and snipped cilantro. Season with salt and black pepper. If desired, serve with fried eggs and fresh cilantro. Makes 6 servings.

**\*NOTE:** To cook potatoes, remove eyes from potatoes. Cut potatoes into quarters. Cook, covered, in enough boiling lightly salted water to cover for 20 to 25 minutes or until tender. Drain.

**Healthy** Each serving: 263 cal., 6 g total fat (2 g sat. fat), 45 mg chol., 189 mg sodium, 28 g carbo., 4 g fiber, 24 g pro. Daily Values: 16% vit. A, 51% vit. C, 6% calcium, 23% iron.

### HEARTY WINTER BREAKFAST

Warm Citrus Fruit with Brown Sugar (page 29)
Beef Hash with a Spicy Kick (above)
Fried eggs
Toasted English muffins with berry preserves
Hot coffee or hot spiced tea

BY JEANNE AMBROSE PHOTOGRAPHS BY COLLEEN DUFFLEY FOOD STYLING BY STEPHANA BOTTOM

# Timberline Lodge Fare

Nestled halfway up Mt. Hood, 55 miles east of Portland, Oregon, is a big, toasty bear's den of a lodge. It's perfect for lazy-day hibernating families or outdoor enthusiasts. With snow guaranteed pretty much year-round, skiers and snowboarders make up most of the visitors, but some families come merely for the getaway. Many make the trek solely for the food. "People who come here expect the food to have a lodgy feel, especially in this majestic, outdoorsy setting in the Cascades," says Chef Leif Benson.

Benson's signature hot chocolate has its own following, providing an instantaneous feel-good warm-up from the blustery cold. Served in gigantic glass mugs, the steamy bittersweet drink is topped with bits of toffee and a melty mound of whipped cream.

The lodge has a great homey feel that you'll notice even before you enter the front door. That just-like-home sensation repeats itself each morning in the dining room where fixings for make-your-own Belgian waffles are waiting. Most takers top them with a spoonful of deep purple marionberry compote, a house specialty.

If you'd rather someone else do the cooking, there are plenty of hearty choices to start your day. The menu includes French toast with a crunchy topcoat of granola; an omelet full of smoky ham, cheese, and onion wrapped in featherlight crepes; and grapefruit and orange sections sprinkled with brown sugar and butter, and broiled until caramelized. Once guests are fortified, it's time to bundle up and head for the hills.

Like the first Timberline Lodge chefs who began cooking for families and other visitors in the 1930s, Benson seeks out the freshest ingredients from the Pacific Northwest. "We have rabbit, venison, and bison, along with salmon, and Hood River apples and pears. You can't help but be inspired in these surroundings to create great food," he says.

Even if you can't get to Timberline Lodge, you can re-create the lodgy food at home. Feel free to skip straight to dessert. A spoonful or two of the Bittersweet Mousse served after a lodge-inspired brunch offers a taste of decadence. Or start the morning with a spicy skillet of beef hash and head outdoors to pretend you're in the snowy mountains of the Pacific Northwest.

## Crisp Potato Cakes with Salmon

Both powdered wasabi (Japanese horseradish) and panko (coarse dried bread crumbs) can be found in Asian markets.

**PREP:** 30 minutes **COOK:** 6 minutes per batch

| | |
|---|---|
| 1 recipe Wasabi Cream (below) | 3/4 tsp. salt |
| 3 medium Yukon Gold potatoes (about 1 lb.) | 1/2 tsp. ground black pepper |
| 2 eggs, slightly beaten | 2/3 cup panko (Japanese-style) bread crumbs or coarse dry bread crumbs |
| 1/4 cup snipped fresh chives | 1/4 to 1/3 cup cooking oil |
| 4 slices bacon, crisp-cooked, drained, and crumbled | 1 3-oz. pkg. thinly sliced, smoked salmon (lox-style) |
| 2 Tbsp. dairy sour cream | |

**1.** Prepare Wasabi Cream. Cover and chill in the refrigerator up to 6 hours. Meanwhile, in a medium saucepan cook potatoes, covered, in enough boiling lightly salted water to cover for 15 to 20 minutes or until almost tender. Drain; cool slightly. Peel and remove eyes. Shred potatoes.

**2.** In a large bowl combine shredded cooked potatoes, eggs, chives, bacon, sour cream, salt, and pepper. Shape into eighteen 2-inch patties. Place panko bread crumbs in a shallow bowl. Coat patties, 1 at a time, on both sides.

**3.** In a large skillet heat the oil over medium-high heat. Carefully place patties in the hot oil (cook half of the patties at a time). Cook for 6 to 8 minutes or until crisp and brown, turning once. Remove from skillet. Place patties in a single layer on a baking sheet; keep warm in a 300° F oven. Repeat with remaining potato patties, adding more oil if needed.

**4.** To serve, place a dollop of Wasabi Cream on each potato patty. Top with smoked salmon. Makes 6 servings.

**WASABI CREAM:** In a small bowl combine 2 teaspoons wasabi powder with 2 teaspoons lime juice to form a paste. Stir in 1/2 cup dairy sour cream and a dash of salt.

Each serving: 266 cal., 18 g total fat (6 g sat. fat), 87 mg chol., 750 mg sodium, 16 g carbo., 1 g fiber, 9 g pro. Daily Values: 7% vit. A, 17% vit. C, 4% calcium, 6% iron.

## Bittersweet Mousse with Cinnamon Poached Pears

**PREP:** 30 minutes **COOK:** 12 minutes **COOL:** 15 minutes
**CHILL:** 2 hours

| | |
|---|---|
| 8 oz. bittersweet or semisweet chocolate, coarsely chopped | 1 1/2 cups whipping cream |
| 2 egg yolks, beaten | 1 recipe Cinnamon Poached Pears (below) |
| 1/3 cup sugar | Whipped cream (optional) |
| 1/4 cup water | Chocolate shavings (optional) |

**1.** In a small saucepan combine chopped chocolate, egg yolks, sugar, water, and 1/2 cup of the whipping cream. Cook and stir over medium heat until mixture starts to bubble around edges. Remove from heat. Pour into a large bowl set in a bowl of ice water. Cool 15 to 20 minutes, stirring frequently.

**2.** In a chilled mixing bowl beat remaining 1 cup whipping cream with chilled beaters just until thickened (do not beat to soft peaks or mousse will be too stiff). Fold into cooled chocolate mixture. Cover and chill in the refrigerator 2 to 24 hours.

**3.** Spoon the mousse into individual bowls. Serve with Cinnamon Poached Pears. If desired, top mousse with additional whipped cream and chocolate shavings. Makes 8 servings.

Each serving (mousse and pear): 576 cal., 27 g total fat (16 g sat. fat), 115 mg chol., 26 mg sodium, 70 g carbo., 5 g fiber, 4 g pro. Daily Values: 15% vit. A, 6% calcium, 13% iron.

## Cinnamon Poached Pears

**PREP:** 20 minutes **COOK:** 15 minutes **CHILL:** 2 hours

| | |
|---|---|
| 8 small to medium pears (about 3 lb. total) | 1 cup sugar |
| 1 750-ml bottle dry white wine or 3 cups apple juice | 1 2-inch piece peeled fresh ginger, cut into strips |
| 2 cups water | 3 inches stick cinnamon, broken |

**1.** Peel pears, leaving stems intact. Cut a thin slice from the bottom of each pear so pears stand up. If desired, use a melon baller to remove the core through the bottom of each pear.

**2.** Meanwhile, in a 4-quart Dutch oven combine the wine, water, sugar, ginger, and cinnamon. Cook, uncovered, over medium heat until gently boiling, stirring occasionally to dissolve sugar. Add the pears. Return liquid just to boiling. Reduce heat. Simmer, covered, about 15 minutes or until pears are just tender. Remove from heat and cool pears slightly in syrup. Transfer to a very large bowl. Cover and chill 2 to 24 hours. Drain pears to serve. Makes 8 servings.

**Crisp Potato Cakes with Salmon**

**Bittersweet Mousse with
Cinnamon Poached Pears**

**Stuffed Omelet Crepes**

## Stuffed Omelet Crepes

Look for Black Forest ham in the deli section of your market.

**START TO FINISH:** 30 minutes (if using purchased crepes)

| | |
|---|---|
| 1 recipe Crepes (below) or eight 6-inch purchased crepes | ½ cup chopped green and/or red sweet pepper |
| 6 eggs, lightly beaten | ¼ cup chopped onion |
| ⅓ cup water | 2 oz. Tillamook cheddar cheese or cheddar cheese, shredded (½ cup) |
| ⅛ tsp. salt | |
| ⅛ tsp. ground black pepper | Bottled salsa |
| 2 Tbsp. butter or margarine | |
| 6 oz. Black Forest ham or smoked ham, diced (1¼ cups) | |

**1.** Prepare homemade crepes, if using. (Extra crepes may be stacked with waxed paper in between, placed in freezer containers, and chilled up to 3 days or frozen up to 3 months.)

**2.** Meanwhile, in a medium bowl combine eggs, water, salt, and pepper; set aside. In a large nonstick skillet heat butter over medium heat. Cook ham, sweet pepper, and onion in hot butter for 3 to 4 minutes or until vegetables are tender.

**3.** Pour egg mixture over ingredients in skillet. Cook over medium heat without stirring until mixture begins to set on the bottom and around edge. Using a large spatula, lift and fold partially cooked egg mixture so that the uncooked portion flows underneath. Continue cooking and folding over medium heat for 2 to 3 minutes or until egg mixture is cooked through but is still glossy and moist. Remove from heat. Sprinkle with cheese. Cover and let stand 2 minutes until cheese melts.

**4.** To serve, divide egg mixture into 4 portions. On each of 4 plates overlap 2 crepes, browned sides down. Spoon 1 portion of the egg mixture onto overlapped crepes on each plate. Roll crepes around egg mixture.* Top with salsa. Makes 4 servings.

**CREPES:** In a small mixing bowl combine 1 beaten egg, ¾ cup milk, ½ cup all-purpose flour, 1 teaspoon cooking oil, and a dash of salt; beat with a fork or whisk until smooth. Heat a lightly greased 6-inch skillet over medium heat; remove from heat. Spoon in 2 tablespoons batter; lift and tilt skillet to spread batter. Return to heat; brown on 1 side only. (Or cook on a crepe maker according to manufacturer's directions.) Invert over paper towels to remove crepe. Repeat with remaining batter, lightly greasing skillet occasionally. Makes 11 or 12 crepes.

***TEST KITCHEN TIP:** If crepes are difficult to roll, warm them for a few seconds, 1 at a time, in an 8-inch skillet over medium heat.

Each serving: 375 cal., 23 g total fat (11 g sat. fat), 415 mg chol., 911 mg sodium, 13 g carbo., 1 g fiber, 27 g pro. Daily Values: 22% vit. A, 25% vit. C, 19% calcium, 13% iron.

## CHEF BENSON

Leif Benson, who has been executive chef at Timberline Lodge for 23 years, occasionally uses his family to test out new ideas for the lodge menu. His wife, Shelby, and their four children, ranging in age from 5 to 16, have a variety of food preferences. "One thing I always like to do is go for the wow factor," Leif says. "A little extra spice or herb can make an incredible difference in flavor."

At home, however, the younger children like foods with a more subtle flavor. So to accommodate those who like a bit more zip in their meals, Benson often sets out a range of condiments, including spices and a variety of hot sauces. "That way, they can grind, shake, or drizzle on that extra flavor."

Granola French Toast

Warm Citrus Fruit with Brown Sugar

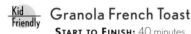

## Granola French Toast

**START TO FINISH:** 40 minutes

| | |
|---|---|
| 3 | eggs, lightly beaten |
| 3/4 | cup milk |
| 1 | Tbsp. granulated sugar |
| 1 | Tbsp. finely shredded orange peel |
| 1/2 | tsp. vanilla |
| 1/4 | tsp. ground cinnamon |
| 12 | 1/2-inch-thick bias-sliced baguette-style French bread |

| | |
|---|---|
| 2 | Tbsp. butter |
| 1 | cup granola, coarsely crushed |
| 1 | recipe Cinnamon-Yogurt Sauce (below) |
| | Maple syrup (optional) |
| | Sifted powdered sugar (optional) |

**1.** In a shallow bowl beat together eggs, milk, granulated sugar, 1 1/2 teaspoons of the orange peel, the vanilla, and cinnamon with a whisk. Dip bread into egg mixture, coating both sides.

**2.** In a skillet or on a griddle melt 1 tablespoon of the butter over medium heat; add half the bread slices. Sprinkle some of the granola on top of each slice of bread in skillet, pressing in gently with spatula. Cook for 3 minutes or until bottom is golden brown. Flip each slice, pressing lightly with the spatula. Cook for 2 minutes more or until golden brown. When removing from pan, flip each slice so granola side is on top.

**3.** Repeat with remaining butter, bread slices, and granola. Serve with Cinnamon-Yogurt Sauce and remaining orange peel. If desired, serve with syrup and sprinkle with powdered sugar. Makes 4 servings.

**CINNAMON-YOGURT SAUCE:** In a bowl combine one 8-ounce container plain low-fat yogurt, 1 tablespoon honey, 1/4 teaspoon ground cinnamon, and 1/4 teaspoon vanilla. Makes 3/4 cup.

Each serving: 501 cal., 16 g total fat (7 g sat. fat), 183 mg chol., 516 mg sodium, 70 g carbo., 6 g fiber, 20 g pro. Daily Values: 12% vit. A, 5% vit. C, 25% calcium, 22% iron.

## Warm Citrus Fruit with Brown Sugar

Use only broiler-safe bakeware for this breakfast compote.

**PREP:** 15 minutes **BROIL:** 5 minutes

| | |
|---|---|
| 2 | medium red grapefruit, peeled and sectioned, or 1 1/2 cups refrigerated grapefruit sections, drained |
| 2 | medium oranges, peeled and sectioned |

| | |
|---|---|
| 1 | cup fresh pineapple chunks or one 8-oz. can pineapple chunks, drained |
| 1/4 | cup packed brown sugar |
| 2 | Tbsp. butter, softened |

**1.** In a medium bowl combine grapefruit, oranges, and pineapple. Transfer to 4 individual broiler-safe au gratin dishes or a 1-quart broiler-safe au gratin dish or casserole.

**2.** In a small bowl stir together brown sugar and butter until well mixed; sprinkle on fruit. Broil about 4 inches from the heat for 5 to 6 minutes until sugar is bubbly. Makes 4 servings.

Each serving: 192 cal., 6 g total fat (4 g sat. fat), 16 mg chol., 68 mg sodium, 35 g carbo., 4 g fiber, 2 g pro. Daily Values: 14% vit. A, 146% vit. C, 6% calcium, 4% iron.

**Oregon Hazelnut Cheesecake**

## Oregon Hazelnut Cheesecake

Sometimes hazelnuts are called filberts. Whole nuts have a brown skin that needs to be removed.

**PREP:** 35 minutes **BAKE:** 55 minutes **COOL:** 2 hours
**CHILL:** 4 hours

| | | | |
|---|---|---|---|
| 1 | recipe Hazelnut Crumb Topping (below) | ½ | cup half-and-half or light cream |
| 2 | tsp. butter | ⅓ | cup honey |
| ¾ | cup hazelnuts (filberts), toasted* and finely ground | 4 | eggs, slightly beaten |
| 3 | 8-oz. pkg. cream cheese, softened | ½ | cup hazelnuts (filberts), toasted* and coarsely chopped |
| 1 | cup sugar | | |
| 2 | Tbsp. sifted cake flour or all-purpose flour | | |

**1.** Prepare Hazelnut Crumb Topping. Set aside.

**2.** Preheat oven to 400° F. For crust, use the butter to grease bottom and 1½ inches up the sides of a 9-inch springform pan. Press ground hazelnuts onto the bottom and sides of the pan. Chill while preparing filling.

**3.** For filling, in a large mixing bowl beat cream cheese, sugar, and flour with an electric mixer until smooth. Stir in half-and-half, honey, eggs, and coarsely chopped hazelnuts.

**4.** Pour filling into nut-lined pan. Place pan in a shallow baking pan. Bake for 20 minutes. Carefully sprinkle Hazelnut Crumb Topping evenly over top of cheesecake. Reduce oven temperature to 300° F and bake for 35 to 40 minutes more or until center appears nearly set when shaken.

**5.** Cool springform pan on a wire rack for 15 minutes. Loosen the crust from the sides of pan; cool for 30 minutes more. Remove the sides of the pan; cool cheesecake completely. Cover and chill at least 4 hours or overnight before serving. (Top may crack upon cooling.) Makes 12 to 16 servings.

**HAZELNUT CRUMB TOPPING:** In a bowl stir together ¼ cup packed brown sugar, 2 tablespoons all-purpose flour, and ⅛ teaspoon ground cinnamon. Using a pastry blender, cut in 2 tablespoons butter until mixture resembles coarse crumbs. Stir in ½ cup toasted hazelnuts (filberts),* chopped.

**\*NOTE:** To toast hazelnuts, preheat oven to 350° F. Spread in a single layer in a shallow baking pan. Bake, uncovered, for 8 to 10 minutes, stirring once or twice, until portions of nuts visible through skin appear lightly browned. Immediately pour out onto a clean kitchen towel. Fold towel over nuts; rub gently with towel to remove skins.

Each serving: 500 cal., 37 g total fat (16 g sat. fat), 144 mg chol., 223 mg sodium, 36 g carbo., 2 g fiber, 10 g pro. Daily Values: 21% vit. A, 2% vit. C, 9% calcium, 12% iron.

**Timberline Hot Chocolate**

## Kid Friendly Timberline Hot Chocolate

This beverage requires a major dollop of *schlag*, the German word for whipped cream.

**Fast!** **START TO FINISH:** 20 minutes

| | | | |
|---|---|---|---|
| 4 | cups milk | 1 | recipe Schlag (below) (optional) |
| ½ | cup water | | English toffee, crushed (optional) |
| ½ | cup sugar | | Unsweetened cocoa powder (optional) |
| 8 | oz. bittersweet or semisweet chocolate, coarsely chopped | | |

**1.** In a saucepan combine milk, water, and sugar. Stir over medium heat until mixture comes just to boiling. Remove from heat. Stir in chocolate. Beat with an immersion blender, rotary mixer, or whisk until chocolate is melted and mixture is frothy.

**2.** To serve, pour hot chocolate into cups. If desired, top with Schlag, English toffee, and cocoa powder. Makes 4 to 6 servings.

**SCHLAG (WHIPPED CREAM):** In a mixing bowl combine 1 cup whipping cream, 2 tablespoons sugar, and 2 teaspoons vanilla. Beat until soft peaks form (tips curl).

Each serving: 491 cal., 24 g total fat (15 g sat. fat), 20 mg chol., 127 mg sodium, 67 g carbo., 4 g fiber, 12 g pro. Daily Values: 10% vit. A, 4% vit. C, 32% calcium, 11% iron.

# Little Bites of
# WONDERFUL

**Lemon-Rose Cookies**

FEBRUARY IS THAT LOVE-IS-IN-THE-AIR MONTH WHEN
EVERYONE SEEMS TO BE SHARING SWEET SOMETHINGS.
SO JOIN IN. OFFER UP A DECADENT DESSERT OR TWO.

# Decadent Treats

Sharing dessert has become an after-dinner ritual because few people have the inclination to consume an entire portion solo. Instead, couples say, "One dessert, two forks, please." So why not think small from the start—but in a big way?

These two-bite treats are just the right size to satisfy that basic human need for a hint of something sweet. There are must-have chocolate, sugared cookies, sips of champagne or sparkling fruit juice over teensy scoops of sorbet, gooey caramel-nut shortbread cookies, or miniature cherry-topped cupcakes. For a bigger crowd, mix and match several of these small wonders to make a huge impression.

**Bittersweet Cheese Truffle**

## Lemon-Rose Cookies

You can find edible flowers in many supermarkets. Be sure any flowers you use have never been sprayed or treated.

**PREP:** 1 hour **BAKE:** 12 minutes per batch

| | |
|---|---|
| ½ cup butter, softened | 2 tsp. finely snipped rose |
| ¼ cup sugar | petals or other edible |
| 1 Tbsp. finely shredded | flowers |
| lemon peel | Coarse sugar or granulated |
| 1 Tbsp. rose water or lemon | sugar |
| juice* | Decorative heart-shape |
| 1¼ cups all-purpose flour | candy sprinkles |
| | Red shoestring licorice |
| | (optional) |

**1.** Preheat oven to 350° F. In a mixing bowl beat the butter with an electric mixer on medium speed for 30 seconds. Beat in ¼ cup sugar until combined. Beat in lemon peel and rose water. Beat in as much flour as you can with the mixer. Using a wooden spoon, stir in any remaining flour and 2 teaspoons rose petals. Form dough into a ball, kneading if necessary until smooth.

**2.** On a lightly floured surface roll half of the dough at a time to about ¼-inch thickness. Using 1½-inch cookie cutters or a pastry wheel, cut dough into desired shapes. Sprinkle each cookie with coarse sugar and top with a heart-shape candy. Place cookies on ungreased cookie sheets.

**3.** Bake for 12 to 15 minutes or until edges are just lightly browned. Transfer cookies to a wire rack to cool completely. If desired, for gift giving, stack pairs of cookies together and tie with shoestring licorice. Makes about 48 cookies.

***NOTE:** If using lemon juice in the dough, decrease lemon peel to 2 teaspoons.

**Healthy** Each cookie: 33 cal., 2 g total fat (1 g sat. fat), 5 mg chol., 21 mg sodium, 3 g carbo., 0 g fiber, 0 g pro. Daily Values: 2% vit. A, 1% vit. C, 1% iron.

## Bittersweet Cheese Truffle

Vivid orange French Mimolette cheese is similar to Dutch Edam in flavor and texture. Aged, dry cheeses, including Parmigiano-Reggiano, taste best with the chocolate, although Swiss cheese is pretty tasty too. A light, fruity red wine makes a perfect companion for these cheesy little numbers.

**PREP:** 30 minutes **CHILL:** 15 minutes

| | |
|---|---|
| 4 oz. French Mimolette, | 3 Tbsp. finely chopped dried |
| aged (dry) Jack, or white | mango, dried apricot, or |
| cheddar cheese | finely chopped pistachio |
| 3 oz. bittersweet chocolate, | nuts |
| chopped | |

**1.** Cut cheese into bite-size chunks; set aside.

**2.** In a small heavy saucepan melt chocolate over low heat, stirring constantly. Dip each cheese piece into chocolate, coating bottom half of cheese. Allow excess chocolate to drip off. Sprinkle with chopped dried fruit or pistachio nuts. Place each piece in a paper candy cup.

**3.** Chill, uncovered, 15 minutes or until chocolate is set. (If not serving immediately, place chocolate-dipped cheese in covered containers and store in the refrigerator up to 24 hours. Let stand at room temperature 15 minutes before serving.) Makes 18 to 24 truffles.

Each truffle: 51 cal., 4 g total fat (2 g sat. fat), 2 mg chol., 42 mg sodium, 3 g carbo., 0 g fiber, 2 g pro. Daily Values: 3% vit. A, 5% calcium, 1% iron.

### Sparkling Sorbet Floats

*Fast!* **START TO FINISH:** 10 minutes

**1.** Place 2 melon-ball-size scoops of mango, peach, and/or strawberry sorbet in the bottom of a cordial or shot glass. Fill glass with chilled champagne or carbonated fruit juice. Makes 1 float.

Each serving: 132 cal., 0 g total fat (0 g sat. fat), 0 mg chol., 3 mg sodium, 18 g carbo., 0 g fiber, 0 g pro. Daily Values: 12% vit. A, 6% vit. C, 1% calcium, 5% iron.

Sparkling Sorbet Floats

## Apricot Cakes for Two

Pick your flavor: For an adult treat, try apricot brandy or raspberry liqueur in the cake batter. Apricot nectar or raspberry juice blend makes a yummy alcohol-free version.

**PREP:** 1 hour **BAKE:** 15 minutes **COOL:** 1 hour

| | | | |
|---|---|---|---|
| 1 | 16-oz. pkg. pound cake mix | 2 | eggs |
| ½ | cup water | 1 | recipe Apricot Butter Frosting (below) |
| ¼ | cup apricot brandy, raspberry liqueur, apricot nectar, or raspberry juice blend | | Edible flower petals or whole edible flowers (optional) |

**1.** Preheat oven to 350° F. Grease and lightly flour a 15×10×1-inch baking pan. Set aside.

**2.** In a large mixing bowl combine cake mix, water, brandy, and eggs. Beat with an electric mixer on low speed for 30 seconds; beat on medium speed for 3 minutes. Spread batter in the prepared pan. Bake about 15 minutes or until a toothpick inserted near center comes out clean. Remove pan to wire rack and cool for 10 minutes. Remove cake from pan and cool completely. Transfer cake to large cutting board.

**3.** Using a 2- to 2½-inch round cutter, cut cake into 12 rounds. (Cube remaining cake scraps to serve another time with fruit, ice cream, or yogurt.) For each cake, spread 1 tablespoon of the frosting on top of 1 cake round. Top with a second cake round. Spread a thin coating of frosting* on the sides of the cake to seal in any crumbs. Let cakes stand, uncovered, 1 hour or until crumb coat is set.

**4.** To frost cake, carefully pick up each cake and add a thicker coating of frosting around the sides. Place cake on serving plate and frost top. Top each cake with edible flower petals. Makes 6 cakes (2 servings per cake).

**APRICOT BUTTER FROSTING:** In a large mixing bowl beat ³⁄₄ cup softened butter until smooth. Add 2 cups sifted powdered sugar, beating well. Slowly beat in ⅓ cup apricot nectar or raspberry juice blend. Gradually beat in 7 cups sifted powdered sugar. Beat in enough additional nectar or raspberry juice blend to reach spreading consistency. Tint frosting a pale peach or pink color.

**\*TEST KITCHEN TIP:** For the thin coating of frosting, transfer ³⁄₄ cup of frosting to a small bowl. Stir in enough apricot nectar or raspberry juice blend (about 1 tablespoon) to make frosting of glazing consistency.

Each serving: 530 cal., 16 g total fat (9 g sat. fat), 56 mg chol., 220 mg sodium, 97 g carbo., 0 g fiber, 2 g pro. Daily Values: 12% vit. A, 3% calcium, 3% iron.

Apricot Cakes for Two

### Kid Friendly  Cherry Baby Cakes

If you make the mini cakes, you'll have plenty to stash—unfrosted—in the freezer in tightly covered containers for up to three months. Thaw and frost the mini cakes when ready to eat more. Or use the batter to make about 16 cupcakes.

**PREP:** 40 minutes  **BAKE:** 12 minutes

| | |
|---|---|
| 1¹/₃ cups all-purpose flour | ²/₃ cup cherry marmalade or cherry preserves, large pieces snipped if necessary |
| ²/₃ cup sugar | |
| 2 tsp. baking powder | |
| ¹/₄ tsp. salt | |
| ²/₃ cup milk | 60 maraschino cherries with stems, drained |
| ¹/₄ cup butter, softened | |
| 1 egg | 1 recipe Powdered Sugar Icing (below) |
| 1 tsp. vanilla | |

**1.** Preheat oven to 350° F. Line sixty 1³/₄-inch muffin cups with miniature paper bake cups;* set aside.

**2.** In a large mixing bowl combine flour, sugar, baking powder, and salt. Add milk, butter, egg, and vanilla. Beat on low speed until combined. Beat on medium speed for 1 minute. Spoon 1 scant teaspoon of batter into each muffin cup. Add ¹/₂ teaspoon of cherry marmalade and top with ¹/₂ teaspoon additional batter.

**3.** Bake cupcakes about 12 minutes or until toothpick inserted in centers comes out clean. Cool in pans on a wire rack for 5 minutes. Remove from pans; cool completely on wire rack.

**4.** Pat cherries dry with clean paper towels. Drizzle each cupcake with about ¹/₂ teaspoon icing. Dip half of each cherry into remaining icing; place on top of cakes. Makes about 60.

**POWDERED SUGAR ICING:** In a small bowl combine 2¹/₂ cups sifted powdered sugar, ¹/₂ teaspoon vanilla, and 2 tablespoons milk. Stir in additional milk, 1 teaspoon at a time, until icing reaches drizzling consistency.

**\*TEST KITCHEN TIP:** If you don't have 1³/₄-inch muffin cups, line sixteen 2¹/₂-inch muffin cups with paper bake cups. Prepare batter as directed. Spoon 1 tablespoon batter into each prepared muffin cup. Add 1 teaspoon of marmalade and another tablespoon of batter. (You will only use about ¹/₃ cup marmalade.) Bake about 15 minutes or until toothpick inserted in centers comes out clean. Frost with Powdered Sugar Icing. Add a cherry as directed in Step 4. (You will need 16 cherries.)

Each cake: 63 cal., 1 g total fat (1 g sat. fat), 6 mg chol., 36 mg sodium, 13 g carbo., 0 g fiber, 0 g pro. Daily Values: 1% vit. A, 1% calcium, 1% iron.

### Peanut Butter Mousse

As an option to piping the mousse into small portions, place it in a bowl and let everyone dip into it with chunks of chocolate.

**PREP:** 30 minutes  **CHILL:** 2 hours

| | |
|---|---|
| 1 2- to 3-oz. bittersweet or semisweet chocolate bar | 2 Tbsp. milk |
| ¹/₃ cup whipping cream | ¹/₂ cup sifted powdered sugar |
| ¹/₂ of an 8-oz. pkg. cream cheese, softened | ¹/₂ tsp. vanilla |
| ²/₃ cup creamy peanut butter (do not use natural peanut butter) | 1 recipe Chocolate Ganache (below) |

**1.** For chocolate curls, with a vegetable peeler scrape along the edge of the chocolate bar to get small shavings; set aside.

**2.** In a chilled small mixing bowl beat whipping cream with chilled beaters of an electric mixer on low to medium speed until soft peaks form; set aside.

**3.** In a medium mixing bowl beat cream cheese, peanut butter, and milk with an electric mixer until combined. Beat in powdered sugar and vanilla until mixture is smooth. Gently fold in beaten whipped cream, half at a time, until mixture is smooth. Cover and chill for 2 hours or up to 24 hours.

**4.** To serve, using a pastry bag* fitted with a large star tip, pipe peanut butter mousse into the bowls of 16 teaspoons. Using a pastry bag fitted with a small round tip, pipe Chocolate Ganache over peanut butter mousse on spoons. Sprinkle mousse with chocolate curls. Makes 16 servings.

**CHOCOLATE GANACHE:** In a small saucepan bring 3 tablespoons whipping cream just to boiling over medium-high heat. Remove from heat. Add 1¹/₂ ounces chopped bittersweet or milk chocolate (do not stir). Let stand 5 minutes. Stir until smooth.

**\*TEST KITCHEN TIP:** Instead of a pastry bag, fill a plastic sandwich bag with mousse. Snip 1 of the bottom corners and squeeze the mousse from the bag. The technique works for ganache too.

Each serving: 146 cal., 12 g total fat (5 g sat. fat), 19 mg chol., 75 mg sodium, 8 g carbo., 1 g fiber, 4 g pro. Daily Values: 4% vit. A, 2% calcium, 2% iron.

## SHOWING OFF THE BITES

Showing off your valentine creations is half the fun. Search out pink or red vellum to wrap up a nibble or two. Muffin-size paper bake cups in silver are perfect containers for individual bites. Serve the tiny bites on a pedestal. To make a mini pedestal, flip a votive candleholder upside down and top it with a dessert or salad plate. Or find an oversize pillar candlestand to raise the tiny desserts to new levels. Even teaspoons can be used as individual serving "bowls" for dollops of creamy mousse; line the spoons up on a small platter for serving.

**Cherry Baby Cakes**

**Peanut Butter Mousse**

Bread Pudding and a Kiss

## Bread Pudding and a Kiss

This treat was inspired by a creation of pastry chef Dan Hahn of Taste on Melrose in Iowa City, Iowa. His bread puddings have a rich chocolate truffle tucked into the center and are topped with a drizzle of caramel sauce.

**PREP:** 20 minutes **BAKE:** 40 minutes **COOL:** 30 minutes

| | | | |
|---|---|---|---|
| 1 | 1-lb. loaf banana bread (purchased or homemade) | 1/4 | cup sugar |
| 4 | egg yolks, beaten | 25 | milk chocolate kisses or chocolate truffles |
| 2 | cups half-and-half or light cream | | |

**1.** Preheat oven to 350° F. Cut banana bread into 1-inch cubes; place in an ungreased 2-quart square (8×8×2-inch) baking dish.

**2.** In a medium mixing bowl beat together egg yolks, half-and-half, and sugar. Pour egg mixture evenly over bread mixture.

**3.** Bake, uncovered, for 40 to 45 minutes or until puffed and a knife inserted off-center comes out clean (center will appear moist but will set up with standing). Immediately cut into 25 squares (about 1½×1½ inches) in dish. Place a chocolate kiss on top of each bread pudding square. Cool 30 minutes before serving. Makes 25 servings.

**MAKE-AHEAD DIRECTIONS:** Prepare recipe through Step 2. Cover and chill in the refrigerator up to 24 hours. Uncover and bake in a 350° F oven for 45 to 50 minutes or until puffed and a knife inserted off-center comes out clean (center will set up with standing).

Each serving: 128 cal., 6 g total fat (3 g sat. fat), 50 mg chol., 68 mg sodium, 16 g carbo., 0 g fiber, 2 g pro. Daily Values: 4% vit. A, 1% vit. C, 4% calcium, 2% iron.

**Nutty Shortbread**

Make someone feel extra special by creating a gift tag to present along with some little bites of wonderful. Use pink, white, or ivory papers in layers. Snip and embellish the tags with glittery stick-ons or tiny bows or ribbons. Finish by penning a love note.

## Nutty Shortbread

The warm, gooey nut mixture is also fantastic over ice cream. The chipotle powder gives it a touch of heat, but it's tasty without it too.

**PREP:** 20 minutes **COOL:** 15 minutes

| | | | |
|---|---|---|---|
| 2 | Tbsp. butter | 1/4 | tsp. smoked chipotle powder or smoked paprika (optional) |
| 1/4 | cup packed brown sugar | | |
| 2 | Tbsp. light-colored corn syrup | 1/2 | tsp. vanilla |
| 3/4 | cup lightly salted mixed nuts | 8 | 2³/4×1-inch purchased shortbread cookies, cut in half crosswise |

**1.** In a small heavy saucepan combine butter, brown sugar, and corn syrup. Bring to boiling over medium heat. Remove from heat. Stir in mixed nuts, chipotle powder (if using), and vanilla; set aside to cool 15 minutes.

**2.** Spoon warm nut mixture on top of cookies. Let stand at least 15 minutes before serving. Makes 16 servings.

Each serving: 118 cal., 7 g total fat (2 g sat. fat), 8 mg chol., 68 mg sodium, 12 g carbo., 1 g fiber, 2 g pro. Daily Values: 2% vit. A, 1% calcium, 2% iron.

# WINTER WARMS UP TO
# radicchio

## Four ways to cook it

When you're crying for fresh produce in the dead of winter, consider radicchio. It's the brilliant red and creamy white member of the chicory family, and a distant cousin to lettuce. Although available year-round, radicchio has its peak season in January and February. Radicchio adds a delightful splash of color and a slightly spicy bite to green salads, but it also makes a particularly wonderful cooked side dish.

Before cooking radicchio, rid it of its overly bitter flavor by soaking wedges in ice water. Cooked radicchio will easily accompany Italian, Asian, and Southern dishes. Give it a try.

**Poached Radicchio**

Two common varieties of radicchio are Chiogga (*left*), or Verona, which resembles a softball-size head of lettuce, and Treviso (*right*), milder in flavor and similar in appearance to a red Belgian endive. When purchasing radicchio, look for full colored leaves with no browning. Refrigerate it in a plastic bag for up to 1 week.

## Poached Radicchio

**Prep:** 10 minutes **Soak:** 30 minutes **Cook:** 15 minutes

| | |
|---|---|
| 1 | medium radicchio (8 or 9 oz.) |
| 2 | Tbsp. butter |
| ¼ | tsp. kosher salt |
| ¼ | cup water |
| 2 | tsp. fresh lime juice |

¼ tsp. anise seeds
Asiago cheese or Parmesan cheese, shaved
1 Tbsp. pine nuts, toasted
Snipped chives

**1.** Cut radicchio lengthwise into 4 wedges; remove root end. Trim a small amount of the pointed edge of wedge to create a flat side. Soak in ice water 30 to 45 minutes. Drain; pat dry with paper towels.

**2.** In a medium saucepan heat butter until bubbly. Place wedges, trimmed side down, in saucepan. Sprinkle with the kosher salt. Add the water. Bring to boiling; reduce heat.

**3.** Simmer, covered, for 2 minutes. Turn wedges over. Top with lime juice, anise seeds, and a generous amount of shaved Asiago cheese. Cook, covered, about 2 minutes more until cheese melts. Return to boiling and cook, uncovered, for 8 to 10 minutes more until radicchio is tender and most of the liquid has evaporated.

**4.** Transfer radicchio to a serving plate; drizzle with remaining cooking liquid. Sprinkle with pine nuts and chives. Makes 4 servings.

Each serving: 145 cal., 13 g total fat (8 g sat. fat), 31 mg chol., 349 mg sodium, 3 g carbo., 1 g fiber, 5 g pro. Daily Values: 5% vit. A, 8% vit. C, 13% calcium, 3% iron.

## Steamed Radicchio

**Prep:** 10 minutes **Soak:** 30 minutes **Cook:** 5 minutes

| | |
|---|---|
| 1 | medium radicchio (8 or 9 oz.) |
| 1 | tsp. chili oil |
| 3 | or 4 cloves garlic, sliced |

½ tsp. grated fresh ginger
¼ cup bottled Asian peanut sauce

**1.** Cut radicchio lengthwise into 4 wedges; remove root end. Soak radicchio in ice water for 30 to 45 minutes. Drain and pat dry with paper towels.

**2.** Place radicchio wedges in a single layer in a bamboo steamer, steamer basket, or electric steamer. Steam about 5 minutes until tender but not wilted.

**3.** Meanwhile, in a small saucepan heat chili oil until hot. Add garlic and ginger. Cook and stir 15 seconds. Stir in peanut sauce; heat through. Transfer radicchio to a serving plate. Spoon sauce over radicchio; serve immediately. Makes 4 servings.

Each serving: 56 cal., 3 g total fat (0 g sat. fat), 0 mg chol., 323 mg sodium, 6 g carbo., 1 g fiber, 2 g pro. Daily Values: 8% vit. C, 2% calcium, 3% iron.

## Grilled Radicchio

**Prep:** 10 minutes **Soak:** 30 minutes **Cook:** 5 minutes

| | |
|---|---|
| 1 | medium radicchio (8 or 9 oz.) |
| 1 | Tbsp. olive oil |
| | Kosher salt |

Freshly ground black pepper
White cheddar cheese, thinly sliced
Thinly sliced prosciutto

**1.** Cut radicchio lengthwise into 8 wedges; remove root end. Soak wedges in ice water for 30 to 45 minutes. Drain and pat dry with paper towels.

**2.** Preheat a ridged grill pan over medium-high heat.

**3.** Brush radicchio wedges with olive oil. Sprinkle lightly with kosher salt and freshly ground black pepper. Place radicchio wedges, cut side down, on ridged grill pan. Cook 2 to 3 minutes. Turn wedges. Top with a few thin slices of white cheddar cheese and some prosciutto. Cook about 2 minutes more until radicchio is tender and cheese is melted. Serve immediately. Makes 4 servings.

Each serving: 142 cal., 11 g total fat (5 g sat. fat), 27 mg chol., 455 mg sodium, 3 g carbo., 0 g fiber, 8 g pro. Daily Values: 5% vit. A, 7% vit. C, 16% calcium, 3% iron.

## Sautéed Radicchio

**Prep:** 15 minutes **Soak:** 30 minutes **Cook:** 7½ minutes

| | |
|---|---|
| 1 | medium radicchio (8 or 9 oz.) |
| 1 | medium onion, cut into slivers |
| 1 | Tbsp. walnut oil or olive oil |
| 1 | tsp. orange peel, finely shredded |

½ tsp. kosher salt
1 Tbsp. full-flavored molasses
Finely shredded orange peel (optional)

**1.** Cut radicchio lengthwise into 4 wedges; remove root end. Soak in ice water for 30 to 45 minutes. Drain; pat dry with paper towels. Remove core. Separate radicchio leaves. Tear into large pieces; set aside.

**2.** In a large saucepan cook onion in hot oil over medium heat for 5 to 7 minutes until tender, stirring occasionally. Stir in the 1 teaspoon orange peel and kosher salt. Add torn radicchio leaves. Cook and stir for 2 minutes. Add molasses. Cook and stir 30 seconds more.

**3.** Place in a serving bowl. If desired, garnish with additional finely shredded orange peel. Serve immediately. Makes 4 servings.

**Healthy** Each serving: 63 cal., 4 g total fat (0 g sat. fat), 0 mg chol., 255 mg sodium, 8 g carbo., 1 g fiber, 1 g pro. Daily Values: 10% vit. C, 3% calcium, 3% iron.

BY STEPHEN EXEL PHOTOGRAPHS BY GREG SCHEIDEMANN [N] HAUS FOTO FOOD STYLING BY BROOKE LEONARD

# CUPID SIPS

**DAD'S
BERRY BLEND**
Pour a smidge of raspberry or cranberry syrup in a tall glass. Top with Dad's favorite chilled pilsner or lager. Garnish the duo with a skewer of cranberries and apple chunks.

**MOM'S
RUBY FIZZ**
Wet the rim of a champagne flute; dip in coarse red sugar to coat. Pour raspberry or pomegranate syrup into flute. Top with chilled champagne or sparkling wine; stir gently.

**TEEN CANDY
SLUSH**
Freeze a raspberry juice blend in ice trays. Place some of the frozen cubes in a food processor. Process until slushy; spoon into glass. Add chilled lemon-lime carbonated beverage and a red licorice twist.

**KID'S
CHERRY TEMPLE**
Pour raspberry or strawberry syrup into a tall glass. Fill glass with ice. Add chilled pineapple juice to fill the glass halfway. Top with chilled ginger ale. Garnish the drink with a maraschino cherry frozen in an ice cube.

PHOTOGRAPHS BY **GREG SCHEIDEMANN [N] HAUS FOTO**

# HEARTS TO YOU

## From the Test Kitchen

When it comes to Valentine's Day treats, it's smart to put your best heart forward. Whether you make them from scratch or embellish purchased treats, these easy ideas will surely win Cupid's heart. **(Clockwise from far right)**

**A Date to Remember:**
Wax nostalgic with a red velvet chocolate cake covered in buttercream icing. Add glamour by outlining with pink candies.

**Heart Mates:**
Decorate brownies using a heart stencil and pink and red sugars. For each, cover top with one color sugar, then place heart stencil on top and fill in with alternating color.

**Love Me Tender:**
Shower vanilla frosted cupcakes with sweetened, flaked coconut and a sprinkling of edible pink glitter.

**Pretty in Pink:**
Any lollipop bouquet will bloom in a glass of pink jelly beans.

## WHO COULD RESIST THIS OFFER OF LOVE IN THE FORM OF A GRILLED CHOCOLATE-BANANA SANDWICH?

For each sandwich, place an ample piece of a chocolate bar on one piece of white bread. Top with banana slices and a second piece of bread. In a skillet heat a generous slice of butter over medium-low heat just until it begins to bubble. Add the decadent sandwich, chocolate side down. Cover the skillet. Cook until the bread is golden brown. Carefully flip sandwich over and repeat, adding more butter if necessary. Dust with powdered sugar. Serve warm.

# March

GATHER THE FAMILY FOR AN
EVENING OF FUN AND
GOOD FOOD.

# Western Movie Night

# Western
## MOVIE NIGHT

Texas Red Chili and Fry Bread

CORRAL THE FAMILY FOR A NIGHT AT THE FLICKS
WITH A ROUNDUP OF COWBOY-INSPIRED TV MEALS.

BY STEPHEN EXEL PHOTOGRAPHS BY COLLEEN DUFFLEY FOOD STYLING BY BROOKE LEONARD PROP STYLING BY KAREN JOHNSON

## Texas Red Chili

Cornmeal thickens this chili stew. You can make the stew ahead of time and reheat it over low heat, stirring frequently so the cornmeal does not settle to the bottom of the pot.

**PREP:** 35 minutes for chili **COOK:** 1½ hours for chili

| | | | |
|---|---|---|---|
| 2½ | lb. boneless beef chuck roast, cut into ¾-inch cubes | 2 | 15- to 16-oz. cans pinto and/or red kidney beans, rinsed and drained |
| 2 | Tbsp. cooking oil | 1 | recipe Fry Bread (recipe page 48) or flour tortillas |
| 1 | medium onion, chopped (½ cup) | ½ | cup cold water |
| 4 | cloves garlic, minced | ¼ | cup cornmeal or Masa Harina (corn tortilla flour) |
| 2 | 14½-oz. cans diced tomatoes, undrained | ¼ | cup snipped fresh cilantro |
| 1 | 10½-oz. can condensed beef broth | 2 | oz. queso blanco or Monterey Jack cheese, shredded |
| 1 | 10-oz. can enchilada sauce | | |

**1.** In a 5- to 6-quart Dutch oven brown beef cubes, half at a time, in hot oil over medium-high heat, adding onion and garlic with second half of meat. Drain off fat. Return all meat to pan.

**2.** Stir in undrained tomatoes, beef broth, and enchilada sauce. Stir in beans. Bring to boiling; reduce heat. Simmer, covered, for 1 hour, stirring occasionally. (Prepare Fry Bread, if using; keep warm while finishing chili.) Uncover chili; simmer about 30 minutes more or until beef is tender, stirring occasionally.

**3.** In a small bowl stir together the cold water and cornmeal. Stir into stew. Cook, uncovered, 10 minutes more or until thickened, stirring frequently. Stir in cilantro just before serving. To serve, place Fry Bread in bowls. Ladle chili over Fry Bread. Top each serving with some of the cheese. Makes 6 servings.

**SLOW COOKER VARIATION:** Brown the meat, onion, and garlic as directed; drain off fat. Transfer meat mixture to a 4½- to 6-quart slow cooker. Stir in undrained tomatoes, beef broth, and enchilada sauce. Stir in beans. Cover and cook on high-heat setting for 6 to 7 hours. In a small bowl stir together ½ cup cold water and ⅓ cup cornmeal or Masa Harina (corn tortilla flour). Stir into stew in cooker. Cover and cook on high-heat setting for 15 minutes longer. Stir in cilantro just before serving. Serve with Fry Bread and cheese as directed above.

Each serving (chili and bread): 764 cal., 27 g total fat (7 g sat. fat), 123 mg chol., 1,728 mg sodium, 71 g carbo., 9 g fiber, 56 g pro. Daily Values: 19% vit. A, 35% vit. C, 25% calcium, 49% iron.

# Tasty Grub

Westerns work wonders at bringing the family together for a night of TV movies and dinner. The lure of the range brings out the cowpoke in all of us, along with the chance to heap a plate high with some hearty cowboy dishes.

Start with a steaming bowl of Texas Red Chili and Fry Bread (a Native American flatbread) studded with cilantro that sops up the chili's sauce and thickens it as the bread breaks up. Apples, grapes, and dill pickles are stirred together to make a tangy coleslaw called Apple Cowboy Slaw. The sprightly sweet-and-sour combination pays homage to the Western settlers of German heritage.

No question about it, Chicken Fingers with Redeye Ketchup is the quintessential movie-watching food: These crunchy nibbles laced with a hint of heat will last all the way to intermission.

A cast-iron skillet's ability to retain heat and sear meat keeps the beef for Westward Ho Flank Steak Sandwiches tender. Of course, a good cast-iron skillet was an essential piece of equipment for any ranch kitchen.

With the addition of tomatoes, a cidery-sweet vinegar sauce becomes the base for a gooey Mop Sauce Pizza. Mop Sauce gets its name from a utensil similar to a small string mop that the chuck wagon cook would use to baste meats, literally mopping on the sauce while cooking.

With buttermilk widely available to ranch cooks, its thick, tangy flavor showed up in everything from fried chicken to pies and biscuits. Use it for homemade Crunchy Buttermilk Ice Cream, and you'll have a great treat.

For the final scene, slice up a ginger-spiced Apricot and Apple Jelly Stack Cake. Don't be surprised by the pine nuts sprinkled on top—in the Southwest, they're known as piñons and are widely used. Stack Cakes were the wedding cakes of the frontier. With frugality always a concern, guests would bring one cake layer and a "put-up" fruit topping, then the cake was assembled at the feast. It's a potluck-style cake.

When tired rancheros were welcomed back from the range with a big bowl of chili, the evening's entertainment was more likely a hoedown than a movie with the kids. Regardless, it's all about a good meal and the place you call home. Slide in a DVD and pull up a pillow, pardner.

Apple Cowboy Slaw

Fry Bread

## Apple Cowboy Slaw

To save time, use preshredded cabbage. For the pickles, choose the level of sharpness that pleases you most.

**PREP:** 25 minutes  **CHILL:** 2 hours

| | |
|---|---|
| 1/3 cup mayonnaise | 4 cups coarsely shredded |
| 2 Tbsp. cider vinegar or malt | cabbage |
| vinegar | 2 medium tart red |
| 2 Tbsp. sugar | and/or green apples, |
| 2 tsp. coarse-grain brown | cored and chopped |
| mustard | 3 large whole dill pickles, |
| 1/2 tsp. salt | chopped (1 cup) |
| 1/2 tsp. freshly ground black | 1/2 cup seedless green or red |
| pepper | grapes, halved |
| | 1/4 cup chopped onion |

**1.** In a small bowl stir together the mayonnaise, vinegar, sugar, mustard, salt, and pepper.

**2.** In a large bowl combine cabbage, apples, pickles, grapes, and onion. Add the mayonnaise mixture to the cabbage mixture; toss to coat. Cover and chill in the refrigerator for 2 to 6 hours before serving. Stir before serving. Makes 6 to 8 servings.

Each serving: 163 cal., 10 g total fat (1 g sat. fat), 4 mg chol., 713 mg sodium, 18 g carbo., 3 g fiber, 1 g pro. Daily Values: 4% vit. A, 34% vit. C, 3% calcium, 4% iron.

The Fry Bread will be golden brown and have a few surface bubbles when it's finished. Wrap cooked Fry Bread in foil and keep in a warm oven until ready to serve.

## Fry Bread

**START TO FINISH:** 1 hour

| | |
|---|---|
| 1 1/2 cups all-purpose flour | 3/4 cup water |
| 1/2 cup cornmeal | 1/3 cup snipped fresh cilantro |
| 1 tsp. salt | 1 Tbsp. shortening or |
| 1/4 tsp. baking powder | cooking oil |
| 1/4 cup shortening | |

**1.** In a large bowl stir together all-purpose flour, cornmeal, salt, and baking powder. With a pastry blender, cut in shortening until mixture is the consistency of small peas. Add water and cilantro all at once. Stir just until dough forms a ball (dough will be slightly sticky). Divide dough into 6 portions.

**2.** On a floured surface roll each portion to a 7-inch circle. In a 10-inch heavy skillet heat shortening over medium heat. Fry 1 dough circle at a time for 2 to 3 minutes per side or until golden brown, turning once. Add additional shortening as needed. If fry bread begins to brown too quickly, reduce heat to medium-low. Makes 6 servings.

Each serving: 242 cal., 11 g total fat (3 g sat. fat), 0 mg chol., 408 mg sodium, 31 g carbo., 2 g fiber, 4g pro. Daily Values: 6% vit. A, 2% vit. C, 2% calcium, 9% iron.

## Chicken Fingers with Redeye Ketchup

**Kid Friendly**

For the chicken, a cast-iron skillet maintains constant, even heat for the crispiest results, but use your deep-fat fryer for equally good results. Find chipotle chili powder in the spice section of the grocery store.

**PREP:** 1 hour **MARINATE:** 1 hour **COOK:** 5 minutes per batch

| | |
|---|---|
| 1½ to 2 lb. chicken tenders | ½ tsp. chipotle chili powder |
| 1 cup buttermilk | ½ of a 32-oz. pkg. frozen french-fried crinkle-cut potatoes |
| 1 tsp. salt | |
| ¼ to ½ tsp. bottled hot pepper sauce | |
| 1 recipe Redeye Ketchup (below) | 1¼ cups all-purpose flour |
| 2 cups plus 2 Tbsp. peanut oil or cooking oil | 1 cup finely chopped peanuts* |
| 2 Tbsp. snipped fresh cilantro | ¼ cup snipped fresh cilantro |
| | ¾ tsp. freshly ground black pepper |

**1.** Place chicken in a large self-sealing plastic bag set in a large bowl. Combine buttermilk, salt, and hot pepper sauce. Pour over chicken in bag. Close bag. Chill in the refrigerator for 1 to 24 hours, turning bag occasionally. Prepare Redeye Ketchup; cover and chill until serving time.

**2.** In a large mixing bowl combine the 2 tablespoons peanut oil, 2 tablespoons cilantro, and chipotle chili powder. Add french fries and toss to coat. Spread on a baking sheet in a single layer. Bake according to package directions.

**3.** Meanwhile, in a shallow dish combine flour, chopped peanuts, the ¼ cup cilantro, and black pepper. Remove chicken pieces from buttermilk mixture, shaking off excess. Coat a few pieces of chicken at a time with flour mixture.

**4.** In a deep 12-inch cast-iron skillet or extra-large deep skillet heat the remaining 2 cups peanut oil over medium heat until a bread cube dropped into the oil browns quickly. Using tongs, carefully add 4 coated chicken tenders to skillet. (Once the chicken has been added, maintain oil temperature at 325° F.) Fry chicken in hot oil about 5 minutes or until chicken is no longer pink (170° F) and coating is golden brown. Drain on paper towels. Transfer to baking sheet along with fries.

**5.** Reduce oven temperature to 300° F and keep chicken and fries in warm oven while frying remaining chicken. Serve chicken and fries with Red Eye Ketchup. Makes 6 servings.

**REDEYE KETCHUP:** In a small saucepan combine 1 cup ketchup, 2 teaspoons instant coffee crystals, and ⅛ teaspoon chipotle chili powder. Cook and stir over medium heat until coffee crystals are dissolved. Cover and chill until serving time.

***TEST KITCHEN TIP:** To save time, chop the peanuts by pulsing them briefly in a food processor or in a mini food chopper.

Each serving: 822 cal., 49 g total fat (8 g sat. fat), 67 mg chol., 1,101 mg sodium, 60 g carbo., 6 g fiber, 40 g pro. Daily Values: 17% vit. A, 28% vit. C, 10% calcium, 21% iron.

**Chicken Fingers with Redeye Ketchup**

**Westward Ho Flank Steak Sandwiches**

## MOVIE NIGHT SUPPER

Westward Ho Flank Steak Sandwiches (right)

Apple Cowboy Slaw (page 48)

Crunchy Buttermilk Ice Cream (page 55)

Lemonade or soft drinks

## Westward Ho Flank Steak Sandwiches

Sourdough bread was a staple for cowpokes on the trail. Purchase sourdough rolls from your favorite bakery (you can special order square-cut rolls if you like) or serve this sandwich on sliced sourdough bread.

**PREP:** 35 minutes  **COOK:** 30 minutes  **STAND:** 10 minutes

| | | | |
|---|---|---|---|
| 1 | recipe Horseradish Sauce (below) | 2 | cloves garlic, minced |
| 1½ | tsp. dried oregano, crushed | 1 | 1½-lb. beef flank steak or boneless beef top sirloin steak, cut 1 inch thick |
| 1½ | tsp. coriander seeds, crushed | 6 | small romaine lettuce leaves |
| 1 | tsp. salt | | |
| 1 | tsp. freshly ground black pepper | 6 | purchased bakery sourdough rolls or 12 slices sourdough bread, toasted |
| 2 | Tbsp. butter | | |
| 2 | large sweet onions, such as Texas 1015 or Vidalia, cut into ¼-inch-thick slices (about 4 cups) | | |

**1.** Prepare Horseradish Sauce; cover and chill. In a small bowl combine oregano, coriander, salt, and pepper; set aside. In a 12-inch nonstick or cast-iron skillet melt butter over medium-low heat. Add onions, garlic, and half (about 2 teaspoons) of the spice mixture. Cook, covered, for 13 to 15 minutes until onions are tender, stirring occasionally. Uncover; cook and stir over medium-high heat for 5 to 8 minutes more or until onions are golden. Remove from skillet; set aside. Wipe skillet clean.

**2.** If using flank steak, score meat on both sides by making shallow cuts at 1-inch intervals diagonally across steak in a diamond pattern. Rub steak on both sides with the remaining spice mixture. Heat the same skillet over medium-high heat until very hot. Add steak. Cook, uncovered, for 12 to 16 minutes or until meat is medium-rare (145° F), turning once. Remove meat from skillet to cutting board; cover with foil. Let steak stand 10 minutes.

**3.** Thinly slice steak across the grain. To serve, arrange lettuce leaves and steak on bottoms of rolls. Top with onions; dollop with Horseradish Sauce. Add roll tops. Makes 6 sandwiches.

**HORSERADISH SAUCE:** In a small bowl stir together ¾ cup mayonnaise, 1 to 2 tablespoons prepared horseradish, 1 tablespoon lime juice, and ½ teaspoon dried oregano, crushed.

Each sandwich: 399 cal., 14 g total fat (6 g sat. fat), 56 mg chol., 799 mg sodium, 37 g carbo., 4 g fiber, 31 g pro. Daily Values: 18% vit. A, 23% vit. C, 9% calcium, 22% iron.

## Kid Friendly Mop Sauce Pizza

Use the Mop Sauce (without tomatoes) as a basting sauce for some delicious barbecue. Follow the sauce recipe just up to the addition of the tomatoes and tomato paste.

**PREP:** 50 minutes  **BAKE:** 15 minutes

| | |
|---|---|
| 1 recipe Mop Sauce (below) | 4 oz. smoked provolone cheese, shredded (1 cup) |
| 1 2- to 2¼-lb. purchased whole roasted chicken | ¼ cup chopped green sweet pepper |
| 1 12-inch Italian bread shell (such as Boboli) or prebaked pizza crust | 4 slices pepper bacon or regular bacon, cooked, drained, and chopped |

**1.** Prepare Mop Sauce. Meanwhile, remove skin from chicken and discard. Remove meat from bones; discard bones. Use 2 forks to pull chicken into small pieces (you should have about 3 to 4 cups). Set meat aside.

**2.** Preheat oven to 450° F. Place bread shell on a large greased baking sheet. Bake for 5 minutes. Remove from oven. Spread Mop Sauce over bread shell to within ½ to 1 inch of the edge. Sprinkle with 2 cups of the chicken (save remaining chicken for another use), cheese, and sweet pepper. Sprinkle with bacon. Bake for 10 to 12 minutes more or until cheese is just melted and bubbly. Cut into wedges. Serve immediately. Makes 6 servings.

**MOP SAUCE:** In a small saucepan stir together 1 cup apple juice; 1 cup cider vinegar; 1 teaspoon packed brown sugar; 1 clove garlic, minced; ½ teaspoon dry mustard; ½ teaspoon paprika; ½ teaspoon ground cumin; and ½ to 1 teaspoon bottled hot pepper sauce. Bring to boiling; reduce heat. Boil gently, uncovered, about 30 minutes or until mixture is reduced to 1 cup. Add 2 seeded and chopped tomatoes (1½ cups) and half of a 6-ounce can (⅓ cup) tomato paste; stir to combine. Return to boiling; reduce heat. Boil gently, uncovered, about 10 minutes more or until slightly thickened, stirring occasionally. Use immediately or cool; cover and store in the refrigerator up to 1 week.

**TEST KITCHEN TIP:** Make double the amount of sauce in a medium saucepan and use the extra sauce to make another pizza; use the remaining chicken.

Each serving: 433 cal., 15 g total fat (5 g sat. fat), 64 mg chol., 806 mg sodium, 47 g carbo., 1 g fiber, 30 g pro. Daily Values: 19% vit. A, 35% vit. C, 28% calcium, 11% iron.

**Mop Sauce Pizza**

## THEM'S COOKIN' WORDS

Cowboy movie language is as colorful as the movie characters themselves. The campfire had a slang all its own. Here's some cow-kitchen lingo:

| | |
|---|---|
| Belly-wash | weak coffee, whiskey, or soup |
| Canned cow | canned or condensed milk |
| Eatin' iron | a knife, fork, or spoon |
| Hot rock | a biscuit |
| Pig's vest with buttons | salt pork |
| Pooch | a dish made from tomatoes, sugar, and bread |
| Sea plum | an oyster |
| Skunk egg | an onion |
| Spotted pup | a dish made from cooked rice and raisins |

SOURCE: *THE ENCYCLOPEDIA OF AMERICAN FOOD AND DRINK*; JOHN F. MARIANI

# COOKING UP HISTORY

Cowboy food and movies: It's a natural match. In just about every cowboy movie there's a crusty cook commanding the chuck wagon on the trail. And when the boys get back to the ranch, a hardworking woman is there clanging a triangle and calling them to eat.

The rugged heroes and heroines of the plains helped expand a nation and inspired a rich culinary heritage. Born of necessity and ethnic tradition, Western cooking captures the spirit of the American kitchen. Practical, flavorful, and diverse, the influences in Wild West cooking come from Mexican vaqueros (the original cowboys), Texans of German stock, freed slaves, French and English Canadians, and Native Americans.

This blend of cultures plus two months of cooking in one iron kettle on the trail (imagine that!) created the original cowboy cuisine. Even back at the ranch house, there were limited ingredients to be had: beef (and lots of it), beans, flour, onions, potatoes, and cornmeal were mainstays. Vegetables consisted of whatever could be scrounged. Dried chiles provided flavor. Fortunately, our supermarkets aren't as limited, so today's cowboy food is even more diverse.

## Apricot and Apple Jelly Stack Cake

Chilling the prepared cake makes it easier to slice and helps it stand tall. Make sure you run some of the glaze down the sides. The crushed red pepper in the glaze gives you a hit of sweet heat.

**PREP:** 45 minutes **BAKE:** 18 minutes **COOL:** 10 minutes

| | |
|---|---|
| 3 cups all-purpose flour | 1/4 tsp. crushed red pepper (optional) |
| 1 1/2 tsp. ground cinnamon | |
| 1 1/2 tsp. ground ginger | 3 15-oz. cans apricot halves, drained, or one 16-oz. pkg. frozen peach slices, thawed, drained, and cut into 1/4-inch slices |
| 1 tsp. baking powder | |
| 1 tsp. baking soda | |
| 1 cup butter, softened | |
| 1/2 cup packed brown sugar | |
| 2 eggs | 1/4 cup pine nuts, toasted |
| 1 cup mild-flavored molasses | Sweetened whipped cream (optional) |
| 2/3 cup water | |
| 1 18-oz. jar apple jelly or apricot preserves (about 1 1/2 cups) | |

**1.** Preheat oven to 350° F. Grease and flour three 9×1 1/2-inch round baking pans; set aside. In a bowl combine flour, cinnamon, ginger, baking powder, and baking soda; set aside.

**2.** In a large mixing bowl beat butter with an electric mixer on medium speed for 30 seconds. Add brown sugar; beat until fluffy. Add eggs and molasses; beat 1 minute (mixture will appear curdled). Add flour mixture and water alternately to egg mixture, beating on low speed after each addition. Divide batter among the prepared pans (about 2 cups each).

**3.** Bake about 18 minutes or until a wooden toothpick inserted near centers comes out clean. Cool for 10 minutes in pans on wire racks. Remove cakes from pans. Cool completely on racks.

**4.** While cakes cool, in a small saucepan combine jelly and, if desired, crushed red pepper. Heat over medium-low heat until jelly is just melted and spreadable, stirring frequently. Set aside. Place 1 layer on serving platter. Top with one-third of the apricot halves, cut side down. Spoon on one-third of the apple jelly mixture (about 1/2 cup). Repeat with remaining cake layers, apricots, and jelly mixture, finishing with jelly mixture. Sprinkle top layer with toasted pine nuts. Chill cake 4 hours before serving. If desired, serve with whipped cream. Makes 8 to 10 servings.

Each serving: 862 cal., 29 g total fat (16 g sat. fat), 119 mg chol., 517 mg sodium, 148 g carbo., 5 g fiber, 8 g pro. Daily Values: 63% vit. A, 8% vit. C, 17% calcium, 32% iron.

Apricot and Apple Jelly Stack Cake

# TRAIL MIX

What better way to watch a movie than with a big bowl of ranch-style snack mix? This one mixes up some Southwestern flavors and features a snack-bar favorite: chocolate-covered raisins.

# ICEBERG SALAD

Give this classic salad a Western spin with a creamy version of a cucumber relish popular on Texas Hill Country ranches. Buttermilk, a ranch-house staple, gives the dressing its snap. Iceberg lettuce retains its refreshing crunch when the lettuce is well chilled before serving.

**Trail Mix**

**Iceberg Lettuce with Cucumber Dressing**

**Kid Friendly** Trail Mix

**PREP:** 15 minutes **BAKE:** 20 minutes **COOL:** 1 hour

| | |
|---|---|
| 1 | 9- to 9½-oz. pkg. ranch-flavored whole grain crackers or thin wheat crackers |
| 1 | 5-oz. pkg. Southwestern-spiced sweet potato sticks or 3 cups shoestring potatoes |
| 1 | 12-oz. can honey-roasted peanuts (2⅓ cups) |

| | |
|---|---|
| 1 | 3-oz. pkg. freeze-dried roasted sweet corn or one 4-oz. container freeze-dried whole kernel corn |
| ¼ | cup butter |
| 1½ | tsp. dried sage, crushed |
| 1 | 7-oz. pkg. chocolate-covered raisins (1 cup) |

**1.** Preheat oven to 300° F. In a large shallow roasting pan combine crackers, sweet potato sticks, peanuts, and corn.

**2.** In a small saucepan heat butter and sage over low heat until butter is melted. Drizzle butter mixture over cracker mixture; mix well. Bake, uncovered, for 20 to 25 minutes or until lightly toasted, stirring twice. Spread mixture on a large piece of foil to cool. When cool, stir in chocolate-covered raisins. Store in an airtight container up to 2 weeks. Makes about 13 cups.

Each serving (½ cup): 209 cal., 12 g total fat (3 g sat. fat), 7 mg chol., 159 mg sodium, 21 g carbo., 2 g fiber, 5 g pro. Daily Values: 36% vit. A, 1% vit. C, 2% calcium, 3% iron.

## Iceberg Lettuce with Cucumber Dressing

**PREP:** 20 minutes **CHILL:** 1 hour

| | |
|---|---|
| 1 | large head iceberg lettuce, chilled |
| 1 | recipe Cucumber Dressing (below) |

| | |
|---|---|
| 6 | cherry tomatoes |
| | Dill seeds (optional) |

**1.** Peel outer leaves from lettuce. Remove core. Rinse thoroughly and drain. Cut lettuce into 6 wedges. Place on a serving platter; cover and chill up to 4 hours.

**2.** Prepare Cucumber Dressing. Cover and chill 1 to 4 hours to blend flavors.

**3.** To serve, spoon Cucumber Dressing over each wedge. Garnish with a cherry tomato. If desired, sprinkle with additional dill seeds. Makes 6 servings.

**CUCUMBER DRESSING:** Peel, seed, and finely chop 1 large cucumber (about 2 cups). In a medium bowl combine cucumber; ½ cup finely chopped sweet yellow onion; one 8-ounce carton dairy sour cream; ¼ cup snipped fresh mint; 1 tablespoon white wine vinegar; 1 teaspoon dill seeds, crushed; 1 teaspoon salt; 1 teaspoon sugar ( if desired); and ½ teaspoon freshly ground black pepper. Stir to combine.

Each serving: 103 cal., 8 g total fat (5 g sat. fat), 17 mg chol., 416 mg sodium, 6 g carbo., 2 g fiber, 2 g pro. Daily Values: 13% vit. A, 17% vit. C, 7% calcium, 7% iron.

**Kid Friendly** Crunchy Buttermilk Ice Cream

**PREP:** 25 minutes **FREEZE:** about 30 minutes

| | |
|---|---|
| 1 | quart buttermilk |
| 1 | cup whipping cream |
| 1 | cup granulated sugar |
| 1 | Tbsp. vanilla |
| 1 | cup butter |

| | |
|---|---|
| 1⅓ | cups packed brown sugar |
| 2 | Tbsp. water |
| 12 | small ice cream cones |
| | Purchased caramel corn, coarsely crushed |

**1.** In a large bowl combine buttermilk, cream, granulated sugar, and vanilla. Stir until sugar dissolves. Freeze mixture in a 1½- to 2-quart ice cream freezer according to manufacturer's directions. Serve immediately or transfer ice cream to freezer container; cover and freeze up to 24 hours.

**2.** For topping, in a large skillet melt butter; whisk in brown sugar and water until sugar is dissolved and mixture is smooth.

**3.** To serve, scoop ice cream into bowls. Invert an ice cream cone on top of ice cream scoop. Top with sauce and sprinkle with caramel corn. Makes about 1½ quarts (twelve ½-cup servings with 2 tablespoons sauce).

**TO PREPARE IN A 4- TO 6-QUART ICE CREAM MAKER:** Double ice cream ingredients. In a large bowl combine buttermilk, whipping cream, sugar, and vanilla. Freeze according to manufacturer's directions. Ripen about 4 hours. To ripen ice cream after churning, remove the lid and dasher. Cover top of freezer can with plastic wrap, waxed paper, or foil. Plug hole in lid with a piece of cloth; replace lid. Pack outer freezer bucket with enough ice and rock salt to cover top of freezer can, using 4 cups ice to 1 cup salt. Discard water from melted ice and replenish ice and salt as necessary.

Each serving (½ cup ice cream and 2 tablespoons sauce): 464 cal., 26 g total fat (16 g sat. fat), 75 mg chol., 293 mg sodium, 56 g carbo., 1 g fiber, 4 g pro. Daily Values: 19% vit. A, 2% vit. C, 14% calcium, 5% iron.

**Crunchy Buttermilk Ice Cream**

# HEART OF THE KITCHEN

Mama's Marinara and Italian Meatballs

SHARING MEALS WITH HER BIG ITALIAN FAMILY TAUGHT DIANE SCALIA THAT HOMEMADE FOOD—SERVED WITH LOVE—SATISFIES THE BODY AND FEEDS THE SPIRIT.

Diane Scalia (left) and her mother, Donna Scalia

## Mama's Marinara and Italian Meatballs

**PREP (SAUCE):** 25 minutes   **COOK (SAUCE):** 60 minutes
**PREP (MEATBALLS):** 30 minutes   **COOK (MEATBALLS):** 40 minutes

| | |
|---|---|
| 1 large onion, finely chopped (1 cup) | 10 fresh basil leaves, torn |
| 3 large cloves garlic, minced | 1 Tbsp. dried Italian seasoning, crushed |
| 1 carrot, finely chopped (1/2 cup) | 1 tsp. sugar |
| 1 stalk celery, finely chopped (1/2 cup) | 1/2 tsp. crushed red pepper (optional) |
| 2 Tbsp. extra-virgin olive oil | 3 bay leaves |
| 2 15-oz. cans tomato sauce | Kosher salt and freshly ground black pepper |
| 1 Tbsp. tomato paste | 1 recipe Handmade Italian Meatballs (below) |
| 1 cup water | Hot cooked spaghetti |
| 1 cup dry red wine | Finely shredded Parmesan cheese |
| 3 Tbsp. fresh parsley, finely chopped | |

**1.** For Mama's Marinara, in 4-quart Dutch oven cook and stir onion, garlic, carrot, and celery in hot oil for 15 minutes or until vegetables are tender. Stir in tomato sauce, tomato paste, water, wine, parsley, basil, Italian seasoning, sugar, red pepper (if desired), and bay leaves.

**2.** Bring sauce to boiling; reduce heat. Simmer, uncovered, for 45 to 60 minutes or until desired consistency; stir occasionally. Discard bay leaves. Season to taste with salt and pepper.

**3.** Meanwhile, prepare Handmade Italian Meatballs. Serve sauce with meatballs over spaghetti. Sprinkle with Parmesan cheese. Makes 8 servings.

**HANDMADE ITALIAN MEATBALLS:** In a large bowl combine 1 pound ground beef; 12 ounces bulk hot or sweet Italian sausage; 1/2 cup fine dry bread crumbs; 1/4 cup milk; 1 slightly beaten egg; 1/4 cup fresh Italian parsley, finely chopped; 1/4 cup freshly grated Parmesan cheese; 1 teaspoon dried Italian seasoning, crushed; 1 teaspoon kosher salt; and 1/4 teaspoon freshly ground black pepper. Mix until combined. Form mixture into meatballs about 1 1/2 inches in diameter. In a large skillet cook meatballs in 2 tablespoons extra-virgin olive oil over medium heat for 10 minutes or until browned, turning occasionally. Bring Mama's Marinara sauce to boiling. Gently place meatballs into sauce. Stir gently to coat with sauce. Cover and cook over medium-low heat for 30 minutes or until an instant-read thermometer inserted in the meatballs registers 160° F. Makes about 16 meatballs.

Each serving: 669 cal., 29 g total fat (10 g sat. fat), 109 mg chol., 1,537 mg sodium, 60 g carbo., 4 g fiber, 35 g pro. Daily Values: 67% vit. A, 37% vit. C, 19% calcium, 34% iron.

# Comfort Cooking

Diane Scalia talks about her mother's old O'Keefe and Merritt range as if it were a close family member. "There's something about just turning on the heat that brings back a flood of memories," Diane says.

The chrome-and-enamel cookstove has been part of the family since 1958 when Diane's mom, Donna Scalia, moved with her family into the California home where she still lives. "My mother cooked on it every single day." She still does. When the family gathers for Sunday dinners, the range is the hub of the kitchen.

"My mom lives in the house where I grew up, and I learned to cook on that stove," says Diane, who calls herself a "chefpreneur"—an entrepreneur who caters, works as a personal chef, teaches cooking classes, and has written a cookbook. Everything she does stems from her conviction that food nurtures the body and the spirit.

"Homemade foods are healing because they remind us of a time and place we keep close in our hearts, when our lives were not so complicated," Diane says. "My work and life is really about food and family and bringing people to the table. What children want—what their parents want—is to spend time with their family. Being around the table at mealtime feeds them on a level that goes beyond sustenance. Sitting down to dinner is a ritual that builds a strong family, more than being in a car all day going from activity to activity.

"In my personal and professional experience, I've found that people have memories of meals with families, and they go back to those memories in their minds and hearts when their lives get really manic." That's why comfort food is so coveted. It's soothing and homey. In the Scalia home, Thursday night was pasta night. "That was our ritual," Diane says. "To this day pasta to me always tastes good."

The ritual of sharing familiar dishes is a bonding experience that needn't be complicated, she says. Stick with those 10 to 15 meals that your family loves, then tweak them with variations to prevent boredom.

Although Diane's family had pasta every Thursday night, the meals were prepared a variety of ways. Because of that ritual, Diane loves concocting pasta suppers. For instance, she makes "flash-in-the-pan" pasta by combining olive oil, cooked noodles, chunks of cooked meat or tofu, fresh chopped tomato and basil, sea salt, and freshly grated Parmesan cheese.

# IS IT Done YET?

Let these time-tested techniques guide you to just the right moment for taking your food off the fire.

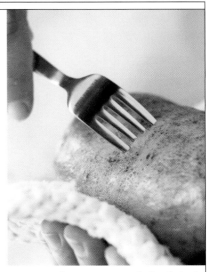

**THE PULL**— Artichokes are ready when the leaves can be pulled easily, not yanked, from base of the vegetable. If leaves resist, cook the artichoke another 5 minutes.

**THE POKE**— Monitor your steak's progress by gently pressing the center— it's time to check the temperature with an instant-read thermometer when you begin to feel resistance.

**THE FORK**— An easy way to tell when baked potatoes are done is with a fork. It will slide in easily all the way to the center.

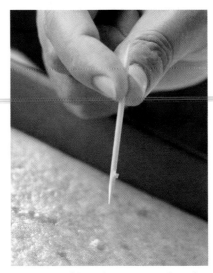

**THE FLAKE**— The "grain" of the fish will separate into clean flakes when it's done. Another test: Peek between the separated flakes— the fish beneath should be opaque.

**THE PICK**— Clean but not spotless: A wooden skewer may still have a few crumbs— but no wet batter adhering to it— when pulled from the cake.

**THE THUMP**— Listen for a hollow sound when you tap baked bread with your fingernail. You can get an idea what it should sound like by tapping on a full bag of flour.

BY **RICHARD SWEARINGER** PHOTOGRAPHS BY **GREG SCHEIDEMANN [N] HAUS FOTO** FOOD STYLING BY **BROOKE LEONARD**

# SEDER PLATES

Passover is the Jewish holiday most associated with food. In fact, the holiday is celebrated with a family feast, the centerpiece of which is the Seder plate. Each Passover plate speaks the language of tradition with its own unique accent. An ornate, antique platter in china, silver, or brass reflects the tastes of a great-grandmother's generation. A bold, artistic platter—newly purchased to hand down to your children—may grace your Passover table with modern intonations that affirm a legacy just begun. Whichever style of plate graces your Seder, it is a self-contained story of the celebration.

Seder plates came into being about 2,000 years ago. Before then, the symbols of the Passover meal were simply placed on a cloth.

- The roasted egg symbolizes renewal, rebirth, and life's eternal circle.
- The roasted lamb shank (or chicken) bone represents the sacrificial Passover lamb.
- Bitter herbs (typically horseradish) describe the bitter suffering of the Jews in Egypt.
- Karpas—celery tops, parsley, or onion—are dipped in salt water to represent the tears of slavery. Another portion of greens (endive or lettuce) symbolizes spring.
- Charoseth, a mixture of apples, nuts, and wine (see Question, *below*), fills the remaining dish.

BY **DAVID FEDER** PHOTOGRAPHS BY **KRITSADA/KRANTZ STUDIOS**

A selection of Seder plates includes a porcelain plate with small bowls, a footed plate, and a metal Seder plate.

## QUESTION:

I have always made charoseth the traditional Eastern European way. Do you have any ideas for updating this favorite Seder recipe?

## ANSWER:

The traditional Passover charoseth—symbolizing the mortar used by Israelite slaves to build monuments in Egypt—is a mixture of 2 cups grated apples and 1/2 cup ground walnuts flavored with 1 cup of sweet wine and 1/2 teaspoon ground cinnamon. Try a Middle Eastern version this year. Substitute finely chopped pitted dates and raisins for half of the apples. Use ground almonds instead of walnuts. Stir in the juice and grated peel of an orange, plus 1/4 teaspoon ground cardamom.

# NO-FAIL
# CHEESE
## COURSE

The three cheeses here are from artisan cheesemakers working in the United States: Mutton Button (left) from the Old Chatham Sheepherding Company in New York, www.blacksheepcheese.com; blue cheese (center) from Point Reyes Farmstead Cheese Company in California, www.pointreyescheese.com; and Seven-Year Cheddar (right) from Carr Valley Cheese in Wisconsin, www.carrvalleycheese.com.

There's something so companionable about a plate of cheeses on the table; it's hard for conversation to lag when there are flavors to compare and plates to be passed.

More and more wonderful cheeses from here and abroad are in supermarket deli cases and specialty cheese shops, but don't be intimidated by the variety. The best plan is to keep it simple and obey the rule of threes. You'll need a soft ripened cheese, such as Brie or Boursault; a firm cheese, such as an aged cheddar or Parmesan; and a blue cheese, such as Roquefort or Gorgonzola. Another strategy is to mix milks: one each of sheep-, goat-, and cow-milk cheeses. And when you're at the cheese case, keep an eye out for cheeses made in your region. Many states now have cheesemakers who craft a delicious array of products.

**SERVING NOTES:** Some people enjoy the cheese course before dinner; some serve it after dinner—either as a substitute for dessert or before or after dessert. Serve it when it suits you. Plan on buying 1 to 2 ounces of each cheese per person. For four people, you will need three 4- to 8-ounce wedges or wheels. Be sure to serve cheese cool, but not cold. A half hour out of the refrigerator is about right.

# TO GET YOU STARTED

Look for these commonly available varieties in the cheese case of your supermarket. Can't find the exact variety? There's bound to be one just as good.

| SOFT | MEDIUM TO HARD | BLUE |
|------|----------------|------|
| Port Salut | Provolone | Danish Blue |
| Bel Paese | Gouda | Blue d'Auvergne |
| Reblochon | Emmentaler | Cashel Blue |
| Muenster | Manchego | Cabrales |
| Brick | Dry Jack | |
| Camembert | Gruyère | |

Look for cheeses from domestic cheesemakers who have gained wide distribution and universal praise, including Vermont Shepherd, Doeling Camembert, Roth Kase Knight's Vail, Maytag Blue, and Wabash Cannonball.

Having trouble finding handcrafted cheeses? Try these sources:
- Cowgirl Creamery; 707/789-2604; www.cowgirlcreamery.com
- Formaggio Kitchen; 888/212-3224; www.formaggiokitchen.com
- Zingerman's; 888/636-8162; www.zingermans.com

Provide guests the luxury of mixing and matching great cheese accompaniments. Those pictured below are some time-tested favorites. Crackers with lots of seeds are welcome with any cheese; small apples add crunch and texture to the richness of creamy cheeses; a pot of honey takes the edge off a pungent variety; paper-thin prosciutto slices draped around hard cheeses add heartiness; and olives provide a salty counterpoint to softer ones.

BY RICHARD SWEARINGER PHOTOGRAPHS BY GREG SCHEIDEMANN [N] HAUS FOTO FOOD STYLING BY CHARLES WORTHINGTON

# April

SPRING IS A TIME WHEN WE CELEBRATE
A NEW SEASON—INCLUDING
SOME GREAT NEW
FOOD FINDS.

# A Luncheon with Flea Market Flair

# A Luncheon

## WITH FLEA MARKET FLAIR

**Honey Shortcakes and Strawberries**
Candlewick-style glass cake stand, circa 1950

CREATE A SPRING GET-TOGETHER WITH OUR MENU AND YOUR COLLECTION OF TABLETOP TREASURES.

## Honey Shortcakes and Strawberries

If using heavy baking pans, watch the baking progress carefully to avoid overbaking.

**PREP:** 30 minutes  **STAND:** 30 minutes  **BAKE:** 15 minutes
**COOL:** 1 hour

| | | | |
|---|---|---|---|
| 2 | eggs | 1 | Tbsp. lime juice |
| 1 | cup all-purpose flour | 3 | cups fresh fruit, such as |
| 1 | tsp. baking powder | | small whole strawberries; |
| 1/4 | tsp. salt | | or peeled, sliced, and/or |
| 3/4 | cup sugar | | chopped mangoes, |
| 1/4 | cup honey | | kiwifruit, pineapple, or |
| 1/2 | cup milk | | bananas |
| 2 | Tbsp. butter | | Sweetened whipped cream |
| 2 | Tbsp. honey | | (optional) |
| 1 | tsp. finely shredded lime peel | | |

**1.** Allow eggs to stand at room temperature for 30 minutes. Meanwhile, grease and flour six 3/4- to 1-cup individual tube pans or 10-ounce custard cups; set pans or cups aside. In a small bowl stir together flour, baking powder, and salt; set aside.

**2.** Preheat oven to 350° F. In a medium mixing bowl beat eggs with an electric mixer on high speed about 4 minutes or until thick. Gradually add sugar, beating on medium speed for 3 to 4 minutes or until light and fluffy. Beat in the 1/4 cup honey. Add the flour mixture; beat on low to medium speed just until combined.

**3.** In a small saucepan heat and stir milk and butter until butter melts; add to batter, beating until combined. Pour batter into the prepared pans.

**4.** Bake for 15 to 20 minutes or until tops spring back when lightly touched. Cool cakes in pans on a wire rack for 10 minutes. Remove cakes from pans and cool completely on wire rack.

**5.** Place cakes on platter or individual plates. Combine 2 tablespoons honey, lime peel, and lime juice; toss with fruit. To serve, spoon fruit mixture over cakes. If desired, top with a dollop of whipped cream. Makes 6 servings.

Each serving: 352 cal., 7 g total fat (3 g sat. fat), 83 mg chol., 239 mg sodium, 71 g carbo., 2 g fiber, 5 g pro. Daily Values: 70% vit. A, 41% vit. C, 9% calcium, 8% iron.

BY RICHARD SWEARINGER PHOTOGRAPHS BY KELLER + KELLER STYLING BY JOSEPH BOEHM AND JACQUELINE FORTIER

# Luncheon Event

Spring is a chance to gather friends and your favorite flea market finds for an afternoon of food and beautiful hats. And lunch is the ideal meal for the occasion: less stress than dinner, less bustle than breakfast. This is especially true because all the tabletop decor you'll need to set a welcoming scene can be found on your keepsake shelves, in your closets, or at antiques malls and charity shops.

The menu is simple, quick to make, and reminiscent of the days when lunch was an event, not just something to be squeezed in between errands. Though all of these recipes would have fit in during the days when women gathered for leisurely camaraderie, they've been streamlined and infused with flavors.

Think of them as the best of department store tearoom cuisine—favorites such as shrimp cocktails, chicken salad, and cheese straws. The inspiration for this menu came from the vintage earthenware and china platters on which it is served. Thus the style of your event is your first decision, whether you prefer the classic appeal of Victorian silver or the whimsical appeal of milk glass.

Once you have a theme in mind, take a moment to inventory the decorative objects you already have around your house, then hit secondhand stores to complete the look you've chosen. In the aisles of the antiques mall is where this potentially inexpensive, fun, and creative mode of party-giving all comes together. Don't worry about matching; your goal is to delight your guests with your sense of style and ability to find new uses for old objects.

Pressed-glass condiment bowls paired with an aqua-glazed California stoneware platter make a graphic backdrop for a shrimp cocktail (page 70). Instead of red cocktail sauce and a bed of ice, this version is presented with three quick stir-together sauces.

Blue-rimmed china plates with a tracery of pink flowers from the '50s are ideal for serving a chicken salad (page 66). The Spring Chicken Salad has been brought up-to-date with a lively blend of spices and a dressing that's much lighter than Mother's.

Minted Pea Salad (page 66) is a ladies' lunch standby. It's drizzled with a mint jelly dressing borrowed from roast lamb, another beloved spring staple. Perched in a 1930s egg cup, it becomes irresistible emerald caviar.

**Minted Pea Salad**

1930s egg cup

## Spring Chicken Salad

Pea shoots are just what they sound like—the deliciously crunchy shoots of young pea vines. Look for them in farmers' markets and grocery stores.

**START TO FINISH:** 35 minutes

| | |
|---|---|
| 1 2- to 2¼-lb. purchased whole roasted chicken | 2 Tbsp. thinly sliced green onion |
| 4 cups coarsely chopped fruit, such as peeled and cored pineapple, peeled and seeded mango, and/or peeled kiwifruit | 1 recipe Creamy Lime Dressing (below) |
| | Bibb lettuce |
| 2 cups coarsely chopped peeled jicama | 2 cups mesclun salad greens, cut into bite-size pieces |
| | Pea shoots or watercress sprigs |

**1.** If desired, remove skin from chicken and discard. Remove meat from bones; discard bones. Coarsely chop chicken (you should have about 3 cups). In a very large bowl combine chicken, pineapple (or other fruit), jicama, and green onion; set aside.

**2.** Prepare Creamy Lime Dressing. Spoon about half the dressing over chicken mixture; toss to coat well.

**3.** Line 6 to 8 individual serving plates with Bibb lettuce. Divide mesclun mix among plates. Arrange some of the chicken mixture on each plate. Top with pea shoots. Drizzle with some of the remaining dressing. Makes 6 to 8 servings.

**CREAMY LIME DRESSING:** In a small bowl stir together ½ cup mayonnaise or salad dressing; ½ teaspoon finely shredded lime peel; 2 tablespoons lime juice; 1 clove garlic, minced; 2 teaspoons Jamaican jerk seasoning or Mediterranean or Greek seasoning; and ¼ teaspoon salt.

Each serving: 401 cal., 25 g total fat (5 g sat. fat), 73 mg chol., 366 mg sodium, 21 g carbo., 2 g fiber, 22 g pro. Daily Values: 4% vit. A, 47% vit. C, 3% calcium, 10% iron.

## Minted Pea Salad

Plunging peas into ice water the second they're done helps them keep their bright green color and fresh flavor.

_Fast!_

**START TO FINISH:** 15 minutes

| | |
|---|---|
| 2 cups shelled baby peas or one 10-oz. pkg. frozen peas | 1 Tbsp. white wine vinegar |
| | ¼ tsp. salt |
| 1 Tbsp. mint jelly | Snipped fresh mint (optional) |

**1.** Half fill a large bowl with water and ice cubes. In a medium saucepan heat a large amount of water to boiling. Add peas and cook 5 minutes for fresh peas or 1 minute for frozen peas. Drain into a strainer; immediately plunge peas in strainer into ice water to stop cooking. Drain well.

**2.** In a small saucepan heat jelly, vinegar, and salt over low heat just until jelly is melted and smooth.

**3.** To serve, divide peas among 4 to 6 large egg cups or demitasse cups. Drizzle peas with mint jelly mixture. If desired, sprinkle with fresh mint. Makes 4 to 6 servings.

Healthy  Each serving: 49 cal., 0 g total fat (0 g sat. fat), 0 mg chol., 100 mg sodium, 9 g carbo., 2 g fiber, 3 g pro. Daily Values: 6% vit. A, 27% vit. C, 1% calcium, 4% iron.

### Spring Chicken Salad

1957 Homer Laughlin "Cavalier" earthenware

### Strawberry Iced Tea

**PREP:** 25 minutes  **COOL:** 2 hours

2  lb. fresh strawberries or two 16-oz. pkg. frozen unsweetened whole strawberries
1  cup packed brown sugar
1  cup water
2  lemons

3  Tbsp. snipped fresh rosemary (optional)
Ice cubes
1  recipe Iced Tea (below) or one 1-liter bottle club soda, chilled
Fresh strawberries (optional)

**1.** In a large saucepan combine fresh or frozen unsweetened strawberries, brown sugar, and water. Cook and stir over medium heat until sugar dissolves.

**2.** Using a vegetable peeler, remove strips of peel from lemons; juice the lemons (should have $1/2$ cup). Add strips of lemon peel, lemon juice, and, if desired, rosemary to mixture in saucepan. Bring mixture just to boiling, stirring occasionally. Remove from heat. Cover; cool to room temperature.

**3.** Press mixture through a fine mesh sieve; discard solids (you should have about 1 quart syrup). To serve, fill glasses with ice. To each glass add $1/2$ cup Iced Tea and syrup to taste (about $1/2$ cup). If desired, garnish with fresh strawberries. Makes about eight (8-ounce) servings.

**MAKE-AHEAD DIRECTIONS:** Syrup may be prepared, covered, and refrigerated up to 3 days.

Each serving: 151 cal., 0 g total fat (0 g sat. fat), 0 mg chol., 14 mg sodium, 39 g carbo., 3 g fiber, 1 g pro. Daily Values: 1% vit. A, 88% vit. C, 4% calcium, 6% iron.

**ICED TEA:** Place 6 tea bags in a heatproof pitcher or glass measuring cup. Add 4 cups boiling water. Let tea steep 3 to 5 minutes; remove tea bags. Cool at room temperature about 2 hours. (After cooling, store in refrigerator. Don't chill quickly or tea will cloud.) Serve over ice with Strawberry Iced Tea syrup.

Each serving (without syrup): 2 cal., 0 g total fat (0 g sat. fat), 0 mg chol., 7 mg sodium, 1 g carbo., 0 g fiber, 0 g pro.

**Strawberry Iced Tea**

# SETTING THE SCENE

Even if you've never thrown a real hats-and-flowers luncheon, don't worry. Your guide to setting the scene for this "newstalgic" style of entertaining is one of the best flea marketers we know—decorator Jacqueline Fortier of Minnesota. When she's not beautifying clients' homes, she's throwing parties for friends. And now she's sharing how she works the aisles of antiques malls to create maximum atmosphere with minimum cash.

Her strategy: Tickle her guests' fancy with tchotchkes. "I think of their interests," says Jacqueline. "Are they younger, older? Are they more formal or informal? If they're gardening buddies, I'll go look for flower-themed elements. If they're bird watchers, then robins are on my list."

A plain stick of butter won't do for this luncheon: Make it special by cutting butter into cubes and sprinkling with a little fresh dill.

# CREATE A MOOD

- If you're a fan of Depression glass, use several colors along with painterly pieces of china from your grandmother. Add soft floral napkins and such frilly flowers as peach or apricot blossoms and pink or white carnations. Depression glass also looks great with mismatched pieces of floral-pattern porcelain or china.
- Are you a fan of 1960s Scandinavian design? Add big, bold flowers with attitude, such as gerbera daisies or tulips, and mix colors and shapes of tableware. Put Abba on the CD player.
- And don't forget the invitation. "I *never* phone," says Jacqueline Fortier. "People get such a kick out of mail. And it really reinforces the mood of specialness that I always try to create for my parties."

## Chive Batter Bread

This recipe, because there's no kneading involved, is a fast way to achieve the rich taste of home-baked yeast bread.

**PREP:** 30 minutes  **RISE:** 20 minutes  **BAKE:** 18 minutes

| | |
|---|---|
| 1 Tbsp. yellow cornmeal | 1/2 tsp. salt |
| 2 cups all-purpose flour | 1 egg |
| 1 pkg. fast-rising active dry yeast | 1/2 cup snipped fresh chives or 1/4 cup finely chopped green onions (green tops only) |
| 1/4 tsp. ground black pepper | |
| 1 cup milk | |
| 2 Tbsp. sugar | 1/3 cup yellow cornmeal |
| 3 Tbsp. butter | |

**1.** Grease the bottoms and sides of twelve 2 1/2-inch muffin cups. Sprinkle bottoms with the 1 tablespoon cornmeal; set aside. In a large mixing bowl stir together 1 1/4 cups of the flour, the yeast, and the pepper; set aside.

**2.** In a small saucepan combine milk, sugar, butter, and salt; heat and stir over medium heat just until mixture is warm (120° F to 130° F) and butter almost melts. Add milk mixture and egg to flour mixture. Beat with an electric mixer on low to medium speed for 30 seconds, scraping bowl constantly. Beat on high speed for 3 minutes. Stir in the chives and the 1/3 cup cornmeal. Stir in remaining flour. (The batter will be soft and sticky.) Cover and let rest in a warm place for 10 minutes.

**3.** Preheat oven to 350° F. Spoon batter into prepared muffin cups. Cover loosely. Let rise in a warm place for 20 minutes.

**4.** Bake, uncovered, about 18 minutes or until rolls sound hollow when tapped. Cool in muffin cups 5 minutes; loosen edges and remove from muffin cups. Serve warm. Makes 12 rolls.

**Healthy** Each roll: 140 cal., 4 g total fat (2 g sat. fat), 28 mg chol., 144 mg sodium, 21 g carbo., 1 g fiber, 4 g pro. Daily Values: 6% vit. A, 2% vit. C, 3% calcium, 6% iron.

### SPRINGTIME LUNCHEON

Roasted Shrimp with Three Sauces (page 70) or
Spring Chicken Salad (page 66)
Chive Batter Bread (above) – butter or
Cheese Straws (page 73)
Honey Shortcakes and Strawberries (page 65)
Strawberry Iced Tea or Iced Tea (page 67)

**Chive Batter Bread**

**Roasted Shrimp with Three Sauces**

1930s Depression glass ramekins on a
Catalina Pottery platter, circa 1950

## Fruit Juice Gels

Kid Friendly

For best results use a fresh fruit juice or fruit-juice blend such as strawberry-banana. Drinks from Naked Juice Co. or Odwalla, Inc., work well. They are generally sold in the produce section of supermarkets. Look in freestanding coolers or in the vegetable case. Do not use fruit juices containing papaya or pineapple because they can prevent the gelatin from firming up.

**PREP:** 15 minutes  **CHILL:** 2 hours

| | |
|---|---|
| 1/4 cup sugar | 1 15.2-oz. bottle fruit juice |
| 1 envelope unflavored | blend (1³/4 cups) |
| gelatin | Edible flowers (optional) |

**1.** In a small saucepan combine sugar and gelatin. Stir in 1 cup of the juice. Cook and stir over medium heat until sugar and gelatin are dissolved. Remove from heat; stir in remaining juice.

**2.** Divide gelatin mixture among six 3- to 4-ounce glasses or small dishes. Chill in the refrigerator for 2 to 3 hours or until set. If desired, garnish with edible flowers. Makes 6 servings.

Healthy Each serving: 73 cal., 0 g total fat (0 g sat. fat), 0 mg chol., 4 mg sodium, 17 g carbo., 0 g fiber, 1 g pro. Daily Values: 29% vit. C, 1% calcium, 1% iron.

## Roasted Shrimp with Three Sauces

Feel free to substitute your favorite cocktail sauce or to use just one or two of the sauces given here.

**PREP:** 30 minutes  **BAKE:** 10 minutes  **COOL:** 15 minutes
**CHILL:** overnight  **STAND:** 30 minutes

| | |
|---|---|
| 3 lb. fresh or frozen uncooked jumbo shrimp, peeled and deveined, leaving tails intact; or one 2¹/2- to 3-lb. fresh or frozen skinless center-cut salmon fillet, about 1 inch thick | 1 tsp. coarse kosher salt or 1/2 tsp. salt |
| | 3/4 tsp. coarsely ground black pepper |
| | 1 recipe Bread-and-Butter Pickle Sauce (below) |
| | 1 recipe Mango-Tomato Sauce (below) |
| 2 Tbsp. cooking oil or olive oil | 1 recipe Avocado Sauce (below) |

**1.** Move oven rack to upper third of oven (6 to 8 inches from top of oven). Preheat oven to 475° F. Thaw shrimp or salmon, if frozen. Rinse and pat dry.

**2.** For shrimp: In a lightly greased baking pan arrange shrimp in a single layer. Brush with cooking oil. Sprinkle with salt and pepper. Bake, uncovered, for 10 minutes or until opaque, turning once. Cool in pan on a wire rack for 15 minutes. Transfer to a large bowl, cover tightly, and chill overnight. (For salmon: Brush salmon with oil; sprinkle with salt and pepper. Place in a shallow roasting pan. Roast, uncovered, about 15 minutes or until fish flakes easily when tested with a fork in thickest portion. Cool 30 minutes. Wrap in plastic wrap and chill overnight.)

**3.** Prepare Bread-and-Butter Pickle Sauce and Mango-Tomato Sauce; cover and chill overnight.

**4.** About 30 minutes before serving, remove shrimp or salmon from refrigerator and transfer to a serving bowl or platter. Prepare Avocado Sauce.

**5.** Serve shrimp with the three sauces. If serving salmon, place cooked fish on a serving platter and arrange sauces around the fish. Guests may cut off portions of fish with a serving spatula or fork. Makes 6 servings.

**BREAD-AND-BUTTER PICKLE SAUCE:** In a small bowl combine 1 cup mayonnaise; 1/2 cup drained bread-and-butter pickles, chopped; and 1 tablespoon finely shredded orange or lemon peel. Cover and chill overnight.

**MANGO-TOMATO SAUCE:** In a small bowl combine 1 medium mango, peeled, seeded, and chopped; 1/2 cup chopped grape tomatoes; and 1/2 cup finely chopped red onion. Cover and chill the sauce overnight.

**AVOCADO SAUCE:** In a small bowl combine 2 avocados, halved, seeded, peeled, and chopped; 1/3 cup chopped green onions; and 1 tablespoon lime juice.

Each serving with sauce: 635 cal., 47 g total fat (7 g sat. fat), 272 mg chol., 897 mg sodium, 17 g carbo., 4 g fiber, 36 g pro. Daily Values: 42% vit. A, 39% vit. C, 11% calcium, 26% iron.

**Fruit Juice Gels**

1930s Anchor Hocking juice glasses

## SOFT TOUCHES

Fabric is a great ally, says Jacqueline. A striped scarf becomes a runner (left), and a half yard of silk can be tied around a pitcher in the style of an obi, a broad sash worn with a kimono.

Cheese Straws

## Cheese Straws

Extra straws may be tightly wrapped and frozen for up to three months. To reheat, bake in a 375° F oven for 5 to 10 minutes.

**PREP:** 15 minutes **BAKE:** 18 minutes

| | |
|---|---|
| 1 | 17¼-oz. pkg. frozen puff pastry, thawed (2 sheets) |
| 1 | egg white, slightly beaten |
| 1 | tsp. cracked black pepper |
| 1½ | cups finely shredded white cheddar, dill Havarti, or Monterey Jack with jalapeño peppers |

**1.** Line a baking sheet with parchment paper; set aside. Unfold pastry on a lightly floured surface; brush lightly with some of the egg white. Sprinkle lightly with half of the pepper. Sprinkle with half of the cheese. Top with second sheet of puff pastry. Brush with egg white and sprinkle with remaining pepper and cheese. With a rolling pin, roll puff pastry to seal the sheets together and press cheese into the pastry.

**2.** Preheat oven to 375° F. Cut the pastry into long ½-inch strips. Gently twist each strip several times. Transfer to prepared baking sheet, pressing down ends. Bake for 18 to 20 minutes or until golden brown. Transfer to a wire rack and let cool. Makes about 20 straws.

Each straw: 142 cal., 10 g total fat (2 g sat. fat), 9 mg chol., 147 mg sodium, 9 g carbo., 0 g fiber, 3 g pro. Daily Values: 2% vit. A, 6% calcium.

## PLAYFUL FINDS

"If you see a lot of similar items when you're out hunting and gathering, let it inspire you to create the party," says Jacqueline. "It can range from a trove of safari-themed ceramics or desert-motif china to a whole aisle of nothing but aqua blue."

When rolling the cheese into the puff pastry, press lightly and make a few passes to get cheese to stick firmly.

Cutting strips is easy with a pizza wheel. Use a straight-sided chopstick or ruler as a guide to make straight cuts.

## Blue Beauty

Be sure to use cream of coconut rather than coconut milk. Cream of coconut is a canned, sweetened coconut product that's usually found in drink-mix section of supermarkets and liquor stores.

**Fast!** **START TO FINISH:** 10 minutes

| | | | |
|---|---|---|---|
| 1 | cup white rum | 1/4 | cup cream of coconut** |
| 1/4 | cup blue curaçao* | 3 | cups ice cubes |
| 2 | 6-oz. cans pineapple juice (1½ cups) | | |

**1.** In a blender combine rum, blue curaçao, pineapple juice, cream of coconut, and ice. Cover and pulse until smooth. Adjust sweetness with additional pineapple juice, if desired. Makes 6 servings.

**\*NOTE:** If you don't have blue curaçao, substitute 1/4 cup triple sec plus 3 to 4 drops blue food coloring.

**\*\*NOTE:** Stir in can before measuring.

Each serving: 184 cal., 4 g total fat (3 g sat. fat), 0 mg chol., 3 mg sodium, 11 g carbo., 0 g fiber, 1 g pro. Daily Values: 11% vit. C, 1% calcium, 2% iron.

**Blue Beauty**

## Spicy Spring Vegetables

The secret to keeping these appetizers standing tall in a goblet or celery vase is to avoid overcooking.

**PREP:** 30 minutes **CHILL:** 2 hours

| | | | |
|---|---|---|---|
| 1 | lb. asparagus spears | 1/2 | tsp. salt |
| 1 | lb. short or medium length carrots | 1/2 | tsp. red chili paste |
| 1/4 | cup red wine vinegar | 1/4 | tsp. freshly ground black pepper |
| 1/4 | cup olive oil | 1/4 | cup sliced radishes |
| 1 | Tbsp. snipped fresh tarragon or 2 Tbsp. snipped fresh basil | | Small sprigs of fresh tarragon or small basil leaves |
| 1 | clove garlic, minced | | Salt and freshly ground black pepper |

**1.** Snap off and discard woody bases from asparagus; trim asparagus. Set aside. If using medium carrots, quarter lengthwise. Cut the carrot quarters in half crosswise or short carrots lengthwise to make carrot sticks. In a large skillet bring 1 inch of lightly salted water to boiling. Add asparagus; return to boiling. Cook, uncovered, 2 to 3 minutes or until just crisp-tender. Using tongs, remove asparagus from boiling water. Immediately plunge asparagus in a large bowl filled with ice water. Let stand until completely chilled; drain well. Pat dry with paper towels.

**2.** Add carrots to boiling water in skillet; return to boiling. Cook, uncovered, 3 to 4 minutes or until just crisp-tender. Remove carrots from boiling water. Immediately plunge in ice water. Let stand until completely chilled; drain well. Pat dry with paper towels. Place drained asparagus and carrots in a self-sealing plastic bag set in a baking dish or place in a shallow dish.

**3.** In a screw-top jar combine vinegar, oil, snipped fresh tarragon, garlic, the 1/2 teaspoon salt, chili paste, and pepper. Cover and shake well. Pour into bag or dish with asparagus and carrots. Add radishes. Seal bag or tightly cover dish and chill 2 to 4 hours, turning occasionally.

**4.** Transfer mixture to a tall goblet or serving dish. Top with sprigs of tarragon. Season to taste with additional salt and pepper. Makes 6 servings.

**Healthy** Each serving: 126 cal., 9 g total fat (1 g sat. fat), 0 mg chol., 230 mg sodium, 8 g carbo., 3 g fiber, 2 g pro. Daily Values: 342% vit. A, 26% vit. C, 3% calcium, 4% iron.

**Spicy Spring Vegetables**
Dakota-pattern water goblet,
circa 1875, made in Pittsburgh

CAKES ARE LIKE BOOKS:
THERE ARE NEW ONES
YOU WANT TO READ AND
OLD FAVORITES YOU
WANT TO REREAD.

– Ellen Rose

**Garden Lavender Pound Cake**

# HEALING, GIVING, BAKING

## Garden Lavender Pound Cake

**PREP:** 15 minutes  **STAND:** 30 minutes  **BAKE:** 45 minutes
**COOL:** 2 hours

| | | | |
|---|---|---|---|
| 1 | recipe Lavender Sugar (below) | ¼ | tsp. salt |
| 4 | eggs | ½ | cup granulated sugar |
| 1 | cup unsalted butter | 1 | Tbsp. vanilla |
| ¾ | cup dairy sour cream | 1 | tsp. finely shredded lemon peel |
| 2½ | cups all-purpose flour | 1 | cup sifted powdered sugar |
| 1 | tsp. baking powder | 1 | Tbsp. butter, melted |
| ½ | tsp. baking soda | 3 | to 4 tsp. lemon juice |

**1.** Prepare Lavender Sugar. Preheat oven to 325° F. Let eggs, the 1 cup butter, and sour cream stand at room temperature for 30 minutes. Meanwhile, grease and flour two 8×4×2-inch loaf pans; set aside. In a medium bowl stir together the flour, baking powder, baking soda, and salt; set aside.

**2.** In a large mixing bowl beat the Lavender Sugar, granulated sugar, 1 cup butter, and vanilla with an electric mixer on high speed about 4 minutes or until light and fluffy, scraping down sides of the bowl frequently.

**3.** Add the eggs, 1 at a time, beating on medium speed for 20 to 30 seconds after each addition. Alternately add flour mixture and sour cream to butter mixture, beating on low speed after each addition until just combined. (Batter will be thick.) Stir in lemon peel. Spread mixture in the prepared pans. Bake about 45 minutes or until a wooden toothpick inserted near centers comes out clean. Cool in pans on wire rack for 10 minutes. Remove from pans and cool completely.

**4.** In a small bowl mix powdered sugar with 1 tablespoon melted butter and enough lemon juice to make of drizzling consistency. Spoon over cake, letting some of it drip down the sides. Makes 24 servings (two 8-inch loaves).

**LAVENDER SUGAR:** In a spice grinder or food processor, grind ½ cup sugar with 1 to 2 tablespoons dried lavender blossoms.

Each serving: 194 cal., 11 g total fat (6 g sat. fat), 61 mg chol., 87 mg sodium, 22 g carbo., 0 g fiber, 3 g pro. Daily Values: 9% vit. A, 1% vit. C, 3% calcium, 4% iron.

BY **SHARON OVERTON** PHOTOGRAPHS BY **EDMUND BARR** PRODUCED BY **LAURA HULL**

# Baking therapy

Back when she owned only three cookbooks, Ellen Rose took them to bed with her at night and devoured the contents under the covers. It wasn't so much about the recipes themselves as the reassurance they brought, the promise that if you assembled all the ingredients carefully and followed the directions to the letter, everything would turn out well in the end.

Now that she owns a Los Angeles bookstore, the Cook's Library, full of nothing but cookbooks—8,000 titles in all—Ellen still turns to them for comfort. But several years ago when she was going through a rough patch in her life, she did more than that. She started baking cakes, about one a day for more than a year. "On really bad days," she says, "I baked two."

Ellen still bakes lots of cakes. But these days, it is more likely to be on a happy occasion—such as a gathering of her five dearest girl friends—rather than for therapy. They fill their plates with slices of lavender-scented pound cake, streusel-topped coffee cake, lemon buttermilk cake, and a rich chocolate cake.

About 20 years ago, she started keeping a journal of recipes she's tried and dinner parties she's given. Tucked inside the rubber-band-wrapped notebooks are magazine clippings, family photos, and motherly advice addressed to her daughter, to whom Ellen plans to give the journals.

The beneficiaries of all that binge baking were girl friends and neighbors, as well as customers and staff at the highly regarded cookbook store that Ellen has owned since 1989. Like her home, the store atmosphere is warm and inviting, with books stacked everywhere and lots of places to curl up and read.

**Ellen Rose**

## Lemony Pecan-Buttermilk Cake

Ellen Rose prefers to use Meyer lemons in this recipe; they're a thin-skinned, less tart cross between a lemon and a mandarin orange, and their taste has a hint of orange. Lemon oil is available through www.lorannoils.com. Or check the Web for a retailer near you.

**PREP:** 40 minutes **BAKE:** 1 hour **COOL:** 10 minutes

| | |
|---|---|
| 3 cups sifted cake flour | ¼ cup finely shredded lemon |
| 2 tsp. baking powder | peel |
| ½ tsp. salt | ½ cup lemon juice |
| 1 cup butter, softened | (4 to 6 regular lemons or |
| 2 cups granulated sugar | 8 to 10 Meyer lemons) |
| 1¼ tsp. vanilla | 1½ cups chopped pecans, |
| ¼ tsp. lemon oil (optional) | toasted |
| 5 eggs | 1 recipe Lemon Glaze |
| ⅔ cup buttermilk | (below) |

**1.** Preheat oven to 350° F. Grease and flour a 10-inch fluted tube pan. Set pan aside.

**2.** In a medium bowl combine the cake flour, baking powder, and salt; set aside.

**3.** In a large mixing bowl beat the softened butter with an electric mixer on high speed for 30 seconds. Add the 2 cups granulated sugar, vanilla, and, if desired, lemon oil; beat about 4 minutes or until light and fluffy.

**4.** Add eggs, 1 at a time, beating for 20 to 30 seconds after each addition. Alternately add the flour mixture and buttermilk to the butter mixture, beating on low speed after each addition and starting and ending with flour. Beat just until combined. Using a wooden spoon, stir in lemon peel and the ½ cup lemon juice. Stir in pecans. Spoon batter into prepared pan.

**5.** Bake for 1 hour or until a wooden toothpick inserted near the center of the cake comes out clean and the top springs back when lightly touched.

**6.** Cool cake in pan on a wire rack for 10 minutes. Invert cake onto wire rack set over a shallow baking pan. Poke holes in the top of the cake with a toothpick or wooden skewer. Spoon Lemon Glaze over cake. Cool completely. Makes 12 to 16 servings.

**LEMON GLAZE:** In a small saucepan heat and stir ¼ cup granulated sugar and 2 tablespoons lemon juice until sugar is dissolved.

Each serving: 517 cal., 28 g total fat (12 g sat. fat), 133 mg chol., 371 mg sodium, 61 g carbo., 2 g fiber, 7 g pro. Daily Values: 15% vit. A, 15% vit. C, 9% calcium, 15% iron.

**Lemony Pecan-Buttermilk Cake**

**Kid Friendly** ## One-Bowl Chocolate Cake
**PREP:** 20 minutes **BAKE:** 30 minutes **COOL:** 1 hour

| | | | |
|---|---|---|---|
| 1 | cup all-purpose flour | ¼ | teaspoon salt |
| 1 | cup sugar | ³/4 | cup milk |
| ½ | cup unsweetened cocoa powder | ⅓ | cup cooking oil |
| | | 1 | teaspoon vanilla |
| ½ | teaspoon baking soda | 1 | egg |
| ¼ | teaspoon baking powder | | Sifted powdered sugar |

**1.** Preheat oven to 350° F. Grease and lightly flour a 9×1½-inch round or 8×8×2-inch baking pan.

**2.** In a large mixing bowl combine flour, sugar, cocoa powder, baking soda, baking powder, and salt. Add milk, oil, and vanilla. Beat with an electric mixer on low speed just until combined. Beat on medium speed for 2 minutes. Add egg and beat 2 minutes more. Pour batter into prepared pan.

**3.** Bake for 30 to 35 minutes or until a wooden toothpick inserted near center comes out clean. Cool cake in pan on wire rack for 10 minutes. Remove cake from pan. Cool thoroughly on wire rack. To serve, sprinkle with powdered sugar. Makes 8 servings.

Each serving: 272 cal., 11 g total fat (2 g sat. fat), 28 mg chol., 179 mg sodium, 39 g carbo., 0 g fiber, 4 g pro. Daily Values: 1% vit. A, 9% calcium, 8% iron.

**One-Bowl Chocolate Cake**

Ellen chose a few of her favorite simple recipes for the buffet of sweets, including (left, from left to right) Best Coffee Cake, Lemony Pecan-Buttermilk Cake, One-Bowl Chocolate Cake, and Garden Lavender Pound Cake.

For years, Ellen has kept journals (above) to record her experience with new recipes and to chronicle parties she has given. Many of the entries track her cake-a-day therapy (right).

## Best Coffee Cake

The purpose behind buttering the cake pan is to provide something for the pecans to stick to, so coat generously. If the nuts aren't sticking, add more butter or chill the pan for a minute or two.

**STAND:** 30 minutes **PREP:** 35 minutes
**BAKE:** 65 minutes **COOL:** 2 hours

| | | | |
|---|---|---|---|
| 1 | recipe Pecan Streusel (below) | $1/2$ | tsp. salt |
| 4 | eggs | $3/4$ | cup butter, softened |
| 6 | Tbsp. butter, softened | 1 | 8-oz. pkg. cream cheese, softened |
| $1^1/2$ | cups chopped pecans | $1^1/2$ | cups sugar |
| $2^1/4$ | cups all-purpose flour | 2 | tsp. vanilla |
| $1^1/2$ | tsp. baking powder | | |

**1.** Prepare Pecan Streusel. Preheat oven to 325° F. Let eggs stand at room temperature for 30 minutes. Generously butter the inside of a 10-inch tube pan or 10-inch fluted tube pan using as much of the 6 tablespoons butter as possible. Coat the inside of the pan with the pecans, pressing the nuts into the butter as necessary; set aside.

**2.** In a medium bowl combine the flour, baking powder, and salt; set aside.

**3.** In a large mixing bowl beat the $3/4$ cup butter and cream cheese with an electric mixer on medium to high speed for 30 seconds. Add the sugar and vanilla; beat 4 to 5 minutes until light and fluffy.

**4.** Add eggs, 1 at a time, beating for 10 to 20 seconds after each addition and scraping bowl well. Beat in flour mixture, one-third at a time, until just combined.

**5.** Spoon one-third to one-half of the batter into the prepared pan, spreading evenly. Sprinkle with half of the Pecan Streusel. Spoon the remaining batter over the Pecan Streusel, spreading evenly. Sprinkle evenly with remaining Pecan Streusel.

**6.** Bake for 65 to 70 minutes or until cake pulls away from sides of pan and top springs back when lightly touched and/or a wooden toothpick inserted near the center comes out clean.

**7.** Cool in pan on a wire rack for 15 to 20 minutes. Remove from pan. Turn upright, cool completely on rack. Makes 12 servings.

**PECAN STREUSEL:** In a small bowl combine $1/2$ cup chopped pecans, $1/4$ cup sugar, 1 tablespoon unsweetened cocoa powder, and $1^1/2$ teaspoons ground cinnamon.

Each serving: 568 cal., 40 g total fat (17 g sat. fat), 141 mg chol., 411 mg sodium, 48 g carbo., 2 g fiber, 8 g pro. Daily Values: 22% vit. A, 8% calcium, 12% iron.

Best Coffee Cake

# April
# FOOLS

DON'T BE FOOLED
BY THE LUSCIOUS
LOOK OF THESE
DESSERTS. THEY'RE
LIGHT FOR
SPRINGTIME
ENJOYMENT.

**Strawberry-Lime Fool**

**Mango-Papaya Fool**

**Blueberry-Kiwi Fool**

# What's a Fool?

## Blueberry-Kiwi Fool

**Fast!** **Prep:** 20 minutes **Chill:** up to 2 hours

| | |
|---|---|
| 2 cups fresh or frozen unsweetened blueberries, thawed | 1/2 cup whipping cream |
| | 1 Tbsp. sugar |
| 1/8 tsp. ground cinnamon | 3 to 4 kiwifruit, peeled and cut up (1 cup) |

**1.** In a shallow dish mash 1 cup of the blueberries with a potato masher. (Or puree with a mini food chopper, food processor, or blender.) Stir cinnamon into mashed blueberries.

**2.** In a medium bowl beat whipping cream and sugar until cream is stiff. Fold in mashed blueberries.

**3.** In individual 6- to 7-ounce glasses or dishes, layer whipped cream mixture and remaining blueberries and kiwifruit. Serve immediately or cover and chill up to 2 hours before serving. Makes 6 servings.

**Healthy** Each serving: 122 cal., 8 g total fat (5 g sat. fat), 27 mg chol., 12 mg sodium, 14 g carbo., 2 g fiber, 1 g pro. Daily Values: 8% vit. A, 59% vit. C, 2% calcium, 1% iron.

## Mango-Papaya Fool

**Fast!** **Prep:** 20 minutes **Chill:** up to 2 hours

| | |
|---|---|
| 3 to 4 medium fresh mangoes and/or papayas, seeded, peeled, and chopped (about 3 cups) | 1/2 cup whipping cream |
| | 1 Tbsp. sugar |
| | 1/8 tsp. ground nutmeg |

**1.** In a shallow dish mash 1 cup of the chopped mango with a potato masher. (Or puree with a mini food chopper, food processor, or blender.)

**2.** In a medium bowl beat whipping cream, sugar, and nutmeg until cream is stiff. Fold in mashed mango.

**3.** In individual 6- to 7-ounce glasses or dishes, layer whipped cream mixture and remaining 2 cups chopped mango. Serve immediately or cover and chill up to 2 hours before serving. Makes 6 servings.

**Healthy** Each serving: 131 cal., 8 g total fat (5 g sat. fat), 27 mg chol., 9 mg sodium, 17 g carbo., 1 g fiber, 1 g pro. Daily Values: 70% vit. A, 38% vit. C, 2% calcium, 1% iron.

Fools, charmingly old-fashioned English desserts of puréed and whole fruit combined with whipped cream, can still hold some surprises. This simple, comforting dessert has a certain sweet nostalgia. It was all the rage during Victorian times and has enjoyed a few renaissances in popularity since its slightly silly name first appeared in print in 1590. The name probably comes from the French word "fouler," which means "to mash."

Originally made with gooseberries, fools can have just about any fresh fruit and a hint of spice or citrus in today's versions. For convenience, you can prepare them up to two hours ahead.

## Strawberry-Lime Fool

**Fast!** **Prep:** 20 minutes **Chill:** up to 2 hours

| | |
|---|---|
| 4 cups fresh strawberries, stems removed and quartered (about 3 cups quartered berries) | 1 Tbsp. sugar |
| | 1/4 tsp. finely shredded lime peel |
| 1/2 cup whipping cream | 1 lime, cut into 6 to 8 wedges |

**1.** In a shallow dish mash 1 cup of the quartered strawberries with a potato masher. (Or puree with a mini food chopper, food processor, or blender.)

**2.** In a medium bowl beat whipping cream, sugar, and lime peel until cream is stiff. Fold in mashed strawberries.

**3.** In individual 6- to 7-ounce glasses or dishes layer whipped cream mixture and remaining strawberries. Top with fresh lime wedge. Serve immediately or cover and chill up to 2 hours before serving. Makes 6 servings.

**Healthy** Each serving: 114 cal., 8 g total fat (5 g sat. fat), 27 mg chol., 9 mg sodium, 11 g carbo., 3 g fiber, 1 g pro. Daily Values: 7% vit. A, 116% vit. C, 3% calcium, 3% iron.

# BBQ BRISKET

**Chef Dean's Never-Fail Brisket**

BY RICHARD SWEARINGER PHOTOGRAPHS BY COLLEEN DUFFLEY

Learn the secrets to a barbecue classic from one of America's greatest chefs, Dean Fearing.

## Mansion Margaritas

**Fast!** **PREP:** 10 minutes

**1.** In a 4-cup glass measure stir together $1/2$ cup lime juice; 1 cup orange liqueur, such as Cointreau, Grand Marnier, or triple sec; and 1 cup quality tequila. Fill glasses with ice. Stir and pour into glasses. Makes 4 to 6 servings.

Each serving: 309 cal., 0 g total fat (0 g sat. fat), 0 mg chol., 1 mg sodium, 20 g carbo., 0 g fiber, 0 g pro. Daily Values: 15% vit. C.

### WHAT'S A SMOKER?

Smokers are different from grills because they're built to do a single job: provide low, steady heat over a long period of time. They come in various shapes. The two most common are the upright vertical water smoker, which is shaped something like a bullet, and the horizontal barrel smoker, which usually has a separate firebox attached at one end of the barbecue.

# A Barbecue Classic

A day spent tending a big beef brisket in the barbecue will help you reclaim the calm side of your weekend. The melding of meat, spice, heat, and smoke requires several hours and an attitude of watchful patience.

Grilling directly over a healthy bed of coals or with the gas grill on "high" is quick, but this is slow-smoking— a gentle method that gradually coaxes the toughness out of the meat. Your reward: plenty of tender slices.

"You can grill a steak and know it's going to be delicious," says Dean Fearing, chef and grill enthusiast. "But a brisket, done right, you can't stop eating it."

Dean is one of the nation's most respected chefs who, for the last 19 years, has run the restaurant at the Mansion on Turtle Creek hotel in Dallas. On the job he creates such Southwest-modern dishes as lobster tacos and silky corn chowder, but at home it's beef brisket.

A beloved Texas barbecue staple for decades, brisket— at up to about 12 pounds—is one of the largest cuts of meat available to the home cook. It is fairly easy to cook if you follow some basic rules. Picking a brisket is done by eye. "You want a big, fat brisket," Dean says. "You want to look for a brisket with the most fat, because it protects and bastes the meat naturally. That's where you get the best meat flavoring from—the fat."

Your choice of equipment is flexible: Use either a smoker or your charcoal or gas grill. However you grill, be sure to use the indirect cooking method. To ensure gentle, even heat, the food isn't placed directly over the coals or gas burners. Push the lit coals to either side of the grill. For gas, turn off at least one burner (either the center burner or one of the side burners). For charcoal, place a disposable pan between the coals, fill it with water, replace the grill racks, then place food over the pan. For gas, set water pan next to the food.

Taking the brisket off the grill at the right time is easy when you use a thermometer. The meat is done when a thermometer inserted in the thickest part of the meat registers 185° F. However, some backyard chefs cook it to 210° F. As the meat approaches 210° F, it will become more tender but less moist.

The most important ingredient is patience. "You have to let the barbecue do its job," he says. "You have to give it time. This isn't something you can decide to do at three in the afternoon."

## Chef Dean's Never-Fail Brisket

We've included directions for all three methods: smoker, charcoal grill, and gas grill. Dean's equipment of choice is a Hasty-Bake Charcoal Oven (www.hastybake.com).

**PREP:** 45 minutes  **CHILL:** overnight
**GRILL:** 8 hours for smoker,
4 hours on grill

| | |
|---|---|
| 2 Tbsp. paprika | 1/2 tsp. dry mustard |
| 1 Tbsp. chili powder | 1/2 tsp. dried thyme, crushed |
| 1 tsp. ground coriander | 8 to 10 mesquite or hickory |
| 1 tsp. ground cumin | wood chunks |
| 1 tsp. sugar | 1 10- to 12-lb. fresh beef |
| 1 tsp. salt | brisket |
| 1/2 tsp. ground black pepper | 2 cups of your favorite |
| 1/2 tsp. cayenne pepper | barbecue sauce |
| 1/2 tsp. curry powder | |

**1.** For rub, in a small bowl combine paprika, chili powder, coriander, cumin, sugar, salt, black pepper, cayenne pepper, curry powder, mustard, and thyme.

**2.** The night before smoking, soak wood chunks in enough water to cover. Drain before using.

**3.** Do not trim fat from brisket. One day before smoking, remove 1 tablespoon of the rub mixture and stir into 2 cups of your favorite barbecue sauce. Cover and chill. Sprinkle brisket with remaining rub mixture. Wrap meat tightly in plastic wrap and refrigerate overnight.

**SMOKER DIRECTIONS***

Arrange preheated coals, half of the drained wood chunks, and the water pan as directed in manufacturer's directions. Fill pan with hot water. Place brisket, fat side up, on grill rack over pan. Cover and smoke for 8 to 10 hours until a fork can easily be inserted into the center of the meat and a thermometer registers 185° F. Add more coals as needed, but do not add any more wood chips after the first 3 hours. (Too much smoke makes meat bitter.) Remove brisket from smoker. Cover; let stand 15 minutes.

*Read and follow the instructions that came with your smoker.

**GAS AND CHARCOAL GRILL DIRECTIONS**

For a grill, prepare a 4 1/2- to 5-pound brisket as directed above, except use only half of the rub ingredients. At least 1 hour before grilling, soak 8 to 10 wood chunks in enough water to cover.

**FOR A CHARCOAL GRILL:** Prepare grill for indirect grilling. Arrange medium hot coals around a drip pan. Fill drip pan with hot water. Test for medium-low heat above the drip pan. Add half of the wood chunks. Place brisket, fat side up, on the grill rack over the drip pan. Cover and grill for 2 1/2 hours. Turn brisket and continue grilling for 1 1/2 to 2 hours until a fork can be easily inserted in the center of the meat and an instant-read thermometer registers 185° F. Add coals (about 8 to 12 per hour) and wood as needed to maintain temperature and smoke. (Do not add any more wood after 2 hours of grilling.)

**FOR A GAS GRILL:** Start with a full tank of fuel. Adjust heat according to manufacturer's directions for indirect cooking over low heat. Add soaked wood chunks according to manufacturer's directions. (Or wrap chunks in foil and place packets directly over heat on the lava rocks, ceramic briquettes, or metal heat-diffusing bars.) Place a small coffee can or pan of hot water on the side of the grill rack over a lit burner. Place brisket, fat side up, on a rack in a roasting pan; set the pan on the grill rack over the unlit burner. Cover and grill for 2 1/2 hours or until meat is dark, dark brown. Wrap brisket in foil; return to grill directly on grill rack. Cook meat an additional 1 1/2 to 2 hours until a fork can be easily inserted in the center of the meat and thermometer registers 185° F.

**TO SERVE** Heat barbecue sauce in a small saucepan over low heat. To serve brisket, trim away crusty outer layer, if desired. Starting at the brisket's wide end, find the seam of fat running through the meat and cut along it, slicing the meat in half horizontally. Trim excess fat. Slice each section across the grain. Pass with heated barbecue sauce.

Makes 15 to 18 servings using a 10- to 12-pound brisket or 7 to 9 servings with a 4 1/2- to 5-pound brisket.

Each serving: 470 cal., 18 g total fat (5 g sat. fat), 177 mg chol., 623 mg sodium, 6 g carbo., 1 g fiber, 66 g pro. Daily Values: 18% vit. A, 5% vit. C, 3% calcium, 35% iron.

Patting the rub into the meat gives the best coverage and the most consistent result.

Replenish wood when smoke goes away; a handful per hour is usually plenty (for only the first 3 hours).

The meat is done when a fork inserted into the thickest part can be twisted easily.

Chef Dean prefers to cut away much of the blackened exterior of the finished brisket. "I like a little cleaner cut of brisket," he says. "Then you're down to that beautiful smoked meat."

# CHILE PEPPER PRIMER

## SCIENTISTS CALL THEM CAPSICUMS, COOKS CALL THEM HOT PEPPERS, AND TASTE BUDS THE WORLD OVER CALL THEM MAGIC.

When Christopher Columbus returned from the New World with chile peppers, he introduced a flavor revolution that continues to grow. In America, salsa—with its peppery kick—has become as familiar as mild-mannered ketchup. Chile peppers have given us a variety of other dishes.

Without chiles, Szechwan food would have no fire, Thai menus would have no warnings, and curries would be mild. There are hundreds of known varieties, but a handful of popular chiles dominates the market (see varieties, right).

By and large, the bigger the pepper, the milder it is; the smaller, the hotter. The ribs of the peppers are where most of the capsaicin—the chemical that causes the chile burn—is concentrated, but the seeds also contain a bit of the hot stuff. Removing the ribs will tone down the heat tremendously.

The redder a pepper is, the sweeter it is likely to be. This is a function of ripening, just as with other fruits. It also means that the flesh has been in contact with the ribs and seeds longer, so reds will be hotter as well as sweeter than their green former selves.

A pepper's heat is often measured by the Scoville heat index. Invented by pharmacist Walter Scoville in 1912, the index measures the impact of peppers on the tongue. Scoville gave peppers a score based on the amount of sugar water necessary to cancel the burn. If a pepper is rated at 5,000 Scoville units, that means the capsaicin extracted from it needs 5,000 times its volume in sugar water to neutralize it.

An effective quencher for burning palates is milk. Capsaicin is soluble in fat and alcohol, but barely at all in water. Starch helps, beer is good, yogurt and milk are great—but water just spreads the flames around.

### ANAHEIM
**500–1,000 SCOVILLE UNITS\***
Long and pale-to-bright green, this chile has medium-thick flesh with a heat that varies from negligible to hot, with most chiles falling somewhere in the middle.
▪ Tasty both raw and cooked, this pepper roasts well and can be stuffed.

### YELLOW
**4,000–6,000 SCOVILLE UNITS\***
Though sometimes mistaken for mild banana peppers, yellow chiles are actually light skinned to almost white-blonde. They are waxy with a sharp, spicy flavor.
▪ This chile is used often in salsas, salads, or mole sauces. It's great pickled too.

### FRESNO
**5,000–7,000 SCOVILLE UNITS\***
A versatile, sweet, thick-fleshed pepper, the Fresno looks like a red jalapeño, but it has broader shoulders, tapers more, and is hotter.
▪ Good cooked, raw, and pickled. Easy to roast and peel for tossing in sauces.

### SERRANO

**5,000–15,000 SCOVILLE UNITS\***

When jalapeños are no longer enough, move up the heat scale to the serrano. This pepper has a pleasant, crisp taste combined with blistering heat.

- Try it raw in coleslaw, salads, and salsas.

### POBLANO

**2,500–3,000 SCOVILLE UNITS\***

A large, mild, thick-fleshed pepper, the poblano (also called pasilla) is best roasted to bring out its earthy and rich flavor. Its dried form is the ancho, often used to make mole.

- The poblano is the most popular pepper for both roasting and stuffing.

### JALAPEÑO

**3,500–7,000 SCOVILLE UNITS\***

The most popular pepper in the country, it is sweet and thick-fleshed. When smoked and dried it is called a chipotle. Watch for new, vivid purple jalapeños in markets.

- Both green and red jalapeños add a gentle boost to guacamole. They're good roasted or pickled.

\*The higher the number the hotter the pepper.

# ROASTING TO REVEAL FLAVOR

Fire is magic for fresh chile peppers: It transforms their flavor from fresh, crisp, and clear to rich, earthy, and smoky. Use thicker-fleshed chiles, such as poblanos, and allow their skin to blacken and blister without burning through the flesh. Try roasted chiles with pizzas, omelettes, salads, sandwiches, and soups.

**1.** Use a grill or a broiler to roast your chiles. Don't worry if direct flame touches the skin; you'll be peeling it off in a few minutes. Roast with high heat, turning chiles as they blacken. Watch the color: brown is OK, black is better, white means they have stayed on the flame too long.

**2.** When blackened, put chiles in a mixing bowl, cover it tightly with plastic wrap, and let them sit for 10 minutes. Some liquid will seep to the bottom of the bowl; stir it into mayonnaise and use it on a sandwich.

**3.** Gently scrape off the skins with a knife, or pull them off with your (gloved) fingers. (You can also rinse the skins off under running water, but purists say this washes out some of the flavor.) Scrape the seeds and ribs from the inside, and cut off the stem. Stuff the chile peppers, or chop them and use as desired. They also freeze well.

## HANDLE WITH CARE

Take care when handling chile peppers. Wear gloves to keep the capsaicin off your skin. Wash the cutting board and utensils thoroughly in hot soapy water. Don't touch your eyes or other sensitive areas until your hands are completely clean using soap and water.

# HOW TO
# Pan-Sear

## THIS EASY, SPEEDY METHOD YIELDS PERFECT BROWNING; BIG, NATURAL FLAVOR; AND A CRUNCHY, CRISPY CRUST.

Pan-searing: You've probably seen the term, and yet not many people are familiar with this simple cooking technique that brings out a food's best flavor. Basically, this method uses high heat to quickly seal in the natural juices of food by searing the outside, resulting in a golden brown color and a texture that's lightly crisp. Moreover—and here's the not-so-secret secret that you'll discover—the food tells you when it's done by releasing itself from the surface of the pan.

To pan-sear, you need little more than a hot pan, a spatula or tongs, and a good cut of fish, meat, or poultry. Choose a pan that's an appropriate size for the number of items to be cooked. A 12-inch skillet will nicely accommodate dinner for four. A hard-anodized aluminum, stainless-steel, or a cast-iron skillet is a premium choice for the high heat retention that makes this approach work.

Add this technique to your weeknight repertoire by honing your skills with the Pan-Seared Tilapia with Almond Browned Butter and Snow Peas recipe (page 91). If tilapia isn't available, substitute perch, sole, or other white fish. You don't need to include the browned butter or snow peas; experiment with any sauce or vegetable that strikes your fancy.

To create a favorite combination of your own, choose a vegetable at its peak, such as asparagus. Make an easy pan sauce by stirring balsamic vinegar, broth, or wine into the pan after removing the meat, scraping up any brown crusty bits and adding a dash of a sassy spice. That's all the accompaniment necessary for a dish that's perfect in its understatement.

**GET IT HOT**—Get the empty pan hot enough that a drop of water rolls and jumps on its surface. Remove pan from heat; add a small amount of butter or oil to coat the surface. It should sizzle or bubble, but not burn. Add the fish or meat; return pan to heat.

**DO THE FLIP**—When the fish can be lifted without sticking, use a spatula to turn the fish and cook the other side. When the flip side is done, you'll know it's time to take it out of the pan by the simple fact that the fish will flake easily and release itself.

## Pan-Seared Tilapia with Almond Browned Butter and Snow Peas

**Fast!** **START TO FINISH:** 20 minutes

| | |
|---|---|
| 3 cups snow pea pods, trimmed | 1 tsp. all-purpose flour |
| 4 4- to 5-oz. skinless fresh tilapia fillets or other white fish | 1 Tbsp. olive oil |
| | 2 Tbsp. butter |
| Sea salt and freshly ground black pepper | ¼ cup coarsely chopped almonds |
| | 1 Tbsp. snipped fresh parsley |

**1.** In a large saucepan bring lightly salted water to boiling. Add pea pods. Cook for 2 minutes. Drain and set aside.

**2.** Meanwhile, season fish with salt and pepper; sprinkle with flour. Heat a large skillet over medium-high heat. When the pan is hot (a drop of water should sizzle or roll) remove from heat and add olive oil, tilting pan to coat. Return pan to heat and add fish (if necessary, cook half the fish at a time). Cook fish for 4 to 5 minutes or until it is easy to remove with spatula. Gently turn fish and cook for 2 to 3 minutes more or until fish flakes easily when tested with a fork. Arrange peas on a serving platter; arrange fish on top of peas.

**3.** Reduce heat to medium. Add butter to skillet. When butter begins to melt, stir in almonds. Cook for 30 to 60 seconds or until butter is melted and nuts are lightly toasted (do not let butter burn). Spoon the butter mixture over fish fillets. Sprinkle with parsley. Makes 4 servings.

Each serving: 266 cal., 15 g total fat (5 g sat. fat), 71 mg chol., 210 mg sodium, 7 g carbo., 3 g fiber, 24 g pro. Daily Values: 9% vit. A, 8% vit. C, 5% calcium, 6% iron.

**Pan-Seared Tilapia with Almond Browned Butter and Snow Peas**

**IT'S NOT READY!**—If you try to turn the fish and find there is some resistance, that's your clue to leave it alone—note the bits sticking to pan.

**FINISHING TOUCH**—The golden crust you see here is what pan-searing is all about—it locks in flavor and natural juices.

# EAT WELL

## GET-UP-AND-GO FOODS REV UP YOUR FAMILY TO LAUNCH THE DAY WITH NOURISHING VIGOR.

Breakfast perks up your metabolism, wards off midmorning snack attacks, and even boosts performance, creativity, and memory. Breakfast skippers tend to have a higher percentage of body fat than those who eat a meal at day's beginning. So heed the wake-up call and give your family a healthy start with these easy eats.

**NO-COOK FRUITY OATMEAL:** In-a-hurry moms can fix old-fashioned oats in a newfangled way. Pour oats in a bowl with some cinnamon, nutmeg, and brown sugar. Cover it all with a big slosh of cold milk and let it sit for 15 minutes or so. Top with fresh chopped fruit, a handful of trail mix, and a squirt of honey.

BY **JEANNE AMBROSE** PHOTOGRAPHS BY **KIM CORNELISON** FOOD STYLING BY **CHARLES WORTHINGTON**

**Chai-Mango Smoothie**

**Banana Breakfast Tostadas**

# BREAKFAST ON THE GO

▲ CHAI-MANGO SMOOTHIE : A frosty drink will tempt rushed teens. For each smoothie: In a blender combine one 8-ounce carton vanilla yogurt, 1 cup liquid chai tea concentrate, 1 cup chopped fruit (we love mango, but bananas are great with an added drizzle of chocolate sauce), and 1 cup ice cubes. For a thicker smoothie, start with frozen fruit and/or double the ice.

▼ BANANA BREAKFAST TOSTADAS: The youngsters at home will find these fruit and nut temptations irresistible, plus they'll start the day with a good serving or two of fruit. Slather wedges of whole wheat tortillas with light strawberry cream cheese (or another favorite flavor). Top with half a banana slice, a mound of chopped fresh fruit, and chunks of nuts.

▶ PROTEIN-PACKED BACON-'N'-EGG SALAD: Make egg salad the night before with light mayo, light dairy sour cream, and a dab of mustard. Add a handful of matchstick carrots, plus fresh snipped dill and chives. Cover and refrigerate. In the a.m., crisp up bacon in the microwave oven. Serve it for a burst of energy-producing protein. Bagel crisps are optional.

**Bacon-'n'-Egg Salad**

# May

PLAN A SPECTACULAR
OUTDOOR GATHERING TO CELEBRATE
A SPRING GRADUATION.

# Graduation Rites

**Plus**

# GRADUATION RITES

**Wasabi Party Mix**

THEY'RE SPARKLING WITH ENTHUSIASM, BRIMMING WITH ACCOMPLISHMENT, AND FULL OF CONFIDENCE ABOUT THE FUTURE. GIVE YOUR GRADUATE A PARTY WITH A LITTLE POMP AND CIRCUMSTANCE.

## Wasabi Party Mix

To make your own wasabi-flavored peas, place 5 cups of dried peas in a bowl. Lightly coat peas with nonstick cooking spray. Sprinkle with 2 to 3 teaspoons wasabi powder; toss to coat.

**Fast!** **PREP:** 15 minutes

| | |
|---|---|
| 5 cups purchased wasabi-flavored dehydrated peas* | 4 cups sesame sticks |
| | 4 cups honey-roasted peanuts |
| 4 cups bite-size toasted rice cracker mix | 2 cups shredded coconut |

**1.** In a bowl combine all ingredients. Store in an airtight container until ready to serve. Mixture can be made ahead and stored at room temperature up to 2 weeks or in the freezer up to 4 months. Makes 20 cups (eighty 1/4-cup servings).

**\*NOTE:** Wasabi peas can be found at grocery stores or at www.vinetreeorchards.com. Dried peas can be found at grocery stores or www.justtomatoes.com.

Each serving (1/4 cup): 99 cal., 6 g total fat (2 g sat. fat), 0 mg chol., 134 mg sodium, 9 g carbo., 1 g fiber, 3 g pro. Daily Values: 2% vit. A, 8% vit. C, 1% calcium, 2% iron.

BY STEPHEN EXEL PHOTOGRAPHS BY COLLEEN DUFFLEY FOOD STYLING BY BROOKE LEONARD PROP STYLING BY CAROL HACKER

# Planning the party

Graduation Day. It happens so quickly. The wide-eyed child you walked to the kindergarten door is now a high school senior walking down the aisle in a cap and gown.

So how will you get it all together for a knockout party? First order of business? Hold a brainstorming session with the guest of honor to glean ideas about the party. Invitations need to go out about five weeks before the big day. It's likely there will be more than one party to attend; you don't want your invitation to get lost in the shuffle.

Next, pick a spring-fresh palette for the party—or let school colors inspire one. Take a trip to the local discount store, office supply store, and crafts shop. You'll find a treasure trove of inexpensive items that can be employed in ways other than they were intended. For instance:

Think of white plastic in-boxes for serving food. Use plastic catch-all trays for stylish plates. Coordinate with inexpensive plastic flatware and colorful paper napkins.

When you plan the menu, consider older and younger tastes and appetites. Teens can be adventurous. But, being teens, an overstuffed sandwich and an interesting snack mix also rate high on their scorecard.

For convenience, recipes that can be made ahead are a necessity. When refrigerator space becomes premium, don't be afraid to ask a neighbor for help.

To start off, welcome everyone with a glass of Chai Punch and serve Wasabi Party Mix.

For salads, serve Melon-Radish Salad with watercress-honey dressing. Tone-on-tone Seven Layer Noodle Salad crowned with a peanut-sour cream dressing provides a bright, fresh note. Spiky Cucumber Salad lives up to its name by hitting the cool cukes with a blast of red pepper.

Consider making two sandwiches—a Smoked Roast Beef as well as a Ham and Mango. Four-ingredient Cold Roasted Salmon is an elegant counterpoint with its topping of crumbled bacon and goat cheese.

For dessert, serve smoky-sweet Grilled Apricots and Pineapple. And, of course, there's cake. But make it easy on yourself. Cover various size store-bought cakes with purchased white rolled fondant. Decorate with additional fondant cutouts and trim, and top with fresh berries.

The hard work is done. Now it's only tuition and four more years until your young adult's next rite of passage.

**Ham and Mango Sandwiches and
Smoked Roast Beef Sandwiches**

## Ham and Mango Sandwiches

For convenience, have the deli slice the ham for you.
**PREP:** 35 minutes  **CHILL:** up to 24 hours

| | | | |
|---|---|---|---|
| $2/3$ | cup coarse-grain Dijon-style mustard | $1\frac{1}{2}$ | lb. cooked smoked ham, thinly sliced |
| $1/4$ | cup sliced, pitted kalamata olives or other ripe olives | 2 | cups refrigerated sliced mango (9 oz.) |
| $1/4$ | cup snipped fresh parsley | | |
| 12 | sourdough and/or whole wheat mini rolls, split and toasted, if desired | | |

**1.** For olive spread, in bowl combine mustard, olives, and parsley.
**2.** Spread the cut sides of roll tops with olive spread. Place ham on the roll bottoms. Top ham with mango slices (cut slices to fit, if necessary). Replace roll tops over mango. Makes 12 sandwiches (using 2 ounces ham per sandwich).

Each sandwich: 371 cal., 4 g total fat (1 g sat. fat), 31 mg chol., 1,600 mg sodium, 56 g carbo., 0 g fiber, 23 g pro. Daily Values: 6% vit. A, 23% vit. C, 1% calcium, 16% iron.

## Smoked Roast Beef Sandwiches
**SOAK:** 1 hour  **PREP:** 30 minutes  **SMOKE:** $1\frac{1}{2}$ hours
**STAND:** 15 minutes  **CHILL:** up to 24 hours

| | | | |
|---|---|---|---|
| 2 | cups mesquite wood chips | 2 | Tbsp. prepared horseradish |
| 1 | 3- to 4-lb. boneless beef sirloin roast | 12 | sourdough and/or whole wheat mini rolls, split and toasted, if desired |
| 2 | tsp. chipotle chili powder or chili powder | 1 | cup purchased roasted red sweet peppers, cut into strips |
| $1/2$ | tsp. salt | | |
| $1/2$ | tsp. ground black pepper | | |
| $1/2$ | tsp. ground cumin | 2 | cups arugula leaves, rinsed and dried |
| $2/3$ | cup purchased onion jam or onion relish | | |

**1.** At least 1 hour before cooking, soak wood chips in enough water to cover. Trim fat from sirloin roast. For rub, in a small bowl combine the chipotle chili powder, salt, black pepper, and cumin. Sprinkle rub evenly over meat; rub in with your fingers. Insert a meat thermometer into the thickest part of the meat.
**2.** Drain wood chips. For a charcoal grill, arrange medium-hot coals around a drip pan. Test for medium heat above the pan. Sprinkle wood chips over coals. Place beef roast on grill rack over the drip pan. Cover; smoke for $1\frac{1}{2}$ to 2 hours or until desired doneness (meat thermometer registers 140° F for medium-rare doneness or 155° F for medium doneness). Cover beef roast with foil. Let stand 15 minutes before carving. (Meat's temperature will rise 5° F during standing.) Thinly slice beef. Place slices in a covered container; chill up to 24 hours.
**3.** In a small bowl combine the onion jam and horseradish.
**4.** Spread the cut roll tops with onion jam mixture. Place sliced roast beef on roll bottoms. Top roast beef with roasted red pepper strips and arugula; add prepared roll tops. Cover and chill any remaining beef up to 2 days. Makes 12 sandwiches (2 ounces cooked meat per sandwich).

**MAKE-AHEAD DIRECTIONS:** Sirloin roast may be smoked ahead and frozen whole or refrigerated up to 1 week prior to serving. Beef slices more easily when it is cold.

Each sandwich: 453 cal., 6 g total fat (2 g sat. fat), 54 mg chol., 682 mg sodium, 63 g carbo., 1 g fiber, 35 g pro. Daily Values: 5% vit. A, 62% vit. C, 2% calcium, 27% iron.

### GRADUATION PARTY

Wasabi Party Mix (page 97)
Ham and Mango Sandwiches (left) and/or
Smoked Roast Beef Sandwiches (above)
Cold Roasted Salmon (page 100)
Spiky Cucumber Salad (page 100),
Seven Layer Noodle Salad (page 101),
Melon-Radish Salad (page 102)
Grilled Apricots and Pineapple with
Mint Syrup (page 102)
Graduation cake
Chai Punch (page 99)

## Chai Punch

Chai is a blend of tea, milk, and spices. Chai concentrate can be found in the tea section of the grocery store.

**PREP:** 10 minutes  **CHILL:** 4 hours

| | |
|---|---|
| 1 | 32-oz. container chai tea concentrate (black tea) |
| ½ | cup sugar |
| 8 | inches stick cinnamon |
| ¼ | cup fresh basil leaves, torn |
| 1 | medium lime or lemon, sliced |
| 1 | medium orange, sliced |

1 32-oz. bottle club soda, chilled
Ice cubes
Cinnamon sticks (optional)
Sliced orange, lime, and/or Key limes (optional)
Whole basil leaves (optional)

**1.** Pour chai tea concentrate into a large container or pitcher. Stir in sugar. Add 8 inches stick cinnamon, torn basil, sliced lime, and sliced orange. Cover and chill 4 to 24 hours.

**2.** Strain mixture, discarding solids. Just before serving, slowly add club soda to chai mixture. Serve over ice cubes. If desired, garnish with additional cinnamon sticks, citrus slices, and whole basil leaves. Makes ten 6-ounce servings.

Each serving: 100 cal., 0 g total fat (0 g sat. fat), 0 mg chol., 26 mg sodium, 25 g carbo., 0 g fiber, 0 g pro.

Chai Punch

A simple spring buffet will satiate everyone's hunger after the graduation ceremony. Keep the food light and fresh. For serving, purchase several of the same dishes; uniformity adds crispness to the table.

## Spiky Cucumber Salad

This salad is sure to become a standard in your repertoire because of its easy preparation and sharp flavors.

**PREP:** 20 minutes   **CHILL:** 2 hours

| | |
|---|---|
| ½ | cup rice vinegar |
| ¼ | cup olive oil |
| 1 | Tbsp. finely shredded lemon peel |
| 2 | Tbsp. lemon juice |
| 1 | Tbsp. grated fresh ginger |
| 1 | Tbsp. sugar |
| 1½ | tsp. coarsely ground black pepper |
| 1 | tsp. toasted sesame oil |
| 1 | tsp. salt |
| ¼ | tsp. crushed red pepper |
| 8 | medium cucumbers |

**1.** For dressing, in a screw-top jar combine vinegar, olive oil, lemon peel and juice, ginger, sugar, black pepper, sesame oil, salt, and red pepper. Close jar; shake well to combine. Set aside.

**2.** Cut unpeeled cucumbers into bite-size strips or sticks. Place cucumbers in a very large bowl. Drizzle dressing over cucumbers; toss to combine. Cover and refrigerate for at least 2 hours or up to 12 hours, tossing occasionally. Drain to serve. Makes 24 to 26 servings.

**Healthy** Each serving: 27 cal., 1 g total fat (0 g sat. fat), 0 mg chol., 51 mg sodium, 3 g carbo., 1 g fiber, 1 g pro. Daily Values: 4% vit. A, 10% vit. C, 2% calcium, 2% iron.

## Cold Roasted Salmon

Make sure to use the center cut of salmon for uniform-size servings.

**PREP:** 30 minutes   **BAKE:** 15 minutes   **CHILL:** 4 hours

| | | | |
|---|---|---|---|
| | Olive oil | | Chives (optional) |
| 6 | 8-oz. center-cut salmon fillets, skinned | 6 | slices bacon, crisp-cooked, drained, and coarsely crumbled |
| 3 | to 4 Tbsp. peppercorn mustard or tarragon mustard | 3 | oz. goat cheese, crumbled |

**1.** Preheat oven to 475° F. Lightly oil a 15×10×1-inch baking pan with olive oil. Arrange salmon fillets in prepared pan. Turn under any thin portions of salmon to make uniform thickness. Spread tops of salmon fillets with mustard.

**2.** Bake for 15 to 18 minutes or until salmon flakes easily when tested with a fork. Transfer to platter. Cover; chill at least 4 hours or up to 24 hours until ready to serve.

**3.** To serve, cut salmon fillets in half lengthwise to make 12 portions. If desired, line serving platters with chives and arrange salmon on top of chives. Sprinkle salmon with crumbled bacon and goat cheese. (For 24 servings, cut salmon portions in half crosswise again.) Makes 12 servings.

**Healthy** Each serving: 236 cal., 12 g total fat (5 g sat. fat), 72 mg chol., 259 mg sodium, 1 g carbo., 0 g fiber, 26 g pro. Daily Values: 4% vit. A, 4% calcium, 7% iron.

**Spiky Cucumber Salad**

**Cold Roasted Salmon**

## Seven Layer Noodle Salad

To make this into a main-dish salad, add a layer of cooked shrimp or chicken. Daikon is a Japanese radish that has a celerylike flavor. You'll find it in the produce department.

**PREP:** 50 minutes  **CHILL:** up to 8 hours

1   recipe Peanut Dressing (below)
1   6- to 7-oz. pkg. rice sticks, broken
2   cups fresh snow pea pods, trimmed
8   cups shredded napa cabbage or cabbage
½   of a medium daikon, cut into thin bite-size strips (1 cup)
4   cups packaged shredded broccoli (broccoli slaw mix)
1   cup fresh cilantro leaves
½   cup coarsely chopped peanuts

**1.**  Prepare Peanut Dressing; set aside.

**2.**  Prepare rice sticks according to package directions. Drain. Rinse with cold water; drain well. Set aside. Cook pea pods, covered, in a small amount of boiling salted water for 2 minutes until crisp-tender. Drain. Rinse with cold water; drain well. Set aside.

**3.**  In a 4½- to 6-quart clear glass bowl or two 3-quart rectangular baking dishes layer the cabbage, rice sticks, pea pods, daikon, shredded broccoli, and cilantro. Carefully spread Peanut Dressing over the cilantro. Sprinkle the peanuts over dressing mixture. Cover and chill until ready to serve or up to 8 hours. If serving in a large straight-sided bowl, toss salad before serving. If serving in baking dishes, use knife to cut through mixture into serving-size portions. Makes 12 to 16 servings.

**PEANUT DRESSING:** In a medium bowl combine two 8-ounce cartons dairy sour cream, 1 cup bottled Thai peanut sauce, and, if desired, ¼ teaspoon cayenne pepper.

Each serving: 246 cal., 14 g total fat (6 g sat. fat), 17 mg chol., 365 mg sodium, 26 g carbo., 5 g fiber, 6 g pro. Daily Values: 36% vit. A, 94% vit. C, 12% calcium, 6% iron.

**Seven Layer Noodle Salad**

Set up a table for gifts and cards. Potted plants provide a welcoming decor for party guests and serve as departure gifts as well. For risers, purchase metal tins in various diameters and heights from the container department at your local discount store.

## Grilled Apricots and Pineapple with Mint Syrup

**PREP:** 25 minutes  **COOK:** 15 minutes  **GRILL:** 5 minutes
**COOL:** 1 hour

| | |
|---|---|
| 1 | recipe Mint Syrup (below) |
| 12 | ripe medium apricots, halved and pitted (or two 15¼-oz. cans unpeeled apricot halves, drained) |
| 1 | large pineapple, peeled, cored, and sliced into 12 rings |
| | Freshly grated nutmeg |
| | Fresh mint leaves |

**1.** Prepare Mint Syrup; set aside to cool.

**2.** Place a grill wok or grill basket on the rack of an uncovered grill directly over medium coals and heat for 5 minutes. Meanwhile, toss apricots with 2 tablespoons of the Mint Syrup. Brush pineapple rings with 2 tablespoons of the Mint Syrup. Sprinkle apricots and pineapple with nutmeg.

**3.** Place apricots in the preheated grill wok or basket. Place pineapple directly on the grill rack. Grill for 5 to 8 minutes or until heated through, turning gently halfway through cooking time. (For gas grill, preheat grill. Reduce heat to medium. Place grill wok or grill basket on grill rack over heat for 5 minutes. Cover; grill as above.) Remove fruit from grill; cool slightly.

**4.** To serve, quarter the pineapple slices. In a large straight-sided serving bowl toss together the apricots, pineapple, and remaining Mint Syrup. Sprinkle with additional freshly grated nutmeg and garnish with fresh mint. (Fruit mixture can be held at room temperature up to 2 hours.) Makes 12 servings.

**MINT SYRUP:** In a medium saucepan combine 1 cup water, 1 cup sugar, 1 medium bunch (about 12 sprigs or ¾ ounce) fresh mint, and one 3-inch strip lemon peel. Gently crush the mint with the bowl of a ladle or a wooden spoon. Bring to boiling, stirring to dissolve sugar. Reduce heat. Simmer, uncovered, for 10 minutes, stirring occasionally. Remove from heat. Let mixture cool for 1 hour. Strain, discarding mint and lemon peel. Transfer to a glass jar; cover and refrigerate up to 1 week. Makes 1 to 1¼ cups syrup.

**Healthy** Each serving: 104 cal., 0 g total fat (0 g sat. fat), 0 mg chol., 3 mg sodium, 26 g carbo., 1 g fiber, 1 g pro. Daily Values: 18% vit. A, 20% vit. C, 1% calcium, 5% iron.

## Melon-Radish Salad

French breakfast radishes feature a long and slim shape, a mild flavor, and a tender texture.

**PREP:** 30 minutes  **CHILL:** up to 2 hours

| | |
|---|---|
| 1 | small honeydew melon, seeded, peeled, and cut into bite-size pieces (4 cups) |
| 1 | small cantaloupe, seeded, peeled, and cut into bite-size pieces (4 cups) |
| 15 | to 20 red radishes and/or French breakfast radishes, thinly sliced (1¾ to 2¼ cups) |
| ½ | cup fresh watercress leaves |
| 2 | tablespoons honey |
| 1 | 8-oz. carton dairy sour cream |
| ¼ | tsp. salt |
| ¼ | tsp. freshly ground black pepper |

**1.** In bowl combine melon, cantaloupe, and radishes; set aside.

**2.** For dressing, in a blender or mini food processor combine watercress and honey. Cover and process or blend until smooth. In a small bowl stir together watercress mixture, sour cream, salt, and pepper until well combined. Chill until ready to serve.

**3.** To serve, place melon salad in large serving bowl and serve dressing on the side. Or pour dressing over salad and toss to coat; cover and chill up to 2 hours. Makes 9 cups.

**MAKE-AHEAD DIRECTIONS:** Cover and chill cut melon up to 2 days ahead. Prepare dressing as directed. Cover; chill up to 24 hours.

**Healthy** Each serving (¾ cup): 92 cal., 4 g total fat (3 g sat. fat), 8 mg chol., 71 mg sodium, 14 g carbo., 1 g fiber, 1 g pro. Daily Values: 39% vit. A, 65% vit. C, 3% calcium, 1% iron.

**Grilled Apricots and Pineapple with Mint Syrup**

**Melon-Radish Salad**

USING PURCHASED CAKES AND COVERING THEM IN ROLLED FONDANT TAKES THE PRESSURE OFF AT DESSERT TIME.

HIDE THE CARDBOARD EDGES OF THE CAKE BOARDS WITH RIBBONS. FOR PRESENTATION, SET CAKES ON OVERTURNED BOWLS AND STURDY PAPER-COVERED BOXES AT GRADUATED HEIGHTS.

**Cake with rolled fondant decorations**

# HOW TO USE ROLLED FONDANT

Here are some helpful hints for using rolled fondant: • Follow the manufacturer's instructions. • Make sure the cake's surface is smooth. Spread a thin layer of buttercream icing on the cake before applying fondant. • Lightly dust the work surface and rolling pin with powdered sugar before rolling fondant. • Repair any tears by joining the tear with oiled fingertips and smoothing with powdered sugar. • Keep unused rolled fondant covered. • Purchase rolled fondant at a crafts store or www.wilton.com.

Carefully transfer fondant from work surface to cake with your rolling pin.

Trim the fondant with a sharp knife or pizza cutter.

Knead food coloring into white fondant one drop at a time until desired color is achieved. Cut out various shapes.

Attach cutouts to cake by brushing the back with a small amount of water.

# Basil

AROMATIC BASILS SCENT THE AIR WITH LICORICE AND ANISE, MINT AND LEMON. THIS MAGICAL HERB INSPIRES US WHEREVER WE FIND IT: IN THE GARDEN, THE MARKET, AND THE KITCHEN.

**Global pestos: Thai, Indian, and Classic Genovese (page 108)**

*Thai Pesto*

*Indian Pesto*

*Classic*

BY **STEPHEN EXEL** AND **DOUG HALL** PHOTOGRAPHS BY **KIM CORNELISON** AND **KING AU** FOOD STYLING BY **BROOKE LEONARD**

## BASIL BOUQUET

A cluster of basils is both decorative and functional. Snip a few leaves as needed. Each has a distinct flavor.

1. 'Purple Ruffles'—Sweet cinnamon and spice.
2. Variegated basil—Licorice and anise overtones.
3. Sweet basil—Tea and licorice.
4. 'Dark Opal'—Delicate hints of clove and vanilla.
5. Thai basil—Highly scented spicy anise and clove.
6. 'Spicy Globe'—Hints of citrus and mint.
7. Cinnamon basil—Soft cinnamon flavor.

Other fragrant basils include
- 'Magical Michael'—Rich in sweet, fragrant oils.
- 'Mrs. Burns' lemon basil—Intense lemon.
- 'Siam Queen'—Anise and licorice.
- 'Genovese'—Well-rounded, not sweet.
- 'Red Rubin'—Subtle sweet scent.
- Lime basil—Hints of lime.
- 'African Blue'—Traces of tea and camphor.

ILLUSTRATION: STEVE STANKIEWICZ

# Explore the varieties

Basil is a glorious gift of the season. Its fragrance livens the garden air; its flavors bring delight in the kitchen. As farmers' markets start to fill with varieties of basil, the plants beckon us to explore their distinctive looks and tastes. Green basils intrigue with their handsome leaves. The purple-hue plants hold their own attractions. Touch basil leaves and you'll find your hands perfumed with traces of scent from cinnamon and clove to vanilla.

Harvest the tips of stems frequently to keep basil bushy and actively growing. Some gardeners set out new transplants at monthly intervals; the leaves of plants that have been in the garden for several months or have flowered can taste bitter. Young leaves have the best flavor.

Snip off flowering buds, but don't discard them. Scatter them on salads and summer pastas. Or cut buds a small way down the stem and place in a vase. Snip the leaves as you need them.

Let the flavored varieties whet your appetite for creative cooking. Add lemon basil to your best tomato sauce, a handful of cinnamon basil to iced tea. Basil can serve as the foundation for myriad condiments. Beyond the classic style of pesto ('Genovese' is the best basil for this), you can use lemon, 'Siam Queen,' cinnamon, 'Spicy Globe,' and 'Osmin' to create international versions of this spread.

Spread Basil Rouille, a chunky garlicky sauce, or nut-and-licorice-flavored Basil-Walnut Cream Cheese on breads. Roasted, sautéed, and fried meats and vegetables will benefit from the kick of Purple Basil Vinaigrette or the velvety smoothness of Sweet Basil Mayonnaise. Guacamole takes a turn for the best when you stir in a generous amount of 'Genovese' basil. Cinnamon basil crisscrosses its way into savory-sweet Cinnamon Basil Dessert Pesto, an herbaceous complement to soft and cheddar cheeses, and buttery cookies such as shortbread.

Basil is best when it's used soon after snipping; otherwise the leaves may darken. To store a large amount of basil, stand the stems in water and do not refrigerate. Cut basil should last a couple of days. If you grow your own basil, one thing you won't have to worry about, though, is supply. With an herb bed full of these gorgeous plants, you're bound to have plenty through the fall.

# GLOBAL PESTOS

Keep this chart handy for your bumper crop of flavored basils. Included are two additional variations to the pestos pictured on *page 106*.

| | **CLASSIC GENOVESE** | **THAI** | **GREEK** | **INDIAN** | **HARVEST** |
|---|---|---|---|---|---|
| **BASIL** Start with 2 cups firmly packed basil* | Genovese or Sweet | Spicy Globe, Siam Queen, or Thai | Lemon, Mrs. Burns Lemon | Osmin, Red Rubin, or Purple Ruffles | Cinnamon, Osmin, or Ruby Red |
| **OIL** Measure ⅓ to ½ cup of oil | Olive oil | Sesame oil (not toasted) | Olive oil | Olive oil | Walnut oil |
| **CHEESE** Add ½ cup cheese | Grated Parmesan or Romano | Crumbled goat cheese | Crumbled feta cheese | Shredded farmer cheese | Shredded white cheddar |
| **NUTS** Add ½ cup nuts | Pine nuts | Peanuts | Substitute one 2¼-oz. can sliced pitted olives, drained | (no nuts required) | Pumpkin seeds and/or chopped walnuts |
| **SEASONINGS** Add the seasonings | 3 or 4 cloves garlic, peeled and quartered; ¼ tsp. salt; ⅛ tsp. ground black pepper | 1 tsp. finely shredded lime peel; ½ tsp. crushed red pepper; ¼ tsp. salt; ⅛ tsp. ground black pepper | 4 cloves garlic, peeled and quartered; ¼ tsp. salt; ⅛ tsp. ground black pepper | 2 Tbsp. finely shredded orange peel; 1 tsp. ground cumin; ¼ tsp. salt; ¼ tsp. ground coriander; ⅛ tsp. ground black pepper | ¼ tsp. pumpkin pie or apple pie spice; ¼ tsp. packed brown sugar; ⅛ tsp. salt; ⅛ tsp. ground black pepper (optional) |

**METHOD:** In a food processor or blender combine basil, ⅓ cup of oil, cheese, nuts, and seasonings. Cover and process or blend until nearly smooth, stopping and scraping sides as necessary and adding enough remaining oil until desired consistency. Makes about 1 cup. To store, divide pesto into three portions. Place each portion into small, airtight containers and refrigerate 1 to 2 days or freeze up to 3 months. *NOTE: Any of these pestos can be made with commercially available sweet basil.

**Basil Guacamole**

## Basil Guacamole

Basil gives this chunky guacamole a fresh, balanced flavor.

*Fast!* **START TO FINISH:** 25 minutes

| | |
|---|---|
| 2 ripe medium avocados, halved, seeded, and peeled | 1 Tbsp. fresh lime juice |
| | ¼ to ½ tsp. salt |
| ¾ cup snipped fresh basil | ¼ tsp. crushed red pepper or few drops bottled hot pepper sauce |
| ½ cup chopped seeded tomato | Tortilla chips |
| 2 Tbsp. chopped green onion | |

**1.** In bowl mash avocado with a fork. Stir in basil, tomato, green onion, lime juice, salt, and red pepper. Serve immediately with tortilla chips. Makes about 2 cups.

Each serving (2 Tbsp.): 40 cal., 4 g total fat (1 g sat. fat), 0 mg chol., 40 mg sodium, 2 g carbo., 1 g fiber, 1 g pro. Daily Values: 5% vit. A, 6% vit. C, 1% calcium, 2% iron.

Basil Rouille and Basil-Walnut Cream Cheese

## Basil Rouille

Rouille (ROO-ee) is a Provençal condiment that is stirred into stews and fish soups. It's a great spread too. Warning: Lots of garlic!

Fast! **START TO FINISH:** 10 minutes

| | | | |
|---|---|---|---|
| 1 | cup snipped fresh basil | 1 | or 2 fresh small serrano or |
| 1 | small tomato, seeded and | | jalapeño chile peppers, |
| | chopped | | seeded and diced* |
| 1/3 | cup fine dry bread crumbs | 1 | tsp. sea salt or salt |
| 4 | large cloves garlic, minced | 1/2 | cup olive oil |

**1.** In a medium bowl combine basil, tomato, bread crumbs, garlic, chile peppers, and salt; mix well. Gradually stir in olive oil; mix well. Cover and chill. To serve, bring to room temperature and stir before serving. Makes 1½ cups.

**\*NOTE:** When handling chile peppers, wear plastic or rubber gloves. If your bare hands do touch the chile peppers, wash your hands well with soap and water.

Each tablespoon: 46 cal., 5 g total fat (1 g sat. fat), 0 mg chol., 96 mg sodium, 1 g carbo., 0 g fiber, 0 g pro. Daily Values: 2% vit. A, 2% vit. C, 1% calcium, 1% iron.

## Basil-Walnut Cream Cheese

In addition to a cracker and bread spread, this cream cheese is also wonderful warmed slightly in the microwave and dropped in small spoonfuls on a vinaigrette salad.

Fast! **START TO FINISH:** 15 minutes

| | | | |
|---|---|---|---|
| 1 | 8-oz. pkg. cream cheese, | 1 | clove garlic, minced |
| | softened | 1/2 | tsp. crushed red pepper |
| 1/4 | cup butter, softened | 1/4 | tsp. salt |
| 1/2 | cup snipped fresh basil | 1/8 | tsp. freshly ground black |
| 1/4 | cup chopped walnuts | | pepper |
| 1 | Tbsp. white wine vinegar | | |

**1.** In a medium mixing bowl beat cream cheese and butter with an electric mixer on medium speed until smooth. Stir in basil, walnuts, vinegar, garlic, red pepper, salt, and black pepper until well combined. Serve immediately or cover and chill up to 3 days. Makes 1½ cups.

Each tablespoon: 60 cal., 6 g total fat (3 g sat. fat), 16 mg chol., 73 mg sodium, 1 g carbo., 0 g fiber, 1 g pro. Daily Values: 5% vit. A, 1% calcium, 1% iron.

**Sweet Basil Mayonnaise and Purple Basil Vinaigrette**

## Purple Basil Vinaigrette

*Fast!* **START TO FINISH**: 15 minutes

| | |
|---|---|
| 1/3 cup olive oil* or salad oil | 1 Tbsp. freshly grated |
| 1/3 cup red wine vinegar | Parmesan cheese |
| 1/4 cup snipped fresh purple | 1 to 2 tsp. sugar |
| basil or sweet basil | Salt and ground black pepper |
| 1 Tbsp. finely chopped | |
| shallot | |

**1.** In a screw-top jar combine oil, vinegar, basil, shallot, cheese, and sugar. Cover and shake well. Season to taste with salt and pepper. Serve immediately or cover and store in refrigerator up to 3 days. Shake before serving. Makes about 3/4 cup.

**\*NOTE:** If using olive oil, let vinaigrette stand at room temperature for 15 to 20 minutes before using.

Each serving (2 Tbsp.): 113 cal., 12 g total fat (2 g sat. fat), 1 mg chol., 64 mg sodium, 1 g carbo., 0 g fiber, 0 g pro. Daily Values: 2% vit. A, 1% vit. C, 1% calcium, 1% iron.

## Cinnamon Basil Dessert Pesto

Serve this with a young Parmesan cheese, such as Grana Podano; shortbread or waffle cookies; warm Brie; and assorted fruit.

*Fast!* **START TO FINISH**: 20 minutes

| | |
|---|---|
| 1/3 to 1/2 cup walnut oil | 1/2 cup flaked coconut |
| 2 cups firmly packed fresh | 1/4 cup freshly grated Asiago |
| cinnamon or sweet basil | cheese (1 oz.) |
| leaves | 2 tsp. raw sugar or packed |
| 1/2 cup chopped almonds | brown sugar |

**1.** In a food processor or blender combine 1/3 cup of the oil, the basil, almonds, coconut, cheese, and sugar. Cover and process or blend until nearly smooth, stopping and scraping sides as necessary and adding enough remaining oil until of desired consistency. If the pesto is not to be served immediately, divide it into 3 portions. Place each portion in a small airtight container. Refrigerate up to 24 hours or freeze up to 3 months. Makes about 1 1/3 cups.

Each tablespoon: 70 cal., 6 g total fat (2 g sat. fat), 1 mg chol., 24 mg sodium, 2 g carbo., 1 g fiber, 1 g pro. Daily Values: 3% vit. A, 1% vit. C, 3% calcium, 1% iron.

## Sweet Basil Mayonnaise

You can also make a version of this recipe by stirring the basil, white pepper, and mustard into 1 cup of purchased mayonnaise. Add 2 to 3 tablespoons lemon juice to taste.

*Fast!* **START TO FINISH**: 15 minutes

| | |
|---|---|
| 1/2 cup snipped fresh basil | 1 Tbsp. lemon juice |
| 1/4 tsp. salt | 3/4 cup salad oil |
| 1/8 tsp. ground white pepper | 1/4 cup olive oil |
| 1/8 tsp. dry mustard | |
| 1/4 cup refrigerated or frozen | |
| egg product, thawed | |

**1.** In a food processor or blender combine 1/4 cup of the basil, the salt, pepper, mustard, egg product, and lemon juice. Cover and process or blend until combined. Scrape down sides. Combine oils in a 1-cup glass measure. With the machine running, add oils in a thin, steady stream. Transfer mixture to a small bowl; stir in remaining basil. Makes 1 1/4 cups.

Each tablespoon: 98 cal., 11 g total fat (2 g sat. fat), 0 mg chol., 35 mg sodium, 0 g carbo., 0 g fiber, 0 g pro. Daily Values: 2% vit. A, 2% vit. C, 1% calcium, 1% iron.

**Cinnamon Basil Dessert Pesto**

# Crispy IT IS!

**The Best Homemade French Fries**

The best french fries are slender, golden, and so crisp you can hear a "crunch" when you bite down. The surest route to that goal is getting the right balance of the three elements that matter most—oil, potatoes, and heat.

The *Better Homes and Gardens®* Test Kitchen tried several methods and determined the most dependable way to create superlative homemade results.

Start with the right oil. Peanut oil turns out to be the best: It has a faintly nutty taste that gives a pleasing flavor boost to the fries, and it has a very high smoke point, which means it doesn't burn easily. Other cooking oils, such as canola, olive, and soybean, work wonderfully but give a different flavor and texture. Premium oils, such as extra-virgin olive and walnut, aren't practical for frying.

For potatoes, our tests show the best, most widely available, choice is the plain brown russet, also called an Idaho. It has a higher ratio of water to solids than other varieties, so it cooks up with a fluffier interior and doesn't absorb as much oil. Varieties such as fingerlings, Yukon golds, reds, and purple potatoes have more sugar and water in their flesh and can burn more easily; some also go limp after they come out of the fryer.

There are two methods for cooking: your stove or an electric deep-fat fryer. Both work, but electric fryers are more convenient and have built-in thermostats that make getting the right temperature much easier.

The next key is to pick the style of fries you want: The thinner you cut your potatoes—$1/4$ inch thick is a good start—the crisper they'll fry up; the thicker you make them, the more tender they'll be. Some cookbooks recommend frying potatoes twice to get them crisp, but in our tests, thinness was what made the most difference.

Safety notes: If you're using an electric deep-fat fryer, follow the manufacturer's directions. If using a saucepan, use one that holds at least three quarts, don't fill more than halfway with oil, and use a thermometer (it's the surest way to get good results). Also, don't try to improvise—buy a wire mesh or perforated-metal fryer basket that fits the saucepan you'll be using. The oil bubbles up when the potatoes are added, so lower the basket slowly and gently into the oil. Finally, don't try to fry too many potatoes at once. Overload the oil and it will boil over the sides of your pot. If this happens, remove the fries and the boiling will stop.

## Kid Friendly — The Best Homemade French Fries

It's essential to allow 5 minutes or so to let the oil come back up to 365° F between batches. Sea salt or other coarse salt gives the potatoes a pleasing extra layer of texture. Between batches, keep potatoes warm on paper towel-lined baking sheet in a 300° F oven.

**PREP:** 20 minutes **COOK:** about 7 minutes per batch

| | |
|---|---|
| 1½ lb. russet or Idaho baking potatoes | Peanut oil for deep-frying<br>Coarse sea salt, kosher salt, or salt |

**1.** Peel the potatoes, if desired, and cut lengthwise into $1/4$- to $3/8$-inch sticks. Soak in ice water if not ready to fry.

**2.** In a deep-fat fryer, heat peanut oil according to manufacturer's directions to 365° F, or heat oil in a 3-quart or larger saucepan to 365° F (saucepan should be no more than half full).

**3.** Drain the potatoes well. Pat potatoes thoroughly dry on toweling. Fry the potatoes, about one-third at a time, until potatoes are tender in the center and edges are just beginning to color and blister, about 7 to 9 minutes. Remove with a frying basket and drain on paper towels.

**4.** To serve, sprinkle lightly with salt. Makes 4 servings.

Each serving: 220 cal., 14 g total fat (2 g sat. fat), 0 mg chol., 408 mg sodium, 23 g carbo., 2 g fiber, 3 g pro. Daily Values: 32% vit. C, 1% calcium, 5% iron.

BY RICHARD SWEARINGER PHOTOGRAPH BY GREG SCHEIDEMANN [N] HAUS FOTO FOOD STYLING BY CHARLES WORTHINGTON

# WINE CRACKERS

### Sublime Wine Crackers

You can make several herb/spice and wine variations of these crackers. Combinations are described at the end of the recipe. The dough will appear dry but will hold together when gently worked with hands. Avoid adding more liquid than called for because this can result in tough crackers.

**PREP:** 20 minutes **BAKE:** 18 minutes

| | |
|---|---|
| 1 cup all-purpose flour | 1/8 to 1/4 tsp. ground black pepper |
| Desired herb/spice option (below) | 3 Tbsp. wine (below) |
| 1/2 tsp. salt | 2 Tbsp. olive oil |
| | Coarse kosher salt (optional) |

**1.** Preheat oven to 325° F. In a mixing bowl combine flour, desired herb/spice, salt, and pepper. In a medium bowl combine desired wine and olive oil. Gradually add wine mixture to flour mixture, tossing with a fork until combined. Form dough into a ball.

**2.** Transfer dough to a lightly floured surface. Roll into a 12×9-inch rectangle, about 1/8 to 1/16 inch thick (trim any uneven edges, if necessary). Prick dough all over with a fork. Using a pastry wheel, cut into 3×1 1/2-inch rectangles. Gently transfer rectangles to ungreased baking sheet. If desired, sprinkle rectangles lightly with kosher salt.

**3.** Bake about 18 minutes or just until crackers start to brown and are firm to the touch. Cool completely on wire racks. Store in an airtight container up to 1 week. Makes 24 crackers.

**Wine and herb/spice combinations:**

- **Sauvignon Blanc and basil**—1/4 cup snipped fresh basil and 2 tablespoons pine nuts, finely ground.
- **Riesling and tarragon**—2 teaspoons snipped fresh tarragon and 1/4 teaspoon paprika.
- **Cabernet Sauvignon and rosemary**—2 tablespoons snipped fresh rosemary.
- **Champagne and mustard**—2 teaspoons dry mustard.
- **Chardonnay and fennel**—2 teaspoons fennel seeds, crushed. Reduce ground black pepper to 1/8 teaspoon.

Each serving (1 cracker; average per variation): 31 cal., 0 g total fat, (0 g sat. fat), 0 mg chol, 1 mg sodium, 8 g carbo., 1 g fiber, 0 g pro. Daily Values: 7% vit. C.

**Sublime Wine Crackers**

Lately, wine seems to be spilling into recipe ingredient lists where you would least expect it. Take, for example, these delectable little crackers that star a splash of wine. You can make several variations using just 3 tablespoons of wine—ideal if you're opening a bottle for a gathering or have some left over. These crisp, thin, and munchable wine crackers (above) come from a simple recipe that pairs wine with an herb or spice. They'll partner rather nicely with cheeses, dips, chutneys, savory jellies, and party spreads; and they'll slip right into a cheese sampling or wine tasting. Remember to include these crackers when you serve soups and chowders. They'll add an unexpected herbaceous note. And if you're visiting instead of hosting, you've got the "what can I bring?" problem solved.

BY **STEPHEN EXEL** PHOTOGRAPH BY **GREG SCHEIDEMANN [N] HAUS FOTO** FOOD STYLING BY **BROOKE LEONARD**

# SURPRISING FLAVORS

Few of life's simple pleasures can match the taste of a homegrown, sun-ripened tomato picked only minutes before it is to be eaten. Say "tomato" and most gardeners think of the popular big red beefsteak types.

Less known and rapidly gaining ground are the heirloom varieties that come in a variety of colors, sizes, shapes, and most important, different flavors. You can get in on the fun and grow your own tomato harvest even if you don't have an acreage or a large garden patch.

## HERE ARE OUR PICKS

When the time is ripe for tomatoes, do as we did at a staff picnic: Have a tomato tasting. Whether you grow your own or harvest at farmers' markets, gather as many different tomatoes as you can. Also gather your friends and family (or coworkers), sea salt, cutting boards, and knives. You'll be amazed at the range of tastes—and differing responses. Our favorites illustrate this story.

### 'LEMON BOY'

These 8-ounce chunky tomatoes are brilliant yellow through the whole fruit, making it a flashy addition to salads. It's mild tasting yet subtly sweet with a touch of tang. Best sliced and eaten fresh.

### 'GREEN ZEBRA'

Don't let the green color fool you: This stripy show-off is ripe and ready. It tastes outstanding in

**TOMATO SALAD WITH VINAIGRETTE** (photo upper right): Cut up some 'Green Zebra' and toss the pieces together with other sliced tomatoes or whole cherry or grape tomatoes, a handful of fresh basil, cubes of fresh mozzarella, and croutons. Drizzle all with a vinaigrette made from a little finely shredded lemon peel mixed into olive oil with a good splash of balsamic vinegar. Sprinkle with salt and ground black pepper.

### 'BLACK KRIM'

Named for the Crimean peninsula in the Black Sea, this dark red heirloom tomato is definitely sweet, but there is also a surprising hint of saltiness. 'Black Krim' is an outstanding slicer that needs little beyond a touch of salt or perhaps some snipped fresh basil. With enough sun and heat, these hefty tomatoes turn nearly black.

BY ELVIN MCDONALD AND JEANNE AMBROSE PHOTOGRAPHS BY **KRITSADA** FOOD STYLING BY **BROOKE LEONARD**

### 'PINEAPPLE'

When you slice into this yellow-red heirloom tomato that can weigh up to 2 pounds, you'll be rewarded with a stunning golden yellow color marbled with patches of pink and light red. Full of meaty flavor, it's a standout in any salad. The 'Pineapple' tomato really makes an impact in a **BLT SANDWICH** (*right*). Be sure to cut thick slices. And think about adding a dollop of guacamole for a super-fresh and nutritious topper.

### 'YELLOW STUFFER'

The shape and color of this bright tomato is similar to a yellow sweet pepper. Appropriately named, 'Yellow Stuffer' begs to be cut in quarters (cut only about three-quarters of the way down) and stuffed. Tuna salad is the obvious choice, but be creative too. How about a sliver of roast beef and a sprinkle of blue cheese?

### 'LONG TOM'

This meaty tomato is one of the best for making tomato sauces and pastes. It's shaped like a sausage with a point on the bottom end. Use it in your favorite pasta sauce recipe or try this **FRESH TOMATO SAUCE:** In a large saucepan cook 1/4 cup chopped onion and 2 cloves of garlic, minced, in a little hot oil until onion is tender. Add 2 cups of peeled, seeded, and chopped fresh 'Long Tom' tomatoes; season with salt and ground black pepper. Bring to boiling; reduce heat. Cook, uncovered, 15 minutes or so; stir occasionally. Add 2 more cups of peeled, seeded, chopped tomatoes and 1/4 cup snipped fresh basil. Heat through.

### 'WHITE WONDER'

This one's a sweety. The high sugar content of 'White Wonder' makes it choice for juicing and canning. If you like a mild-mannered tomato, just slice and eat. When ripe, this fruit is white inside and out.

# June

LET'S CELEBRATE FATHER'S DAY.
TAKE DAD BY THE HAND,
LEAD HIM TO HIS FAVORITE CHAIR, AND
LET THE PAMPERING BEGIN.

# A Delicious Day for Dad

**Plus**

# A DELICIOUS DAY FOR DAD

**Salsa and Cheese Dip with Crispy Tortilla Chips**

WHAT DOES DAD WANT MOST ON FATHER'S DAY? TO BE SURROUNDED BY FAMILY. OF COURSE, SOME TASTY FOOD IS WELCOME AS WELL.

## Salsa and Cheese Dip

Create a chunky dip by combining sour cream with a bit of salsa and chunks of queso fresco—a white, crumbly Mexican cheese. A swirl of fresh herbs and green onion add a vivid flavor. To scoop up the dip, you'll need a sturdy chip, such as our Crispy Tortilla Chips (page 120) or some of the colorful tortilla chips available in grocery stores.

**PREP:** 15 minutes  **CHILL:** 1 hour

| | |
|---|---|
| ¼ cup fresh Italian parsley leaves | 1 8-oz. carton dairy sour cream |
| 2 Tbsp. fresh cilantro leaves | 2 oz. queso fresco or farmer cheese, crumbled (½ cup) |
| 1 Tbsp. fresh oregano leaves | 3 Tbsp. bottled green salsa |
| 2 Tbsp. pistachio nuts | Few drops bottled hot pepper sauce (optional) |
| 1 green onion (white portion only), cut up | |

**1.** In a food processor or blender combine parsley, cilantro, oregano, 1 tablespoon of the pistachio nuts, and the green onion. Cover and process until finely chopped. Set aside.

**2.** In a small bowl stir together sour cream, queso fresco, salsa, and bottled hot pepper sauce. Stir in herb mixture. Cover and chill 1 to 2 hours or until serving time. To serve, spoon into serving bowl and top with remaining pistachio nuts. Makes about 1½ cups.

Each serving dip (3 tablespoons): 85 cal., 7 g total fat (4 g sat. fat), 15 mg chol., 33 mg sodium, 3 g carbo., 0 g fiber, 2 g pro. Daily Values: 9% vit. A, 7% vit. C, 6% calcium, 2% iron.

BY JEANNE AMBROSE PHOTOGRAPHS BY STEVEN MCDONALD PROP STYLING BY KAREN JOHNSON FOOD STYLING BY SUSIE SKOOG RECIPES BY NANCY BYAL

# Dinner for Dad

Because the cliché is true—the way to a man's heart is through his stomach—plan on making Father's Day extra special by giving Dad the day off and plying him with his favorite foods. Most dads are easy-to-please kind of guys, so it's not necessary to add a lot of fussy food to the dinner menu on the day set aside to honor all fathers.

We've created a slightly macho menu based on Dad's desires, according to those who know him best: you. Nearly 2,500 people responded to a recent *Better Homes and Gardens®* survey about dads that we posted at bhg.com, our website. According to those who took the survey, Dad's favorite meal includes steak and potatoes, corn on the cob, and pie or ice cream—preferably both.

This easy meal means that kids can help Mom with some of the prep work in the kitchen and still have plenty of time to decorate a homemade card or take him outside for a game of catch. Teens in the family might want to burn a compact disc for Dad of his favorite tunes or songs that feature father and family themes.

Because one of Dad's favorite predinner munchies is a bowl of chips with dip, treat him to a homemade version. In this case, the chips are ready in a jiffy, giving the kids plenty of time to stir together the ingredients for a dip. The basic seared steak takes on a bold profile when topped with a thick slice of sizzling bacon and a homemade steak sauce that adds a hint of fruity sweetness.

For dessert, we took a cue from the story of "Goldilocks and the Three Bears" to create Big, Bigger, Biggest Plum Pies. The pies can be made in three sizes: junior pies for the small fries, medium-size pies, or great big Papa Bear portions. Bake one, two, or all three pies, depending on how many people you're serving. Serve with a scoop or two of ice cream for a delicious finish to your Father's Day.

## Sizzling Steak with Peach Steak Sauce

A 6-ounce portion is a pretty hefty serving for a child, so consider splitting steaks into smaller portions for those with pint-size appetites.

**START TO FINISH:** 30 minutes

| | |
|---|---|
| 1 recipe Peach Steak Sauce (page 121) | Salt and ground black pepper Nonstick cooking spray |
| 4 slices thickly sliced bacon, cut crosswise into thirds | 2 fresh peaches, pitted and cut into eighths |
| 4 6-oz. beef boneless flatiron, ribeye, or Delmonico steaks, cut $3/4$ to 1 inch thick | 4 1-inch slices French or Italian bread, toasted |

**1.** Prepare Peach Steak Sauce; set aside. In a large skillet cook bacon until crisp and brown. Remove from skillet. Drain on paper towels. Reserve 1 tablespoon drippings in skillet; set aside.

**2.** Lightly season steaks with salt and pepper. Lightly coat a 12-inch heavy skillet with nonstick cooking spray. Preheat skillet over medium-high heat until very hot. Add meat. Reduce heat to medium and cook, uncovered, for 8 to 15 minutes for medium rare (145° F) to medium (160° F) doneness, turning occasionally. (If meat browns too quickly, reduce heat to medium low.) Use $1/2$ cup of the Peach Steak Sauce to brush on steaks during the last 5 minutes of cooking.

**3.** Meanwhile, in the large skillet heat the reserved 1 tablespoon of bacon drippings. Add peaches and cook over medium-high heat about 3 minutes or until peaches are browned and heated through, stirring and turning the peaches occasionally.

**4.** To serve, place a toast slice on each plate. Top with a steak, peach slices, and bacon. Pass remaining Peach Steak Sauce. Makes 4 servings.

Each serving with sauce: 690 cal., 16 g total fat (6 g sat. fat), 88 mg chol., 840 mg sodium, 87 g carbo., 7 g fiber, 47 g pro. Daily Values: 27% vit. A, 46% vit. C, 9% calcium, 31% iron.

When preparing the tortilla chips, use a sharp knife or a pizza cutter to carefully cut through a small stack of tortillas. Be creative and cut the tortillas into free-form strips, wedges, squares, or other shapes.

## Crispy Tortilla Chips

Flavored tortillas in different colors make a fun treat. Go easy on the salt because these chips can get too salty very quickly.

**PREP:** 10 minutes  **BAKE:** 8 minutes per batch

| | |
|---|---|
| 8 6-inch corn or flour tortillas | 2 tsp. garlic-pepper blend |
| Nonstick cooking spray | $1/2$ tsp. coarse salt (optional) |

**1.** Preheat oven to 425° F. Lightly coat tortillas on both sides with nonstick cooking spray. Sprinkle tortillas on both sides with garlic-pepper blend and coarse salt. Make 2 stacks of 4 tortillas each (see photo, above). With a sharp knife or a pizza cutter, cut each stack into 6 pieces. Place pieces in a single layer on 2 baking sheets.

**2.** Bake 1 sheet at a time for 8 to 10 minutes or until tortillas are lightly browned and crisp. Cool on baking sheets. Serve immediately or store in a tightly sealed container up to 3 days. Makes 8 servings.

Each serving: 69 cal., 1 g total fat (0 g sat. fat), 0 mg chol., 362 mg sodium, 15 g carbo., 1 g fiber, 2 g pro. Daily Values: 3% calcium, 8% iron.

**Sizzling Steak with Peach Steak Sauce; Roasted Potato Kabobs**

## Peach Steak Sauce

Slather this sweet-and-hardy sauce generously over all kinds of beef. Try it on a grilled burger. It's yummy with pork too.

**START TO FINISH:** 25 minutes

| | | | |
|---|---|---|---|
| 2 | medium fresh peaches, peeled, pitted, and cut up | 2 | Tbsp. balsamic vinegar |
| ¼ | cup peach or apricot nectar | 1 | Tbsp. packed brown sugar |
| | | 1 | Tbsp. minced onion |
| 2 | Tbsp. condensed beef consommé or condensed beef broth | ¼ | tsp. ground cinnamon |

**1.** Place the peaches in a food processor or blender. Cover and process until almost smooth.

**2.** In a small saucepan combine pureed peaches, peach nectar, beef consommé, balsamic vinegar, brown sugar, onion, and cinnamon. Bring to boiling; reduce heat. Simmer, uncovered, for 10 minutes or until sauce reaches desired consistency, stirring occasionally. Makes 1 cup.

Each serving (¼ cup): 55 cal., 0 g total fat (0 g sat. fat), 0 mg chol., 43 mg sodium, 13 g carbo., 1 g fiber, 1 g pro. Daily Values: 3% vit. A, 10% vit. C, 2% calcium, 2% iron.

## Roasted Potato Kabobs

Precooking potatoes in a microwave oven gives them a fluffy texture.

**PREP:** 25 minutes   **COOK:** 5 minutes
**ROAST:** 20 minutes

| | | | |
|---|---|---|---|
| 1½ | lb. small potatoes, such as purple, Dutch yellow, fingerlings, or new reds | 2 | Tbsp. olive oil |
| | | 2 | Tbsp. snipped fresh thyme |
| 2 | Tbsp. butter or margarine, melted | ½ | tsp. salt |
| | | ¼ | tsp. freshly ground black pepper |

**1.** Soak four 8-inch wooden skewers in water for 30 minutes. Scrub potatoes. Cut any large potatoes in half. In a large saucepan cook potatoes, uncovered, in boiling salted water to cover for 5 to 10 minutes or until almost tender. Drain. Or place potatoes in a microwave-safe bowl with 2 tablespoons water. Microwave, covered, on 100 percent power (high) for 5 to 7 minutes or until almost tender.

**2.** Preheat oven to 475° F. Thread potatoes on the soaked wooden skewers. Place kabobs on a baking sheet. In a small bowl combine melted butter and olive oil. Brush potatoes with butter mixture. Sprinkle with thyme, salt, and pepper. Roast, uncovered, for 20 to 25 minutes or until golden brown. Makes 4 servings.

Each serving: 241 cal., 13 g total fat (5 g sat. fat), 16 mg chol., 364 mg sodium, 29 g carbo., 3 g fiber, 4 g pro. Daily Values: 6% vit. A, 45% vit. C, 3% calcium, 14% iron.

## Skillet-Toasted Corn Salad

If you love the taste of smoky, charred corn, plan on cooking the corn an additional 5 minutes—but be forewarned that your skillet will blacken along with the corn kernels. Use a cast-iron skillet if you have one. The Cotija cheese used in this recipe is often called Mexican Parmesan cheese. It's white, dry, and crumbly.

*Fast!* **START TO FINISH:** 30 minutes

| | |
|---|---|
| 1 recipe Lemon Dressing (below) | 2 oz. Cotija or Parmesan cheese, finely shredded ($1/2$ cup) |
| 6 fresh ears of corn | |
| 1 Tbsp. olive oil | 1 head romaine lettuce, cut crosswise into 1-inch thick rounds or torn into bite-size pieces |
| 20 baby sweet peppers (10 oz.) or 4 medium red, yellow, and/or green sweet peppers | |

**1.** Prepare Lemon Dressing; set aside. Remove husks from fresh ears of corn; scrub with a stiff brush to remove silks. Cut kernels from corn cobs. In a large skillet cook corn kernels in the 1 tablespoon oil over medium-high heat about 5 minutes or until corn is tender and golden brown, stirring often. Turn down heat as necessary to prevent corn from popping out of the skillet. Remove from heat; keep warm.

**2.** Remove membrane and seeds from sweet peppers. Cut sweet peppers into large pieces or coarsely chop medium sweet peppers. In a large bowl combine sweet peppers, corn, and cheese. Pour Lemon Dressing over mixture; toss lightly to coat. Serve over romaine lettuce. Makes 6 to 8 servings.

**LEMON DRESSING:** In a screw-top jar combine $1/3$ cup olive oil; $1/3$ cup lemon juice; 1 tablespoon Worcestershire sauce for chicken; 3 cloves garlic, minced; $1/2$ teaspoon freshly ground black pepper; $1/4$ teaspoon salt; and a few dashes bottled hot pepper sauce. Cover and shake well; set aside.

Each serving: 260 cal., 19 g total fat (2 g sat. fat), 9 mg chol., 138 mg sodium, 24 g carbo., 4 g fiber, 7 g pro. Daily Values: 90% vit. A, 171% vit. C, 12% calcium, 9% iron.

### FATHER'S DAY DINNER

Sizzling Steak with Peach Steak Sauce (page 120)
Roasted Potato Kabobs (page 121)
Skillet-Toasted Corn Salad (above)
Crispy breadsticks
Big, Bigger, Biggest Plum Pies (page 124)
Hot coffee and/or beer and milk

## SPICY RIMS

Punch up the taste of a basic brew by dressing up the glass rim with flavor. Start with an empty glass. Moisten the rim by rubbing a lime wedge along the top edge. Dip the rim in a mixture of 2 tablespoons coarse salt or sea salt combined with $1/8$ teaspoon chili powder. (Go easy on the chili powder!) Carefully pour Dad's favorite beer into the glass. Then drop the lime wedge in too.

**Skillet-Toasted Corn Salad**

Kid

**Big, Bigger, Biggest Plum Pies**

This recipe makes an 11-inch father of all pies. To make smaller versions, check out the "Pie Chart"(left). If you can find Pluots—a cross between plums and apricots—in your market, give them a try. Pluots have a much higher sugar content than standard plums or apricots, making them spectacularly sweet. Pluots are great in this pie or as a fresh snack.

**PREP:** 30 minutes  **BAKE:** 45 minutes

| | | | |
|---|---|---|---|
| 1 | 15-oz. pkg. folded refrigerated unbaked piecrust (2 crusts) | 4 | medium apricots, pitted and cut into quarters |
| 5 | Tbsp. sugar | 1 | Tbsp. lemon juice |
| 3 | Tbsp. cornstarch | 1 | Tbsp. purchased honey butter, softened |
| 3/4 | tsp. ground cinnamon | | Coarse sugar or sugar (optional) |
| 1/4 | tsp. ground nutmeg | | Vanilla ice cream (optional) |
| 4 | medium red plums or Pluots, pitted and cut into eighths | | |

**1.** Preheat oven to 375° F. Let the piecrusts stand at room temperature as directed on package.

**2.** In a large mixing bowl combine sugar, cornstarch, cinnamon, and nutmeg. Stir in plums, apricots, and lemon juice. Set aside.

**3.** Unfold piecrusts. Place 1 piecrust on a 12-inch pizza pan (unfolded piecrusts should be 11 inches in diameter). Cut out a 3- to 4-inch circle from the center of the remaining piecrust; set aside. Stir fruit mixture. Mound fruit mixture in middle of piecrust on pan, leaving a 2-inch border. Top with remaining piecrust (with the hole at the top of the mound); firmly roll edges of piecrusts together toward filling. Place a double thickness of foil over the exposed fruit.

**4.** Bake for 25 minutes; remove foil. Bake about 20 minutes more or until pastry is brown and fruit is tender. Brush hot crust and fruit with honey butter. Sprinkle crust with sugar. Serve warm with ice cream. Makes 8 servings.

Each serving: 348 cal., 16 g total fat (7 g sat. fat), 14 mg chol., 213 mg sodium, 50 g carbo., 2 g fiber, 2 g pro. Daily Values: 16% vit. A, 18% vit. C, 1% calcium, 2% iron

# PIE CHART

Follow the instructions for Big, Bigger, Biggest Plum Pies (right), but match the ingredient amounts to the size pastry you use. All pies begin with one 15-ounce package unbaked piecrust (2 crusts). Trim the top and bottom pastry to the size indicated *below*. Combine the ingredients and proceed as directed in the recipe. Finish by brushing crust with honey butter.

| | | |
|---|---|---|
| Sugar | 2 Tbsp. | |
| Cornstarch | 1 Tbsp. | **7"** |
| Cinnamon | 1/4 tsp. | **(BIG)** |
| Nutmeg | Dash | **4 SERVINGS** |
| Red plums or Pluots | 2 | |
| Apricots | 2 | |
| Lemon juice | 1 tsp. | |

| | | |
|---|---|---|
| Sugar | 3 Tbsp. | |
| Cornstarch | 2 Tbsp. | |
| Cinnamon | 1/2 tsp. | |
| Nutmeg | 1/8 tsp. | |
| Red plums or Pluots | 3 | |
| Apricots | 3 | |
| Lemon juice | 2 tsp. | |

**9"**
**(BIGGER)**
**6 SERVINGS**

| | | |
|---|---|---|
| Sugar | 5 Tbsp. | |
| Cornstarch | 3 Tbsp. | |
| Cinnamon | 3/4 tsp. | |
| Nutmeg | 1/4 tsp. | |
| Red plums or Pluots | 4 | |
| Apricots | 4 | |
| Lemon juice | 1 Tbsp. | |

**11"**
**(BIGGEST)**
**8 SERVINGS**

## SIZING UP YOUR PIES:

1. To make a medium-size pie, start with a standard pastry (11 inches in diameter); use a 9-inch lid or plate as a guide for trimming to size. Do the same for the top crust. (If you're making the smallest pie, cut 7-inch pastry circles for the top and bottom crusts.)

2. Use a cookie or biscuit cutter to cut a circle in the top pastry.

3. After fruit is piled on the bottom pastry, add the top pastry and tightly roll and seal the edges together. Pile more fruit into the hole so some of it peeks out.

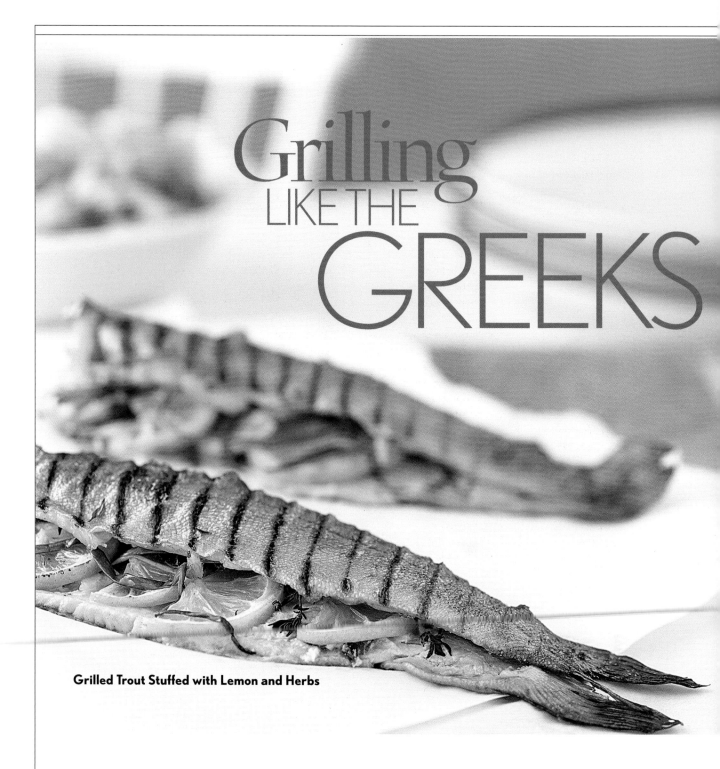

# Grilling LIKE THE GREEKS

**Grilled Trout Stuffed with Lemon and Herbs**

## Grilled Trout Stuffed with Lemon and Herbs

This is a simple way to grill almost any whole fish, with a stuffing—not to be eaten—that flavors the fish from the inside. Although Greek food is typically associated with saltwater fish (sea bass works well with this method), the country's mountain streams make trout popular as well.

**Fast!** **PREP:** 20 minutes **GRILL:** 8 minutes

| | | | |
|---|---|---|---|
| 4 | 8- to 10-oz. fresh or frozen dressed rainbow trout or coho salmon | 2 | Tbsp. snipped fresh oregano, thyme, and/or chives, or 2 tsp. dried oregano or thyme, crushed |
| 1 | Tbsp. olive oil | | |
| 1 | tsp. kosher salt or ½ tsp. salt | 2 | cloves garlic, minced |
| ¼ | tsp. coarsely ground black pepper | 12 | sprigs fresh oregano and/or thyme, and/or chive stems (omit all if using dried herbs) |
| 2 | lemons | | |

**1.** Thaw fish, if frozen. Rinse fish; pat dry with paper towels. If desired, remove the heads of fish. Rub both sides of the fish lightly with olive oil. Sprinkle flesh with salt and pepper; set aside.

**2.** Cut 1 of the lemons in half lengthwise, then cut each half into thin slices. Cut remaining lemon into wedges; set aside.

**3.** In a small bowl stir together the snipped or dried herbs and the garlic. Sprinkle the flesh side of each fish with the herb mixture. Tuck the lemon slices and herb sprigs evenly into center cavity of each fish. Squeeze one of the lemon wedges over fish.

**4.** Grill fish on the rack of an uncovered grill directly over medium coals for 8 to 12 minutes or until fish flakes easily when tested with a fork, turning once. Serve with remaining lemon wedges. Makes 4 servings.

Each serving: 356 cal., 16 g total fat (4 g sat. fat), 133 mg chol., 564 mg sodium, 6 g carbo., 3 g fiber, 48 g pro. Daily Values: 12% vit. A, 80% vit. C, 19% calcium, 6% iron.

BY JONATHON LOCKE PHOTOGRAPHS BY KIM CORNELISON FOOD STYLING BY CHARLES WORTHINGTON

# Focus on freshness

Because the Olympics returned to their birthplace this year, now is a good time to give the backyard grill a decidedly Greek flavor.

If you follow the basic philosophy of Greek cooking—focusing on distinct, fresh flavors in uncomplicated recipes—you'll produce a winning meal. Start with the inseparable trio of lemon, olive oil, and oregano. Add garlic, onions, more fresh herbs, feta cheese, kalamata olives, and bold wine, and you have the makings of a great evening.

In Greece, ingredients for daily meals have long been gathered from the sea as well as local farms and fields. Meals were created, with few exceptions, with what was at hand. They still follow that recipe for success.

The Chickpea Salad (page 128) is a good example of a recipe that has cousins all around the Mediterranean. Chickpeas, or garbanzo beans, are a favorite source of protein in the region. Tomatoes and peppers, although imported from the New World, are so much a part of the local cuisines that they are considered practically indigenous. Garlic and onions are used everywhere, as is cilantro (and its seed, coriander).

Then you must consider the olive and its oil. To a large degree, much of Greek life has revolved around olives for thousands of years. Fine olive oils have always been Greece's source of pride. Today it makes appearances in marinades, salad dressings, and drizzled over vegetables and breads.

Desserts are a celebration of regional ingredients as well, so expect more fruit and honey than chocolate. Ancient Greeks waxed poetic about honey, believing it to be part of the daily fare of the gods. Honey is used in the dessert recipe on page 128 to glaze fresh fruit—an adaptation of a centuries-old technique called *glykó*, the preserving of fruits in a honey-based syrup.

**Orange-Glazed Fruit with Anise Whipped Cream**

mixed greens for a light entrée. If desired, serve with lemon wedges to squeeze over salad. Makes 8 to 10 side-dish servings.

**RED WINE VINEGAR DRESSING:** In a screw-top jar combine 1/4 cup olive oil; 3 tablespoons red wine vinegar; 1 teaspoon kosher salt; 1 clove garlic, minced; and 1/8 teaspoon sugar. Cover and shake well. Season to taste with additional sugar, if desired.

Each serving: 134 cal., 8 g total fat (1 g sat. fat), 0 mg chol., 419 mg sodium, 14 g carbo., 4 g fiber, 4 g pro. Daily Values: 23% vit. A, 57% vit. C, 3% calcium, 6% iron.

## Orange-Glazed Fruit with Anise Whipped Cream

Ouzo, often referred to as the national drink of Greece, is an anise-flavor liqueur.

**PREP:** 20 minutes  **CHILL:** 30 minutes  **GRILL:** 10 minutes

| | |
|---|---|
| 1/4 cup orange juice | 3 cups fruit, such as fresh or |
| 2 Tbsp. sugar | dried figs, tangerine |
| 2 Tbsp. honey | wedges, strips of mango, |
| 1/2 cup whipping cream | or quartered plums or |
| 1 tsp. sugar | apricots |
| 1 tsp. ouzo (anise-flavor | 1 Tbsp. butter or margarine, |
| liqueur), orange liqueur, | melted |
| orange juice, vanilla, or | Chopped almonds (optional) |
| several drops anise | |
| extract | |

**1.** For syrup, in a small saucepan combine orange juice, 2 tablespoons sugar, and honey. Bring to boiling, stirring to dissolve sugar and honey; reduce heat. Simmer, uncovered, for 10 minutes. Set aside.

**2.** In a chilled medium mixing bowl beat whipping cream, 1 teaspoon sugar, and ouzo with an electric mixer on medium speed until soft peaks form (tips curl). Cover and chill the mixture up to 30 minutes.

**3.** In a mixing bowl toss fruit with melted butter. Transfer fruit to a grill pan or a disposable foil pan with small slits cut in the bottom.* For a charcoal grill, place fruit in pan on the rack of an uncovered grill directly over medium coals. Grill for 10 to 12 minutes or until heated through, stirring occasionally. (For a gas grill, preheat grill. Reduce heat to medium. Place grill pan on grill rack directly over heat. Cover and grill as above.)

**4.** To serve, arrange fruit on each of 4 dessert plates. Drizzle with syrup. If desired, sprinkle with almonds. Serve with whipped cream. Makes 4 servings.

***NOTE:** Make a foil pan with a double thickness of heavy foil; fold up sides of foil to form a pan and cut several slits in bottom.

Each serving: 267 cal., 15 g total fat (9 g sat. fat), 49 mg chol., 44 mg sodium, 36 g carbo., 2 g fiber, 2 g pro. Daily Values: 51% vit. A, 44% vit. C, 3% calcium, 1% iron.

## Chickpea Salad

During peak tomato season, the dressing needs just a smidge of sugar. If your tomatoes are a little on the tart side, you might want to add more.

**PREP:** 30 minutes  **CHILL:** 4 hours  **STAND:** 15 minutes

| | |
|---|---|
| 3 cups coarsely chopped tomatoes (about 4 medium) | 1 cup chopped green sweet pepper |
| 1 15-oz. can garbanzo beans (chickpeas), rinsed and drained | 1 cup snipped fresh cilantro |
| | 1/4 cup finely chopped onion |
| | 1 recipe Red Wine Vinegar Dressing (right) |
| 1/2 of a large cucumber, peeled, quartered, and sliced (about 1 cup) | Torn mixed salad greens (optional) |
| | Lemon wedges (optional) |

**1.** In a very large bowl combine chopped tomatoes, garbanzo beans, cucumber, sweet pepper, cilantro, and onion; set aside.

**2.** Prepare Red Wine Vinegar Dressing. Pour dressing over vegetable mixture, tossing to coat. Cover and chill for 4 to 24 hours.

**3.** Let vegetable mixture stand at room temperature about 15 minutes before serving. Serve alone or, if desired, toss with

**Chickpea Salad**

## MARINADES

Marinades are popular throughout the Mediterranean as a versatile way to flavor fish or meat before cooking. Here are two to try:

**LEMON-HERB MARINADE**

Combine $3/4$ cup olive oil, 2 tablespoons lemon juice, 1 tablespoon snipped fresh chives, 1 tablespoon minced garlic, 1 teaspoon kosher salt or $1/2$ teaspoon salt, 1 teaspoon ground black pepper, and 1 tablespoon dried oregano, crushed. Makes 1 cup. Use to marinate 2 pounds of boneless pork, chicken, beef, or lamb.

**YOGURT-MINT MARINADE**

Combine one 8-ounce carton plain yogurt; 1 tablespoon snipped fresh mint or 1 teaspoon dried mint, crushed; 2 teaspoons lemon juice; $1/2$ teaspoon minced garlic; $1/4$ teaspoon salt; and $1/4$ teaspoon ground black pepper. Makes 1 cup. Use to marinate 2 pounds boneless lamb or pork.

**Lemon-Herb Marinade**

# PICKLING
## Primer

**WHEN THE GARDEN AND MARKET OFFER UP A BUSHEL OF CUCUMBERS, CHOOSE PICKLING TO PRESERVE THEIR PEAK FLAVOR.**

Nothing captures the full flavors of a bountiful summer quite like the snap of a fresh, vinegary-sweet homemade pickle. Follow these guidelines for capturing crisp bites of the summer garden:

Canning jars and lids are available in grocery and discount stores. Follow the manufacturer's instructions for sterilization: Boil water in a stockpot, reduce it to a simmer, and place your equipment in the hot water bath (photo 1, page 131). Keep your equipment warm by placing the hot jars in a roasting pan and set in a 200° F. oven until ready to fill. Placing jars, lids, and seals in the dishwasher will get them clean but will not guarantee sterilization.

Avoid jars, such as jelly jars, that were not made for pickling. Vintage canning jars have charm but might not withstand the rigors of modern kitchen equipment. Some canning equipment manufacturers now offer complete kits.

Use produce at its peak. Make sure it is free of blemishes and dirt. Wash well and trim any bad spots. Read recipes completely through; sometimes the process is spread over a couple of days. For food safety, follow the recipe exactly. White and cider vinegars with a high acid level are best for pickling. Pickling salts are recommended; kosher salt is a good alternative. A wide mouth funnel is useful for filling jars (photo 2, page 131).

Leave ½ inch of the jar unfilled (photo 3, page 131). This amount of space between the top of the food and the jar rim is called headspace, essential when canning. Use new lids and make sure the screw-on bands are free of dents, bends, and rust. You want the tightest seal possible. Use a small plastic knife or spatula to release air pockets in the pickle mixture (photo 4, page 131). Process the filled jars in a water bath for at least 10 minutes; remove with a jar lifter and let the jars rest until they cool to room temperature (photo 5, page 131). The jars will be ready to store.

The Bread and Butter Pickles recipe (below) has been a *Better Homes and Gardens®* standard since 1930. For variations, substitute the seeds with anise, fennel, sesame, or caraway (use whole seeds only), and the spices with crushed red pepper, whole peppercorns, fresh dill, or dried juniper berries. Avoid using ground spices because they may turn the brine dark and cloudy.

### Bread and Butter Pickles

For these pickles, be sure to cut the cucumbers into ⅛-inch slices.

**PREP:** 40 minutes  **CHILL:** 3 hours  **PROCESS:** 10 minutes

| | |
|---|---|
| 4 quarts (16 cups) sliced medium cucumbers | Cracked ice |
| 8 medium white onions, sliced | 4 cups sugar |
| ⅓ cup pickling salt | 3 cups cider vinegar |
| 3 cloves garlic, halved | 2 Tbsp. mustard seeds |
| | 1½ tsp. turmeric |
| | 1½ tsp. celery seeds |

**1.** In a 6- to 8-quart stainless-steel stockpot combine cucumbers, onions, pickling salt, and garlic. Add 2 inches of cracked ice. Cover and refrigerate for 3 hours. Drain mixture well. Remove and discard garlic.

**2.** In the same stockpot combine sugar, vinegar, mustard seeds, turmeric, and celery seeds. Heat to boiling. Add cucumber mixture. Return to boiling.

**3.** Pack hot cucumber mixture and liquid into hot, sterilized pint canning jars, leaving a ½-inch headspace. Wipe jar rims; adjust lids. Process in a boiling-water canner for 10 minutes (start timing when water begins to boil). Remove jars and cool on racks. Makes 7 pints (70 servings).

Each serving: 57 cal., 0 g total fat, 0 mg chol., 229 mg sodium, 14 g carbo., 1 g dietary fiber, 0 g protein. Daily Values: 1% vit. A, 3% vit. C, 1% iron.

BY STEPHEN EXEL PHOTOGRAPHS BY GREG SCHEIDEMANN [N] HAUS FOTO FOOD STYLING BY CHARLES WORTHINGTON

**Bread and Butter Pickles**

# THE HEART OF THE
# Artichoke

**Warm Artichoke and Salsa Dip**

**Artichoke Omelet**

**Fried Artichoke Hearts with Marinara Sauce**

Take that jar of marinated artichoke hearts out of the cupboard (and off the antipasto platter) and make it your new best friend. This grocery shelf item has many uses. What makes this convenience product really convenient? You don't have to go rooting through the thistle-like leaves of fresh whole artichokes to get to the heart, and the oil-based marinade gives the hearts a silky texture and a tangy, vinegary taste to dress a whole lot of favorite foods.

Give some familiar dishes a zippy spin with these little green hearts.

- Warm Artichoke and Salsa Dip adds pucker to a salsa-based spread.
- The Artichoke Omelet is a lively version of a Denver omelet.
- A crispy pile of Fried Artichoke Hearts with Marinara Sauce is a great match to an ice cold brew at a party.

## Artichoke Omelet

If you don't have a 12-inch skillet, use an 8-inch nonstick skillet to make two smaller omelets. Divide the egg, filling mixture, and butter in half and cook them one at a time.

**Fast! START TO FINISH:** 25 minutes

| | |
|---|---|
| 1 6-oz. jar marinated artichoke hearts | 2 oz. cooked boneless ham, cut into 1/2-inch pieces (1/3 cup) |
| 1/2 cup thin wedges red or yellow onion | 4 eggs |
| 1/2 of a green sweet pepper, cut in bite-size strips (1/2 cup) | 1/4 cup water |
| | 1/4 tsp. salt |
| | 1/4 tsp. freshly ground black pepper |
| | 1 Tbsp. butter |

**1.** Drain artichoke hearts, reserving 2 tablespoons of the liquid. In a bowl combine artichoke hearts, onion, sweet pepper, and ham; toss with the reserved liquid. Heat a skillet over medium-high heat. Add artichoke mixture to skillet. Cook and stir about 6 minutes or until ham and vegetables begin to char. Remove from heat; set aside.

**2.** Meanwhile, in a bowl combine eggs, water, salt, and pepper. Beat mixture with a fork or rotary beater until frothy. Heat a 12-inch nonstick skillet with flared sides over medium-high heat. Add butter to skillet; melt butter swirling to coat pan. Add egg mixture; reduce heat to medium. Stir egg mixture gently but continuously until mixture resembles small pieces of cooked egg surrounded by liquid egg. Stop stirring. Cook 30 to 60 seconds more or until egg is set but shiny.

**3.** Spoon filling mixture onto one half of the omelet. With a spatula, lift and fold opposite side over filling. Invert onto a serving plate. Gently cut in half. Makes 2 servings.

Each serving: 317 cal., 23 g total fat (7 g sat. fat), 455 mg chol., 1,080 mg sodium, 13 g carbo., 4 g fiber, 18 g pro. Daily Values: 22% vit. A, 89% vit. C, 6% calcium, 2% iron.

### HEART OF THE MATTER

Drain marinated artichoke hearts well, but don't rinse them before using them.

- Sliver artichoke hearts and toss them over roasted fish or into couscous or pasta.
- Chop them and stir into creamy soups.
- Crush artichoke hearts with black olives and parsley for a spread or topping.
- Stuff quartered artichoke hearts and chopped garlic inside a pork chop.
- Roll artichoke hearts with pastrami for a simple hors d'oeuvre.

## Warm Artichoke and Salsa Dip

Select a green salsa with a heat level that will satisfy you.

**Fast! START TO FINISH:** 15 minutes

| | |
|---|---|
| 1 12-oz. jar or two 6-oz. jars marinated artichoke hearts | 1/2 cup shredded Monterey Jack or white cheddar cheese (2 oz.) |
| 1/3 cup sliced green onion | 1/4 cup dairy sour cream |
| 2 Tbsp. bottled green salsa | 1/4 cup snipped fresh cilantro |

**1.** Drain artichokes; discarding marinade. Coarsely chop artichoke hearts. In a small saucepan combine chopped artichoke hearts, green onion, and salsa. Cook over medium heat until heated through, stirring frequently. Remove from heat. Stir in cheese, sour cream, and cilantro. Serve immediately. Makes 1 1/2 cups (six 1/4-cup servings).

Each serving: 144 cal., 13 g total fat (5 g sat. fat), 12 mg chol., 256 mg sodium, 5 g carbo., 0 g fiber, 3 g pro. Daily Values: 7% vit. A, 14% vit. C, 9% calcium, 1% iron.

## Fried Artichoke Hearts with Marinara Sauce

**START TO FINISH:** 45 minutes

| | |
|---|---|
| 1 recipe Marinara Sauce (below) | 2/3 cup fine dry bread crumbs |
| 2 12-oz. or four 6-oz. jars marinated artichoke hearts | 2 Tbsp. snipped fresh oregano |
| 1/2 cup all-purpose flour | 1/2 tsp. crushed red pepper |
| 2 eggs | 1/4 tsp. freshly ground black pepper |
| 2 Tbsp. water | Cooking oil for deep-fat frying |

**1.** Prepare Marinara Sauce; keep warm. Drain artichoke hearts, discarding marinade; set artichokes aside. Place flour in a shallow dish. In a small bowl beat eggs lightly with the water. In another shallow dish combine bread crumbs, oregano, and peppers. Dip artichokes in flour, egg mixture, and then bread crumb mixture to coat completely.

**2.** In a deep-fat fryer heat oil to 365° F. Fry coated artichoke hearts, about 6 at a time, for 1 to 2 minutes or until golden brown. Drain on paper towels. Transfer to serving plate. Serve warm with Marinara Sauce. Makes 6 appetizer servings.

**MARINARA SAUCE:** In a small saucepan heat 1 1/4 cups purchased marinara sauce just until bubbly. Stir in 1 tablespoon. snipped fresh oregano and 1/4 teaspoon crushed red pepper (optional). Serve warm with fried artichokes. Makes 1 1/4 cups.

Each serving: 299 cal., 20 g total fat (2 g sat. fat), 71 mg chol., 806 mg sodium, 28 g carbo., 1 g fiber, 7 g pro. Daily Values: 9% vit. A, 44% vit. C, 7% calcium, 14% iron.

BY **STEPHEN EXEL** PHOTOGRAPHS BY **GREG SCHEIDEMANN [N] HAUS FOTO** FOOD STYLING BY **BROOKE LEONARD**

# SUMMER
# Pudding

Summer pudding has its origins in England, where the word "pudding" sometimes substitutes for the word "dessert." Traditionally, summer pudding is a delicious chilled combination of lightly cooked fresh summer berries and their juices hiding under a "crust" of familiar white bread.

## Three-Fruit Summer Pudding
**PREP:** 30 minutes  **COOK:** 5 minutes  **CHILL:** overnight

| | |
|---|---|
| 8 to 10 slices firm-texture white bread | 2 Tbsp. snipped fresh lemon thyme or lemon verbena, or 1 tsp. finely shredded lemon peel |
| Nonstick cooking spray | |
| 3 cups sliced fresh strawberries | 2 Tbsp. kirsch or cherry brandy |
| 3 cups fresh blackberries or blueberries | 1 recipe Mascarpone Topping (below) |
| 3 cups fresh red or golden raspberries | Assorted fresh berries (optional) |
| ½ cup sugar | |

**1.** Remove crusts from bread. Cut slices into triangles. Spray interior of 6- to 7-cup mold or bowl with nonstick cooking spray. Line with plastic wrap. Arrange slices in the bottom and up the sides of the mold so that the interior is covered. (Tear slices into small pieces to fill any gaps.) Press slices gently. Set aside.

**2.** In a saucepan combine berries, sugar, lemon thyme, and kirsch. Cook over medium heat about 5 minutes or until berries begin to release juices, stirring occasionally. Remove from heat. Strain berries, reserving juices. Let berries cool slightly.

**3.** Carefully spoon berries into bread-lined mold. Spoon half of the reserved juices over the berries, reserving remaining juices to use later. Top berries with a layer of bread triangles, filling any gaps with small pieces. Cover with plastic wrap. Place a small plate on top of plastic wrap; weigh down with a heavy can. Chill in the refrigerator overnight.

**4.** Prepare Mascarpone Topping. To serve, unmold pudding just before serving (see steps 2 and 3 below). Drizzle remaining fruit juices over top. Top with Mascarpone Topping and, if desired, additional berries. Makes 6 servings.

**MASCARPONE TOPPING:** In chilled mixing bowl combine ¼ cup mascarpone cheese, ¼ cup whipping cream, and 2 teaspoons honey. Beat with chilled beaters of electric mixer on high speed until soft peaks form.

Each serving: 335 cal., 8 g total fat (4 g sat. fat), 20 mg chol., 245 mg sodium, 61 g carbo., 9 g fiber, 6 g pro. Daily Values: 6% vit. A, 110% vit. C, 7% calcium, 11% iron.

For a perfect pudding, proper chilling holds the key.
1. Spray interior of mold with nonstick cooking spray; line mold with plastic wrap before filling with bread slices. Use small, torn pieces of bread to fill in any gaps. 2. To unmold pudding, remove chilled pudding from refrigerator; remove weight, plate, and top layer of plastic wrap. Place a serving platter upside down on top of mold. 3. Holding mold and platter together, carefully invert. Lift away mold and plastic wrap.

### It's-a-Breeze Tropical Soup

**PREP:** 20 minutes   **COOK:** 5 minutes   **CHILL:** 2 hours

| | |
|---|---|
| 3 | cups unsweetened pineapple juice |
| 1/3 | cup sugar |
| 2 | to 3 Tbsp. light or dark rum (optional) |
| 1 | or 2 small banana peppers or jalapeño chile peppers, seeded and finely chopped (about 1 to 2 tsp.) (see page 89) |
| 1 | 1-inch piece fresh ginger, quartered |
| 8 | inches stick cinnamon, broken |
| 1/2 | medium pineapple, peeled, cored, and cut into bite-size chunks |
| 1 | mango, pitted, peeled, and chopped (1 cup) |
| 2 | small bananas, peeled and cut into 1/2-inch slices |
| 1/2 | cup fresh litchis, shelled, halved, and seeded, or canned litchis, drained and halved |
| | Coconut shards, toasted* |

**1.** In a medium saucepan combine pineapple juice, sugar, rum (if using), peppers, ginger, and cinnamon. Bring to boiling; reduce heat. Simmer, covered, 5 minutes. Remove ginger and cinnamon; discard. Cool slightly. Stir in pineapple. Cover; chill in the refrigerator 2 to 24 hours. Remove from refrigerator; add mango, banana, and litchis. To serve, ladle soup into bowls. Garnish with coconut shards. Makes 8 appetizer servings.

**\*NOTE:** To toast coconut shards, arrange shards on baking sheet. Bake in a 350° F oven for 2 to 3 minutes or until edges just start to brown.

**Healthy** Each serving: 147 cal., 0 g total fat (0 g sat. fat), 0 mg chol., 2 mg sodium, 37 g carbo., 2 g fiber, 1 g pro. Daily Values: 10% vit. A, 52% vit. C, 1% calcium, 3% iron.

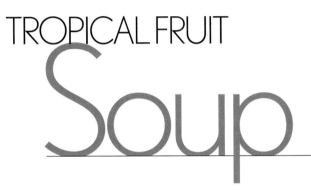

# TROPICAL FRUIT
# Soup

Cool down a steamy summer day with this fruit-packed chilled soup. It's great as a light lunch with a green salad or as a dessert with dinner. Pineapple, bananas, mango, and litchis (exotic, yes, but available fresh or canned at grocery stores) team up in a cinnamon, rum, and ginger-flavored broth. Banana peppers add just the right amount of zing.

RESOLUTIONS 2004

# EAT WELL

## PUCKER UP AND WRAP YOUR LIPS AROUND SOME SNACKS THAT SMACK OF SUMMER.

Our grab-and-gobble munchies satisfy those between-meal hunger attacks. When snacking, be sure to stick to the same healthful eating guides you follow at mealtimes, reaching for nibbles that emphasize naturally sweet fruits and fresh veggies.

**ICY TROPICAL POPS** These super-fruity treats are high in vitamin C. For 12 pops, blend together 1 cup guava nectar, 1 cup pineapple juice, and 1 cup fresh pineapple chunks. Drop raspberries or cut-up kiwifruit into molds or small paper cups. Pour blended fruit juice over fruit. Add sticks, cover, and freeze. (For paper cups, cover with foil; make a slit for a stick.)

BY JEANNE AMBROSE. PHOTOGRAPHS BY **GREG SCHEIDEMANN [NJ HAUS FOTO** FOOD STYLING BY **CHARLES WORTHINGTON** RECIPES BY **JENNIFER KALINOWSKI**

# SNACKS ON THE GO

### ▲ HERBED RICOTTA AND CRACKERS

A great mini meal for busy parents, these snacks combine protein, carbs, and whole grains to boost energy levels. Stir together a couple tablespoons of snipped fresh basil and 1 cup of light ricotta cheese. Add salt and pepper to taste. Spread the herbed cheese on whole grain crackers. Top with cherry or grape tomatoes.

### ▼ BAG O' TEDDIES WITH YOGURT

Kids will have some fun with this sweet snack that gives them a bit of calcium plus fruit. Just snip open a little bag of bear-shaped grahams or animal crackers, spoon in some low-fat yogurt, and top with fresh fruit.

### ▶ VEGGIES ON THE GO

The vending machine won't be as alluring to teens who tote these dippers to after-school activities. Spruce up purchased light dill vegetable dip with a bit of finely shredded lemon peel. Spoon it into a plastic cup and add crunchy vegetable sticks. If you cut the veggies to fit below the top of the cup (or use a tall cup) and cover tightly, the snack is ready to tote. Be sure to keep it chilled.

# July

CELEBRATE SUMMER WITH A BACKYARD BARBECUE. FIRE UP THE GRILL, THEN JAZZ UP YOUR MENU WITH BOLD AND REFRESHING FLAVORS.

# Savor the Summer

**Plus**

# SAVOR THE SUMMER

GRILLING RECIPES THAT PACK ENOUGH GARDEN-FRESH INGREDIENTS, SIMPLE TECHNIQUES, AND BOLD FLAVORS TO CARRY YOU THROUGH A SEASON IN THE SUN.

**Shishless Kabob**

## Shishless Kabob

It's an easy after-work meal—fast and no skewers. The slices of ripe tomato soften slightly from the warmth of the grilled ingredients as the food sits a few moments before being devoured.

**PREP:** 35 minutes  **GRILL:** 35 minutes

| | | | |
|---|---|---|---|
| 2 | 12- to 16-oz. pork tenderloins | 1 | cup bottled honey-mustard barbecue sauce |
| 2 | fresh ears of corn | 3 | Tbsp. snipped fresh sage or 2 tsp. dried sage, crushed |
| 2 | small red onions | | |
| 1½ | lb. zucchini and/or yellow summer squash, cut in half lengthwise | 1 | tsp. crushed red pepper |
| | | 3 | large tomatoes, cut into thick slices |

Salt
Freshly ground black pepper

**1.** Cut each tenderloin crosswise into 3 to 4 pieces. Remove husks from corn; scrub with a stiff brush to remove silks. Rinse. Peel and cut onions into wedges, leaving root end intact (helps wedges stay together). Sprinkle tenderloin pieces, corn, onions, and zucchini lightly with salt and pepper.

**2.** For brush-on sauce, in a bowl combine barbecue sauce, sage, and crushed red pepper. Divide mixture in half; set aside.

**3.** For a charcoal grill, arrange hot coals around a drip pan. Test for medium-hot heat above the pan. Place pork on grill rack over the drip pan. Cover and grill for 35 to 40 minutes or until an instant-read thermometer registers 160° F. Arrange corn, onions, and squash halves directly over coals around edge of grill rack for the last 20 minutes of grilling or until tender and browned, turning occasionally. Brush pork and all the vegetables with half of the brush-on sauce the last 10 minutes of grilling. (For gas grill, preheat grill. Reduce heat to medium-hot. Adjust heat for indirect cooking. Grill as above.)

**4.** To serve, cut corn and squash into bite-size pieces. Arrange tomato slices in a bowl and top with vegetables and pork. Heat the remaining sauce in a small saucepan on the grill, or microcook remaining sauce in a microwave-safe bowl, covered, for 20 seconds or until heated through; stir before passing with pork and vegetables. Makes 6 servings.

Each serving: 264 cal., 4 g total fat (1 g sat. fat), 73 mg chol., 764 mg sodium, 30 g carbo., 4 g fiber, 27 g pro. Daily Values: 23% vit. A, 51% vit. C, 5% calcium, 14% iron.

BY **RICHARD SWEARINGER** PHOTOGRAPHS BY **COLLEEN DUFFLEY** FOOD STYLING BY **ANNE DISRUDE** PROP STYLING BY **KAREN JOHNSON**

# Adventure
# in grilling

Combine classic grilling fare with new and unexpected tastes guaranteed to make your dinner unforgettable. Dinner is done with more fun than work by using a few everyday ingredients and tapping into a spirit of cooking adventure. There's nothing drastic or dramatic, just small changes. They're small steps, but they can take you a long way to a memorable outdoor meal.

**START EARLY:** For the best results, use fresh herbs and vegetables from your garden. Before the day's heat bakes their essence away, pick tomatoes, peppers, green onions, mint, rosemary, and basil. Gardenless? Take a Saturday morning stroll through your local farmer's market or the produce section of the grocery store while the aisles are calm and quiet and the lettuce is still standing tall.

**UPDATE YOUR STAPLES:** Keep an eye out for new versions of old favorites: sausages with enticing ingredient combinations, salad greens you've never seen before, pastas in unusual shapes or colors, and vegetables and peppers arriving in ever-increasing variety. And check out the sauces; there are dozens of appealing blends that can be brushed on during the last 5 minutes on the grill.

**THE SOONER THE BETTER:** Time puts flavor into food, so do marinating, rubbing, and mixing. Spice rubs, sauces, and relishes love extra blending time; chiles get hotter as they release their oils into the mix, and herbs give up more of their perfume.

**MODERATE THE HEAT:** Now that you've built in great flavors, don't cook them away. Done is done—not charred. That's why indirect cooking, where food sits on the grill away from the heat, is such a good idea. Charcoaling it? Invest in a chimney starter, which simultaneously measures the perfect amount of coals to avoid a too-hot fire and lights them quickly. Leave a spot open on the grill where you can shift food if it's cooking too quickly or flames flare up.

**PULLING IT ALL TOGETHER:** On the table, provide more opportunities for big flavor with seasoned salts to sprinkle and pepper for cracking. Finish off the meal by halving and pitting fresh plums, nectarines, peaches, or big strawberries, sprinkling the cut sides with sugar, and grilling them directly over low coals or gas burners on low for 5 minutes or so (just until they're softened slightly and have light grill marks). Serve the treats over big bowls of ice cream.

## Game Hens

More guests than expected? Use kitchen shears to snip game hens in half before serving. Half a hen is still a satisfying portion.

**PREP:** 30 minutes **MARINATE:** 12 hours
**GRILL:** 50 minutes **STAND:** 10 minutes

| | | | |
|---|---|---|---|
| 4 | 1¼- to 1½-lb. Cornish game hens or 4 medium chicken breast halves (about 2 lb. total) | 1½ | cups snipped fresh herbs, such as oregano and basil |
| 2 | lemons | 1 | tsp. kosher salt or sea salt or salt |
| | | ½ | tsp. freshly ground black pepper |

**1.** Thaw Cornish game hens, if frozen. Finely shred enough lemon peel from 1 of the lemons to make 2 teaspoons peel. In a small bowl combine herbs, salt, pepper, and lemon peel; set aside. Cut 1½ of the lemons into slices; cut remaining lemon half into quarters.

**2.** To prepare Cornish hens, remove giblets, if present. If desired, remove skin from hens. Rinse hens; pat dry. Place hens on a plate or baking dish. Place 1 lemon quarter in each hen cavity. (If using chicken breasts, omit lemon quarters.) Tie drumsticks to tail using heavy kitchen string. Twist wing tips under the back. Generously pat outside of birds with herb mixture. Lay lemon slices over top. Wrap tightly with plastic wrap and chill in the refrigerator for 12 to 24 hours.

**3.** For a charcoal grill, arrange medium-hot coals around a drip pan. Test for medium heat above the pan. Place Cornish hens, breast side up, on grill rack over drip pan. (Place chicken breasts, bone side down, over drip pan.) Cover and grill for 50 to 60 minutes or until meat is tender, no longer pink, and an instant-read thermometer inserted into thigh muscle registers 180° F. (For a gas grill, preheat grill. Reduce heat to medium. Adjust for indirect cooking; see "Indirect Grilling" at left. Grill as above.)

**4.** Remove Cornish game hens from grill. Cover with foil and let stand 10 minutes before carving. Makes 4 servings.

Each serving: 676 cal., 45 g total fat (12 g sat. fat), 346 mg chol., 651 mg sodium, 3 g carbo., 0 g fiber, 60 g pro. Daily Values: 10% vit. A, 28% vit. C, 9% calcium, 14% iron.

## INDIRECT GRILLING

A great method for slow cooking large cuts of meat, whole chickens, and Cornish game hens, indirect cooking means food is positioned on the grill rack away from the burning charcoal or gas flames. The result: Food cooks evenly with few flare-ups.

### CHARCOAL GRILL

The easiest setup for indirect cooking on a charcoal grill is to light the coals, push them to either side of the grill (see photo, *above*), and place a drip pan (a disposable foil pan or garage sale baking pan works well) between the two banks of coals.

### GAS GRILLS

For a grill with three or more burners, do not light the center burner. Methods vary for two-burner grills, so consult the owner's manual. When cooking indirectly, it's important to maintain the temperature by keeping the grill covered, so do not lift the lid until directed.

### SUNDAY DINNER

Game Hens (above)
Sage-Roasted Root Vegetables (page 147)
Tossed salad greens with creamy salad dressing
Chive Batter Bread (page 68) and butter
Homemade ice cream with sliced fresh peaches
Strawberry Iced Tea (page 67)

**Game Hens**

## DIP INTO THE GARDEN

Lure neighbors for an after-work get-together with the aroma of grilling red peppers or green onions. Combine the vegetables with sour cream for a tangy dip to serve with tender grilled shrimp or scallops, or thick kettle-cooked potato chips.

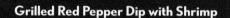

**Grilled Red Pepper Dip with Shrimp**

## A BOWL ON THE GRILL

Portobello Pasta Bowls are qiant mushrooms made tender by the fire and filled with a tidy twirl of pasta—spinach fettuccine or spaghetti. The pasta sauce gets its deep red color, body, and smoky zing from fresh tomatoes grilled alongside the mushrooms.

**Portobello Pasta Bowls**

## Grilled Red Pepper Dip with Shrimp

Another time, serve the dip as a sauce with grilled fish or chicken.

**PREP:** 20 minutes  **GRILL:** 15 minutes peppers; 9 minutes shrimp
**STAND:** 15 minutes  **CHILL:** 1 hour.

| | | | |
|---|---|---|---|
| 2 | lb. fresh or frozen jumbo shrimp in shells (about 32) | 1 | 8-oz. carton dairy sour cream |
| 1 | Tbsp. olive oil | 1/4 | tsp. salt |
| 2 | medium red sweet peppers or 16 whole green onions, trimmed | 1/4 | tsp. coarsely ground black pepper |

**1.** Thaw shrimp, if frozen. Peel and devein shrimp, leaving tails intact, if desired. Thread shrimp onto eight 8-inch skewers, leaving 1/4 inch space between pieces (you should have 3 or 4 shrimp per skewer). Brush lightly with some of the olive oil; set aside.

**2.** Lightly brush sweet peppers or onions with remaining olive oil. For a charcoal grill, grill shrimp skewers and vegetables on the rack of an uncovered grill directly over medium coals. Grill shrimp for 9 to 11 minutes or until shrimp turn opaque, turning once halfway through. Grill peppers for 15 minutes or until charred, turning occasionally. Grill onions about 5 minutes or until limp and slightly charred, turning once halfway through. (For a gas grill, preheat grill. Reduce heat to medium. Place peppers or onions and shrimp directly over heat. Cover and grill as above.) Wrap peppers in foil and let stand about 15 minutes or until cool and skin loosens. Remove stems and seeds from peppers. Using a sharp paring knife, peel peppers. Place shrimp skewers on a tray; cover and chill in the refrigerator 1 to 24 hours.

**3.** In a blender or food processor combine peppers or onions, sour cream, salt, and black pepper. Cover and blend or process with a few on/off turns to coarsely chop the mixture. Transfer to a small bowl. (Or coarsely chop the vegetables. In a small bowl stir together the sour cream, vegetables, salt, and black pepper.) Cover and chill in the refrigerator for 1 to 24 hours. Serve dip with shrimp on skewers. Makes 8 servings (about 1 1/2 cups dip).

Each serving (1 tablespoon dip plus 3 ounces shrimp): 176 cal., 9 g total fat (4 g sat. fat), 142 mg chol., 218 mg sodium, 4 g carbo., 1 g fiber, 19 g pro. Daily Values: 10% vit. A, 12% vit. C, 10% calcium, 14% iron.

## Portobello Pasta Bowls

The gills on the underside of portobello mushroom caps can discolor the other ingredients in the recipe; that's why they should be scraped away with a teaspoon.

*Fast!*  **PREP:** 20 minutes  **GRILL:** 6 minutes

| | | | |
|---|---|---|---|
| 6 | 4-inch diameter fresh portobello mushrooms (about 1 1/4 lb.), stems removed | 1/4 | cup olive oil |
| | | 2 | Tbsp. lemon juice |
| | | 1 | tsp. snipped fresh oregano |
| 2 | medium yellow or red tomatoes | 1/2 | tsp. salt |
| 3 | Tbsp. olive oil | 1/2 | tsp. freshly ground black pepper |
| Salt | | | |
| Freshly ground black pepper | | 2 | Tbsp. snipped fresh oregano or 1/4 cup snipped fresh basil |
| 6 | oz. dried spinach fettuccine or spaghetti | | |

**1.** Using a teaspoon, gently scrape gills out of the bottom of the mushroom caps. Lightly rinse mushroom caps. Pat dry with paper towels. Cut tomatoes in half; remove seeds and stems.

**2.** Brush top and underside of the mushrooms and all sides of tomatoes with the 3 tablespoons olive oil. Sprinkle the mushrooms and tomatoes lightly with salt and pepper.

**3.** For a charcoal grill, grill mushroom caps and tomato halves, cut sides up, on the rack of an uncovered grill directly over medium coals for 6 to 8 minutes or until tender, turning once halfway through grilling. (For a gas grill, preheat grill. Reduce heat to medium. Place mushroom caps and tomato halves on the grill rack over heat. Cover and grill as above.) Remove from grill.

**4.** Cook pasta according to package directions. Drain; return the cooked pasta to pot and keep warm.

**5.** For dressing, coarsely chop the grilled tomatoes. In a blender or food processor combine the tomatoes, the 1/4 cup olive oil, lemon juice, the 1 teaspoon oregano, 1/2 teaspoon salt, and 1/2 teaspoon pepper. Cover and blend or process until smooth. Drizzle pasta with 2 tablespoons of the dressing.

**6.** To serve, place mushroom caps on serving plates. Divide pasta among mushrooms. Drizzle with remaining dressing. Sprinkle with additional snipped fresh herbs. Makes 6 servings.

Each serving: 284 cal., 18 g total fat (2 g sat. fat), 0 mg chol., 324 mg sodium, 26 g carbo., 2 g fiber, 7 g pro. Daily Values: 15% vit. C, 4% calcium, 11% iron.

**Grilled Green Beans**

## Grilled Green Beans

Green beans become sweet and substantial when drizzled with olive oil and roasted over the fire with hunky cloves of garlic and slivers of red chiles. Keep this recipe handy throughout the summer harvest cycle; it also works with zucchini, tomatoes, and peppers.

**PREP:** 20 minutes  **Grill:** 25 minutes

| | |
|---|---|
| 12 oz. green beans, trimmed | 2 tsp. lemon-flavored olive |
| 8 unpeeled cloves garlic | oil (or 1½ tsp. olive oil and |
| 1 Tbsp. water | ½ tsp. lemon juice) |
| 1 tsp. cooking oil | Salt |
| 1 or 2 fresh jalapeño chile | |
| peppers, cut into thin | |
| strips (do not seed)* | |

**1.** In a large bowl toss together beans, garlic, water, cooking oil, and jalapeño pepper; set aside. Fold a 36×18-inch piece of heavy foil in half to make an 18-inch square. Place bean mixture in center of foil. Bring together 2 opposite edges of foil; seal with a double fold. Fold remaining edges together to enclose the beans, leaving space for steam to build.

**2.** For a charcoal grill, place bean packet on the rack of an uncovered grill directly over medium coals. Grill for 20 minutes, turning once. Remove packet from the grill and cool slightly. Carefully open packet (some steam will escape). Return open foil packet to the grill rack. Continue grilling 5 minutes more or until beans are just browned and crisp-tender, stirring occasionally. (For a gas grill, preheat grill. Reduce heat to medium. Place packet on grill rack. Cover and grill as above.)

**3.** Transfer beans to a serving bowl. Drizzle with lemon-flavored olive oil. Season to taste with salt. To serve, remove peel from garlic cloves, mash lightly, and divide cloves among servings of beans. Makes 4 servings.

**\*NOTE:** Jalapeño peppers contain volatile oils that can burn your skin and eyes, so avoid direct contact with the peppers as much as possible. When working with chiles, wear plastic or rubber gloves.

**Healthy** Each serving: 59 cal., 4 g total fat (0 g sat. fat), 0 mg chol., 78 mg sodium, 7 g carbo., 3 g fiber, 2 g pro. Daily Values: 10% vit. A, 21% vit. C, 3% calcium, 5% iron.

## Fire-Roasted Acorn Squash

**PREP:** 10 minutes  **Grill:** 45 minutes

| | |
|---|---|
| 1 Tbsp. olive oil | 2 Tbsp. butter or margarine, |
| ½ tsp. salt | melted |
| ¼ tsp. ground black pepper | 2 tsp. snipped fresh tarragon |
| 2 small acorn squash, cut | or ½ tsp. dried tarragon, |
| crosswise into 1-inch rings | crushed |
| and seeded | |

**1.** In a small bowl combine olive oil, salt, and pepper; brush over squash rings. In another small bowl stir together melted butter and tarragon; set aside.

**2.** For a charcoal grill, arrange medium-hot coals around a drip pan. Test for medium heat above the pan. Place squash rings on grill rack over drip pan. Cover and grill about 45 minutes or until squash is tender, turning squash occasionally and brushing with butter mixture after 30 minutes of grilling. (For a gas grill, preheat grill. Reduce heat to medium. Adjust for indirect cooking. Grill as above.) Makes 4 servings.

Each serving: 153 cal., 10 g total fat (4 g sat. fat), 16 mg chol., 358 mg sodium, 18 g carbo., 3 g fiber, 1 g pro. Daily Values: 16% vit. A, 27% vit. C, 6% calcium, 7% iron.

## Sage-Roasted Root Vegetables

**PREP:** 25 minutes  **Grill:** 6 minutes

| | |
|---|---|
| 1 Tbsp. honey | 16 baby carrots or 4 medium |
| 1 Tbsp. balsamic vinegar | carrots, cut into 2-inch |
| 2 tsp. Dijon-style mustard | pieces |
| 2 tsp. snipped fresh sage or | 8 tiny new potatoes |
| 1 tsp. dried sage, crushed | 8 pearl onions, peeled, or |
| | 1 small onion, cut into |
| | small wedges |

**1.** In a small bowl stir together honey, vinegar, mustard, and sage; set aside. In a large saucepan combine carrots and potatoes; add enough water to cover. Bring to boiling over high heat. Add onions. Reduce heat; simmer, covered, for 3 to 5 minutes or until potatoes, carrots, and onions are slightly tender. Drain vegetables; let stand until cool enough to handle. On 4 metal skewers alternately thread carrots, potatoes, and onions, leaving ¼ inch space between the pieces.

**2.** For a charcoal grill, place kabobs on the rack of an uncovered grill directly over medium coals for 6 to 8 minutes or until potatoes are tender, turning once halfway through grilling and brushing frequently with honey-sage mixture. Makes 4 servings.

**Healthy** Each serving: 108 cal., 0 g total fat (0 g sat. fat), 0 mg chol., 77 mg sodium, 24 g carbo., 2 g fiber, 2 g pro. Daily Values: 29% vit. C, 2% calcium, 7% iron

## Two-Pepper Tomato Relish

Serrano peppers are slender, extremely hot peppers. They are 1 to 3 inches long and turn orange or red as they ripen. In this recipe, red was chosen to match the colors of the other ingredients, but green serranos or jalapeños may be substituted.

**PREP:** 20 minutes **CHILL:** up to 2 hours

| | |
|---|---|
| 2 small red sweet peppers, chopped (1 cup) | 2 Tbsp. balsamic vinegar |
| 1 large tomato, seeded and chopped (1 cup) | ½ to 1 red or orange serrano chile pepper, seeded and finely chopped* |
| 1 medium onion, finely chopped (½ cup) | ¼ tsp. salt |

**1.** In a medium bowl combine all ingredients. Cover and chill in the refrigerator up to 2 hours. Makes about 2½ cups.

**\*NOTE:** Serrano peppers contain volatile oils that can burn your skin and eyes, so avoid direct contact with the peppers as much as possible. When working with chiles, wear plastic or rubber gloves.

**Healthy** Each ¼-cup serving: 12 cal., 0 g total fat (0 g sat. fat), 0 mg chol., 50 mg sodium, 3 g carbo., 0 g fiber, 0 g pro. Daily Values: 16% vit. A, 45% vit. C, 2% calcium, 1% iron.

## Fresh Mango Chutney

Serve this refreshing condiment with grilled steaks, burgers, pork chops, ham slices, or chicken breasts.

**PREP:** 15 minutes **COOK:** 10 minutes **CHILL:** up to 1 week

| | |
|---|---|
| ¼ cup packed brown sugar | ⅛ tsp. ground cloves |
| ¼ cup finely chopped onion | 2 cups chopped, peeled mangoes or peaches |
| ¼ cup golden raisins | |
| ¼ cup cider vinegar | 2 Tbsp. water |
| ½ tsp. ground nutmeg | 2 Tbsp. lemon juice or lime juice |
| ½ tsp. ground cinnamon | |
| ¼ tsp. salt | |

**1.** In a medium saucepan combine sugar, onion, raisins, vinegar, nutmeg, cinnamon, salt, and cloves. Bring to boiling; reduce heat. Simmer, uncovered, for 5 minutes, stirring occasionally.

**2.** Stir in mangoes and water. Return to boiling; reduce heat. Simmer, uncovered, about 5 minutes more or until slightly thickened, stirring frequently. Remove from heat. Stir in lemon juice. Let cool. Cover and chill in the refrigerator for up to 1 week. Makes about 2 cups.

**Healthy** Each tablespoon: 18 cal., 0 g total fat (0 g sat. fat), 0 mg chol., 18 mg sodium, 5 g carbo., 0 g fiber, 0 g pro. Daily Values: 5% vit. A, 6% vit. C.

## Fresh Kraut

When chopping cabbage, cut pieces bite-size for neater eating.

**PREP:** 20 minutes **CHILL:** 2 hours

| | |
|---|---|
| 2 tsp. mustard seeds | ¼ cup white wine vinegar |
| 4 cups shredded and coarsely chopped green cabbage | 4 cloves garlic, minced |
| | 1 tsp. sugar |
| | ½ tsp. salt |

**1.** In a small skillet or saucepan toast mustard seeds over medium-low heat, stirring constantly, for 2 minutes or until fragrant. In a large bowl combine cabbage, white wine vinegar, garlic, sugar, salt, and the toasted mustard seeds. Cover and chill in the refrigerator for 2 to 24 hours. Makes about 2½ cups.

**Healthy** Each ¼-cup serving: 13 cal., 0 g total fat (0 g sat. fat), 0 mg chol., 100 mg sodium, 2 g carbo., 0 g fiber, 0 g pro. Daily Values: 13% vit. C, 1% calcium, 3% iron.

## Overnight Cucumber Pickles

**PREP:** 20 minutes **CHILL:** 2 hours

| | |
|---|---|
| 1 cup cider vinegar | 2 medium pickling cucumbers or 2 small cucumbers (4 to 5 inches long), coarsely chopped (about 2 cups) |
| ⅓ cup sugar | |
| 1 tsp. salt | |
| 1 tsp. fennel seeds, crushed | |
| 1 tsp. celery seeds | |
| | 1 medium fennel bulb, coarsely chopped (1 cup) |

**1.** In a large bowl combine cider vinegar, sugar, salt, fennel seeds, and celery seeds. Stir in cucumbers and chopped fennel. Cover and chill in the refrigerator 2 hours or up to 3 days. Serve with a slotted spoon. Makes about 3 cups.

Each ¼-cup serving: 13 cal., 0 g total fat (0 g sat. fat), 0 mg chol., 200 mg sodium, 3 g carbo., 2 g fiber, 0 g pro. Daily Values: 1% vit. A, 4% vit. C, 1% calcium, 1% iron.

### A MUST-HAVE TOOL

Mastering the outdoor grill requires keeping the heat consistent cookout after cookout. The easiest way to achieve that is with a chimney starter. These inexpensive tools both measure your charcoal and light it quickly without the need for lighter fluid. They are made by several manufacturers and are available at hardware stores, home centers, and barbecue specialty outlets.

## Grilled Frankfurters

The sausages and frankfurters sold fully cooked require just a brief warming on the grill; uncooked varieties require longer grilling.

**PRECOOKED SAUSAGE GRILLING TIME:** 3 minutes
**UNCOOKED SAUSAGE GRILLING TIME:** 20 minutes

6   frankfurters or sausages in flavors such as chicken pesto, curry, roasted-pepper pork, or Mediterranean lamb
6   ficelles or thin baguettes, split, toasted, and cut to the length of frankfurters or sausages; or hot dog buns, split and toasted*

Assorted toppings, such as Overnight Cucumber Pickles, Fresh Kraut, and Two-Pepper Tomato Relish (recipes, page 148)

**1.** To grill frankfurters or fully cooked sausages: For a charcoal grill, place frankfurters or sausages on the rack of an uncovered grill directly over medium coals; grill for 3 to 7 minutes or until heated through, turning once halfway through grilling. (For a gas grill, preheat grill. Reduce heat to medium. Place frankfurters or sausages on grill over heat. Cover and grill as above.)

**2.** To grill uncooked sausages: Prick sausages with a fork. For a charcoal grill arrange medium-hot coals around a drip pan. Test for medium heat above the pan. Place sausages on grill rack over the drip pan. Cover and grill for 20 to 30 minutes or until temperature registers 160° F on an instant-read thermometer inserted horizontally into sausage. (For a gas grill, preheat grill. Reduce heat to medium. Adjust heat for indirect cooking. Grill sausages as above.)

**3.** Place frankfurters or sausages in buns. Spoon on assorted toppings. Makes 6 servings.

**\*NOTE:** To toast buns on the grill: Grill directly over medium heat about 1 minute. Watch carefully; they can burn quickly.

Each serving: The nutritional analysis of frankfurters and sausages varies widely so check individual packages.

## Greek Tomato Relish

**PREP:** 15 minutes

3   roma tomatoes, seeded and finely chopped
½   cup chopped, pitted kalamata olives
⅓   cup finely chopped red onion

2   Tbsp. olive oil
1   Tbsp. snipped fresh oregano
1   Tbsp. red wine vinegar
Ground black pepper

**1.** In a small bowl combine tomatoes, olives, onion, oil, oregano, and vinegar. Season to taste with pepper. Makes about 1½ cups.

Each tablespoon: 17 cal., 2 g total fat (0 g sat. fat), 0 mg chol., 32 mg sodium, 1 g carbo., 0 g fiber, 0 g pro. Daily Values: 2% vit. A, 2% vit. C.

**Grilled Frankfurters**

## NEW FLAVOR ADDITIONS

Fresh Kraut, Overnight Cucumber Pickles, and Two-Pepper Tomato Relish are snazzy extras for summer's easiest main course. In the grocery store, look for hot dogs and bun-size sausages with flavor accents and fillings, such as onion, red pepper, cheddar cheese, mango, andouille, and lime-infused tequila chicken.

## Bunless Burger

To cook burgers evenly, it's important that they be surrounded by the heat, so don't peek for the first 18 minutes of grilling.

**PREP:** 20 minutes **GRILL:** 18 minutes

| | |
|---|---|
| 2 lb. 85% lean ground beef | Salt |
| 8 oz. bulk mild or hot Italian sausage | Ground black pepper |
| 3 oz. Parmesan cheese, cut into 1×1/4-inch slices | Lettuce leaves |
| 3/4 cup roasted red sweet peppers, cut into 1-inch pieces | 6 cherry tomatoes (optional) |

**1.** In a large bowl combine ground beef and sausage with your hands (it is not necessary to get it perfectly blended; it will mix further as patties are shaped). Shape meat mixture into 12 evenly sized balls. Pat each ball onto waxed paper to form a flat patty 4 1/2 inches in diameter. Place Parmesan pieces and chopped red sweet peppers on top of 6 of the patties. Top with remaining meat patties to make 6 burgers. Press gently to seal edges. Season with salt and black pepper.

**2.** For a charcoal grill, arrange medium-hot coals around a drip pan. Test for medium heat above the pan. Place patties on grill rack over drip pan. Cover and grill for 18 to 22 minutes or until an instant-read thermometer inserted slightly away from the center of the burger registers 160° F. (For gas grill, preheat grill. Reduce heat to medium. Adjust for indirect cooking. Grill as above.) If desired, brown the top of the patties by moving the burgers directly over the coals for the last 2 to 3 minutes of cooking.

**3.** To serve, place each burger between lettuce leaves on individual plates. If desired, use toothpicks to attach a cherry tomato to each. Makes 6 servings.

Each serving: 391 cal., 26 g total fat (11 g sat. fat), 107 mg chol., 604 mg sodium, 2 g carbo., 0 g fiber, 33 g pro. Daily Values: 2% vit. A, 86% vit. C, 19% calcium, 15% iron.

## Snapper with Sausage

For this hearty dish, any firm white-flesh fish, such as cod or rockfish, can be substituted for the snapper. Cooking time is the same. If using frozen fish, thaw in the refrigerator overnight.

**PREP:** 20 minutes **GRILL:** 20 minutes

| | |
|---|---|
| 4 6-oz. fresh or frozen, skinless red snapper fillets, 1/2 to 3/4 inch thick | 1/2 of a medium fresh pineapple, peeled, cored, and cut into bite-size chunks (2 cups), or one 20-oz. can pineapple chunks (juice pack), drained |
| 3 Tbsp. olive oil | |
| 1 tsp. smoked paprika or paprika | |
| 1/4 tsp. salt | |
| 1/4 tsp. ground cardamom | 6 oz. pepperoni, diced (1 3/4 cups) |
| 1/4 tsp. ground black pepper | 2 Tbsp. snipped fresh cilantro |
| 3 medium sweet potatoes (1 1/4 lb.), peeled and thinly sliced (4 cups) | |

**1.** Thaw fish, if frozen. In a small bowl combine olive oil, paprika, salt, cardamom, and pepper; set aside.

**2.** Cut four 18×24-inch pieces of heavy foil. Fold in half to make 18×12-inch rectangles. Arrange 1 cup sweet potato slices in the center of each piece of foil.

**3.** Rinse fish; pat dry. Top sweet potatoes with a fish fillet, tucking under any thin edges of fillets. Top fish with pineapple and pepperoni. Drizzle with oil mixture. Bring together 2 opposite edges of foil; seal with a double fold. Fold remaining edges together to enclose mixture, leaving space for steam to build.

**4.** For a charcoal grill, place packets on the rack of an uncovered grill directly over medium coals. Grill for 20 to 25 minutes or until fish flakes easily when tested with a fork and potatoes are tender (do not turn packets). (For a gas grill, preheat grill. Reduce heat to medium. Place packets on grill rack. Cover and grill as above.) To serve, carefully open packets. Transfer contents of package with juices to 4 shallow bowls. Sprinkle with cilantro. Makes 4 servings.

Each serving: 634 cal., 33 g total fat (9 g sat. fat), 95 mg chol., 1,176 mg sodium, 37 g carbo., 4 g fiber, 47 g pro. Daily Values: 380% vit. A, 45% vit. C, 7% calcium, 14% iron.

**Bunless Burger**

## BUILD A BETTER BURGER
Two pounds of ground beef with a taste infusion from a half-pound of sausage becomes the knife-and-fork Bunless Burger. Roasted sweet peppers and cheese are concealed within the burger. A bun is optional; the flavors are exceptional.

## PACKAGE MAKES PERFECT
Ingredients of many flavors join forces to make Snapper with Sausage. Chunks of yellow pineapple, slices of sweet potato, red snapper, and pepperoni are layered in foil and coated with a cardamom and smoked paprika drizzle; 20 minutes of grilling, and dinner is done.

**Snapper with Sausage**

**Grilled Skillet Corn Bread**

## Grilled Skillet Corn Bread

Serve the grilled bread with a slightly sweetened nectarine mixture. To shorten prep time a bit, the bread can also be made with a mix.

**PREP:** 25 minutes  **GRILL:** 35 minutes  **COOL:** 10 minutes

| | | | |
|---|---|---|---|
| 4 | medium nectarines, pitted and coarsely chopped | 1½ | tsp. baking powder |
| 3 | Tbsp. granulated sugar | 1 | tsp. salt |
| 2 | small sprigs fresh basil | ¼ | tsp. baking soda |
| 2 | Tbsp. cooking oil | 3 | eggs, beaten |
| 2 | medium or 3 small onions, cut into ½-inch slices (do not separate onion slices into rings) | 1 | cup buttermilk |
| | | 3 | Tbsp. cooking oil |
| | | 2 | fresh ears of corn* or 1 cup frozen corn kernels, thawed |
| 1 | cup yellow cornmeal | 1 | Tbsp. packed brown sugar |
| ¾ | cup all-purpose flour | 1 | Tbsp. snipped fresh basil |

**1.** For a charcoal grill, arrange medium-hot coals around the outside edge of the grill. Test for medium heat in center of grill where corn bread will bake. (For a gas grill, preheat grill. Reduce heat to medium. Adjust for indirect cooking according to manufacturer's instructions.)

**2.** Meanwhile, place nectarines in a medium bowl. Add granulated sugar and basil sprigs; toss to coat. Fold a 36×18-inch piece of heavy foil in half to make an 18-inch square. Place nectarine mixture in center of foil. Bring together 2 opposite edges of foil; seal with a double fold. Fold remaining edges together to enclose the nectarines, leaving space for steam to build; set aside.

**3.** Place the 2 tablespoons cooking oil in a 10-inch round or square cast-iron skillet. Arrange onion slices in bottom of skillet. Place skillet on grill rack away from direct heat (not over lit coals or burners). Cover grill. Grill for 5 minutes. Carefully turn onion slices; grill for 5 minutes more (onions will be partially cooked).

**4.** Meanwhile, in a bowl combine cornmeal, flour, baking powder, salt, and baking soda. In a small bowl stir together eggs, buttermilk, and the 3 tablespoons cooking oil. Add buttermilk mixture to cornmeal mixture; stir until combined. Stir in corn.

**5.** Sprinkle brown sugar over onions in skillet on grill rack. Spoon corn bread batter into the hot skillet and spread evenly over onions with the back of the spoon. Place foil pouch of nectarines on grill rack over direct heat (over lit coals or burner). Cover and do not remove grill lid or open grill for 20 minutes. After 20 minutes, open lid. Carefully remove foil packet; set aside. Check doneness of corn bread (a toothpick inserted near the center should come out clean). If needed, give pan a half turn, replace cover and grill for 5 to 15 minutes more or until a toothpick inserted near the center comes out clean. Cool in skillet for 10 minutes.

**6.** Meanwhile, carefully open foil packet. Remove and discard basil sprigs. Transfer nectarines to a small bowl. Mash mixture slightly with a fork. Stir in the 1 tablespoon snipped basil. To serve, run a knife around edge of skillet; invert corn bread onto a serving plate. Serve warm with nectarine mixture. Makes 8 servings.

**\*NOTE:** Remove husks from fresh ears of corn; scrub with a stiff brush to remove silks. Rinse. Cut kernels from cob.

**EASY GRILLED SKILLET CORN BREAD:** Prepare onions and nectarines as at left. Instead of making the corn bread batter, prepare two 8½-ounce packages corn muffin mix according to package directions. Spoon over the hot onions. Grill as at left.

Each serving: 303 cal., 12 g total fat (2 g sat. fat), 81 mg chol., 466 mg sodium, 44 g carbo., 4 g fiber, 8 g pro. Daily Values: 16% vit. A, 11% vit. C, 10% calcium, 7% iron.

## Grill-Roasted Fresh Figs

**PREP:** 15 minutes  **GRILL:** 20 minutes

| | | | |
|---|---|---|---|
| 6 | large fresh figs, halved, or 6 medium fresh plums, pitted and halved, or 3 small fresh peaches, pitted and quartered | 1 | Tbsp. water |
| | | 1 | Tbsp. sugar |
| | | 2 | Tbsp. slivered almonds, toasted |
| 2 | Tbsp. honey | 1 | Tbsp. lemon juice (optional) |
| 1 | Tbsp. butter, melted | ½ | cup mascarpone cheese |

**1.** Place figs in a 12×8-inch disposable foil pan. Drizzle with honey, melted butter, and water. Cover pan tightly with foil.

**2.** For a charcoal grill, arrange medium-hot coals around the edge of the grill. Test for medium heat above the center of the grill. Place the prepared foil pan on grill rack in the center of the grill. Cover and grill about 15 minutes or until figs are heated through. Remove foil cover from pan. Brush figs with any juices that have collected in the bottom of the pan. Sprinkle sugar and almonds evenly over figs in pan. Cover pan with foil. Return pan to grill. Cover grill and continue grilling 5 minutes more. (For a gas grill, preheat grill. Reduce heat to medium. Adjust for indirect cooking. Place pan on grill rack away from heat. Grill as above.)

**3.** Carefully remove figs and liquid to a serving dish. If desired, sprinkle with lemon juice. Serve figs with mascarpone cheese. Makes 4 servings.

Each serving: 274 cal., 18 g total fat (9 g sat. fat), 44 mg chol., 39 mg sodium, 28 g carbo., 3 g fiber, 7 g pro. Daily Values: 4% vit. A, 3% vit. C, 4% calcium, 3% iron.

# FROZEN **TREATS**

**White Chocolate Berry Pops**

KIDS OF ALL AGES WILL LOVE THESE PUDDING POPS. WHAT COULD BE MORE REFRESHING THAN A FROSTY TREAT FOR INDEPENDENCE DAY OR ANY SUMMER DAY IN JULY.

## COOL AND REFRESHING

These homemade frozen treats combine the best of quick prep and great taste. Name your flavor. You'll find fruit flavors as well as chocolate in this selection. For added variety, seek out unusual frozen pop molds for the fruity pops or use readily available paper or plastic drink cups.

BY STEPHEN EXEL PHOTOGRAPH BY SHAUN SULLIVAN FOOD STYLING BY POUKÉ PROP STYLING BY AARON HOM

### Kid Friendly — White Chocolate Berry Pops

**PREP:** 20 minutes  **STAND:** 5 minutes  **FREEZE:** 4 hours

| | |
|---|---|
| 2 cups milk | 1 cup fresh or frozen blueberries, chopped strawberries, or whole raspberries |
| 1/2 cup whipping cream | |
| 1 4-serving-size pkg. instant white chocolate pudding mix | |
| 5 to 8 drops blue or red food coloring (optional) | 8 to 10 3-oz. paper or plastic drink cups or pop molds |
| | 8 to 10 wooden sticks |

**1.** In a blender combine milk, whipping cream, and pudding mix. Cover and blend until smooth. For blue pops, add 5 to 8 drops blue food coloring. For pink pops, add 5 to 8 drops red food coloring. Cover and blend until combined.

**2.** Transfer blended mixture to a medium bowl. Let stand for 5 minutes before stirring in berries so they won't sink.

**3.** Pour or spoon mixture into the paper or plastic drink cups or frozen pop molds. Cover cups with foil; cut a slit in the foil and insert wooden sticks (or cover pop molds according to manufacturer's directions). Freeze 4 hours or overnight. To serve, remove foil and tear paper cups away or remove pops from plastic cups or molds. Makes 8 to 10 pops.

Each pop: 137 cal., 7 g total fat (4 g sat. fat), 25 mg chol., 212 mg sodium, 17 g carbo., 0 g fiber, 2 g pro. Daily Values: 7% vit. A, 5% vit. C, 9% calcium.

### Kid Friendly — Banana Crunch Pops

**PREP:** 15 minutes  **FREEZE:** 2 hours  **STAND:** 10 minutes

| | |
|---|---|
| 1/3 cup fat-free yogurt (any flavor) | 1/2 cup crisp rice cereal or chocolate-flavored crisp rice cereal |
| 1/8 tsp. ground cinnamon | 1 banana (halved crosswise) |
| | 2 wooden sticks |

**1.** Place yogurt in small shallow dish; stir in cinnamon. Place cereal in another small shallow dish. Insert a wooden stick into each banana piece. Roll banana in yogurt mixture, covering entire piece of banana. Roll in cereal to coat. Place on baking sheet lined with waxed paper. Freeze about 2 hours or until firm. When frozen, wrap each in freezer wrap. Store in freezer. Before serving, let stand for 10 minutes at room temperature. Makes 2 pops.

Healthy  Each pop: 99 cal., 0 g total fat (0 g sat. fat), 1 mg chol., 94 mg sodium, 23 g carbo., 2 g fiber, 3 g pro. Daily Values: 4% vit. A, 21% vit. C, 7% calcium, 4% iron.

### Kid Friendly — Eskimo-Cicles

**PREP:** 20 minutes  **FREEZE:** 6 hours

| | |
|---|---|
| 2 1/2 cups cubed, seeded watermelon, cantaloupe, or honeydew melon | 1/4 cup sugar |
| | 1 Tbsp. lemon juice |
| 1/2 cup fresh or frozen raspberries | 8 3-oz. paper or plastic drink cups or pop molds |
| | 8 wooden sticks |

**1.** In a blender combine the melon, raspberries, sugar, and lemon juice. Cover and blend until smooth.

**2.** Pour mixture into drink cups or frozen pop molds. Cover cups with foil; cut a slit in foil and insert wooden sticks (or cover pop molds according to manufacturer's directions). Freeze 6 hours or overnight or until firm. To serve, remove foil and tear paper cups away or remove from plastic cups or molds. Makes 8 pops.

Healthy  Each pop: 50 cal., 0 g total fat (0 g sat. fat), 0 mg chol., 4 mg sodium, 12 g carbo., 1 g fiber, 0 g pro. Daily Values: 4% vit. A, 13% vit. C, 1% calcium, 1% iron.

### Kid Friendly — Rocky Road Pops

**PREP:** 20 minutes  **CHILL:** 1 hour  **FREEZE:** 4 hours  **STAND:** 10 minutes

| | |
|---|---|
| 1 4-serving-size pkg. regular chocolate pudding mix or chocolate fudge pudding mix | 1/2 cup miniature semisweet chocolate pieces |
| | 1/2 cup chopped walnuts or peanuts (optional) |
| 2 1/2 cups chocolate-flavored milk | 9 3-oz. paper or plastic drink cups |
| 3/4 cup miniature marshmallows | 9 wooden sticks |

**1.** In a medium saucepan combine pudding mix and milk; cook and stir over medium heat until mixture is bubbly (use a whisk, if necessary, to smooth mixture). Transfer to a large bowl; cool slightly. Cover surface with plastic wrap. Chill in the refrigerator for 1 hour.

**2.** Stir in marshmallows, chocolate pieces, and, if desired, nuts. Spoon about 1/3 cup of the mixture into each drink cup. Cover cups with foil; cut a slit in foil and insert a wooden stick into each. Freeze about 4 hours or until firm. To serve, let pops stand at room temperature for 10 minutes. Remove foil and tear paper cups away or remove pops from plastic cups. Makes 9 pops.

Healthy  Each pop: 153 cal., 5 g total fat (3 g sat. fat), 8 mg chol., 94 mg sodium, 27 g carbo., 1 g fiber, 3 g pro. Daily Values: 1% vit. A, 1% vit. C, 8% calcium, 4% iron.

# Farmer's market supper

The menu for your reunion feast doesn't have to be fancy. In fact, it should play on family favorites. After a trip to the farmer's market, feed the family well at the reunion or other summer get-together by taking advantage of fresh produce finds. For example, you might add fresh fruits to a beverage, fresh corn and other veggies to a coleslaw mix, snipped herbs to fried chicken, and berries to top a pan of brownies. (See photos.)

For an easy-on-the-cook meal, add your own touch to baked goods, take-out chicken, and deli items. Let the whole family pitch in with the menu preparations since there's no complicated measuring involved with these fix-ups. Use disposable plates, napkins, cups, and eating utensils to simplify cleanup.

## BERRY COOLER

Wet your whistle with a sparkling cooler made from a 12-ounce can of frozen juice concentrate—such as lime, lemon, cranberry, or orange—and 48 ounces of chilled seltzer water. Top off the blend with your favorite fresh fruit. For starters, try raspberries, lemons, and limes.

## SUMMER CHICKEN

Who doesn't like fried chicken? It's good hot or cold, and whether it's homemade or take-out from your favorite market or restaurant, you can spruce it up in a snap. Sprinkle with a handful of chopped fresh parsley, basil, and chives, and squeeze on some fresh lemon juice.

## CORN SLAW

Toss together a sweet-and-crunchy corn salad with fresh-off-the-cob corn (each ear yields about a cup) and any combo of preshredded coleslaw mix, chopped red and green sweet peppers, shredded carrots, ripe olives, sliced scallions, fresh herbs, or fresh lime juice. Add salt, freshly ground black pepper, and your favorite vinaigrette.

### QUESTION

I love the idea of making sun tea. Isn't this the perfect time of year to brew tea outdoors?

### ANSWER

Although brewing tea in the hot sun may seem like a good idea, the practice should be avoided because it encourages the growth of bacteria. If you plan to brew a pitcher of iced tea, you have two options. The first is to make tea with boiling water. Allow it to cool, then serve over ice.

The second option is even simpler. Just place 6 to 8 tea bags in a 2-quart glass container. Add 1½ quarts cold water; cover and let tea brew in the refrigerator about 24 hours. Remove tea bags. Serve tea over ice cubes. Sweeten to taste.

For a flavor boost, add fresh herbs to your iced tea. Mint leaves are a favorite standby, but experiment with lemon-thyme sprigs, pineapple sage, or cinnamon basil. A stalk of lemongrass makes a perfect swizzle stick. Be sure to crush the stalk first to release its citrusy flavor. Or drop a few raspberries or blueberries into the glass.

## BROWNIES DELUXE

Boxed brownies are anything but humble topped with raspberry preserves and fresh raspberries. Other ideas: caramel sauce with toasted chopped walnuts, cherry pie filling with toasted slivered almonds, peanut butter with sliced bananas and chopped peanuts. Bake the brownies in a disposable foil pan for easy cleanup.

# August

A CROWD-PLEASING FEAST IS ALWAYS ON THE MENU WHEN THIS MARYLAND FAMILY INVITES OVER FRIENDS AND NEIGHBORS.

# Blockbuster BBQ

# Blockbuster BBQ

Creamy-Crunchy Corn (page 162)
Pesto Green Beans and Tomatoes (page 162)
Quita's Egg-Battered Fried Chicken

MY NEIGHBORS ARE ALWAYS COMING BY AND WANTING TO KNOW: WHEN'S YOUR NEXT PARTY? —QUITA HIGHSMITH

BY JEANNE AMBROSE PHOTOGRAPHS BY **JAMES CARRIER** FOOD STYLING BY **MICHAEL PEDERSON** PROP STYLING BY **KAREN JOHNSON**

<sup>Kid</sup>
<sup>Friendly</sup> Quita's Egg-Battered Fried Chicken

The flour mixture for coating the chicken is simple to make, but a purchased variety speeds the process. A secret to moist fried chicken, Quita Highsmith says, is to use tongs for turning the pieces, rather than a fork.

**PREP:** 25 minutes **COOK:** 30 minutes

| | |
|---|---|
| ½ of a 10-oz. pkg. all-purpose batter fry mix* (about ¾ cup) | 2½ to 3 lb. meaty chicken pieces (breast halves, thighs, and drumsticks), skinned if desired |
| 4 eggs | Salt and ground black pepper |
| | Peanut oil or cooking oil |
| | Bottled hot pepper sauce |

**1.** Place the batter fry mix in a shallow bowl; set aside. In another shallow bowl slightly beat eggs; set aside.

**2.** Season chicken pieces with salt and pepper. Dip chicken pieces, 1 at a time, into beaten eggs; coat with fry mix. Dip into the beaten eggs and coat with fry mix again. Repeat with remaining chicken pieces, beaten eggs, and fry mix.

**3.** Add oil to a 12-inch heavy skillet to a depth of ⅓ to ½ inch. Heat over medium-high heat until hot enough to sizzle a drop of water. Carefully add chicken to skillet. (Do not crowd chicken. If necessary, use 2 skillets.) Cook, uncovered, over medium heat for 30 minutes, turning about halfway through to brown evenly. (Cook to 170° F for breasts; 180° F for thighs and drumsticks.) Drain chicken pieces on paper towels.

**4.** Pass bottled hot pepper sauce with chicken. Serves 6.

**\*FRY MIX OPTION:** In a shallow bowl combine ⅔ cup all-purpose flour, 3 tablespoons cornmeal, ¼ teaspoon salt, and ¼ teaspoon ground black pepper. Use in place of the fry mix as directed above.

Each serving: 546 cal., 38 g total fat (9 g sat. fat), 249 mg chol., 417 mg sodium, 14 g carbo., 1 g fiber, 35 g pro. Daily Values: 9% vit. A, 4% vit. C, 3% calcium, 14% iron.

# Backyard Barbecue

When Quita Highsmith and her father, James Beeler, fire up the grill, they're likely to have 30 or more folks over for some of their savory family recipes. That's because many of the people living near this multigenerational home in Fort Washington, Maryland, are like family. "It's the closest-knit neighborhood we've ever lived in," says Quita. The sentiment is echoed by James, who finds as much joy in cooking for a crowd as he does in joining them at the table. When James and Quita put on a backyard feast, everyone knows it's going to be special. James, who ran a soul-food restaurant for 20 years, flavors dishes using his secret ingredient—tradition.

If you listen to James, you'll soon believe that feeding a crowd is no more difficult than cooking a meal for immediate family. "Do as much as you can ahead, and then reheat it," he says. That's one of the secrets to throwing a feast that lets you prepare lots of food and still have time to relax and mingle with guests. He also employs a few shortcuts, such as using purchased salad dressings, especially on salads that have plenty of flavor, and sprucing up bottled barbecue sauce with dashes of mustard and honey.

Another secret for big-batch cooking? Plan a menu that's familiar. Making favorite family recipes is James' strategy for serving dozens of guests. The more times you make a particular dish, the easier it is to master—especially when you need lots of it. His trademark delights—honey-laced baked beans, bone-sucking-good ribs, and kid-pleasing gooey mac and cheese—can be traced to his grandmother's home cooking in Kentucky. Favorites such as fried chicken, barbecued pork, and creamy corn are reliable staples that James has made for years. They're perfect for an all-day gathering where people nibble their way through catch-up conversations.

## Creamy-Crunchy Corn

This is one of Quita's specialties; it's reminiscent of old-fashioned creamed corn, but with a surprising crispiness.

**PREP:** 15 minutes **COOK:** 30 minutes **STAND:** 10 minutes

| | |
|---|---|
| 5 fresh ears of corn or one 20-oz. pkg. frozen whole kernel corn | 2 to 4 Tbsp. sugar |
| | 1 Tbsp. cornmeal |
| ¼ cup butter | Salt and ground black pepper |

**1.** If using fresh corn, remove husks and silk; cut kernels from cobs (you should have about 2½ cups). In a large heavy skillet melt butter. Stir in corn, sugar, and cornmeal. Cover and cook over medium-low heat for 30 minutes, stirring occasionally.

**2.** Season to taste with salt and pepper. Let stand for 10 minutes before serving. Makes 6 servings.

Each serving: 152 cal., 9 g total fat (4 g sat. fat), 22 mg chol., 254 mg sodium, 19 g carbo., 2 g fiber, 2 g pro. Daily Values: 8% vit. A, 6% vit. C, 1% calcium, 2% iron.

## Pesto Green Beans and Tomatoes

Two main ingredients drizzled with one herb-saturated vinaigrette make for a happy side dish.

**Fast!** **PREP:** 20 minutes **COOK:** 10 minutes

| | |
|---|---|
| 1½ lb. fresh green beans, trimmed | ¼ cup Pesto Vinaigrette (recipe, right) |
| 1 pint small tomatoes, such as red grape, halved | Salt and freshly ground black pepper |

**1.** Cook beans, covered, in a small amount of boiling salted water for 10 to 15 minutes or until crisp-tender. Drain and rinse under cool water. Drain and pat dry with paper towels.

**2.** In a large bowl toss green beans and tomatoes with Pesto Vinaigrette. Add additional vinaigrette, if desired. Season to taste with salt and pepper. Serve immediately or chill in the refrigerator up to 8 hours. Makes 6 to 8 servings.

**Healthy** Each serving: 128 cal., 8 g total fat (1 g sat. fat), 1 mg chol., 275 mg sodium, 13 g carbo., 5 g fiber, 4 g pro. Daily Values: 23% vit. A, 48% vit. C, 4% calcium, 8% iron.

## Pesto Vinaigrette

Another time, use this vinaigrette to add super flavor to a plate of sliced tomatoes sprinkled with green onions and feta cheese.

**Fast!** **PREP:** 5 minutes

| | |
|---|---|
| ½ cup Jaye's Basil Pesto (recipe, below) or purchased basil pesto | 1 Tbsp. fresh lemon juice |
| | ¼ cup extra-virgin olive oil |
| 3 Tbsp. white wine vinegar | Salt and ground white pepper |

**1.** In a bowl combine pesto, vinegar, and lemon juice. Slowly add olive oil in a thin stream, whisking until combined. Add salt and pepper to taste. Refrigerate up to 3 days. Makes about ¾ cup.

Each tablespoon: 115 cal., 11 g total fat (1 g sat. fat), 1 mg chol., 102 mg sodium, 2 g carbo., 0 g fiber, 1 g pro. Daily Values: 1% vit. C.

## Jaye's Basil Pesto

Quita's sister Jaye Jelier makes this when summer basil is at its peak. The secret is the baby spinach, which adds a mellow, fresh flavor.

**Fast!** **PREP:** 10 minutes

| | |
|---|---|
| ½ cup extra virgin olive oil | ½ cup walnuts or pine nuts |
| 1½ cups fresh baby spinach, stems removed | 6 oz. Asiago cheese, grated |
| ¾ cup fresh basil leaves | 3 large cloves garlic, peeled and quartered |

**TO PREPARE IN A FOOD PROCESSOR:** Combine 2 tablespoons of the oil, the spinach, basil, walnuts, cheese, and garlic. Cover and process until nearly smooth, stopping processor and scraping sides as necessary. Drizzle in remaining olive oil until mixture is smooth.

**TO PREPARE IN A BLENDER:** Coarsely chop spinach, basil, walnuts, and garlic on a cutting board. In a blender combine all ingredients. Cover and blend until mixture is smooth. Makes about 1¾ cups.

**TO STORE:** Place pesto in an airtight container. Cover and refrigerate for 1 or 2 days or freeze up to 1 month.

Each tablespoon: 77 cal., 8 g total fat (2 g sat. fat), 6 mg chol., 68 mg sodium, 1 g carbo., 0 g fiber, 2 g pro. Daily Values: 3% vit. A, 1% vit. C, 6% calcium, 1% iron.

### BACKYARD BBQ

Smoky Spice-Rubbed Ribs (page 165)
Quita's Egg-Battered Fried Chicken (page 161)
Creamy-Crunchy Corn (above left)
Big Jim's Baked Beans (page 169)
Pesto Green Beans and Tomatoes (above left)
Rosy Berries and Melon Salad (page 164)
Lime-Coconut Chess Pie (page 167)
Frosty Blackberry-Lemon Ice (page 167)
Iced tea and soft drinks

**Creamy-Crunchy Corn
Pesto Green Beans and Tomatoes**

## Rosy Berries and Melon Salad

Any fresh fruit works in this salad. All red fruit makes a vivid impact, but a version with sliced peaches, honeydew melon, and blueberries also is a welcome combination.

**START TO FINISH:** 35 minutes

- 1 recipe Candied Pecans (below) or 3/4 cup purchased glazed almonds or walnuts
- 1/2 cup mayonnaise or fat-free mayonnaise dressing
- 1/4 cup regular or fat-free dairy sour cream
- 1/3 cup milk
- 2 Tbsp. Champagne vinegar, Chardonnay vinegar, or white wine vinegar
- 2 Tbsp. finely chopped crystallized ginger
- 1/4 tsp. salt
- 1/4 tsp. ground ginger
- 1 10-oz. pkg. mixed salad greens
- 2 1/2 cups thinly sliced seedless watermelon wedges
- 1 cup fresh raspberries
- 1 cup halved or quartered fresh strawberries

**1.** Prepare Candied Pecans, if using; set aside. For dressing, in a small bowl whisk together mayonnaise, sour cream, milk, vinegar, crystallized ginger, salt, and ground ginger. Use immediately or cover and chill in the refrigerator up to 24 hours.

**2.** Line a platter with salad greens. Arrange fruit in rows on top of greens. Sprinkle with Candied Pecans. Pass dressing to drizzle over salad. Makes 8 to 10 servings.

**CANDIED PECANS:** Line a baking sheet with parchment paper or foil. In a medium heavy skillet combine 1/2 cup coarsely chopped pecans and 1/4 cup sugar. Cook over medium-high heat, shaking skillet occasionally, until sugar begins to melt. Do not stir. Reduce heat to low. Continue cooking until sugar is completely melted and golden brown, stirring occasionally. Remove skillet from heat. Pour nut mixture onto prepared baking sheet. Cool completely. Break nuts into pieces. Store tightly covered in the refrigerator up to 3 weeks.

Each serving: 230 cal., 18 g total fat (3 g sat. fat), 12 mg chol., 167 mg sodium, 18 g carbo., 3 g fiber, 2 g pro. Daily Values: 40% vit. A, 40% vit. C, 4% calcium, 5% iron.

## Peanut-Crusted Crab Cakes

These chunky crab cakes get a Southern embellishment and extra crunch with a coating of chopped peanuts.

**PREP:** 30 minutes **CHILL:** 1 hour **COOK:** 6 minutes per batch

- 1/4 cup chopped onion
- 1 Tbsp. butter
- 1/3 cup finely shredded carrots
- 1/2 cup finely crushed saltine crackers or cracker meal
- 1 egg
- 1/4 cup mayonnaise
- 1 Tbsp. yellow mustard
- 1 tsp. Old Bay seasoning
- 1 lb. fresh lump crabmeat, flaked, or three 6 1/4- to 6 1/2-oz. cans lump crabmeat, drained, flaked, and cartilage removed
- 1/3 cup finely chopped honey-roasted peanuts
- 1/2 cup peanut oil

**1.** In a medium skillet cook onion in butter for 3 to 5 minutes or until tender. In a large mixing bowl combine onion, carrots, 1/4 cup of the cracker crumbs, the egg, mayonnaise, mustard, and Old Bay seasoning. Add crabmeat. Use hands to mix well.

**2.** Line a baking sheet with waxed paper; set aside. In a shallow dish or pie plate combine finely chopped nuts and remaining 1/4 cup cracker crumbs. Mound about 1/3 cup of the crab mixture on top of the cracker mixture. Flatten and turn the crab cake, coating both sides with the cracker mixture. Place crab cake on the prepared baking sheet. Repeat with remaining crab mixture and crumb mixture. Cover crab cakes with another piece of waxed paper; chill in refrigerator for 1 to 2 hours.

**3.** In a large skillet heat peanut oil until hot. Cook crab cakes, half at a time, over medium heat for 6 to 8 minutes or until golden brown, turning halfway through cooking. Add additional oil during cooking, if necessary. Drain on paper towels. Makes 10.

Each crab cake: 239 cal., 20 g total fat (4 g sat. fat), 95 mg chol., 414 mg sodium, 5 g carbo., 0 g fiber, 12 g pro. Daily Values: 23% vit. A, 1% vit. C, 6% calcium, 2% iron.

Rosy Berries and Melon Salad

**Smoky Spice-Rubbed Ribs**

**Peanut-Crusted Crab Cakes**

## Smoky Spice-Rubbed Ribs

These falling-off-the-bone-tender ribs are rubbed with spices and roasted in the oven for ease, then finished off on the grill for a burst of smoky flavor.

**PREP:** 25 minutes **ROAST:** 1 hour 20 minutes **GRILL:** 10 minutes

| | | | |
|---|---|---|---|
| 5 | to 6 lb. pork loin back ribs or meaty pork spareribs | 2 | tsp. garlic pepper seasoning |
| 4 | tsp. dry mustard | 2 | tsp. celery seeds, crushed |
| 1 | Tbsp. coarse kosher salt or 2 tsp. salt | 2/3 | cup honey |
| 1 | Tbsp. chili powder | 2/3 | cup strong brewed coffee or apple juice |
| 1 | Tbsp. finely shredded lemon peel | 2/3 | cup bourbon |
| 3 | tsp. fennel seeds, crushed | 1/2 | cup finely chopped onion |
| | | 1/4 | cup Worcestershire sauce |
| | | 1 | 15-oz. can tomato sauce |

**1.** Preheat oven to 350° F. Rinse ribs; pat dry. In a small bowl combine 2 teaspoons of the dry mustard, the salt, chili powder, lemon peel, 2 teaspoons of the crushed fennel seeds, the garlic pepper seasoning, and crushed celery seeds. Rub mixture onto ribs.

**2.** Place ribs, meaty side up, in a large roasting pan. Roast, uncovered, for 1 hour and 20 minutes or until meat is tender.

**3.** Meanwhile, for barbecue sauce, in a large saucepan stir together remaining 2 teaspoons dry mustard, the remaining 1 teaspoon of fennel seeds, the honey, coffee, bourbon, onion, and Worcestershire sauce. Bring to boiling. Add tomato sauce. Return to boiling; reduce heat. Simmer, uncovered, about 15 minutes or until slightly thickened.

**4.** For a charcoal grill, place ribs, meaty side down, directly over medium-low coals. (For a gas grill, preheat grill. Reduce heat to medium-low. Place ribs, meaty side down, on grill.) Grill for 5 minutes; brush with barbecue sauce. Turn meaty side up. Brush with barbecue sauce and grill for 5 to 10 minutes more or until ribs are glazed and deep brown in color.

**5.** Cut ribs into 2- to 3-rib portions. Heat any remaining barbecue sauce and pass with ribs. Makes 8 servings.

Each serving: 450 cal., 13 g total fat (4 g sat. fat), 84 mg chol., 1,382 mg sodium, 30 g carbo., 1 g fiber, 40 g pro. Daily Values: 7% vit. A, 5% vit. C, 4% calcium, 16% iron.

Lime-Coconut Chess Pie

## Lime-Coconut Chess Pie

The coconut sprinkled on the bottom of the pie crust rises during baking to form a golden-brown topping.

**PREP:** 45 minutes **BAKE:** 45 minutes **COOL:** 1 hour
**CHILL:** 3 hours

| | |
|---|---|
| 1 recipe Pastry for Single-Crust Pie (below) | 2 tsp. finely shredded lime peel |
| 1 cup granulated sugar | 2 Tbsp. lime juice |
| ½ cup packed brown sugar | ½ tsp. vanilla |
| 2 Tbsp. all-purpose flour | 1 cup coconut |
| 5 eggs | 1 cup whipping cream |
| ⅓ cup unsalted butter, melted | |

**1.** Preheat oven to 325° F. Prepare pastry as directed. On a lightly floured surface, use your hands to slightly flatten dough. Roll dough from center to edges into a circle about 12 inches in diameter. To transfer pastry, wrap it around the rolling pin. Unroll pastry into a 9-inch pie plate. Ease pastry into pie plate without stretching it. Trim pastry to ½ inch beyond edge of pie plate. Fold under extra pastry. Crimp edge as desired. Do not prick pastry; set aside.

**2.** In a large mixing bowl combine granulated sugar, brown sugar, and flour. Using an electric mixer, beat in eggs, 1 at a time, until combined. Beat in melted butter, lime peel, lime juice, and vanilla until combined.

**3.** Sprinkle ¾ cup of the coconut over the bottom of the pie crust. Pour filling over coconut in crust. Bake for 45 minutes or until top appears set when lightly shaken. Cool pie on wire rack for 1 hour. Chill in the refrigerator for 3 to 6 hours.

**4.** Meanwhile, toast the remaining ¼ cup coconut in a shallow baking pan in a 350° F oven for 5 to 10 minutes or until light golden brown. Watch carefully and stir once or twice so coconut doesn't burn. Just before serving, in a chilled mixing bowl beat whipping cream with an electric mixer on medium speed until soft peaks form. Spread whipped cream over center of chilled pie and sprinkle with toasted coconut. Makes 8 servings.

**PASTRY FOR SINGLE-CRUST PIE:** In a medium bowl stir together 1¼ cups all-purpose flour and ¼ teaspoon salt. Using a pastry blender, cut in ⅓ cup shortening until pieces are pea-size. Sprinkle 1 tablespoon water over part of the flour mixture; gently toss with a fork. Push moistened dough to the side of the bowl. Repeat moistening flour mixture, using 1 tablespoon water at a time, until all the flour mixture is moistened (4 to 5 tablespoons total water). Form dough into a ball.

Each serving: 554 cal., 34 g total fat (18 g sat. fat), 196 mg chol., 133 mg sodium, 57 g carbo., 2 g fiber, 7 g pro. Daily Values: 19% vit. A, 4% vit. C, 6% calcium, 12% iron.

## Frosty Blackberry-Lemon Ice

Eat this with a spoon, or turn it into a slushy drink by pouring club soda or sparkling water over a scoop in a glass.

**PREP:** 15 minutes **COOK:** 2 minutes **FREEZE:** 2½ hours

| | |
|---|---|
| 1 cup water | ¼ cup fresh lemon juice |
| ½ cup sugar | 2 Tbsp. finely shredded lemon peel |
| 4 cups fresh blackberries or frozen unsweetened blackberries | |

**1.** In a medium saucepan combine water and sugar; bring to boiling, stirring frequently. Boil gently, uncovered, for 2 minutes. Remove from heat and cool slightly.

**2.** In a blender or food processor combine blackberries, the warm sugar mixture, and lemon juice. Cover and blend or process until almost smooth. Strain mixture through a fine mesh sieve, discarding seeds. Stir in 1 teaspoon of the lemon peel.

**3.** Transfer the mixture to a 3-quart rectangular baking dish or a 13×9×2-inch baking pan. Place in the freezer, uncovered, for 1½ hours or until almost solid.

**4.** Remove berry ice from freezer. Using a fork, break up the ice into a somewhat smooth mixture. Freeze 1 hour more.* Break up the ice with a fork and serve in cups. Top each serving with remaining shreds of lemon peel. Makes 6 to 8 servings.

**\*NOTE:** If mixture remains in the freezer longer than the additional 1 hour, let it stand at room temperature about 20 minutes before breaking up mixture with a fork and serving.

**Healthy** Each serving: 115 cal., 0 g total fat (0 g sat. fat), 0 mg chol., 2 mg sodium, 29 g carbo., 5 g fiber, 1 g pro. Daily Values: 3% vit. A, 46% vit. C, 4% calcium, 3% iron.

**Frosty Blackberry-Lemon Ice**

Shrimp Pasta Salad

Big Jim's Baked Beans

## Shrimp Pasta Salad

James Beeler uses spaghetti when he makes this dish for a crowd, but just about any shape of pasta does the trick.

**PREP:** 30 minutes **CHILL:** 2 hours

| | | | |
|---|---|---|---|
| 10 | oz. dried campanelle pasta, spaghetti, or bow tie pasta (about 3 cups) | 1 | 2¼-oz. can sliced pitted ripe olives, drained |
| 1½ | lb. cooked, peeled, and deveined shrimp | 4 | roma tomatoes, cut into thin wedges |
| 1 | cup chopped celery | 1 | recipe Citrus Vinaigrette (below) or 1¼ cups bottled Italian salad dressing |
| ½ | cup chopped red onion | | |
| ½ | cup chopped green sweet pepper | | |

**1.** Cook pasta according to package directions; drain. Rinse with cold water; drain again.

**2.** In a large bowl combine pasta, shrimp, celery, onion, sweet pepper, and olives. Stir in tomato wedges. Pour Citrus Vinaigrette over pasta mixture and toss gently to coat. Cover and chill in the refrigerator for 2 to 24 hours. Stir before serving. Makes 10 to 12 servings.

**CITRUS VINAIGRETTE:** In a screw-top jar combine ³/₄ cup grapefruit juice; ½ cup salad oil; 2 tablespoons honey; 1 tablespoon snipped fresh thyme or 1 teaspoon dried thyme, crushed; ¼ teaspoon salt; and ¼ teaspoon ground black pepper. Cover and shake well to mix.

Each serving: 308 cal., 13 g total fat (2 g sat. fat), 133 mg chol., 280 mg sodium, 29 g carbo., 2 g fiber, 18 g pro. Daily Values: 10% vit. A, 36% vit. C, 5% calcium, 19% iron.

## Kid Friendly Three-Cheese Macaroni

No Southern-style barbecue is complete without it. For this super-easy version, just stir the ingredients together and bake.

**PREP:** 30 minutes **BAKE:** 20 minutes **STAND:** 10 minutes

| | | | |
|---|---|---|---|
| 12 | oz. dried elbow macaroni (2²/₃ cups) | 8 | oz. sharp cheddar cheese, shredded (2 cups) |
| 1½ | cups milk | 2 | oz. mozzarella cheese, shredded (½ cup) |
| ¼ | cup butter, melted | 20 | rich round crackers, crushed |
| ½ | tsp. ground white pepper | | |
| ¼ | tsp. salt | | |
| 8 | oz. American cheese, cut into ½-inch cubes | | |

**1.** Preheat oven to 350° F. Cook macaroni following package directions; drain. Return pasta to pan. Add milk, butter, pepper, and salt. Stir in cheeses. Transfer to a greased 2-quart casserole.

**2.** Bake, uncovered, for 15 minutes. Carefully stir mixture. Sprinkle with crushed crackers. Bake 5 minutes more or until crackers are browned and mixture is just heated through (don't overheat or mixture will curdle). Let stand for 10 minutes before serving. Makes 8 to 10 side-dish servings.

Each serving: 512 cal., 29 g total fat (17 g sat. fat), 81 mg chol., 841 mg sodium, 40 g carbo., 2 g fiber, 23 g pro. Daily Values: 21% vit. A, 1% vit. C, 50% calcium, 11% iron.

## Kid Friendly Big Jim's Baked Beans

James says the kids love it when he adds chunks of all-beef hot dogs to his beans.

**PREP:** 20 minutes **BAKE:** 50 minutes

| | | | |
|---|---|---|---|
| 6 | slices bacon | 1 | 15- to 16-oz. can butter, black, or pinto beans, rinsed and drained |
| ⅓ | cup chopped green sweet pepper | | |
| ⅓ | cup chopped onion | ½ | cup ketchup |
| 1 | 21-oz. can pork and beans in tomato sauce, drained | ¼ | cup honey |
| | | 1 | Tbsp. packed brown sugar |

**1.** Preheat oven to 350° F. In a large skillet cook bacon over medium heat until crisp. Drain bacon on paper towels, reserving 1 tablespoon drippings in skillet. Crumble bacon; set aside.

**2.** Cook sweet pepper and onion in reserved hot bacon drippings about 5 minutes or until tender.

**3.** In a 1½-quart casserole combine pork and beans, butter beans, half the crumbled bacon, and the sweet pepper mixture. In a small bowl combine ketchup, honey, and brown sugar. Pour over bean mixture; stir gently to coat.

**4.** Bake, uncovered, for 50 to 60 minutes or until heated through. Stir gently and sprinkle with remaining crumbled bacon before serving. Makes 8 servings.

Each serving: 195 cal., 3 g total fat (1 g sat. fat), 11 mg chol., 804 mg sodium, 37 g carbo., 6 g fiber, 8 g pro. Daily Values: 6% vit. A, 18% vit. C, 7% calcium, 18% iron.

**Three-Cheese Macaroni**

# GARDEN-TO-TABLE
# PARTY

Break bread with others and the world will be a better place, says Anne Otterson. Her casual dinners, flavored with herbs from her California garden, prove the point.

Anne Otterson has studied cooking in Bangkok, worked as the director of the Perfect Pan cooking school in San Diego, toured wineries in Turkey and Italy, and knows the value of freshly picked food as a part of culture and celebration. "That's why, even after all my exotic travels, I really love coming home," she says.

For Anne, fresh foods, cooking, and gardening intertwine in happy harmony. Her garden in La Jolla, California, is designed as four outdoor rooms where she loves to entertain and serve culinary delights made from fresh ingredients.

Growing up in Minnesota with parents who grew vegetables and loved to cook, Anne learned early on that fresh food is integral to health and celebration. "I never ate a pea that had been off the vine more than 15 minutes," she says. When she moved to California 30 years ago, Anne missed the peonies and birches from her home state, yet found that herbs provided a connection to the land.

Those herbs now spill over a flagstone path in a side yard, where Anne first planted salad greens and English lavender. She tends prolific beds of basil, parsley, garlic, rosemary, cilantro, oregano, and lemongrass, all of which make their way into her cooking.

Anne's frequent garden parties give her ample opportunities to keep the fast-growing garden in check. Whether she's entertaining friends or family, she often chooses to hold the gatherings on quiet Sunday afternoons, when guests can linger outdoors. To complement her garden-fresh menus, Anne makes use of leaves, petals, and sprigs of plants to fashion decorations and party favors.

## Goat Cheese Tart

Serve this savory treat with a salad tossed together from ingredients gathered at the farmer's market. Good choices include baby mustard or other peppery greens tossed with tomato slices and slightly steamed green beans. Edible viola flowers add color.

**PREP:** 25 minutes  **BAKE:** 30 minutes

| | |
|---|---|
| 1 Tbsp. butter, softened | 1 tsp. snipped fresh parsley |
| 2 Tbsp. fine dry bread crumbs | 1 tsp. snipped fresh lemon verbena* |
| 4 eggs | ½ tsp. snipped fresh rosemary |
| 8 oz. fresh goat cheese (chèvre) | ½ tsp. snipped fresh lemon thyme* |
| ½ cup crème fraîche | |
| 1 Tbsp. snipped fresh basil | ½ teaspoon salt |
| 1 Tbsp. snipped fresh chives | 1 clove garlic, minced |

**1.** Preheat oven to 300° F. Use the 1 tablespoon butter to grease a 9-inch quiche dish. Sprinkle with crumbs; set aside.

**2.** Separate eggs. Place whites in a medium mixing bowl; set aside. In a large mixing bowl beat the yolks with an electric mixer on medium to high speed for 3 minutes or until thick and lemon color. Add goat cheese, beating just until smooth and creamy. Add crème fraîche, herbs, salt, and garlic; beat just until combined.

**3.** Wash beaters thoroughly. Beat egg whites with an electric mixer on medium speed until stiff peaks form. Gently fold beaten whites into goat cheese mixture. Pour into prepared dish.

**4.** Bake for 30 to 35 minutes or until tart is puffed and golden brown and a knife inserted near the center comes out clean. Serve warm. Makes 8 servings.

***NOTE:** If you can't find lemon verbena or lemon thyme, substitute 1 teaspoon finely shredded lemon peel and ½ teaspoon snipped fresh thyme.

Each serving: 174 cal., 14 g total fat (8 g sat. fat), 136 mg chol., 347 mg sodium, 2 g carbo., 0 g fiber, 9 g pro. Daily Values: 5% vit. A, 1% vit. C, 7% calcium, 6% iron.

BY DEBRA LANDWEHR ENGLE PHOTOGRAPHS BY EDMUND BARR PRODUCED BY ANDREA CAUGHEY

## Lemon Geranium Pound Cake

Scented geranium leaves vary in size; the object is to pluck enough leaves to line the bottom of the pan.

**PREP:** 30 minutes **BAKE:** 60 minutes **COOL:** 10 minutes

| | | | |
|---|---|---|---|
| 1 | cup butter | 1 | cup sugar |
| 4 | eggs | 2 | Tbsp. lemon juice |
| 15 | to 20 whole fresh lemon, rose, or ginger geranium leaves | 2 | Tbsp. finely shredded lemon peel |
| 2 | cups all-purpose flour | ¼ | cup snipped fresh lemon geranium leaves (optional) |
| 1 | tsp. baking powder | | Lavender gelato, fruit ice |
| ¼ | tsp. salt | | cream, or sorbet; or fresh |
| ⅛ | tsp. baking soda | | summer berries and whipped cream (optional) |

**1.** Preheat oven to 325° F. Let butter and eggs stand at room temperature for 30 minutes. Generously butter a 9×5×3-inch loaf pan; line the bottom with whole geranium leaves. In a medium bowl combine flour, baking powder, salt, and baking soda.

**2.** In a large mixing bowl beat butter with an electric mixer on medium speed for 30 seconds. Gradually add sugar, beating until light and fluffy, about 6 minutes. Beat in lemon juice. Add eggs, 1 at a time, beating 1 minute after each egg. Gradually add flour mixture, beating on low speed until combined. Stir in lemon peel and, if desired, snipped geranium leaves.

**3.** Carefully pour batter over leaves in pan. Bake for 60 to 65 minutes or until a wooden toothpick inserted near center comes out clean. Cool cake in pan on a wire rack for 10 minutes. Remove from pan and cool completely on rack.

**4.** If desired, serve with lavender gelato, fruit-based ice cream, sorbet, or fresh summer berries and whipped cream. Makes 12 to 14 servings.

Each serving: 301 cal., 18 g total fat (9 g sat. fat), 114 mg chol., 221 mg sodium, 31 g carbo., 1 g fiber, 4 g pro. Daily Values: 12% vit. A, 4% vit. C, 2% calcium, 7% iron.

**Goat Cheese Tart**

**Lemon Geranium Pound Cake**

Toasted Coconut-Macadamia Cream Pie

Hawaiian Pulled Pork, Speckled Rice

Tomato and Salmon Salad

# LAZY AFTERNOON
# Luau

IT'S SIMPLE TO SAVOR THE FLAVORS—AND FUN—OF THE ALOHA STATE. NO GRASS SKIRTS REQUIRED.

### Tomato and Salmon Salad

**PREP:** 25 minutes **COOK:** 3½ minutes **CHILL:** 2 hours

| | | | |
|---|---|---|---|
| 4 | 4-oz. fresh or frozen skinless, boneless salmon fillets | 4 | medium tomatoes, chopped (about 4 cups) |
| 1 | teaspoon sea salt or salt | 1 | cup sliced green onions or finely chopped red onion |
| 2 | lemons | | Snipped fresh cilantro |
| 1 | cup cilantro leaves, chopped | | |

**1.** Thaw fish, if frozen; rinse and pat dry with paper towels. Halve each fillet horizontally. In a 2-quart square microwave-safe baking dish place half of the fish, leaving no space between the pieces. Sprinkle with ¼ teaspoon of the salt. Thinly slice 1 of the lemons. Lay the lemon slices and 1 cup cilantro leaves on the fish in baking dish. Top with remaining fish. Sprinkle with ¼ teaspoon of the salt. Add 2 tablespoons water to the bottom of the dish. Cover dish with waxed paper.

**2.** Microwave on 100% power (high) for 3½ to 4½ minutes or until fish flakes easily when tested with a fork, turning dish halfway through cooking, if necessary. Cool slightly. Transfer fish to a serving platter. Cover with plastic wrap; chill for 2 to 4 hours.

**3.** In a medium bowl combine tomatoes, onions, and remaining ½ teaspoon salt. Toss gently to combine. Cover and chill.

**4.** To serve, spoon tomato mixture next to fish. Cut remaining lemon in half; squeeze over fish and tomato mixture. Sprinkle with cilantro. Makes 8 side-dish servings.

**Healthy** Each serving: 105 cal., 4g total fat (1 g sat. fat), 30 mg chol., 100 mg sodium, 6 g carbo., 2 g fiber, 13 g pro. Daily Values: 30% vit. A, 36% vit. C, 4% calcium, 6% iron.

## LUAU TO-DO LIST

A cooking schedule reduces stress when entertaining.

**SATURDAY**

1. Bake the pastry shell for the Toasted Coconut-Macadamia Cream Pie. Set aside.
2. Increase oven temperature to 450° F. Prepare Hawaiian Pulled Pork for roasting.
3. Roast pork. An hour before pork is done, prepare pie filling.
4. When pork is done, reduce oven temperature to 350° F. Fill and bake the pie. Cool and chill the pie.

**SUNDAY**

1. Make Tomato and Salmon Salad; refrigerate.
2. Prepare Chile Pepper Water; refrigerate.
3. Reheat Hawaiian Pulled Pork.
4. Prepare Speckled Rice.

BY **STEPHEN EXEL** PHOTOGRAPHS BY **ANNE STRATTON** FOOD STYLING BY **SUSAN BROWN DRAUDT** PROP STYLING BY **KAREN JOHNSON**

# Summer Entertaining

Slip into the aloha mood with brightly patterned shirts and flip-flops, then gather friends for a laid-back Sunday afternoon luau. Capture the spirit of the paradise islands with three easy recipes and a breezy decor. To make this luau one of the easiest gatherings you'll ever host, you can prepare some of the food the day before.

For decorations, you don't need to build a tiki hut or invest in island props. Choose a light-hearted, beachy color scheme and punch it up with a few tropical flowers ordered in advance from the florist, such as bromeliads, ginger, and anthurium, and a few large banana leaves. Tropicals are dramatic; one or two make a bold statement. Use everyday dishes—summer brights or whites look great. An inexpensive splash of color comes from the napkins. Add a funky flea market find, such as the teak leaf dish pictured on page 172.

A luau marks any special occasion in Hawaii. Its signature dish, kalua pig, inspired the slow-cooked Hawaiian Pulled Pork recipe. Smoky and fork-tender, this dish cooks in the oven for several hours without tending, freeing time for other details. Best of all, it can be made a day ahead and reheated. Accompany the pork with a side of Speckled Rice, a miniature pitcher of Chile Pepper Water (recipes on page 175) to splash on the meat, and pineapple spears.

Tomato and Salmon Salad, a version of the classic luau dish lomi lomi salmon, will please fish lovers in the crowd. To make the dish heartier, we substituted a generous portion of poached salmon for the usual flaked salmon and served the dish's tomato-onion mixture on the side. For a more traditional presentation, flake the salmon and toss it with the tomato and onion.

Toasted Coconut-Macadamia Cream Pie is a knockout finale to your luau feast. Luscious describes this rich, velvety smooth combination of two favorite island flavors. Make sure to ask the guests, "Are you *pau*?" ("Are you finished?") or whether they'd like *hana hou* (another round).

The "to-do" list will help you plan the afternoon with minimal stress. Put on a Don Ho CD, mix the mai tais, and you're on your way to a festive afternoon that conjures up ocean breezes and barefoot walks in the sand.

## Hawaiian Pulled Pork

Reheat the pork and juices in a slow cooker set on high or in a roasting pan, tightly covered with foil, in a 350° F oven. Stir occasionally.

**PREP:** 20 minutes **ROAST:** 3½ to 4 hours **STAND:** 10 minutes

| | |
|---|---|
| 1 | 4- to 5-lb. boneless pork butt or shoulder roast |
| 5 | cloves garlic, halved |
| 10 | thin slices of fresh ginger |
| 1 | to 2 Tbsp. Hawaiian red sea salt or sea salt |

| | |
|---|---|
| 1 | pound kale, banana leaves, or 1 small head cabbage |
| | Chile Pepper Water (page 175) |
| | Speckled Rice (page 175) |
| | Fresh pineapple spears |

**1.** Preheat oven to 450° F. Cut 20 slits on all sides of pork roast at 1-inch intervals with a sharp knife. Fill slits alternately with garlic halves and ginger slices. Rub salt evenly over pork. Wrap entire roast with kale. Tie with 100-percent-cotton string to secure leaves to pork.

**2.** Place pork, fat side up, in center of a large sheet of foil. Gather foil up and around roast so it is completely wrapped. Place wrapped pork on a rack in a large roasting pan. Place pan in oven. Pour about 1 inch of water in bottom of roasting pan. Roast for 30 minutes; reduce heat to 375° F. Roast for 3 to 3½ hours more or until meat is fork-tender. Watch carefully; add water to bottom of pan as needed to maintain water level (do not let roasting pan boil dry).

**3.** Remove pan from oven and let pork stand for 10 minutes. Carefully transfer wrapped roast to a large container with sides high enough to collect juices, reserving juices in pan. Unwrap roast and remove string and cooked leaves; discard. Using 2 forks, shred pork. Skim fat from pan juices; discard fat. Serve shredded pork with combined juices, Chile Pepper Water, Speckled Rice, and pineapple spears. Makes 8 to 10 servings.

Each serving: 528 cal., 16 g total fat (5 g sat. fat), 151 mg chol., 1,082 mg sodium, 44 g carbo., 2 g fiber, 48 g pro. Daily Values: 12% vit. A, 60% vit. C, 5% calcium, 32% iron.

## Toasted Coconut-Macadamia Cream Pie

Find cream of coconut in the drink mix section of the market.

**PREP:** 40 minutes **BAKE:** 15 minutes **COOL:** 1 hour **CHILL:** 3 hours

| | |
|---|---|
| ½ | of a 15-oz. pkg. refrigerated unbaked piecrust (1 crust) |
| ⅓ | cup finely chopped macadamia nuts |
| 3 | eggs |
| ⅔ | cup sugar |
| ¼ | cup cornstarch |
| ¼ | tsp. salt |

| | |
|---|---|
| 2 | cups milk |
| ¾ | cup cream of coconut |
| 2 | Tbsp. butter |
| 1 | cup flaked coconut, toasted |
| 2½ | tsp. vanilla |
| ¼ | tsp. cream of tartar |
| 1 | Tbsp. flaked coconut |
| | Coconut shards (below) (optional) |

**1.** Unfold pie crust; press half of macadamia nuts into dough. Transfer to pie plate; flute edges. Bake according to package directions; cool. Set aside.

**2.** Separate egg yolks from whites; set whites aside for meringue. For filling, in a medium saucepan combine ⅓ cup of the sugar, the cornstarch, and salt. Stir in milk and cream of coconut. Cook and stir over medium heat until thickened and bubbly. Cook and stir for 2 minutes more. Remove from heat. In a small bowl beat egg yolks slightly. Gradually stir about 1 cup of the hot milk mixture into the beaten egg yolks, stirring constantly. Return all of the mixture to saucepan. Cook and stir until bubbly. Cook and stir for 2 minutes more. Remove from heat. Stir in butter. Stir in the 1 cup toasted coconut and 2 teaspoons of the vanilla. Keep filling warm; prepare meringue.

**3.** Preheat oven to 350° F. For meringue topping, in a mixing bowl beat egg whites, remaining ½ teaspoon vanilla, and the cream of tartar on medium speed of an electric mixer until soft peaks form (tips curl). Gradually add remaining ⅓ cup sugar, 1 tablespoon at a time, beating until stiff peaks form.

**4.** Pour warm filling into baked pastry shell. Spread meringue evenly over hot filling; seal to pastry edge. Sprinkle with remaining macadamia nuts and 1 tablespoon flaked coconut. Bake for 15 minutes. Cool on a wire rack for 1 hour. If desired, top with coconut shards. Chill for 3 to 6 hours before serving; cover and chill in the refrigerator for longer storage. Makes 8 servings.

**COCONUT SHARDS:** With a vegetable peeler, shave curls of fresh peeled coconut. Spread in a single layer in a shallow baking pan; bake in a 350° F oven for 5 minutes or until light brown.

Each serving: 473 cal., 30 g total fat (18 g sat. fat), 97 mg chol., 297 mg sodium, 44 g carbo., 2 g fiber, 7 g pro. Daily Values: 6% vit. A, 1% vit. C, 9% calcium, 6% iron.

## PULLED PORK GO-WITHS

**CHILE PEPPER WATER:** Chop 1 small red Thai chile pepper (see page 89). In a small pitcher, cruet, or shaker bottle stir together chopped pepper (with seeds), 1 whole Thai chile pepper, and 1 cup water. Cover and refrigerate for 1 to 4 hours.

**SPECKLED RICE:** In a saucepan bring 2 cups short grain rice, 4 cups water, $1/4$ cup pineapple juice, and 1 teaspoon salt to boiling. Reduce heat; simmer, covered, for 20 minutes or until rice is tender. Stir in $1/3$ cup snipped fresh pineapple mint, regular mint, or lemon basil; 1 cup chopped red sweet pepper; $1/4$ cup pineapple juice; and $1/4$ teaspoon ground black pepper. Serve warm.

# HOMEMADE
# Ice Cream

School's out, so this is just the right time for a summer session in ice cream making. Sharing the magic that transforms milk, cream, sugar, and flavorings into frozen dreams-come-true is sure to earn you an A⁺.

To make ice cream with the kids, involve them in the measuring, stirring, and pouring. Let them help you pack the ice cream maker with rock salt and ice. The machine does the rest of the work. While the churning and freezing is going on, give the children a cool trivia lesson (see "The Cold Facts" at right).

The origin of ice cream goes back some 2,000 years, but for most of its history it was a treat reserved for the wealthy. It wasn't until 1847 that it became generally available when New England homemaker Nancy Johnson invented the first hand-cranked ice cream churn.

Today, of course, having homemade ice cream ready and available is simple. Aficionados choose an electric ice cream maker that uses ice and rock salt to freeze the milk and cream mixture. Another popular unit freezes the creamy concoction in a container surrounded by a chilled chemical mixture.

If there's any left over, store it in the main part of the freezer. Keeping ice cream in the door exposes it to fluctuating temperatures. Likewise, allowing ice cream to soften and refreeze causes a crust of ice to form across the top.

## THE COLD FACTS

- The United States tops the world in ice cream consumption. In fact, 98 percent of American households enjoy the creamy, frozen dessert.
- Vanilla beats chocolate as the most popular flavor. According to several sources, positions three, four, and five are up for grabs between butter pecan, Neapolitan, chocolate chip, and strawberry.
- Children ages 2 through 12 and adults over 45 eat the most ice cream per person.
- It takes the average person 50 licks to finish an ice cream cone.
- Speaking of the ice cream cone, 2004 marks the 100th anniversary of when it took America by storm. An Italian immigrant in New York City patented a machine that formed cones for ice cream in 1903, but the treat lingered on the fringes of popularity. It was at the 1904 St. Louis World's Fair that an ice cream vendor ran out of serving dishes and enlisted the help of a nearby wafflemaker, who rolled waferlike pastries into cones to help out.

## Chocolate Toffee Crunch Ice Cream

**Kid Friendly**

**START TO FINISH:** 30 minutes

| | | |
|---|---|---|
| 1 | cup sugar | 1/8 tsp. salt |
| 1/4 | cup unsweetened cocoa powder | Cubed or crushed ice |
| 2 | cups whipping cream | Rock salt* |
| 1 | cup milk | 3/4 cup chocolate-covered toffee pieces |
| 1 | tsp. vanilla | |

1. In canister container for a 4-quart ice cream freezer, combine sugar and cocoa powder. Stir in cream, milk, vanilla, and salt. Whisk thoroughly until sugar is dissolved.

2. Place lid over ice cream freezer container. Place container in bucket. Attach motor piece to lid and sides of bucket according to manufacturer's directions. Pack 6 cups of ice around the container. Sprinkle ice with 1 cup rock salt. Repeat packing with 6 cups ice and sprinkling with 1 cup rock salt until bucket is filled to the top of the container. Plug in electric ice cream maker. When motor comes to a stop, unplug immediately. Stir in toffee pieces. Serve immediately or place in the freezer to harden ice cream; use ice cream within 1 week. Makes about 4 cups (eight 1/2-cup servings).

**FOR A NO-ICE, NO-SALT ICE CREAM MAKER:** In a large mixing bowl combine 1/2 cup sugar and 2 tablespoons cocoa powder. Stir in 1 cup whipping cream, 1/2 cup milk, 1/2 teaspoon vanilla, and a dash of salt. Whisk thoroughly until sugar is dissolved. Freeze according to manufacturer's directions. When finished, stir in 1/3 cup chocolate-covered toffee pieces. Makes about 2 1/3 cups.

**\*NOTE:** Rock salt is available in the salt section of supermarket.

Each serving: 448 cal., 30 g total fat (17 g sat. fat), 92 mg chol., 165 mg sodium, 42 g carbo., 0 g fiber, 3 g pro. Daily Values: 19% vit. A, 1% vit. C, 11% calcium, 2% iron.

**Chocolate Toffee Crunch Ice Cream**

# CHILLY BURGERS

When you want a creative treat that kids can put together themselves, use purchased ice cream and sandwich it between store-bought cookies. One pint of ice cream makes about twelve 2-inch sandwich cookies or about six 3- to 4-inch sandwich cookies. Wrap each sandwich in plastic wrap or foil; freeze at least 6 hours or until firm. Let stand about 10 minutes before eating.

**CARAMEL CRUNCH BRRRWICH:** Stir a crushed chocolate-covered English toffee candy bar into softened vanilla ice cream. Spoon some of the ice cream mixture onto the flat side of a pecan shortbread cookie. Spread caramel ice cream topping on the flat side of another cookie. Place cookie, caramel side down, on top of ice cream to make a sandwich.

**DOUBLE COOKIE DOUGH BLAST:** Spoon softened cookie dough ice cream onto the flat side of a soft chocolate chip cookie. Spread chocolate or fudge ice cream topping on the flat side of another cookie. Place cookie, fudge side down, on top of ice cream to make a sandwich. Roll ice cream sides in miniature semisweet chocolate pieces.

**OOEY-GOOEY ROCKY ROAD:** Spoon softened chocolate ice cream onto the flat side of a soft chocolate cookie. Spread marshmallow creme on the flat side of another cookie. Sprinkle salted peanuts on top of the marshmallow creme. Place cookie, marshmallow creme side down, on top of ice cream.

# CHEF SALAD

Fans of the Atlanta cook's market Star Provisions know it's peak salad season when fresh-from-the-farm produce appears in the shop. "Salads fit summer perfectly," says the shop's co-owner Anne Quatrano. A seasoned chef, Anne and her partner grow most of the produce that's sold in the store on their nearby 60-acre farm. They also oversee all selections for the meat, seafood, cheese, wine, bread, pasta, and tableware sections of the market. Anne offers these salad-making tips.

▪ Simple preparations and presentations are best. If you use the freshest quality, you don't have to do much to make a beautiful salad.

▪ Every salad benefits from olive oil and lemon juice. Drizzle them separately. Sea salt is a must.

▪ Salads aren't just for vegetables. Toss in peaches or berries.
Star Provisions, 1198 Howell Mill Rd., Atlanta, GA. 404/365-0410.

# SPREAD THE NEWS

After 5,000 years of butter eating, you'd think we'd have run out of ways to fine tune the flavor, but the butter case in the grocery store has more choices than ever. Some new labels you might be seeing: "European-style" and European imports have a little more butterfat, creating a smoother texture and a butter that won't burn as quickly. "Cultured" means the butter is made from cream that's been fermented, resulting in a stronger, buttery, nutty flavor. "Organic" means that the cow herds are raised free of antibiotics, hormones, and pesticides.

Check out these sources: Vermont Butter and Cheese, www.vtbutterandcheeseco.com; Organic Valley, www.organicvalley.coop; Plugra, Keller's Creamery, www.kellerscreamery.com; Straus Family Creamery, www.strausmilk.com.

**IN AGAIN**

# BUTTER FANCIES

With the morning rush to get everyone up, fed, and out the door, it hardly seems possible that families once took time for a breakfast with all the accoutrements, including butter dishes and knives.

During the early 1800s, the first meal of the day was an elaborate affair complete with fresh butter and toast. Butter was considered a delicacy because it was perishable and a chore to make. When factory or "creamery" production began in the 1860s, it was possible to purchase this special morning treat from a butter-and-egg man. Specialized dishes were designed to accommodate the standard one-pound slab, which was about four inches round. A serving knife was used to cut individual pats so that only it would be used in the communal dish. Next, small dishes for individual servings of bread and butter evolved, giving rise to the butter knife as a standard part of silver tableware service in the 1880s. Ever wonder about the curious saberlike shape of a butter knife? The design allows you to cut and maneuver a slice onto the plate with a quick twist. Because butter comes in multiple forms and few diets rely on it as a staple, you can extend the use of the small knives to assorted cheeses and pâté. These pretty knives and spreaders also make great hostess gifts. *From top to bottom:* English carved mother-of-pearl butter knife, circa 1890; English mother-of-pearl spreader with sterling ferrules; English carved mother-of-pearl butter knife, circa 1890; sterling butter spreader, circa 1875.

# September

GATHER THE FAMILIES
AND OTHER WEDDING
PARTICIPANTS FOR AN
EVENING OF GOOD
FOOD TO MAKE A
MEMORABLE OCCASION.

# Romantic Rehearsal Dinner

# Romantic
## rehearsal dinner

**Bourbon-Infused Honey with assorted cheeses, crackers, and fruit**

SEND THE BRIDE AND GROOM OFF TO THEIR WEDDING FROM THE HEART OF YOUR HOME WITH A RELAXED, INTIMATE, AND SIMPLE REHEARSAL DINNER.

BY JENNIFER WILKINSON AND STEPHEN EXEL PHOTOGRAPHS BY MIKI DUISTERHOF STYLED BY CHRISTINA WRESSELL FOOD STYLING BY ALISON ATTENBOROUGH PRODUCED BY JESSICA THOMAS

## Bourbon-Infused Honey

Serve this with blue cheese and juicy seedless red grapes. You can also use it to sweeten iced tea or to drizzle over cakes or ice cream.

**PREP:** 5 minutes **COOK:** 5 minutes **COOL:** 1 hour

| | |
|---|---|
| 1 cup honey | ¼ cup bourbon |
| 1 large bay leaf | |

**1.** In a small saucepan heat honey and bay leaf over medium heat just until mixture bubbles around the edges. Reduce heat to low and cook for 5 minutes. Remove from heat. Stir in bourbon. Set aside to cool, about 1 hour. Remove and discard bay leaf. Transfer honey to a jar and store overnight or up to 5 days in the refrigerator. Makes 1 cup.

Each tablespoon: 73 cal., 0 g total fat (0 g sat. fat), 0 mg chol., 1 mg sodium, 17 g carbo., 0 g fiber, 0 g pro.

## Autumn Punch

**PREP:** 20 minutes **CHILL:** 4 hours

| | |
|---|---|
| 2 tsp. whole cloves | 4 medium purple and/or green plums, pitted and sliced |
| ½ of a vanilla bean, split lengthwise | |
| 1 64-oz. bottle apple-cranberry juice | 1 750-ml. bottle Gewürztraminer or other fruity white wine* |
| | Ice cubes |

**1.** Place cloves and vanilla bean in center of a double-thick 6-inch square of 100-percent-cotton cheesecloth. Bring corners of cloth together; tie closed with clean string. Pour apple-cranberry juice into a large container or pitcher. Add plums and spice bag. Cover and chill for 4 to 24 hours.

**2.** Remove and discard cheesecloth bag. Stir in Gewürz-traminer. Serve beverage and plum slices over ice. (Or omit the ice and heat the juice mixture and wine in a 4-quart Dutch oven until hot. Serve in heatproof mugs.) Makes 10 to 12 servings.

**\*NONALCOHOL OPTION:** Substitute two 12-ounce cans chilled ginger ale for the Gewürztraminer.

Each serving: 180 cal., 0 g total fat (0 g sat. fat), 0 mg chol., 30 mg sodium, 33 g carbo., 1 g fiber, 1 g pro. Daily Values: 5% vit. A, 109% vit. C, 1% calcium, 2% iron.

# A casual get-together

Special in its own way, the rehearsal dinner is when families and friends gather one final time before newly-weds begin their lives together. A gathering at home is a wonderful way to send off the bride and groom with a sense of warmth and family. It's the welcome prelude to the joy and excitement of the wedding day.

Although traditionally the groom's family hosts this event, that's not always the case today. An aunt or uncle, close friends, the parents of the groom or bride, or even the bride and groom themselves might serve as hosts.

If you like, subtly introduce the color scheme of the wedding in the home. Continue the color scheme on your tables, mixing fresh flowers from the market with those blooming in your garden. Combine them with grapes, plums, green apples, and seasonal foliage for an easy, beautiful centerpiece. Use the same cut flowers to make the bride's rehearsal bouquet. Napkins and handwritten place cards in similar shades finish the effortless setting.

For the menu, choose recipes that are homey in style, play on autumn flavors different from the wedding menu, and can serve a large group. Dishes that are made ahead or get a jump start from ready-made ingredients keep last-minute preparations to a minimum.

Let your take-away gifts carry out the harvest theme with simply wrapped half-bottles of wine or jars of seasonal jam. This is also the time to share other presents: the bride's and groom's gifts for the bridal party or the presentation of an heirloom piece from mother to daughter or father to son. Sharing stories, memories of the bridal couple, special toasts, and unique memen-tos fosters the bonding of two families in the relaxed setting of home. It's a quiet moment for shared times during the whirlwind of wedding events.

## Chicken and Duck Hunter Stew

Israeli couscous, available in most grocery stores and specialty food stores, is large and has a slightly "toothy" texture.

**PREP:** 1 hour **COOK:** 45 minutes

| | |
|---|---|
| 12 chicken drumsticks (about 3 lb.), skinned if desired | 3 medium green sweet peppers, cut into 1-inch pieces |
| 3 boneless duck breast halves, skinned and quartered* | 1½ cups dry Marsala or beef broth |
| ¼ cup olive oil | 1 6-oz. can tomato paste |
| 3 cups assorted sliced fresh mushrooms, such as crimini, shiitake, oyster, and/or button | ¾ cup pitted kalamata olives and/or green olives |
| 2 medium onions, sliced | 2 Tbsp. balsamic vinegar |
| 3 cloves garlic, minced | 1 tsp. salt |
| 6 medium tomatoes, seeded and chopped (about 3 cups) | ¼ tsp. ground black pepper |
| | ¼ cup snipped fresh oregano or marjoram |
| | 2 Tbsp. snipped fresh rosemary |
| | 6 cups hot cooked Israeli couscous or couscous |

**1.** In a 6-quart Dutch oven cook drumsticks and duck, half at a time, in hot oil about 15 minutes or until lightly browned, turning to brown evenly. Remove chicken and duck, reserving drippings in the Dutch oven; set drumsticks aside. Cover and chill the duck in the refrigerator.

**2.** Add mushrooms, onions, and garlic to drippings in the Dutch oven. Cook and stir about 5 minutes or until vegetables are just tender. Return drumsticks to Dutch oven.

**3.** Meanwhile, in a large bowl combine tomatoes, sweet peppers, Marsala, tomato paste, olives, vinegar, salt, and black pepper. Pour over drumsticks in Dutch oven. Bring to boiling; reduce heat. Simmer, covered, for 20 minutes. Add duck; return to boiling. Reduce heat and simmer 25 to 30 minutes more or until poultry is tender. Just before serving, stir in oregano and rosemary. Serve stew with couscous. Makes 12 servings.

**MAKE-AHEAD TIP:** Prepare stew as above, adding herbs before freezing, if desired. Chill the stew quickly by placing the Dutch oven in a sink of ice water. Divide mixture between two 2½- to 3-quart freezer containers. Seal, label, and freeze up to 1 month. To reheat, place freezer containers in refrigerator overnight to partially thaw. Place mixture in Dutch oven.

Cook over medium-low heat until mixture is completely thawed. Increase heat to medium and cook just until bubbly, about 35 to 40 minutes total (do not overcook or duck may toughen). Add herbs just before serving if not added before freezing.

**\*NOTE:** To make this stew with all chicken, substitute 12 chicken thighs for the duck; add the thighs and drumsticks back into the Dutch oven all at once.

Each serving: 393 cal., 14 g total fat (3 g sat. fat), 129 mg chol., 407 mg sodium, 28 g carbo., 3 g fiber, 33 g pro. Daily Values: 11% vit. A, 62% vit. C, 4% calcium, 22% iron.

## Three-Cheese Lasagna

The ricotta gives the lasagna a slightly grainy texture.

**PREP:** 50 minutes **BAKE:** 35 minutes **STAND:** 15 minutes

| | |
|---|---|
| 2 medium eggplants (2 lb.), chopped (11 cups) | 1 15-oz. carton ricotta cheese |
| 2 large red onions, halved crosswise and thickly sliced (about 2 cups) | 12 oz. goat cheese (chèvre) |
| 2 cloves garlic, minced | 1 cup whipping cream |
| 1 cup snipped fresh sweet basil or purple basil | 2 eggs |
| ¼ cup olive oil | ½ tsp. salt |
| 12 dried lasagna noodles | ½ tsp. ground black pepper |
| 8 oz. Gruyère cheese, finely shredded (2 cups) | ¼ tsp. crushed red pepper |
| | 2 tsp. finely shredded lemon peel |

**1.** Preheat oven to 450° F. In a roasting pan combine chopped eggplant, onion, and garlic. Add ½ cup of the snipped basil and the oil; toss to coat. Roast, uncovered, for 30 to 35 minutes or until vegetables are very tender, stirring once; set aside.

**2.** Meanwhile, cook lasagna noodles according to package directions; drain and set aside. For filling, in a food processor* combine 1½ cups of the Gruyère cheese, the ricotta cheese, goat cheese, whipping cream, eggs, salt, black pepper, and crushed red pepper. Cover and process until just combined.

**3.** Reduce oven temperature to 375° F. Spoon one-third of the eggplant mixture evenly in the bottom of a 3-quart rectangular baking dish. Layer with 4 noodles and one-third of the filling. Repeat layers twice, starting with eggplant and ending with filling. Sprinkle with remaining ½ cup Gruyère cheese. Cover with nonstick aluminum foil. Bake for 20 minutes; uncover and bake for 15 to 20 minutes more or until heated through. Let stand for 15 minutes before serving. Sprinkle top with remaining ½ cup basil and the lemon peel. Makes 12 servings.

**MAKE-AHEAD TIP:** Prepare lasagna as directed but do not bake. Cover and refrigerate up to 24 hours. Bake, covered, in a 375° F oven for 40 minutes; uncover and bake for 20 to 25 minutes more or until heated through. Let stand for 15 minutes before serving. Top as directed above.

**\*NOTE:** If you do not have a food processor, combine filling ingredients in a large bowl. Beat with an electric mixer on low speed until combined.

Each serving: 439 cal., 30 g total fat (16 g sat. fat), 114 mg chol., 315 mg sodium, 23 g carbo., 3 g fiber, 20 g pro. Daily Values: 18% vit. A, 6% vit. C, 34% calcium, 11% iron.

**Three-Cheese Lasagna**

**Chicken and Duck Hunter Stew**

## SET THE SCENE

Gather the elements for the centerpiece: beeswax candles, bunches of grapes, pears, plums, and small bowls of flowers. Spread them along the center of the dining room table on a base of grapevines. A runner of brown wrapping paper provides a neutral background to the sumptuous shades of plum and green.

**Mixed Greens with Cardamom-Curry Dressing**

## Mixed Greens with Cardamom-Curry Dressing

Preparing the dressing in advance saves time and allows the flavors to mellow and blend.

*Fast!* **START TO FINISH:** 10 minutes

| | | | |
|---|---|---|---|
| 1 | 8-oz. carton dairy sour cream | ¼ | to ½ tsp. ground black pepper |
| ½ | cup grapefruit juice or ruby red grapefruit juice | ⅓ | cup salad oil |
| 1 | Tbsp. honey | | Freshly ground black pepper (optional) |
| 1 | tsp. curry powder | 20 | cups mesclun or other |
| 1 | tsp. ground cardamom | | torn salad greens |
| ½ | tsp. ground cinnamon | | (about 2½ 5-oz. pkg.) |

**1.** For dressing, in a blender or food processor combine sour cream, grapefruit juice, honey, curry powder, cardamom, cinnamon, and pepper. Cover and blend or process until combined. With blender or processor running, slowly add salad oil in a steady stream until mixture is thickened. Cover and chill until ready to serve. Dressing can be prepared up to 3 days ahead.

**2.** Before serving, stir dressing to combine. If desired, sprinkle with additional freshly ground pepper. Serve dressing with mesclun. Makes 12 servings.

Each serving: 128 cal., 12 g total fat (4 g sat. fat), 10 mg chol., 15 mg sodium, 5 g carbo., 0 g fiber, 1 g pro. Daily Values: 6% vit. A, 10% vit. C, 4% calcium, 2% iron.

## Apple-Garlic Loaves

Slice bread in large chunks to keep topping contained on each piece.

*Fast!* **PREP:** 20 minutes **BAKE:** 10 minutes

| | | | |
|---|---|---|---|
| 3 | medium Granny Smith apples (about 1 lb.), cored | ½ | cup packed brown sugar |
| 1 | Tbsp. butter | 1 | Tbsp. lemon juice |
| 4 | large cloves garlic, coarsely chopped | 2 | 20-oz. loaves purchased ciabatta bread or other crusty bread |
| ½ | cup rolled oats | 3 | Tbsp. butter, melted |

**1.** Thinly slice 1½ of the apples; coarsely chop remaining apples. In a large skillet melt the 1 tablespoon butter. Add apples, garlic, and oats. Cook over medium heat for 5 to 8 minutes or until apples start to soften, stirring occasionally. Remove from heat; stir in brown sugar and lemon juice. Use immediately to top bread or transfer to a medium bowl; cover and chill up to 24 hours.

**2.** Preheat oven to 375° F. Place loaves on a large baking sheet.* Brush tops of loaves with melted butter. Spoon half the apple mixture onto each loaf, pressing mixture in slightly. Bake, uncovered, for 10 minutes or until warmed through. Transfer to a cutting surface. Slice carefully to avoid dislodging apples. Makes 24 servings.

**\*NOTE:** If the loaves do not have flat tops, slice off the rounded portions to make flat surfaces.

Each serving: 180 cal., 4 g total fat (1 g sat. fat), 5 mg chol., 293 mg sodium, 32 g carbo., 2 g fiber, 5 g pro. Daily Values: 1% vit. A, 2% vit. C, 4% calcium, 9% iron.

### TOP IT OFF

Use your fingers to press the apple-garlic topping onto the ciabatta loaf. The topping is meant to be loose, but it will adhere better with a little help.

### REHEARSAL DINNER

Cheese with Bourbon-Infused Honey (page 183)
Chicken and Duck Hunter Stew (page 184)
Three-Cheese Lasagna (page 184)
Mixed Greens with
Cardamom-Curry Dressing (above left)
Apple-Garlic Loaves (above)
Grape Pie (page 188)
Autumn Punch (page 183), coffee, iced tea

**Chicken and Duck Hunter Stew with couscous**

**Three-Cheese Lasagna**

**Apple-Garlic Loaves**

**Mixed Greens with Cardamom-Curry Dressing**

# REHEARSAL DINNER TIMELINE

Keep your rehearsal dinner stress free by following this timeline. The day of the party, you'll need just over an hour to get the food together.

## ONE MONTH BEFORE OR LESS

- Prepare Chicken and Duck Hunter Stew (1 hour). Freeze.
- Five days before the party, make Bourbon-Infused Honey (10 minutes). Refrigerate.
- Three days before the party, make Cardamom-Curry Dressing (5 minutes). Refrigerate.

## ONE DAY BEFORE

- Make Grape Pie (45 minutes). Bake (55 minutes). While the pie bakes, prepare Three-Cheese Lasagna (50 minutes); do not bake the lasagna. Refrigerate.
- Prepare base for Autumn Punch (20 minutes). Prepare topping for Apple-Garlic Loaves (20 minutes). Refrigerate both.
- Thaw stew overnight in the refrigerator.

## DAY OF PARTY

- Bring cheeses for the appetizer tray to room temperature; set up with Bourbon-Infused Honey.
- Add wine to Autumn Punch. Pour the punch into pitchers (do not add ice until serving).
- Clean salad greens (5 minutes). Refrigerate.
- Bake lasagna (1 hour). Let stand 15 minutes.
- While lasagna bakes, reheat the stew (35 minutes).
- Top Apple-Garlic Loaves and bake (20 minutes).
- Prepare couscous (10 minutes). Let stand; fluff before serving.
- Before dinner, whip cream for pie (3 minutes). Refrigerate.

## CURVY CRUST

To crimp the bottom and top crust together into this whimsical piecrust rim, pinch the bottom and top crusts together with your thumb and forefinger and give a little twist. Work your way around the pie.

## Grape Pie

To shorten preparation time, you can use 2 refrigerated unbaked piecrusts instead of preparing the pastry. If desired, serve the baked pie with sweetened whipped cream topped with chopped walnuts.

**PREP:** 45 minutes **BAKE:** 50 minutes **COOL:** 6 hours

| | |
|---|---|
| 1 recipe Pastry for Double-Crust Pie (below) | 7 cups seedless red or black grapes, halved |
| 1/2 cup packed brown sugar | 2 to 3 Tbsp. snipped fresh sage or 1 teaspoon ground sage |
| 1/4 cup all-purpose flour | |
| 1/4 cup port or red grape juice | 1 egg white |
| 2 Tbsp. cornstarch | 1 Tbsp. water |
| | Granulated sugar (optional) |

**1.** Preheat oven to 375° F. Prepare Pastry for Double-Crust Pie. For filling, in a 5- or 6-quart Dutch oven stir together the brown sugar, flour, port, and cornstarch. Stir in grapes. Cook, stirring constantly over medium heat, until thickened and bubbly (about 10 minutes). Stir in sage.

**2.** Transfer the filling to the pastry-lined pie plate. Roll remaining dough into a circle about 12 inches in diameter. Cut slits to allow steam to escape. Place pastry on the filling; trim to 1/2 inch beyond edge of plate. Fold top pastry under bottom pastry. Crimp edge as desired (photo lower left). Place pie on a baking sheet.

**3.** In a small bowl combine egg white and water. Brush top of pie with egg white mixture. If desired, sprinkle lightly with granulated sugar. Cover edge of pie with foil. Bake for 25 minutes; remove foil. Bake for 25 to 30 minutes more or until top of pastry is golden brown and filling bubbles through slits in crust. Remove from oven; cool at least 6 hours. Pie can be baked up to 24 hours ahead. Loosely cover; store at room temperature. Makes 8 servings.

**PASTRY FOR DOUBLE-CRUST PIE:** In a medium bowl stir together 2 1/4 cups all-purpose flour and 3/4 teaspoon salt. Using a pastry blender, cut in 2/3 cup shortening until pieces are pea-size. Sprinkle 1 tablespoon cold water over part of the flour mixture; gently toss with a fork. Push moistened dough to side of bowl. Repeat, using 1 tablespoon water at a time, until all the flour mixture is moistened (about 8 to 10 tablespoons water total). Divide dough in half. Form each half into a ball. On a lightly floured surface, use your hands to slightly flatten 1 dough ball. Roll dough from center to edges into a 12-inch circle. To transfer pastry, wrap it around the rolling pin; unroll into a 9-inch pie plate. Ease pastry into pie plate, being careful not to stretch pastry. Trim pastry even with rim of pie plate. Fill pie; continue as directed.

**FOOD PROCESSOR METHOD:** Place steel blade in a food processor bowl. Add flour, salt, and shortening. Cover; process with on/off turns until most of mixture resembles cornmeal but a few larger pieces remain. With processor running, quickly add 6 tablespoons water through feed tube. Stop processor when all water is added; scrape down sides. Process with 2 on/off turns. Remove dough from bowl; shape into a ball. Divide in half. Continue as directed above.

Each serving: 453 cal., 18 g total fat (4 g sat. fat), 0 mg chol., 235 mg sodium, 69 g carbo., 2 g fiber, 5 g pro. Daily Values: 2% vit. A, 25% vit. C, 4% calcium, 14% iron.

**Grape Pie**

# THAT'S A WRAP

This clever wrapping for take-away gifts is easy to assemble. You'll need kraft paper torn into a triangle, a square of fabric, leather cord, and a note card. Wrap the bottle with the paper; secure it with adhesive tape. Fold down the top of the fabric square, wrap over the paper, and secure it with the leather cord. Tie on a note card with cord. Every bottle need not be identical.

**Greens and Roasted Chicken**

# BIG
# SALADS
## IN A FLASH

A MEAL-IN-ITSELF SALAD IS JUST A MATTER OF
TUMBLING GREAT GREENS WITH TOSS-IN EXTRAS
YOU'VE GRABBED AT THE MARKET.

BY **LINDA WOODRUM** PHOTOGRAPHS BY **GREG SCHEIDEMANN [N] HAUSFOTO** FOOD STYLING BY **CHARLES WORTHINGTON**

## Greens and Roasted Chicken

**Fast!** **START TO FINISH:** 20 minutes

1  2¼-lb. purchased whole roasted chicken, chilled
1  5-oz. pkg. mixed salad greens (about 8 cups)
2  cups sliced fresh strawberries or blueberries
4  oz. Gorgonzola or blue cheese, crumbled (1 cup)
½  cup honey-roasted cashews or peanuts
1  lemon, halved
3  Tbsp. olive oil
¼  tsp. salt
¼  tsp. ground black pepper

**1.** Remove and discard skin from chicken. Remove meat from bones; discard bones. Shred meat (you should have about 3½ cups chicken).

**2.** Place greens on a platter. Top with chicken, strawberries, cheese, and nuts. Drizzle with juice from lemon and oil; sprinkle with salt and pepper. Makes 6 main-dish servings.

Each serving: 376 cal., 27 g total fat (8 g sat. fat), 81 mg chol., 454 mg sodium, 9 g carbo., 2 g fiber, 27 g pro. Daily Values: 7% vit. A, 53% vit. C, 12% calcium, 10% iron.

## Spinach-Pasta Salad with Shrimp

**Fast!** **START TO FINISH:** 20 minutes

1  cup dried shell pasta or elbow macaroni
1  lb. frozen cooked shrimp, thawed, or 1 lb. cooked shrimp
1  cup chopped red sweet peppers
⅓  cup bottled creamy onion or Caesar salad dressing
2  Tbsp. snipped fresh dill (optional)
   Salt and freshly ground black pepper
1  6-oz. pkg. baby spinach
4  oz. goat cheese (chèvre), sliced, or feta cheese, crumbled

**1.** Prepare pasta according to package directions; drain.

**2.** In an extra-large bowl combine pasta, shrimp, and sweet peppers. Drizzle with the salad dressing. If desired, sprinkle with dill. Toss to coat. Season to taste with salt and black pepper.

**3.** Divide spinach among 6 shallow bowls or plates. Top with shrimp mixture and cheese. Makes 6 main-dish servings.

Each serving: 247 cal., 10 g total fat (4 g sat. fat), 156 mg chol., 435 mg sodium, 17 g carbo., 2 g fiber, 23 g pro. Daily Values: 72% vit. A, 95% vit. C, 9% calcium, 23% iron.

# Explore the varieties

Rip open a bag of crisp greens; toss them into a big bowl along with flavor-packed extras such as berries, cheese, nuts, and chicken; then add a splash of dressing; and call it dinner. With a bag of greens as a base, you can have a main-dish salad ready in about 20 minutes. A loaf of bread or warm tortillas completes the meal.

Most grocery stores carry a variety of greens—from mildly sweet to fiercely spicy, in vivid greens and shades of burgundy. Some lettuce blends contain added dill, cilantro, or other herbs to provide fresh bursts of flavor. Look for combinations that include added carrots or other veggies for a healthful boost of crunch and taste. If you can't find a mixed bag that suits your family's palate, add their favorite vegetables from the produce section or, better yet, reach for ready-to-toss ingredients at a supermarket salad bar.

Although most greens are prewashed, we suggest rinsing them again at home. A salad spinner eliminates the moisture after washing the lettuce, but a quick pat-down with paper towels works too. Make sure the lettuce is as dry as possible so oil-based salad dressings cling.

When shopping for your salad fixings, look for vibrant greens free of wilting and dark spots. Check the bag for a freshness date. When it's time to assemble, simply open the bag and get started. It should only take minutes from bag to plate.

**Spinach-Pasta Salad with Shrimp**

Tuna Salad with Capers

## Tuna Salad with Capers

*Fast!* **START TO FINISH:** 20 minutes

½ cup mayonnaise or salad dressing
2 Tbsp. capers, drained
2 Tbsp. lemon juice
1 Tbsp. snipped fresh tarragon
1 tsp. Cajun seasoning or pepper blend
1 12-oz. can solid white tuna, drained

2 Tbsp. milk
1 10-oz. pkg. torn mixed salad greens (romaine blend) or 8 cups torn romaine
2 cups shredded cabbage with carrot (coleslaw mix)
3 small tomatoes, cut into wedges

**1.** In a small bowl combine mayonnaise, capers, lemon juice, tarragon, and Cajun seasoning. Set aside.

**2.** In a large bowl flake tuna into large chunks; toss with 3 tablespoons of the mayonnaise mixture. Stir milk into remaining mayonnaise mixture. To serve, divide greens among 6 plates; top with shredded cabbage, tuna mixture, and tomato wedges. Serve with the dressing. Makes 6 main-dish servings.

Each serving: 228 cal., 17 g total fat (3 g sat. fat), 38 mg chol., 455 mg sodium, 5 g carbo., 2 g fiber, 15 g pro. Daily Values: 9% vit. A, 26% vit. C, 4% calcium, 6% iron.

## Asian Chicken Salad

*Fast!* **START TO FINISH:** 15 minutes

1 10-oz. pkg. torn mixed salad greens
8 oz. cooked chicken, cut into bite-size pieces
⅓ cup bottled Asian vinaigrette salad dressing

1 11-oz. can mandarin orange sections, drained
3 Tbsp. sliced almonds, toasted

**1.** In a large bowl combine salad greens and chicken. Add salad dressing; toss to coat.

**2.** Divide salad mixture among 4 plates. Top with mandarin orange sections and almonds. Serve immediately. Makes 4 main-dish servings.

**Healthy** Each serving: 218 cal., 9 g total fat (1 g sat. fat), 50 mg chol., 502 mg sodium, 15 g carbo., 2 g fiber, 19 g pro. Daily Values: 5% vit. A, 15% vit. C, 4% calcium, 9% iron.

# NIBBLE ON THESE GREENS

Here's a guide to varieties you might find in the produce section of your supermarket.

**LOLLO ROSA** The small greens have ruffled edges and a burgundy tint that make them a gorgeous salad addition. The flavor is mild and fresh.

**RED OAK LEAF LETTUCE** As the name implies, this lettuce has leaves that resemble those of an oak tree. Red oak is mild in flavor and great for piling onto a homemade sandwich or adding color to a salad.

**TATSOI** Also called rosette bok choy or spoon cabbage, this Asian green has dark spoon-shaped leaves and a strong, slightly sweet and nutty flavor.

**FRISÉE (FREE-SAY)** This sassy green is a member of the chicory family. Frisée is feathery with slender outer green leaves, paler middle leaves, and delicate white center leaves. Because it has a mildly bitter flavor, frisée is often used in combination with other salad greens.

Lollo Rosa

Red Oak Leaf Lettuce

Tatsoi

Frisée

# ROSH HASHANAH COUSCOUS

**Couscous with
Seven Vegetables**

When Jews of Mediterranean origin celebrate the Jewish New Year, Rosh Hashanah, you're likely to find Couscous with Seven Vegetables on the holiday table. This dish is a natural combination of cooking and tradition: Seven is considered a lucky number for Jewish people; couscous is a staple of the Mediterranean region.

The choice of seven vegetables has its own New Year's significance: nothing black, such as eggplant or olives, to prevent sorrow; and at least one golden vegetable, such as carrot, pumpkin, or squash, to signify prosperity. Some of the vegetables are cut into coinlike shapes to represent a coming year that is full and rounded.

The recipe is simple. Stir cooked onion, carrots, sweet potato, yellow summer squash, zucchini, green sweet pepper, and tomato into quick-cooking couscous. You can also use artichoke hearts, turnips, cabbage, green beans, or leeks. For a sweet version, try a combination of seven dried and fresh fruits.

## Couscous with Seven Vegetables

Cut the carrots, summer squash, and zucchini into coinlike shapes.

**PREP:** 25 minutes **COOK:** 10 minutes

| | | | |
|---|---|---|---|
| 1 | large yellow onion, slivered (1½ cups) | 1 | small yellow summer squash, sliced (1 cup) |
| 2 | cloves garlic, minced | 1 | small zucchini, sliced (1 cup) |
| 1 | Tbsp. olive oil | | |
| 1 | cup sliced carrots | 1 | large green sweet pepper, chopped (1 cup) |
| 1 | medium sweet potato, peeled and cubed (1 cup) | ³/₄ | cup cherry tomatoes, quartered |
| 2 | tsp. ground turmeric | | |
| 2 | tsp. ground cumin | 1 | 10-oz. pkg. quick-cooking couscous |
| ½ | tsp. salt | | |
| ³/₄ | cup water | ½ | cup snipped fresh mint |

**1.** In a 4-quart Dutch oven cook onion and garlic in hot oil over medium heat until tender. Add carrots, sweet potato, turmeric, cumin, and salt. Add water. Bring to boiling; reduce heat. Cook, covered, for 5 minutes, stirring occasionally. Add yellow summer squash, zucchini, and sweet pepper. Cover and cook for 5 minutes more or until vegetables are tender. Stir in tomatoes.

**2.** Meanwhile, prepare couscous with optional salt according to package directions. Transfer couscous to a large bowl. Add vegetable mixture; stir gently. Stir in snipped mint. Serve immediately. Makes 10 servings.

Each serving: 159 cal., 2 g total fat (0 g sat. fat), 0 mg chol., 134 mg sodium, 31 g carbo., 3 g fiber, 5 g pro. Daily Values: 64% vit. A, 42% vit. C, 4% calcium, 9% iron.

BY STEPHEN EXEL PHOTOGRAPH BY GREG SCHEIDEMANN [+1] HAUSFOTO FOOD STYLING BY CHARLES WORTHINGTON

# ALL THE BUZZ

Mani Niall knew he was a full-fledged honey guru when he declared that his favorite honey was from a wildflower plant in New Mexico that only blooms every few years. "That honey had a wonderful caramel and fruit flavor with smoky, mesquite overtones," says Niall, describing a few nuances. "Honey isn't a one-note food. It's just like olive oil, wine, coffee, or chocolate—the more you taste and learn, the less you know. The floral source makes all the difference in the flavor, and any plant that produces a flower can make honey. All plants flower—even weeds. Dandelion honey is amazing."

To fully enjoy the flavor of honey, Niall suggests a tasting party. Start with three varietals. Taste from the lightest to the darkest. Or offer honey from three sources, such as local beekeepers. "To taste, place just a drop in the middle of the tongue and let it dissolve."

# HONEY POTS

## HONEY, THE DELECTABLE CONCOCTION OF BEES, IS AGAIN A STAPLE OF THE TABLE.

Some might argue it never left: Honey was one of the first foods harvested. Archaeologists of the 18th century found jars of honey stored in Egyptian tombs, ready for the awakening of the pharaohs. That's a contrast to a typical household today where a honey pot sits on the counter waiting for Winnie the Pooh fans to rouse from their nighttime slumber. Basic honey pot shapes mimic early domed beehives made of layers of coiled straw. Usually the close-fitting cover is adorned with one or more bees for a natural look.

A universal sweetener, honey is used in many cultures. Evidence of the use of honey in ancient Greece is revealed in one of Aesop's fables—a tale of flies whose feet become trapped in the sticky, sweet substance when they come upon an overturned honey pot.

In the 18th century, elegant silver pots were popular on English tables for use at breakfast and teatime. Colorful ceramic versions appeared in the 1850s when the Victorian taste for novelty tableware took hold. A surge in honey pot production naturally followed the publication in the 1920s of the Winnie the Pooh poems and stories. With the rise of gourmet specialty honeys, made by pointing bees in the direction of fields of specific flowers, honey pots are once again on the market. For a special morning greeting, shop flea markets for the Pooh version labeled "HUNNY!"

## Date-Walnut Honey Bars

**PREP:** 40 minutes **BAKE:** 25 minutes **CHILL:** 30 minutes

| | | | |
|---|---|---|---|
| 1 | recipe Oatmeal Crust (below) | 1/2 | tsp. baking powder |
| 3/4 | cup honey | 1/2 | tsp. salt |
| 3/4 | apple jelly | 4 | eggs, lightly beaten |
| 1/4 | cup unsalted butter | 1 | tsp. vanilla |
| 1/4 | cup packed brown sugar | 2 1/2 | cups coarsely chopped walnuts |
| 1/4 | cup all-purpose flour | 2 | cups chopped pitted dates |

**1.** Preheat oven to 350° F. Prepare Oatmeal Crust.

**2.** In a saucepan combine honey, jelly, and butter. Cook over low heat for 5 minutes or until butter and jelly are melted, stirring often. Remove from heat. In a mixing bowl stir together brown sugar, flour, baking powder, and salt. Add eggs and vanilla; beat until smooth. Stir in honey mixture.

**3.** Pour half of the filling over each prepared crust. Spread evenly. Top each with the walnuts and dates. Bake for 25 minutes. Cool in pans on wire racks. Chill for 30 minutes. Cut each pan into 18 bars. Makes 36 bars.

**OATMEAL CRUST:** Place 3/4 cup regular rolled oats, 3/4 cup sugar, and 1/2 teaspoon salt in a blender or food processor. Blend or process until oats are finely chopped. Transfer to a large mixing bowl. Stir in 2 cups all-purpose flour. Using a pastry blender, cut 1 cup unsalted butter into flour mixture until mixture resembles coarse crumbs. Sprinkle 1 tablespoon water over mixture. Continue to blend until mixture forms loose crumbs. Press evenly into bottom of 2 greased 13×9×2-inch baking pans. Bake each pan on center rack of oven for 12 minutes. Cool on wire racks.

Each bar: 254 cal., 13 g total fat (5 g sat. fat), 42 mg chol., 84 mg sodium, 34 g carbo., 2 g fiber, 3 g pro. Daily Values: 8% vit. A, 1% vit. C, 3% calcium, 5% iron.

# EAT WELL

## RESOLVE TO KEEP YOUR FAMILY COOL AND WELL HYDRATED WITH SPLASHY DRINKS.

After a workout—or anytime of the day—thirst-quenching sippers sweetened with fruit or veggies offer a burst of refreshing flavor plus a bonus of nutrients.

BY JEANNE AMBROSE PHOTOGRAPHS BY GREG SCHEIDEMANN [N] HAUSFOTO PROPS STYLING BY CARRIE NAUMANN FOOD STYLING BY CHARLES WORTHINGTON RECIPES JENNIFER KALINOWSKI

## FIZZY ICED TEA

Teens get a boost of antioxidants in this brew. Steep 4 green tea bags in 2 cups boiling water according to package directions. Discard tea bags. Stir in a 12-ounce can of frozen juice concentrate (such as cranberry-raspberry or apple-cherry). Cover and chill. To serve, fill a glass of ice one-quarter full with the tea mixture. Top off with chilled club soda. Add fresh berries. Makes 6 to 8 servings.

## FROSTY FRUITY MILK

▶ Use fruit as the base for a frothy "milk shake" full of calcium, protein, and fiber without ice cream. In a blender place 1 cup fat-free milk, 1 cup frozen fruit (such as blueberries and/or peeled peach slices), and ½ teaspoon vanilla. Cover and blend until smooth. Pour into glasses and top with fresh berries. Makes 2 servings.

## MELON-MINT WATER

◀ Mom will love a soothing splash of this refresher after her workout. Cut a small, clean, unwaxed cucumber into slices. Place slices, a few wedges of peeled honeydew melon, and a handful of mint leaves in a large pitcher. Fill pitcher with water. Cover and chill up to 3 days. Strain water, reserving melon and cucumbers to nibble on. Pour water into tall glasses over ice. Makes 8 servings.

## GARDEN VEGGIE SPLASH

▶ Spice up Dad's day with lycopene-rich garden veggies. Seed and cut up 1 jalapeño chile pepper (see note, page 89) and one-quarter of a red sweet pepper. Add to blender with 1½ cups chopped tomato, the white part of a green onion, and the juice of half a lime. Cover and blend until smooth. Add salt, black pepper, and bottled hot pepper sauce to taste. Top with a pickled banana pepper. Makes 2 servings.

# October

WITH CRISPNESS IN THE FALL AIR, IT'S A
WONDERFUL TIME TO GATHER FOR AN
AFTERNOON OF PUMPKIN DECORATING
AND AN AUTUMN MEAL.

# Gathering at the Pumpkin Patch

gathering at the

# PUMPKIN
# PATCH

A SAN FRANCISCO MOM BRINGS TOGETHER FRIENDS AND FAMILY
FOR A DAY OF CREATIVE DECORATING AND CAPS IT OFF
WITH AN AUTUMN-INSPIRED DINNER.

## Kid Friendly Cranberry-Apple Crush

This versatile sipper can be served warm on a chilly autumn day or cold on a balmy summer afternoon.

**Fast!** **START TO FINISH:** 15 minutes

| | |
|---|---|
| 5 cups apple cider or apple juice | 1 tsp. ground ginger |
| 5 cups cranberry juice | ½ tsp. ground cinnamon |
| 1½ cups guava juice or mango nectar | ½ tsp. ground allspice |
| ¼ cup lime juice | Honey (optional) |
| | Lime slices (optional) |
| | Kumquats (optional) |

**1.** In a 4-quart Dutch oven combine apple cider, cranberry juice, guava juice, lime juice, ginger, cinnamon, and allspice. Bring to boiling; reduce heat. Simmer, uncovered, for 5 minutes, stirring occasionally. If desired, sweeten to taste with honey.

**2.** To serve, pour into mugs. If desired, garnish with lime slices and kumquats. Makes 8 to 10 servings.

Each serving: 182 cal., 0 g total fat (0 g sat. fat), 0 mg chol., 28 mg sodium, 46 g carbo., 0 g fiber, 0 g pro. Daily Values: 88% vit. C, 1% calcium, 4% iron.

**Cranberry-Apple Crush**

# Autumn in the air

Donata Maggipinto gets her family in the act to decorate for her annual pumpkin pageant. She sends husband Courtney Reeser and 5-year-old son Reyn to hunt for autumn leaves and wild flowers. With items they bring back, Donata sets the stage for a celebration of her favorite season.

Donata invites eight best friends plus their kids for an afternoon of pumpkin decorating, leisurely lunching, and a ghost story or two. Jack-o'-lantern making is the main attraction of the day. When guests arrive at the house a few miles north of the Golden Gate Bridge, they fortify themselves with hot mugs of Cranberry-Apple Crush and apple wedges spread with Blue Cheese-Ricotta Dip. Then they meander down to the family pumpkin patch to make their selections. Back at the house, a decorating station is set up. Because so many kids are involved, Donata makes it a no-carve project.

Both the setting and the foods take cues from the season. To maximize her enjoyment of the party, Donata preps some of the food the day before, and the meal is served family-style. A few of the dishes served include a green salad enriched with avocados, tangerines, and pumpkin seeds, sweet potatoes with caramelized onions, and a pork roast.

Despite its casual setting, Donata says the event relies on three elements: planning, a simple menu, and a timetable that takes cues from the guests as well as the clock.

"I always plan for my own sanity," says Donata, who gained her expertise during years as an author, lifestyle correspondent for NBC's *Today* show, and former creative director for the Williams-Sonoma specialty cookware retailer. "I give the decorating about an hour. Then the kids are bored, and the adults want to eat and have adult time." After the meal, she gives the kids time to go back and finish their pumpkins, which provides the adults time to talk.

As twilight falls, Donata switches on the strings of orange lights hung along the porch beams to illuminate the day's creations, and she tells a ghost story or two to accompany dessert. For dessert, homey Pear Upside-Down Cake is served, complemented by Pumpkin Ice Cream, on the side or in a chocolate-dipped cone.

Before leaving, guests fill paper party-favor cones with penny candy from a black cast-iron pot, then amble into the night with their treats and freshly decorated pumpkins.

## Blue Cheese-Ricotta Dip

Donata Maggipinto likes to serve this simple but sumptuous spread alongside green apple slices, crackers, and breadsticks. For children who might find the blue cheese too strong, serve wedges of cheddar cheese with the apple slices.

**STAND:** 1 hour **PREP:** 10 minutes

1   15-oz. container ricotta cheese

8   oz. blue cheese, such as Gorgonzola or Maytag, crumbled (2 cups)

2   Tbsp. apple cider or milk

Freshly ground black pepper

Snipped fresh chives or your favorite herb

Green and/or red apple slices

Breadsticks and/or crackers (optional)

**1.** Allow ricotta and blue cheese to stand at room temperature for 1 hour. In a medium bowl stir together the cheeses, mashing with a fork until well combined. Stir in the apple cider. Add pepper to taste. Spoon into a serving bowl. Sprinkle with chives. Serve with apple slices and, if desired, breadsticks and/or crackers. Makes 8 servings.

Each serving without apples: 195 cal., 15 g total fat (10 g sat. fat), 48 mg chol., 440 mg sodium, 3 g carbo., 0 g fiber, 12 g pro. Daily Values: 9% vit. A, 26% calcium, 2% iron.

Donata's house (above) overlooks her pumpkin patch. Courtney, Donata's husband, helps with the pumpkin picking, a highlight of the day for many participants at the gathering. As an alternative, Donata suggests asking guests to bring their own pumpkins and letting the host supply the decorating materials.

Searching for empty quail eggs, colored rocks, and other "kid treasures" along the creek and in the meadow behind the house is a favorite after-lunch activity (right).

## Kid Friendly   Mashed Sweet Potatoes with Caramelized Onions

**PREP:** 30 minutes **COOK:** 30 minutes

1/2   cup unsalted butter or butter

2   lb. yellow onions, peeled, halved, and thinly sliced (7 cups)

1/2   tsp. salt

1/2   tsp. freshly ground black pepper

4   lb. sweet potatoes or white potatoes, peeled and cut into 1/2-inch cubes (about 10 cups)

1/2   cup milk

1/3   cup dairy sour cream

Salt and ground black pepper

**1.** To caramelize the onions, in a large skillet heat 1/4 cup of the butter. Add the onions and cook, stirring frequently over very low heat, about 30 minutes or until golden brown. Season with the 1/2 teaspoon salt and 1/2 teaspoon pepper. Remove from the heat; set aside.

**2.** Meanwhile, cook the potatoes in a large pot, covered, in boiling lightly salted water for 12 minutes or until tender; drain.

**3.** Add the remaining 1/4 cup butter to the pot in which the potatoes were cooked and let it melt. Return potatoes to the pot and mash with a potato masher until smooth. Stir in the milk, sour cream, and salt and pepper to taste. Stir in caramelized onions, reserving a few onions for garnish. Cook and stir over low heat until heated through. Transfer to a serving dish. Top with reserved onions. Makes 8 to 10 servings.

**MAKE-AHEAD DIRECTIONS:** Prepare potatoes through stirring in the caramelized onions in Step 3 but do not heat through. Transfer to a 2 1/2- to 3-quart casserole. Cover and chill in the refrigerator up to 24 hours ahead of baking. Before serving, bake potato-onion mixture in a 325° F oven for 55 to 60 minutes or until heated through.

Each serving: 299 cal., 14 g total fat (9 g sat. fat), 37 mg chol., 182 mg sodium, 40 g carbo., 6 g fiber, 4 g pro. Daily Values: 413% vit. A, 56% vit. C, 10% calcium, 7% iron.

**Blue Cheese-Ricotta Dip**

**Mashed Sweet Potatoes with Caramelized Onions**

**Pecorino Romano cheese, fruit, and pumpernickel bread**

Donata Maggipinto (above) sees her party as an opportunity to recapture the magic of autumn she felt when she was growing up, unite friends and family, and teach her son, Reyn, 5, about the seasons of the year.

**Pork Roast with Harvest Fruits**

## Pork Roast with Harvest Fruits

Pork shoulder is an ideal cut of meat for slow cooking because it retains its moistness and delivers a lot of flavor. Here, it's braised in balsamic vinegar and red wine, both of which balance the sweetness of the fruit and contribute a delectable kick to the sauce.

**PREP:** 30 minutes **ROAST:** 3 hours

| | |
|---|---|
| 1 5- to 6-lb. boneless pork shoulder roast, trimmed and tied to retain its shape | 1 cup balsamic vinegar |
| | 1 cup dry red wine |
| | 1½ cups pitted dried plums and/or dried apricots |
| 3 Tbsp. olive oil | 1½ cups dried figs, halved |
| Salt | |
| Freshly ground black pepper | 1 quince, peeled, cored, and coarsely chopped (optional) |
| 1 large yellow onion, finely chopped (1 cup) | |
| 3 bay leaves | 4 medium apples, such as Granny Smith, peeled, cored, and quartered |
| 2 Tbsp. snipped fresh rosemary | |

**1.** Preheat oven to 325° F. In a 6- to 8-quart oval roasting pan brown meat on all sides in hot oil. Remove the meat from the pan and pour off all but 2 tablespoons of the fat. Sprinkle meat lightly with salt and pepper; set aside. Reduce the heat to medium.

**2.** Add onion to the pan and cook about 5 minutes or until tender. Add the bay leaves, rosemary, vinegar, wine, dried plums and/or apricots, figs, and, if desired, quince. Bring to boiling and cook for 1 minute. Remove pan from heat.

**3.** Return the meat to the pan. Cover pan and place in oven for 2¾ hours. Add apples. Cover and bake 15 minutes more or until meat and apples are tender. Remove meat and fruit from the pan using a slotted spoon; cover meat and fruit loosely with foil to keep warm. Remove and discard bay leaves from pan.

**4.** For sauce, place pan on range top and simmer, uncovered, over medium-high heat about 15 minutes or until the liquid is reduced to 1¼ cups, stirring and scraping the bottom of the pan to release any brown bits.

**5.** To serve, slice the pork and arrange it on a platter with the fruit. Spoon some of the sauce over the pork. Pass remaining sauce. Makes 8 to 10 servings.

Each serving: 724 cal., 22 g total fat (7 g sat. fat), 183 mg chol., 394 mg sodium, 67 g carbo., 8 g fiber, 59 g pro. Daily Values: 14% vit. A, 16% vit. C, 11% calcium, 31% iron.

Donata's favorite pumpkin varieties include (photo at right, from top left): 'Cinderella,' 'Lumina,' 'Cheese,' 'New Zealand Blue,' field pumpkin, 'Peek-A-Boo,' and 'Mini.'

**TO PREPARE PUMPKINS FOR PIES:** Cut 6 pounds of pumpkins into 5-inch-square pieces (or halve small pumpkins). Remove seeds and fibrous strings. Arrange in a single layer, skin side up, in a shallow baking pan. Cover with foil; roast in a 375° F oven for 1 to 1½ hours or until tender. Scoop pulp from rind. Puree pulp in a blender or food processor; place puree in a cheesecloth-lined strainer and press out the liquid. Makes 2 cups.

When Donata sets the table she drapes stadium blankets over the chair backs in case the day turns chilly.

CINDERELLA · LUMINA · MINI · CHEESE · PEEK-A-BOO · FIELD · NEW ZEALAND BLUE

## Autumn Salad

A cumin-scented sherry vinaigrette enhances a harmony of flavors and textures in this colorful autumn salad.

**PREP:** 35 minutes

| | |
|---|---|
| 4 tsp. sherry wine vinegar or red wine vinegar | 3 medium seedless tangerines, peeled and sectioned |
| 3/4 tsp. ground cumin | |
| 1/4 cup extra-virgin olive oil | 1 medium red onion, thinly sliced |
| 1/8 tsp. salt | |
| 1/8 tsp. freshly ground black pepper | 2 medium avocados, halved, seeded, peeled, and cut into chunks |
| 2 medium heads red leaf lettuce, torn (about 12 cups) | 8 Tbsp. Cumin-Toasted Pumpkin Seeds (below) |

**1.** For dressing, in a large salad bowl whisk together the vinegar and cumin. Gradually whisk in olive oil in a slow, steady stream. Add the salt and pepper.

**2.** Add lettuce, tangerines, onion, avocados, and 6 tablespoons of the pumpkin seeds to the salad bowl. Toss lightly to coat with dressing. Sprinkle with the remaining 2 tablespoons pumpkin seeds. Serve at once. Makes 8 to 10 servings.

Each serving: 244 cal., 20 g total fat (3 g sat. fat), 0 mg chol., 140 mg sodium, 13 g carbo., 6 g fiber, 7 g pro. Daily Values: 131% vit. A, 50% vit. C, 5% calcium, 18% iron.

## Cumin-Toasted Pumpkin Seeds

A 10- to 14-pound pumpkin will yield about 1 cup raw seeds. Pumpkin seeds may also be purchased in health food stores, Hispanic grocery stores, and some supermarkets.

**PREP:** 15 minutes **BAKE:** 1 hour 10 minutes

| | |
|---|---|
| 1 cup raw pumpkin seeds or shelled sunflower seeds | 2 tsp. cooking oil |
| | 1/2 tsp. ground cumin |
| | 1/2 tsp. salt |

**1.** Preheat oven to 325° F. Rinse pumpkin seeds in water until pulp and strings are washed off; drain.

**2.** Spread seeds in a parchment paper-lined 8×8×2-inch baking pan. Bake, uncovered, for 1 hour. Remove parchment paper. Add oil, cumin, and salt; stir to coat.

**3.** Bake, uncovered, 10 to 15 minutes more or until toasted, stirring once. Transfer seeds to paper towels to cool. Makes 1 cup.

Each 2-tablespoon serving: 104 cal., 11 g total fat (2 g sat. fat), 0 mg chol., 148 mg sodium, 2 g carbo., 0 g fiber, 4 g pro. Daily Values: 1% vit. C, 1% calcium, 9% iron.

## Pear Upside-Down Cake

**PREP:** 40 minutes **BAKE:** 40 minutes **COOL:** 5 minutes

| | |
|---|---|
| 1/4 cup butter | 3/4 tsp. ground cloves |
| 1/2 cup packed brown sugar | 1/4 tsp. salt |
| 4 medium fresh pears, peeled, halved, and cored | 2/3 cup butter, softened |
| | 1/2 cup packed brown sugar |
| 1/4 cup chopped crystallized ginger | 2 eggs |
| | 1/2 cup full-flavored molasses |
| 2 cups all-purpose flour | 2 Tbsp. grated fresh ginger |
| 2 tsp. ground ginger | 3/4 cup buttermilk |
| 1 tsp. baking powder | Chopped crystallized ginger (optional) |
| 1 tsp. baking soda | |
| 3/4 tsp. ground cinnamon | |

**1.** Preheat oven to 350° F. In a 10-inch cast-iron or oven-going skillet melt the 1/4 cup butter over medium heat.* Stir in the 1/2 cup brown sugar, stirring until sugar is no longer grainy; remove from heat. Arrange the pear halves, cut side up, in the skillet. Sprinkle with the 1/4 cup crystallized ginger; set aside.

**2.** In a medium bowl combine the flour, ground ginger, baking powder, baking soda, cinnamon, cloves, and salt; set aside.

**3.** In a large mixing bowl beat the 2/3 cup butter with an electric mixer on medium to high speed for 30 seconds. Beat in 1/2 cup brown sugar until well combined. Add eggs, 1 at a time, beating after each addition. Beat in molasses and fresh ginger. Alternately add flour mixture and buttermilk to molasses mixture, beating on low speed after each addition just until combined. Spread the thick batter evenly over the pears (photo at right).

**4.** Bake about 40 minutes or until a wooden toothpick inserted near center comes out clean. Cool in skillet on a wire rack for 5 minutes. Loosen cake from skillet; invert onto a large serving plate. Serve warm or at room temperature. If desired, top with chopped crystallized ginger. Makes 8 to 10 servings.

**\*NOTE:** If you don't have a cast-iron or oven-going skillet, prepare brown sugar-butter mixture in a small saucepan. Pour the mixture into a 2-quart rectangular glass baking dish, spreading evenly. Continue as above, baking for 45 minutes or until a wooden toothpick inserted near center comes out clean. Cool and serve as above.

Each serving: 567 cal., 24 g total fat (12 g sat. fat), 113 mg chol., 483 mg sodium, 85 g carbo., 4 g fiber, 6 g pro. Daily Values: 16% vit. A, 7% vit. C, 13% calcium, 19% iron.

**Autumn Salad with
Cumin-Toasted Pumpkin Seeds**

**Pear Upside-Down Cake**

## AUTUMN DINNER

Pecorino Romano and cheddar cheeses
Blue Cheese-Ricotta Dip (page 202)
Cranberry-Apple Crush (page 201)
Pork Roast with Harvest Fruits (page 205)
Mashed Sweet Potatoes with
Caramelized Onions (page 202)
Autumn Salad with
Cumin-Toasted Pumpkin Seeds (page 206)
Pear Upside-Down Cake (page 206) and/or
Pumpkin Ice Cream (page 209)

In addition to the pumpkins,
guests leave with their pick
of colorful Halloween candy
in decorative baskets (left).

A PARTY LIKE THIS ENGAGES YOUR SENSES: THE SOUND OF PEOPLE LAUGHING, THE SMELL OF SPICES, THE SIGHT OF A GREAT FROSTY ICE CREAM CONE FILLED WITH THE FLAVORS OF A PUMPKIN PIE. DONATA MAGGIPINTO

**Pumpkin Ice Cream in Chocolate-Dipped Ice Cream Cones**

### Kid Friendly Pumpkin Ice Cream

The spices that infuse this ice cream are the same ones found in the best pumpkin pies. Splendid with the Pear Upside-Down Cake, it's spectacular on its own too.

**PREP:** 20 minutes **CHILL:** 3 hours
**FREEZE:** according to manufacturer's directions plus 3 hours

| | | | |
|---|---|---|---|
| 2 | cups whipping cream | 1 | tsp. vanilla |
| 3/4 | cup packed dark brown sugar | 1 | Tbsp. cognac or brandy (optional) |
| 5 | egg yolks | 1 | cup canned pumpkin |
| 1/2 | tsp. ground cinnamon | | Plain ice cream cones or |
| 1/4 | tsp. ground nutmeg | | 1 recipe Chocolate- |
| 1/4 | tsp. ground allspice | | Dipped Ice Cream |
| 1/4 | tsp. ground cloves | | Cones (below right) |
| 1/4 | tsp. salt | | (optional) |

**1.** In a medium saucepan combine the whipping cream and brown sugar. Cook over medium heat about 5 minutes or until bubbles form around the edges of the pan, stirring to dissolve sugar.

**2.** In a small mixing bowl beat the egg yolks, cinnamon, nutmeg, allspice, cloves, and salt. Gradually whisk about 1/2 cup of the hot cream mixture into the egg mixture and continue to whisk until smooth. Pour the egg mixture into the cream mixture in the pan. Cook and stir over medium heat until the mixture coats a metal spoon (photo below), 4 to 6 minutes. Do not boil. Strain through a fine mesh sieve into a bowl. Stir in the vanilla and, if desired, the cognac. Whisk the pumpkin into the egg mixture. Cover surface with plastic wrap to prevent a skin from forming; refrigerate until chilled, at least 3 hours or overnight.

**3.** Pour the pumpkin custard into a 1 1/2- or 2-quart ice cream freezer and freeze according to the manufacturer's directions. Remove and pack the ice cream into a freezer-safe container. Cover and freeze until firm, at least 3 hours or up to 3 days, before serving. Makes 1 1/4 quarts (ten 1/2-cup servings).

Each serving (without cone): 269 cal., 20 g total fat (12 g sat. fat), 168 mg chol., 89 mg sodium, 21 g carbo., 1 g fiber, 3 g pro. Daily Values: 93% vit. A, 2% vit. C, 7% calcium, 5% iron.

The cooked pumpkin mixture is ready to remove from the heat when it's thick enough to leave a clear trail on the back of a spoon when you draw your finger through it.

## FLOWER CENTERPIECE

To create a pumpkin-looking centerpiece, you'll need a 6- or 8-inch-diameter floral foam ball; approximately 60 to 75 marigolds, orange carnations, or button mums (carnations are the most readily available); the stem of a pumpkin; and a long blackberry cane or other vine.

Slice off the bottom of the foam sphere to make a firm base; trim top to ensure finished result will look like a pumpkin. Soak the sphere in cold water until completely soaked. Make holes in the foam about 1 inch apart with a skewer or length of wire before inserting stems (depending on size of blooms, you may have to adjust spacing between the flowers for complete coverage). Leave space to insert the pumpkin stem at the top of the arrangement.

When the entire surface of the sphere is covered with flowers, arrange blackberry cane around the top. Place on a cake stand or platter with a lip that will hold water to keep flowers fresh. Add water to base.

**CHOCOLATE-DIPPED ICE CREAM CONES:** Place 1/2 cup semisweet chocolate pieces (or 3 ounces semisweet chocolate, chopped) in a small microwave-safe bowl or ramekin. Microwave, uncovered, on 70% power (medium-high) for 1 minute; stir. Microwave for 1 1/2 to 3 minutes more, stirring after every 15 seconds, until chocolate is melted and smooth. Spoon chocolate over open end of cone to cover about one-quarter of sides. (If chocolate is too thick to spread, stir in 1 teaspoon shortening.) Transfer to a waxed paper-lined baking sheet until set, about 1 hour at room temperature or 15 minutes in the refrigerator.

**Chicken and
Squash Tagine**

The exotic cities of Morocco—Casablanca, Tangier, and Marrakech—conjure legendary liaisons among romance, spice, aroma, and intrigue. And that's just the food. At your next gathering, do a little globe-trotting without leaving your city by sampling Morocco's most popular dish: hearty, fragrant tagine. It's an enticing, easy-to-prepare company supper. Basically, it's a stew.

Tagines, and Moroccan cooking in general, combine elements of North African, Arabian, and Southern European cuisines. Versatile and pleasing tagines meld savory and sweet, use such familiar spices as cilantro and cinnamon, and can feature chicken, beef, or lamb. Tagines also can include almonds, chickpeas, dried fruits, and olives.

Tagines are spiced with *ras el hanout*, an aromatic blend consisting of about 30 different spices. A simpler version is used (below) for our Chicken and Squash Tagine. Its subtle perfume suggests the warm spiciness of cloves and cardamom.

A side dish to a tagine dinner would be a Tomato and Mint Salad (page 211). Although couscous is also a Moroccan staple, surprisingly, it isn't usually served with a tagine.

Traditionally, tagines are prepared in a vessel of glazed earthenware or terra-cotta with a conical lid (the vessel is also called a tagine), although tagines turn out fine cooked in a Dutch oven. The secret is slow cooking in a pot with a tight lid. The tagine's cone-shape lid traps the steam generated during the long cooking time and results in a succulent, tender dinner. (And if you want to know the answer to the "which came first" question, the culinary dish is named after the utensil.)

# DINNER IN
# MOROCCO

EXPERIENCE THE HEADY
CUISINE OF NORTH AFRICA.
THE ENCHANTING SUBTLE
SPICES WILL CARRY YOU AWAY.

**MOROCCAN SPICE MIXTURE:** In a bowl mix together 2 teaspoons salt; 1 teaspoon each crushed red pepper, ground cardamom, ground cloves, turmeric, ground cinnamon, ground ginger; and 1/2 teaspoon ground black pepper. Makes about 3 tablespoons.

## Chicken and Squash Tagine

**PREP:** 50 minutes  **COOK:** 1 hour 10 minutes

| | |
|---|---|
| 1 | recipe Moroccan Spice Mixture (page 210) |
| 2 | lb. meaty chicken pieces (breast halves, thighs, and drumsticks), skinned |
| 3 | tsp. olive oil |
| 2 | medium onions, cut into wedges |
| 6 | large cloves garlic, halved lengthwise |
| 5 | to 6 threads saffron, crushed |
| 1 | 2½- to 3-lb. butternut squash, seeded, peeled, and cut into 1-inch chunks |
| ¼ | cup chicken broth or water |
| 1 | cup golden raisins |
| 3 | Tbsp. honey |
| ¼ | cup snipped fresh parsley |

**1.** Prepare Moroccan Spice Mixture. Rub chicken pieces with 1 tablespoon of the spice mixture.

**2.** Place the tagine vessel bottom on a heat deflector on the stove top over medium to medium-high heat. (To use a Dutch oven, see directions below.) Add 2 teaspoons of the oil to hot tagine. Carefully add chicken, half at a time if necessary, and cook, uncovered, for 6 to 8 minutes or until browned, turning once. Remove chicken; set aside. Add remaining oil, onions, garlic, and saffron to vessel. Cook and stir over medium heat for 2 minutes.

**3.** Place squash over onion mixture. Sprinkle with 2 teaspoons of the spice mixture (reserve remaining spice mixture for another use); toss lightly. Top with chicken; pour broth over all. Bring to boiling; reduce heat to medium to medium-low. Simmer, covered, for 1 hour. Add raisins; cook for 10 to 25 minutes more or until chicken is done (170° F in breast portion; 180° F in thigh and leg pieces) and squash is tender.

**4.** To serve, uncover tagine vessel. Drizzle with honey and sprinkle with parsley. Serve directly from vessel. (Or remove chicken and squash to serving platter with slotted spoon; drizzle with honey. Spoon on desired amount of pan juices. Sprinkle with parsley.) Makes 6 servings.

**DUTCH OVEN DIRECTIONS:** Rub chicken with 1 tablespoon of the spice mixture. In a 4-quart Dutch oven heat 2 teaspoons of the oil over medium heat. Add chicken. Cook, uncovered, for 6 to 8 minutes, turning to brown evenly. Remove chicken. Add remaining 1 teaspoon of the oil to Dutch oven. Add onions, garlic, and saffron. Cook and stir over medium heat for 2 minutes. Add squash. Sprinkle with 2 teaspoons of the spice mixture; toss. Add chicken and broth. Bring to boiling; reduce heat. Cover and simmer for 1 hour. Add raisins; cover and cook for 10 to 25 minutes more until chicken is done and squash is tender. Serve as above.

**Healthy** Each serving: 332 cal., 8 g total fat (2 g sat. fat), 61 mg chol., 369 mg sodium, 46 g carbo., 5 g fiber, and 23 g pro. Daily Values: 107% vit. A, 35% vit. C, 8% calcium, 14% iron.

**Tomato and Mint Salad**

## Tomato and Mint Salad

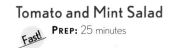 **PREP:** 25 minutes

| | |
|---|---|
| | Salt |
| 1 | large clove garlic |
| ¼ | cup olive oil |
| ½ | tsp. finely shredded lemon peel |
| 1 | Tbsp. lemon juice |
| 1 | Tbsp. white wine vinegar or cider vinegar |
| 3 | large tomatoes, sliced |
| ½ | cup snipped fresh mint |
| | Freshly ground black pepper |

**1.** Sprinkle a pinch of salt on a cutting board. Using the flat blade of a knife, crush garlic into the salt. Finely chop the garlic with the salt to create a chunky paste.

**2.** In a screw-top jar combine the garlic mixture, olive oil, lemon peel, lemon juice, and vinegar. Cover and shake well. Place half the tomato slices in a single layer on a serving platter. Top with half of the mint. Drizzle with half of the dressing. Top with remaining tomato slices and remaining mint. Sprinkle with black pepper and drizzle with remaining dressing. Serve immediately. Makes 6 side-dish servings.

Each serving: 102 cal., 9 g total fat (1 g sat. fat), 0 mg chol., 29 mg sodium, 5 g carbo., 1 g fiber, 1 g pro. Daily Values: 17% vit. A, 31% vit. C, 2% calcium, 9% iron.

# THE COMFORT OF
# BUTTERSCOTCH PUDDING

**Butterscotch Pudding**

The buttery smoothness of Butterscotch Pudding has a familiar, friendly taste that will satisfy the family's sweet tooth on a weekday night and also dress up nicely for company. Here's a velvety dessert that's so rich, creamy, and simple, you'll want to make it over and over. Go ahead—let this no-fuss recipe become one of your star signature dishes.

Butterscotch Pudding takes only 20 minutes to prepare and uses just seven on-hand ingredients, so when the craving hits, indulge yourself. You'll find you pull out this recipe year-round.

Use a wire whisk to thoroughly combine the ingredients and to whisk some of the hot cream mixture into the beaten egg yolks to warm them before adding the yolks to the saucepan. Whisk constantly during cooking to keep mixture from scorching.

Enjoy the pudding on its own, or add a few toppings to suit the occasion and season. For the family, scatter broken candy bars across the top. For company, stir together ⅓ cup goat cheese, ¼ cup crème fraîche, and 1 tablespoon sugar. Spoon some of the mixture on each serving, then sprinkle with a dash of freshly grated nutmeg.

## Butterscotch Pudding

Kid Friendly

**PREP:** 20 minutes   **CHILL:** 4 hours

| | | | |
|---|---|---|---|
| 1 | cup packed light brown sugar | 4 | cups half-and-half or light cream |
| ¼ | cup cornstarch | 5 | egg yolks, slightly beaten |
| ¼ | tsp. salt | ¼ | cup butter, cut up |
| | | 2 | tsp. vanilla |

**1.** In a medium saucepan combine brown sugar, cornstarch, and salt. Whisk in the half-and-half.

**2.** Whisk constantly over medium heat until mixture is thickened and bubbly. Cook and stir 2 minutes more. Remove pan from heat. Gradually whisk about 1 cup of the hot mixture into egg yolks. Add egg yolk mixture to hot cream mixture in the saucepan. Bring to a gentle boil; reduce heat. Cook and whisk constantly for 2 minutes more.

**3.** Remove from heat and whisk in butter and vanilla until combined. Pour pudding into a large bowl. Cover surface of pudding with plastic wrap. Refrigerate 4 to 5 hours or until chilled. Remove plastic wrap and stir. To serve, spoon into dessert dishes. Makes 8 servings.

Each serving: 373 cal., 23 g total fat (13 g sat. fat), 189 mg chol., 182 mg sodium, 38 g carbo., 0 g fiber, 5 g pro. Daily Values: 15% vit. A, 2% vit. C, 17% calcium, 5% iron.

BY STEPHEN EXEL PHOTOGRAPHS BY GREG SCHEIDEMANN FOOD STYLING BY SUSAN BROWN DRAUDT

# HALLOWEEN PARTY

Jan P. Hazard just adores Halloween. Perhaps because she remembers how her grandparents would go to parties all dressed up. "They loved Halloween because it gave them a fun opportunity to try on a new personality," says Hazard, a food consultant, editor, and coauthor of a regular column, "GadgetGals." Nowadays, Hazard honors her grandparents' spirit and celebrates the season by throwing her own party. "My parties vary. Sometimes I do a dinner; other times I keep it simple with just appetizers. Either way, I always serve orange or black food and end with adorable treats," says Hazard. Pulling off an orange menu is easy. According to Hazard, "There are many ready-made food products you can just open and serve. Above all, keep it fun." This year's menu is simple: The curry soup gets a start from frozen squash (*below*). Sweet hot carrots are steamed and tossed with red pepper jelly. Cooked shrimp goes with peach salsa, and frozen meatballs are served in a tomato-vodka sauce. Smoked salmon adds its own orange hue when stirred into cream cheese to make a spread.

## WHAT'S ORANGE IN YOUR PANTRY?

With the package of frozen butternut squash hanging out in Jan P. Hazard's freezer, she created the Curry in a Hurry Soup (left). Simply heat the squash in a saucepan. Add a can of chicken broth until desired consistency. Then stir in ½ to 1 teaspoon curry powder. Top it off with toasted pumpkin seeds or a round of toasted bread cut into a fanciful shape.

## PUMPKIN PERFECT

You can make a pumpkin-patch worth of this pretty little treat in minutes. Use a small pastry brush or art brush to coat purchased meringue cookies with corn syrup. Next sprinkle on a mix of edible orange glitter and decorative sugar. For the leaf topper, cut green fruit leather into a free-form leaf and stem. Then let the fun begin. You can feature your homegrown treats to ring a cake or top off a dessert tart. Or serve them solo on top of a cupcake. Scatter a few over a bowl of pumpkin ice cream or wrap them in cellophane bags to give as party favors. And, for a dinner party, set them at each place setting and attach a place card.

# November

FOR YOUR THANKSGIVING FEAST, TRY SOME LUSCIOUS NEW RECIPES TO SERVE YOUR FAMILY.

# Homegrown Thanksgiving

**Pecorino Shortbread with Rhubarb Sauce (page 218); Hubbard Squash Soup**

# Homegrown Thanksgiving

THE FLOWERS ARE HUNG FOR DRYING; THE FRUITS OF ALL THE SEASONS HAVE BEEN GATHERED AND SEALED INTO TEMPTING JARS. COME ENJOY THE HARVEST TASTINGS OF A 202-YEAR-OLD NEW YORK FARM AND ORCHARD.

BY KEN HAEDRICH PHOTOGRAPHS BY SIMON AND TAMMAR PRODUCED BY JESSICA THOMAS AND NANCY HOPKINS FOOD STYLING BY SUSIE THEODOROU

## Hubbard Squash Soup

**PREP:** 35 minutes **COOK:** 25 minutes

| | | | |
|---|---|---|---|
| 3 | Tbsp. butter | 3 | cups chicken stock or |
| 3 | Tbsp. extra-virgin olive oil | | broth |
| 1 | large onion, sliced (1 cup) | 1½ | cups water |
| 2 | tsp. curry powder | 1 | tsp. salt |
| 5 | lb. Hubbard*, butternut, or | 3 | 2- to 3-inch cinnamon |
| | acorn squash, peeled and | | sticks |
| | cut into 2-inch pieces | 1 | recipe Poached Lady |
| | (about 11 cups) | | Apples (optional) (below) |
| 6 | cloves garlic, minced | | |

**1.** In a 4-quart Dutch oven or pot heat butter and oil over medium heat. Add onion and curry. Cook and stir about 5 minutes or until onion is tender. Add squash pieces and garlic. Cook, uncovered, for 10 minutes, stirring occasionally. Add the stock, water, salt, and cinnamon sticks. Bring to boiling; reduce heat. Simmer, covered, for 25 to 30 minutes or until squash is tender.

**2.** Remove and discard cinnamon sticks. Using a potato masher, coarsely mash mixture, or cool slightly and transfer in batches to a food processor. Cover and process until nearly smooth. Return all to pot. Heat through. If desired, top with Poached Lady Apples. Makes 8 to 10 servings.

**POACHED LADY APPLES:** Cut 2 lady apples or other small apples each into 6 wedges. If desired, core and stem. In a medium skillet combine ½ cup water and 2 tablespoons sugar; bring to boiling, stirring to dissolve sugar. Add apples; cover and cook for 5 minutes or just until tender. Remove with a slotted spoon.

**\*NOTE:** A huge Hubbard squash can be difficult to cut up. Here's a tip from the Machamers. Wash squash; place in a clean, large heavy plastic cooking bag. Fasten bag closed. Drop bag several times onto a hard surface, such as a cement floor. The squash should break safely into small, more manageable pieces.

Each serving: 173 cal., 10 g total fat (3 g sat. fat), 13 mg chol., 701 mg sodium, 21 g carbo., 3 g fiber, 3 g pro. Daily Values: 52% vit. A, 34% vit. C, 7% calcium, 8% iron.

# Harvest Tastings

Ask Amy Machamer to describe a typical day as coproprietor of an 1,100-acre, seventh-generation farm, and she'll oblige by ticking off some of the many hats she wears on the job. As if that weren't enough, the Amherst College grad stays current in horticultural science and the latest advances in food-processing technology, the latter of which probably does not include the method she illustrates for subduing a cumbersome Hubbard squash. "You put it inside a big, sturdy plastic cooking bag, like so. Then just drop it onto a clean hard surface a couple of times."

Amy's demonstration is hardly a measure of her food-processing savvy. But it is a telling reflection of the hands-on relationship that she and her mom-and-business-partner, Susan Hurd Machamer, have with Hurd Orchards outside Holley, New York. When Parmenus Hurd first settled here in the early 1800s, he sunk his roots in prime fruit-growing soil. In the process, he created a legacy that would guide future generations of Hurd farmers. And he set the stage for the current ones, whose life and livelihood revolve around the growing seasons at their unique fruit and flower farm and canning company. "We realize," says Amy, whose father Jeff, husband Joe, and 2-year-old daughter Amelia share the farm as well, "what an incredible privilege it is to be here. There's a powerful sense of walking in our ancestors' shoes."

The sheer abundance and variety of preserved goods in the farm's roadside store reveals the true story of the previous months' efforts. The Machamers' canned goods are the star attraction of what Amy and Susan call, simply, their "tastings," multicourse meals served periodically throughout the growing and harvest seasons. They've become the Machamers' vehicle for sharing their passion for old-fashioned ways in the kitchen.

More than 80 diners will gather at the orchards in November for each of the Machamers' much-anticipated Thanksgiving tastings. At the first of seven such evenings, friends and patrons are greeted by Susan, then led from the farm store to the barn and directed to candlelit tables.

Ultimately, the Machamers say, Hurd Orchards is not just about the products they sell—much as these things matter. It's about a process—a vision that must be constantly nurtured and managed. It's about connections with people, made possible by delectable foods lovingly preserved. And it's about knowing, when someone asks, the best way to deal with a big Hubbard squash.

## Pecorino Shortbread with Rhubarb Sauce

Serve with Hurd Orchards' Spiced Rhubarb Sauce or a favorite jam.

**Prep:** 30 minutes **Chill:** 2 hours **Bake:** 15 minutes

| | | |
|---|---|---|
| 3/4 | cup butter, softened | 2 | tsp. finely shredded lemon peel |
| 2 | cups grated Pecorino Romano* or Parmesan cheese | 1/4 | to 1/2 tsp. cayenne pepper |
| 1 1/2 | cups all-purpose flour | 1/2 | to 1 cup Spiced Rhubarb Sauce or desired fruit |
| 2 | Tbsp. hot or sweet paprika | | chutney or jam |

**1.** In a medium mixing bowl beat butter with an electric mixer on medium speed for 1 minute. Stir in the cheese. Stir in as much of the flour as you can with a wooden spoon. On a lightly floured surface, gradually knead in any remaining flour until smooth.

**2.** Shape dough into a 2 1/2- to 3-inch-diameter roll about 8-inches long. In a small bowl combine paprika, lemon peel, and cayenne. Spread mixture on a sheet of waxed paper. Roll dough in paprika mixture, pressing lightly into dough. Wrap dough in plastic wrap or waxed paper. Chill for 2 to 48 hours or until firm.

**3.** Preheat oven to 325° F. Cut roll of dough into slices about 1/2 inch thick. Place the slices 1 inch apart on an ungreased cookie sheet.

**4.** Bake for 15 to 20 minutes or until set. Remove and cool on a wire rack. Serve with Spiced Rhubarb Sauce or fruit chutney or jam. Makes about 18 slices.

**\*NOTE:** You can buy grated Parmesan cheese. But to get the same fine texture when using Pecorino Romano, cut cheese into chunks; place in a food processor. Cover; process until finely grated.

Each slice: 155 cal., 11 g total fat (6 g sat. fat), 31 mg chol., 183 mg sodium, 11 g carbo., 1 g fiber, 4 g pro. Daily Values: 14% vit. A, 4% vit. C, 10% calcium, 4% iron.

## Herbed Mashed Potatoes

**Prep:** 25 minutes **Cook:** 20 minutes **Stand:** 5 minutes

| | | |
|---|---|---|
| 4 | lb. round red or white potatoes | 2 | Tbsp. snipped fresh thyme |
| 3 | cloves garlic, minced | 2 | Tbsp. snipped fresh rosemary |
| 6 | Tbsp. butter | 1/4 | cup mayonnaise |
| 1 | cup water | 1/4 | cup dairy sour cream |
| 1 | tsp. salt | | Half-and-half, light cream, or milk |
| 2 | Tbsp. snipped fresh parsley | | Salt |
| 2 | Tbsp. snipped fresh chives | | Ground white or black pepper |
| 2 | Tbsp. snipped fresh oregano | | Snipped fresh herbs (optional) |

**1.** Peel potatoes, if desired, and cut up. In a Dutch oven combine potatoes, garlic, 4 tablespoons of the butter, the water, and salt. Bring to boiling; reduce heat. Simmer, covered, for 20 to 25 minutes or until tender. Stir in parsley, chives, oregano, thyme, and rosemary. Let stand 5 minutes.

**2.** Using a potato masher, mash mixture until nearly smooth. Stir in mayonnaise and sour cream. Add enough half-and-half (about 1/2 cup) to desired consistency. Season to taste with salt and pepper (about 1/2 teaspoon each).

**3.** Melt remaining butter and drizzle over potatoes. If desired, sprinkle with additional fresh herbs. Makes 8 to 10 servings.

**TEST KITCHEN TIP:** The mashed potatoes can be prepared ahead and kept warm up to 2 hours in a slow cooker. Transfer prepared potatoes to a slow cooker, then drizzle with butter and sprinkle with herbs. Cover and keep warm on low-heat setting.

Each serving: 269 cal., 15 g total fat (7 g sat. fat), 35 mg chol., 568 mg sodium, 31 g carbo., 3 g fiber, 5 g pro. Daily Values: 11% vit. A, 48% vit. C, 6% calcium, 14% iron.

## Winter Herb and Fennel Slaw

Leftover portions of this slaw are delicious on turkey sandwiches. Add a splash of Fennel Vinegar from Hurd Orchards for extra flavor.

**Prep:** 25 minutes **Chill:** 2 hours

| | | |
|---|---|---|
| 2 | medium fennel bulbs with tops | 1 | cup mayonnaise or salad dressing |
| 1 | medium head cabbage, shredded (about 8 cups) | 1/4 | cup sugar |
| 3 | cups fresh Italian parsley leaves | 1/4 | cup fennel vinegar or cider vinegar |
| | | 1 | Tbsp. dry mustard |
| | | 1/4 | tsp. salt |

**1.** To prepare the fennel, cut off green leafy tops from fennel bulbs. Snip tops and set aside. Cut off and discard upper stalks from fennel. Remove any wilted outer layers from bulbs and cut a thin slice from each fennel base. Thinly slice fennel bulbs, removing the core.

**2.** In 2 very large bowls combine half of each of the sliced fennel, snipped fennel tops, cabbage, and parsley leaves. In a small bowl stir together mayonnaise, sugar, vinegar, mustard, and salt until well combined. Add half of the mayonnaise mixture to cabbage mixture in each bowl, tossing to coat evenly. Cover and chill for 2 to 8 hours before serving. Makes 12 to 14 servings.

**TEST KITCHEN TIP:** If you only have 1 very large bowl, use a Dutch oven to mix the salad.

Each serving: 173 cal., 15 g total fat (2 g sat. fat), 13 mg chol., 186 mg sodium, 9 g carbo., 2 g fiber, 1 g pro. Daily Values: 27% vit. A, 62% vit. C, 5% calcium, 7% iron.

**Herbed Mashed Potatoes**

**Winter Herb and Fennel Slaw**

(Above) Three generations of Machamers—Susan, Amy, and little Amelia—spend days racing between the barn where their November tastings are held and the adjacent farm store.

## Pear-Glazed Roast Turkey

The glorious pear glaze adds flavor to the drippings. It also enhances the color of the roasted bird. Serve the turkey with Pear Almond Preserves from Hurd Orchards or enjoy it with a favorite chutney.

**PREP:** 15 minutes **ROAST:** 2³/₄ hours **STAND:** 15 minutes

| | |
|---|---|
| 1 10- to 12-lb. turkey | Roasted Pear Halves* |
| 1 Tbsp. butter, melted | Pear Almond Preserves or |
| 1 recipe Pear Glaze (below) | desired fruit chutney or |
| 1 recipe Pan Gravy (optional) | relish |
| (below) | |

**1.** Rinse inside of turkey; pat dry with paper towels. If desired, season body cavity with salt. Pull neck skin to back; fasten with skewer. Tuck ends of drumsticks under band of skin across tail. If there is no band of skin, tie drumsticks to tail. Twist wing tips under back.

**2.** Place turkey, breast side up, on a rack in a shallow roasting pan. Brush with the butter. Insert an oven-going meat thermometer into the center of an inside thigh muscle, being careful not to touch bone. Cover turkey loosely with foil.

**3.** Place turkey in a 325° F oven. Roast for 2³/₄ to 3 hours. During the last 45 minutes of roasting, remove foil and cut band of skin or string between drumsticks so thighs cook evenly. During the last 15 minutes of roasting, brush twice with the Pear Glaze. Roast until the thermometer registers 180° F. (The juices should run clear and drumsticks should move easily in their sockets.)

**4.** Remove turkey from oven. If preparing Pan Gravy, reserve drippings. Cover turkey and let stand for 15 to 20 minutes before carving. Garnish platter with Roasted Pear Halves. Carve turkey. Serve with Pear Almond Preserves or desired fruit chutney and, if desired, Pan Gravy. Makes 8 to 10 servings.

**PEAR GLAZE:** In a small saucepan whisk 1 cup pear nectar, 2 tablespoons packed brown sugar, 1 tablespoon Dijon-style mustard, 1 tablespoon Worcestershire sauce for poultry, ¹/₄ teaspoon salt, ¹/₈ teaspoon ground nutmeg, and ¹/₈ teaspoon cayenne pepper. Add 1 tablespoon butter. Bring to boiling; reduce heat. Boil gently, uncovered, for 5 to 8 minutes or until mixture is a glazing consistency .

**PAN GRAVY:** While turkey stands after roasting, pour pan drippings into a large measuring cup. Scrape the browned bits from the pan into the cup. Skim and reserve fat from the drippings. Pour ¹/₄ cup of the fat into a medium saucepan (discard any remaining fat). Stir in ¹/₄ cup all-purpose flour. Add enough chicken broth to remaining drippings in the measuring cup to equal 2 cups; add broth mixture all at once to flour mixture in saucepan. Cook and stir over medium heat until thickened and bubbly. Cook and stir for 1 minute more. Season to taste with salt and black pepper.

**\*NOTE:** To prepare the Roasted Pear Halves used as a garnish, halve small Bosc or other pears; add to pan with turkey the last 10 to 20 minutes of roasting; brush with some of the drippings.

Each serving: 512 cal., 17 g total fat (5 g sat. fat), 283 mg chol., 315 mg sodium, 9 g carbo., 0 g fiber, 77 g pro. Daily Values: 2% vit. A, 9% vit. C, 8% calcium, 27% iron.

## Harvest Buffet

The Thanksgiving tasting menu at the orchards wouldn't be complete without Herbed Mashed Potatoes, heady with garlic and fresh herbs such as parsley, chives, oregano, thyme, and rosemary.

Hurd Orchards' Raspberry Applesauce and Pear Almond Preserves make easy, no-cook go-alongs for almost any holiday dish, especially the Pear-Glazed Roast Turkey.

Susan and Amy always present their tasting dishes on antique pine boards set on collectible linens. The pared-down, yet sophisticated look makes the food all the more inviting.

**Carrots with Grape
and Port Glaze**

## Carrots with Grape and Port Glaze

If you can't find carrots with tops, use small, slender carrots without tops.

**PREP:** 30 minutes  **COOK:** 8 minutes

| | | | |
|---|---|---|---|
| 2 | lb. small whole carrots with tops | 2 | Tbsp. butter |
| 4 | 6-inch fresh rosemary sprigs | ⅓ | cup Wild Grape and Port Jelly* |

**1.** Trim and peel or scrub carrots, leaving about 1½ inches of carrot tops, if present. Halve any thick carrots lengthwise. Place in a 4-quart Dutch oven along with the rosemary sprigs. Add lightly salted water to cover. Bring to boiling; reduce heat. Simmer, covered, for 8 to 10 minutes or until crisp-tender.

**2.** Drain in a colander; remove and discard rosemary sprigs (some rosemary leaves will remain). Add butter to Dutch oven; heat just until butter is melted. Return carrots to Dutch oven and toss gently to coat. Arrange carrots on serving platter. Top with some of the jelly. Pass remaining jelly. Makes 8 to 10 servings.

**\*TEST KITCHEN TIP:** To substitute for the Hurd Orchards' Wild Grape and Port Jelly, whisk together ¼ cup grape jelly and 1 tablespoon port, grape juice, or apple juice.

**Healthy**  Each serving: 102 cal., 3 g total fat (2 g sat. fat), 8 mg chol., 95 mg sodium, 18 g carbo., 3 g fiber, 1 g pro. Daily Values: 221% vit. A, 8% vit. C, 4% calcium, 2% iron.

The Hurd Orchards products were featured in our recipes on these pages. You can use them or try the other delicious options we tested in our kitchens. (Photo at left, clockwise from far left): The Spiced Rhubarb Sauce makes Pecorino Shortbread all the more tempting. And the Fennel Vinegar adds zing to Winter Herb and Fennel Slaw. Raspberry Applesauce and Pear Almond Preserves are delicious with roast turkey; Wild Grape and Port Jelly turns carrots into stars. Hurd Orchards is a fruit and flower farm owed by Susan Hurd Machamer and Amy Machamer. Every product is created at the orchard and is a celebration of the Machamers' joy in their rural heritage. For information and to order products or sign up for upcoming events, contact: Hurd Orchards, 17260 Ridge Rd., Holley, NY 14470-9353; 585/638-8838 or www.hurdorchards.com. Hurd Orchards sells its products in specialty stores across the United States and Canada. Call for a store near you. Products are available in multiple sizes, from $4 to $15.

These harvest candle rings bring together the best of the rose hip harvest at Hurd Orchards. To make them using the harvest finds in your area, Amy recommends you start in your own backyard and gather what is beautiful and lush. It doesn't take much gathering to fill a small grapevine base or a piece of an old coat hanger shaped into a small circle. Using string or wire, attach the gathered pieces to the base and add your favorite open roses or seasonal flowers. (Never leave burning candles unattended.)

**Leeks au Gratin**

At just 2 years old, Amelia knows how to spot a crisp apple. Using baskets of apples for decorations is charming, but ideally, after the harvest, all apples should be kept refrigerated for best quality.

**Quince Pudding**

## Leeks au Gratin

For an extra golden color on top, you may wish to broil for 1 to 2 minutes in a broiler-safe dish. Watch carefully to avoid burning. And, to save prep time, cook eggs ahead and keep them refrigerated.

**PREP:** 35 minutes **COOK:** 15 minutes **BAKE:** 10 minutes

| | | | |
|---|---|---|---|
| 8 | hard-cooked eggs, peeled* | 1/2 | cup white cheddar cheese, shredded (2 oz.) |
| 10 | medium leeks | 1/4 | cup grated Parmesan cheese (1 oz.) |
| 6 | Tbsp. butter | | |
| 2 | Tbsp. all-purpose flour | 1/4 | tsp. cayenne pepper |
| 1 1/2 | cups milk | | Salt and ground black pepper |

1. Preheat oven to 450° F. Quarter eggs lengthwise. Arrange eggs in a single layer in a 1 1/2- to 2-quart round or oval au gratin dish or 10-inch round quiche dish; set aside.

2. Remove green portion from leeks. Halve leeks lengthwise. Wash thoroughly; pat dry. Remove roots from leeks; cut leeks lengthwise into thin strips (you should have about 5 cups). Heat 4 tablespoons of the butter in a large skillet over medium heat; add leek strips. Cook leeks until tender, stirring occasionally. Spoon leeks over eggs in dish.

3. Melt remaining 2 tablespoons butter in skillet; whisk in flour. Add milk; cook until thickened and bubbly, whisking to make smooth. Whisk in 1/4 cup of the white cheddar cheese, the Parmesan cheese, and cayenne pepper. Season to taste with salt and black pepper. Pour sauce over the leeks and eggs in dish. Sprinkle with remaining 1/4 cup white cheddar cheese. Bake, uncovered, about 10 minutes or until edges are bubbly and top begins to brown. Makes 8 to 10 servings.

**\*TEST KITCHEN TIP:** To hard-cook eggs, place 8 eggs in a single layer in a 2-quart saucepan. Add enough cold water to come 1 inch above the eggs. Bring to a rapid boil over high heat (water will have large, rapidly breaking bubbles). Remove from heat, cover, and let stand for 15 minutes; drain. Run cold water over eggs or place them in ice water until cool enough to handle; drain. To peel eggs, gently tap each egg on the countertop. Roll the egg between the palms of your hands. Peel off eggshell, starting at the large end.

Each serving: 333 cal., 22 g total fat (11 g sat. fat), 141 mg chol., 200 mg sodium, 32 g carbo., 2 g fiber, 4 g pro. Daily Values: 181% vit. A, 4% vit. C, 8% calcium, 10% iron.

## Quince Pudding

This dessert isn't a typical "pudding." It's more like dumplings made with a topping filled with quince, sugar, and cardamom, and in the end it looks spiraled like cinnamon rolls.

**PREP:** 45 minutes **BAKE:** 50 minutes

| | | | |
|---|---|---|---|
| 2 | cups sugar | 3/4 | cup butter |
| 2 | cups water | 2/3 | cup milk |
| 1/2 | cup butter | 3 | cups peeled, cored, and chopped quince* |
| 1/4 | tsp. ground cardamom | | |
| 2 | cups all-purpose flour | 1/4 | cup sugar |
| 2 | tsp. baking powder | 1/4 | tsp. ground cardamom |
| 1/2 | tsp. salt | | |

1. For sauce, in a large saucepan combine the 2 cups sugar, water, the 1/2 cup butter, and 1/4 teaspoon cardamom. Bring to boiling; reduce heat. Simmer, uncovered, for 25 minutes (should have about 2 cups sauce). Set aside to cool slightly.

2. Preheat oven to 350° F. For dough, in a large mixing bowl combine flour, baking powder, and salt. Using a pastry blender, cut in the 3/4 cup butter until the pieces are pea-size. Make a well in center. Add milk all at once. Stir just until moistened. Knead dough on a well floured surface for 10 to 12 strokes or until nearly smooth. Roll into a 12×10-inch rectangle.

3. For filling, in a large bowl combine quince, the 1/4 cup sugar, and 1/4 teaspoon cardamom. Sprinkle quince mixture evenly over dough. Roll dough into a spiral, starting from a long side. Pinch seam to seal. Using a serrated knife, cut roll into twelve 1-inch-thick pieces. Place, cut sides down, in a 13×9×2-inch baking pan. Pour sauce over slices. Bake about 50 minutes or until golden.

4. To serve, carefully separate and remove slices and sauce with a wide spatula and place on a large serving platter. Serve warm or at room temperature. Makes 12 servings.

**\*TEST KITCHEN TIP:** Select quinces that are firm and have a pale yellow color all over without blemishes. If quinces are not ripe, let them sit at room temperature until there is no sign of green.

Each serving: 409 cal., 21 g total fat (10 g sat. fat), 55 mg chol., 289 mg sodium, 55 g carbo., 1 g fiber, 3 g pro. Daily Values: 13% vit. A, 6% vit. C, 4% calcium, 6% iron.

## Dried Fruit Tart

**PREP:** 35 minutes  **CHILL:** 1 hour  **BAKE:** 33 minutes  **COOL:** 1 hour

| | |
|---|---|
| 1 recipe Almond Pastry (below) | 1/2 cup dried tart red cherries, dried cranberries, and/or dried blueberries |
| 1 3-oz. pkg. cream cheese, softened | 1/4 cup boiling water |
| 1/2 cup ricotta cheese | 1/2 cup red currant jam or jelly |
| 1 egg | |
| 1 Tbsp. sugar | |
| 1 tsp. finely shredded orange peel | |

**1.** Prepare and chill Almond Pastry. Preheat oven to 450° F. Use your hands to slightly flatten pastry dough on a lightly floured surface. Roll dough from center to edges into an 11-inch circle. Wrap pastry around rolling pin. Unroll into an ungreased 9-inch tart pan with a removable bottom. Ease pastry into tart pan, being careful not to stretch pastry. Press pastry into the fluted side of the tart pan. Trim edge. Line pastry with a double thickness of foil. Bake for 5 minutes; remove foil. Bake about 5 minutes more or until edge of pastry is light brown. Transfer to a wire rack. Reduce oven temperature to 350° F.

**2.** Meanwhile, in a medium mixing bowl beat cream cheese, ricotta cheese, egg, and sugar with an electric mixer until combined. Stir in orange peel. Spread into partially baked pastry. To prevent overbrowning, cover edge of tart with foil.

**3.** Bake about 15 minutes or until filling is slightly puffed on the edges and center is set. Cool on a wire rack for 1 hour.

**4.** Meanwhile, place dried fruit in a small bowl. Add the boiling water. Cover; let stand 30 minutes. Stir jam into dried fruit mixture. To serve, remove sides of tart pan. Spread fruit mixture over cooled tart. Cut into wedges. Makes 8 to 10 servings.

**ALMOND PASTRY:** Preheat oven to 350° F. Place 1/3 cup slivered almonds in a shallow baking pan. Bake, uncovered, for 8 to 10 minutes or until toasted, stirring occasionally. Let cool. Place almonds in a food processor or blender. Cover and process or blend until finely ground. In a medium bowl stir together 3/4 cup all-purpose flour, the ground almonds, 1 tablespoon sugar, and 1/4 teaspoon salt. Using a pastry blender, cut in 1/4 cup cold butter until the pieces are pea-size. Sprinkle 1 tablespoon milk over part of the flour mixture; gently toss with a fork. Push moistened dough to the side of the bowl. Repeat, moistening flour mixture with 1 to 3 tablespoons additional milk until all the flour mixture is moistened. Form dough into a ball. Cover with plastic wrap and chill in refrigerator about 1 hour or until dough is easy to handle.

Each serving: 293 cal., 15 g total fat (7 g sat. fat), 62 mg chol., 178 mg sodium, 33 g carbo., 2 g fiber, 6 g pro. Daily Values: 9% vit. A, 4% vit. C, 7% calcium, 6% iron.

### Pumpkin Custards

This recipe is a favorite of Susan Machamer's mother, Betty. At the orchards, these pumpkin custards are enjoyed warm from the oven or cold with a dollop of whipped cream. Either way, your family will delight in this subtle change from traditional pumpkin pie.

**PREP:** 15 minutes  **BAKE:** 45 minutes

| | |
|---|---|
| 3 eggs, slightly beaten | 1 tsp. pumpkin pie spice |
| 1 15-oz. can pumpkin | 1/2 tsp. salt |
| 1 1/2 cups whipping cream, half-and-half, or light cream | 1/3 cup coarsely chopped pecans, toasted |
| 2/3 cup packed brown sugar | 1/4 cup maple syrup |

**1.** Preheat oven to 350° F. In a large mixing bowl combine eggs, pumpkin, cream, brown sugar, pumpkin pie spice, and salt; mix well with a whisk. Divide mixture among eight 6-ounce custard cups. Place cups in a roasting pan. Pour hot water into pan around custard cups to a depth of 1 inch.

**2.** Bake for 45 to 55 minutes or until set.* Remove cups from water. Cool slightly on a wire rack.

**3.** In a small bowl combine chopped pecans and maple syrup; spoon on top of warm custards. Serve warm or chilled custards in cups. Makes 8 servings.

***TEST KITCHEN TIP:** Check the custards at the end of 45 minutes. If necessary, remove any custards that are firm in the center and continue baking the remaining custards.

Each serving: 333 cal., 22 g total fat (11 g sat. fat), 141 mg chol., 200 mg sodium, 32 g carbo., 2 g fiber, 4 g pro. Daily Values: 181% vit. A, 4% vit. C, 8% calcium, 10% iron.

## THANKSGIVING FEAST

**Pumpkin Custards and
Dried Fruit Tart**

Chicken with Sourdough-Mushroom Stuffing

## Chicken with Sourdough-Mushroom Stuffing

**PREP:** 40 minutes **COOK:** 4 hours on high

Nonstick cooking spray
2 Tbsp. finely shredded lemon peel
1 Tbsp. ground sage
1 Tbsp. seasoned salt
1½ tsp. freshly ground black pepper
8 small chicken legs (thigh-drumstick piece), skinned (about 5 lb.)
¼ cup butter
4 cups quartered or sliced fresh mushrooms, such as crimini, baby portabello, shiitake, and/or button mushrooms

2 cloves garlic, thinly sliced
8 cups sourdough baguette cut into 1-inch pieces (about 10 oz.)
1 cup coarsely shredded carrot
1 cup chicken broth
¼ cup chopped walnuts, toasted
3 Tbsp. snipped fresh Italian parsley

1. Lightly coat the inside of a 5½- or 6-quart slow cooker with cooking spray. Reserve 1 teaspoon of the lemon peel. In a small bowl combine remaining lemon peel, sage, seasoned salt, and pepper. Remove three-quarters of the mixture and rub onto chicken legs. Place chicken in slow cooker.

2. Meanwhile, melt butter in a skillet; add mushrooms and garlic. Cook and stir 3 to 5 minutes or just until tender. Stir in remaining sage mixture. Transfer mushroom mixture to a large bowl. Add bread pieces and carrot. Drizzle with chicken broth, tossing gently. Lightly pack stuffing on top of chicken. Cover and cook on high-heat setting for 4 to 5 hours.

3. Transfer stuffing and chicken to a platter. In a bowl combine reserved lemon peel, walnuts, and parsley; sprinkle over chicken before serving. Makes 8 servings.

Each serving: 412 cal., 17 g total fat (5 g sat. fat), 146 mg chol., 1,450 mg sodium, 27 g carbo., 3 g fiber, 39 g pro. Daily Values: 45% vit. A, 17% vit. C, 7% calcium, 19% iron.

# Company's coming

It may be hurry-scurry Saturday, but when you've got a slow cooker on the counter, all is right with the world. You'll have time to run family errands or spiff up the house while you turn your back on dinner.

You know the slow cooker drill. Toss everything into the pot, cover, and go about your business until dinnertime. That's easy enough for a weekday meal when a big potful of comfort food makes a happy family. But on weekends when company is coming, the "wow" factor needs to be put into play.

To show off with a slow cooker, get started with these ideas:
▪ Start with a roast. Long, slow cooking tenderizes even the toughest cuts. Think beef pot roast, bottom round, or pork shoulder roast. Add broth, juice, or water and some veggies, and dinner is well on its way.
▪ Pop in plenty of potatoes or sweet potatoes with the meat of your choice. When the potatoes are tender, scoop them out and mash them. Serve it all with gravy you make from the juices remaining in the slow cooker.
▪ Make chicken and stuffing in one pot. Dress it up by using big chunks of sourdough bread combined with mushrooms. Finish off the slow-simmered chicken with fresh gremolata. The lemon-peel, parsley, and chopped-walnut topping gives it a fantastic citrusy flavor.
▪ Add a grand richness to your favorite beef stew. A big-flavored red wine—such as Cabernet Sauvignon with its hint of herb—brings a full-bodied flavor to a long-simmered dish.

A key to making slow-cooker meals special for guests lies in the presentation. Be sure to scoop everything out of the pot and into guest-worthy platters and bowls.

**Pork and Apricots with Mashed Sweet Potatoes**

**Beef Stew with Red Wine Gravy**

## Pork and Apricots with Mashed Sweet Potatoes

**PREP:** 35 minutes  **COOK:** 7 hours on low; 3½ hours on high

| | |
|---|---|
| 2½ | lb. sweet potatoes, peeled and cut into 1½-inch chunks |
| 1 | 3½- to 4-lb. boneless pork shoulder roast |
| 1 | tsp. dried tarragon, crushed |
| 1½ | tsp. fennel seeds, crushed |
| 3 | cloves garlic, minced |
| 1 | tsp. freshly ground black pepper |
| 2 | Tbsp. cooking oil |
| 12 | to 16 oz. kielbasa or other smoked sausage links, halved lengthwise and cut into 2-inch pieces |
| 1 | 14-oz. can chicken broth |
| ¾ | cup apricot nectar |
| ½ | cup dried apricots |
| 4 | tsp. cornstarch |
| | Chicken broth |

**1.** Place sweet potatoes in bottom of a 6-quart slow cooker. Trim fat from pork roast. In a small bowl combine tarragon, fennel seeds, garlic, pepper, and 1½ teaspoons salt; rub onto pork roast.

**2.** In a 12-inch skillet brown roast on all sides in hot oil. Drain off fat. Place meat on top of sweet potatoes in cooker. Add sausage. Pour broth and ½ cup of the apricot nectar over all. Cover and cook on low-heat setting for 7 to 9 hours or on high-heat setting for 3½ to 4½ hours, adding apricots the last 30 minutes.

**3.** With a slotted spoon, transfer pork, sausage, and apricots to a serving platter. Transfer sweet potato chunks to a large bowl; mash with a potato masher.

**4.** Strain cooking liquid into a glass measuring cup. Skim fat from liquid; discard fat. Reserve 2 cups liquid (if necessary, add chicken broth to equal 2 cups). In a small mixing bowl whisk together the remaining ¼ cup apricot nectar and the cornstarch. In a medium saucepan combine cooking liquid and the cornstarch mixture. Cook and stir over medium heat until thickened and bubbly; cook and stir 2 minutes longer. Serve with meat and mashed sweet potatoes. Makes 8 servings.

Each serving: 565 cal., 28 g total fat (11 g sat. fat), 159 mg chol., 1,161 mg sodium, 29 g carbo., 4 g fiber, 47 g pro. Daily Values: 263% vit. A, 34% vit. C, 6% calcium, 22% iron.

## Beef Stew with Red Wine Gravy

**PREP:** 30 minutes  **COOK:** 12 hours on low; 6 hours on high

| | |
|---|---|
| 2 | lb. boneless beef chuck roast |
| ¼ | cup all-purpose flour |
| 2 | tsp. dried Italian seasoning, crushed |
| 1 | tsp. salt |
| ½ | tsp. freshly ground black pepper |
| 2 | Tbsp. olive oil |
| 2 | large onions, cut into thin wedges |
| 8 | oz. parsnips, quartered lengthwise and halved |
| 8 | oz. carrots, quartered lengthwise and halved |
| 8 | oz. Jerusalem artichokes (sunchokes), peeled and coarsely chopped |
| 1 | cup Cabernet Sauvignon or beef broth |
| ½ | cup beef broth |
| ¼ | cup tomato paste |
| | Chopped roma tomatoes, golden raisins, and/or red wine vinegar or balsamic vinegar |
| | Crusty bread |

**1.** Trim excess fat from beef; cut into 1-inch cubes. Combine flour, Italian seasoning, salt, and pepper. Coat meat with flour mixture. In a 12-inch skillet brown meat, half at a time, in hot olive oil (add more oil, if necessary).

**2.** In a 4½- to 6-quart slow cooker place onions, parsnips, carrots, and Jerusalem artichokes. Top with browned meat. Combine wine and beef broth; pour over meat.

**3.** Cover and cook on low-heat setting for 12 to 14 hours or on high-heat setting for 6 to 7 hours. Stir in tomato paste. Pass tomatoes, raisins, and/or vinegar to sprinkle on each serving. Serve with crusty bread. Makes 6 servings.

Each serving: 356 cal., 9 g total fat (2 g sat. fat), 90 mg chol., 601 mg sodium, 26 g carbo., 4 g fiber, 35 g pro. Daily Values: 73% vit. A, 20% vit. C, 6% calcium, 33% iron.

DON'T PEAK Those aromas bubbling up out of your slow cooker may tempt you to peek inside. But resist the temptation. An uncovered cooker can lose up to 20 degrees of heat in 2 minutes. If the recipe calls for the addition of an ingredient near the end of cooking, replace the lid as quickly as possible.

# TURKEY ROASTING GUIDE

WITH THANKSGIVING JUST AROUND THE CORNER, KEEP THIS TURKEY-ROASTING REFRESHER HANDY.

| TURKEY WEIGHT | ROASTING TIME (STUFFED TURKEY) |
| --- | --- |
| 8 to 12 lb. | 3 to 3¾ hours |
| 12 to 14 lb. | 3¼ to 4½ hours |
| 14 to 18 lb. | 4 to 5 hours |
| 18 to 20 lb. | 4½ to 5¼ hours |
| 20 to 24 lb. | 4¾ to 5¾ hours |

FOR UNSTUFFED TURKEYS, REDUCE TOTAL COOKING TIME BY 15 TO 45 MINUTES.
VERIFY DONENESS OF POULTRY AND STUFFING WITH A MEAT THERMOMETER.

## GETTING STARTED

**TOOLING UP**   A large, sturdy roasting pan with rack, no more than 2 inches deep; meat thermometer; potholders or oven mitts

**BUYING**   1 to 1½ pounds of turkey per person

**THAWING**   Start in the morning and allow 24 hours for every 4 pounds of bird. Do not count the cooking day as part of the thawing time. Thawed birds keep 2 days in the refrigerator. The bird is ready for roasting when the giblets and neck can be removed and no ice crystals remain in the body cavities.

**STUFFING**   Allow ¾ cup per pound of bird. (That's 11 cups for a 15-pound bird.) Stuff bird just before roasting (not ahead). Loosely spoon stuffing into neck and body cavities; pull neck skin over stuffing; secure to bird's back with a short skewer.

**TRUSSING**   After stuffing, tuck drumsticks under band of skin across tail, reset leg clamp, or tie legs to tail with kitchen string. Twist wing tips under bird's back.

**ROASTING**   Place turkey, breast side up, on the rack of the roasting pan. Brush bird with cooking oil. Cover loosely with foil. Place in a preheated 325° F oven. After two-thirds of the cooking time, cut string between drumsticks. Remove foil the last 30 to 45 minutes of roasting.

## COMMON QUESTIONS

**Q**   **Which is best, a fresh or frozen turkey?**
**A**   They're about equal—base your choice on personal preference. Fresh turkeys take up shelf space in the fridge for a day or two; frozen birds take up to a week to thaw there.

**Q**   **It's Thanksgiving morning and the bird's not thawed.**
**A**   Place the bird in a clean sink full of cold water; change the water every 30 minutes. For food safety, don't thaw the bird at room temperature, in the microwave, or in warm water. When thawed, remove giblets and neck. Rinse bird, if desired. Pat dry with paper towels.

**Q**   **Where do I insert the meat thermometer?**
**A**   Push the thermometer probe into the center of an inside thigh muscle, careful that it does not touch any bone.

**Q**   **How do I know when the turkey is done?**
**A**   When a meat thermometer in thigh registers 180° F and the stuffing is at least 160° F. The drumsticks will move easily in their sockets, and the thickest parts feel soft when pressed. Juices from the thigh look clear when the meat is pierced with a long-tined fork.

**Q**   **What is standing time?**
**A**   After the bird comes out of the oven, it needs a 15 to 20-minute "rest" to make the meat easier to carve and to allow the stuffing temperature to rise to a safe 165° F.

**Q**   **How long can I store turkey leftovers?**
**A**   Refrigerate meat, stuffing, and gravy separately within 2 hours after cooking. Eat or freeze within 2 days.

**Q**   **I still have questions.**
**A**   Try the Butterball Turkey Talk-Line: 800/288-8372 or the USDA Meat and Poultry Hot Line: 800/535-4555.

BY **NANCY BYAL** PHOTOGRAPHS BY **KING AU** FOOD STYLING BY **DIANNA NOLIN**

## CARVING TIPS

**1.** Pull one drumstick away from the body. Cut through skin and meat between thigh and body. To separate thighs and drumsticks, cut through the joints where the drumstick and thigh bones meet.

**2.** With legs and thighs removed, steady the bird with a carving fork. Make a deep horizontal cut into the breast just above each wing. Next, cut from the top of the bird down to the horizontal cut, making thin, even slices of breast meat.

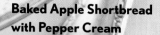

**Baked Apple Shortbread
with Pepper Cream**

# BAKED APPLES

The fall harvest puts an abundance of apples—Rome Beauty, Braeburn, Fuji, Gala, McIntosh, and Jonathan—on your doorstep. Take advantage of this bounty. Turn fresh apples into easy-to-make dishes that can be starters, side dishes, or desserts. These three recipes serve any of those purposes.

Baked Apple Shortbread with Pepper Cream is a showstopper dessert and a delicious side to pork or turkey. Baked Apples with Feta and Thyme makes a charming first course, complements a cider-glazed ham or chicken, and also is an elegant finish to dinner. Serve Molasses-Fig Baked Apples alongside cheeses for a starter, spoon it over ice cream for dessert, or stir it into mashed parsnips or potatoes.

Each recipe serves six and can be increased by doubling or tripling the ingredients—no difficult math required—enabling the recipes to conveniently go from family supper to company dinner to potluck.

**Baked Apples with Feta and Thyme**

**Molasses-Fig Baked Apples**

BY **STEPHEN EXEL** PHOTOGRAPHS BY **GREG SCHEIDEMANN**, **[N] HAUSFOTO** FOOD STYLING BY **CHARLES WORTHINGTON**

## Baked Apple Shortbread with Pepper Cream

As a dessert, serve this recipe with caramel ice cream topping.

**PREP:** 25 minutes  **BAKE:** 20 minutes

| | |
|---|---|
| 1/2 | of a 15-oz. package folded refrigerated unbaked piecrust (1 crust) |
| 6 | small Jonathan apples (2 1/2 to 3 oz. each), peeled if desired, cored, and quartered |
| 2 | Tbsp. lemon juice |

| | |
|---|---|
| 2 | Tbsp. honey |
| 4 | tsp. finely chopped crystallized ginger |
| | Coarsely ground black pepper |
| | Milk |
| 1 | Tbsp. sugar (optional) |
| 1 | recipe Pepper Cream (below) |

**1.** Let piecrust stand at room temperature 15 minutes. Preheat oven to 400° F. Arrange apple quarters in six 6-ounce custard cups or in 4-inch reusable or disposable tart pans. In a small bowl stir together lemon juice, honey, and ginger. Drizzle over apples. Sprinkle lightly with black pepper; set aside.

**2.** Unfold piecrust. Brush lightly with milk. If desired, sprinkle sugar evenly over piecrust. Cut into 12 wedges. Drape 2 pastry wedges over apples in each cup or pan, allowing corners to hang over edge. Place cups in a 15×10×1-inch baking pan. Bake for 20 minutes or until crust is golden brown. Serve warm with Pepper Cream. Makes 6 servings.

**PEPPER CREAM:** In a medium mixing bowl beat 1/2 cup whipping cream, 1/2 teaspoon sugar, and a dash to 1/8 teaspoon cayenne pepper with chilled beaters until soft peaks form. Cover and refrigerate until serving (up to 30 minutes).

Each serving: 285 cal., 10 g total fat (4 g sat. fat), 7 mg chol., 135 mg sodium, 51 g carbo., 5 g fiber, 1 g pro. Daily Values: 2% vit. A, 16% vit. C, 1% calcium, 2% iron.

## Baked Apples with Feta and Thyme

**PREP:** 30 minutes  **BAKE:** 25 minutes  **COOK:** 10 minutes

| | |
|---|---|
| 3 | small to medium cooking apples |
| 2 | tsp. snipped fresh thyme |
| 1 | cup apple cider or apple juice |

| | |
|---|---|
| 1/3 | cup raisins and/or dried cherries |
| 2 | oz. feta cheese, crumbled (1/2 cup) |
| 2 | tsp. olive oil |
| | Apple cider or apple juice |

**1.** Preheat oven to 350° F. Cut apples in half lengthwise and cut out the core to make a deep well. Sprinkle cut sides of apples with 1 teaspoon of the thyme. Place apple halves, cut sides down, in a 2-quart rectangular baking dish. Pour apple cider over apples in baking dish. Bake, covered, 25 minutes.

**2.** Meanwhile, combine raisins, feta cheese, and remaining thyme. Toss mixture with olive oil.

**3.** Remove apples from oven and turn the apples cut sides up. Spoon apple cider in bottom of dish over apples. Spoon raisin mixture into centers of apple halves, mounding filling as needed. Bake apples, uncovered, about 5 minutes more or until the filling is just heated through.

**4.** Transfer apple halves to dessert dishes. If desired, strain juices through a strainer lined with 100-percent-cotton cheesecloth. Measure juices. If necessary, add enough apple cider to make 3/4 cup. In a small saucepan bring to boiling over high heat. Continue boiling about 10 minutes or until mixture is reduced to 1/4 cup and is slightly thickened. Spoon over apple halves. Makes 6 servings.

**Healthy** Each serving: 111 cal., 4 g total fat (2 g sat. fat), 8 mg chol., 107 mg sodium, 19 g carbo., 2 g fiber, 2 g pro. Daily Values: 2% vit. A, 5% vit. C, 6% calcium, 3% iron.

## Molasses-Fig Baked Apples

**PREP:** 20 minutes  **BAKE:** 25 minutes

| | |
|---|---|
| 1/2 | cup mild-flavored molasses |
| 1/2 | cup snipped dried figs |
| 1/4 | cup packed brown sugar |
| 1/4 | cup chopped walnuts |

| | |
|---|---|
| 1 | Tbsp. butter, melted |
| 2 | lb. cooking apples, peeled if desired, cored, and cut into 8 wedges each |

**1.** Preheat oven to 350° F. In a large bowl stir together molasses, figs, brown sugar, walnuts, and butter. Add apple wedges; toss to coat. Spoon mixture into a 2-quart rectangular baking dish.

**2.** Bake, uncovered, for 25 to 30 minutes or until apples are tender, stirring once. Cool slightly before serving. Serve with a slotted spoon. Makes 6 to 8 servings.

Each serving: 242 cal., 6 g total fat (1 g sat. fat), 5 mg chol., 31 mg sodium, 50 g carbo., 4 g fiber, 2 g pro. Daily Values: 2% vit. A, 5% vit. C, 10% calcium, 11% iron.

# THE PIES THAT BIND

The secret to a flaky piecrust is using lard, says Joyce Illian (above right), who learned to bake pies from her mother. Joyce's daughter, Darcy Hosier (left), says she inherited the pie-baking gene.

A PASSION FOR PIES IS SHARED BY EVEN THE YOUNGEST OF THE HOSIER CLAN, WHERE THREE GENERATIONS FIND JOY IN BAKING TOGETHER.

Seven-year-old Betsy Hosier, her face scrunched in concentration, kneels on a kitchen stool and crimps a pint-size piecrust with a deft pinch of little fingers. She dips her hand into the sugar bowl and sprinkles a generous shower of sugar over the top crust.

"That's great," says her mother, Darcy, taking a moment to admire the ready-for-the-oven artistry. Big sister Bella, who's 9, has already finished one pie, rolling out the dough in seconds and piling the center with sugared sliced apples.

Welcome to the Hosier household where piemaking isn't simply a pastime, it's a way of life. In fact, the Hosiers actually moved to a country home outside of Des Moines, Iowa, just so they could grow their pie fillings. Their orchard is full of not-so-perfectly shaped apples in a variety they haven't identified. In the summer, there are raspberries, gooseberries, and rhubarb.

It's common to find a couple of pies in the oven at least once or twice a week at their home. The same goes for Darcy's mother, Joyce Illian, who lives a couple of hours away but visits often for baking sessions. Both mother and daughter—and now the grandchildren—can't resist the allure of tucking seasonal ingredients between layers of pastry.

On pie-baking days, the family piles into the kitchen and awaits an assignment. Everybody wants to help. Bella and Betsy stir together the filling ingredients while their brother Max, 5, cranks the apple peeler. Three-year-old Frank zips in and out, poking, sniffing, sampling, and giggling. Grandma Joyce typically makes the dough.

Pies have been a big part of this family for generations. Joyce remembers being in charge of gathering "whatever I could find" nearly every morning as a child on her parents' farm. "I was the oldest girl of 10 kids," Joyce says. "We always had a list of things to do every morning. One of the options was to go out in the orchard and collect the apples that had dropped or pick raspberries or whatever we could find. Then we made pies with whatever we brought into the house and ate them later in the day. In winter we made cream pies because we had a dairy farm."

Joyce remembers making pies with her grandmother too. So by the time she was a teenager, she was a baker extraordinaire. Now retired, Joyce once baked 20 pies for an office birthday celebration.

At her husband's urging, Darcy asked her mother for lessons. And so they began, mother and daughter—with four little children underfoot—gently combining flour and salt with lard and ice-cold water for the dough. "This was the original Play-Doh," says Joyce, holding up the scraps of pastry trimmed from an oven-ready, just-crimped pie.

### Joyce's Pecan Pie

The Lard-Crust Pastry is incredibly flaky and easy to roll out, but a purchased pastry works if you're in a shortcut mood.

**PREP:** 25 minutes **BAKE:** 35 minutes **COOL:** 2 hours

| | |
|---|---|
| 1 recipe Lard-Crust Pastry (below) or your favorite single crust pastry | 2/3 cup sugar |
| | 1/3 cup butter, melted |
| | 1/2 tsp. salt |
| 3 eggs, slightly beaten | 2 cups pecan halves |
| 1 cup light-colored corn syrup | |

**1.** Preheat oven to 375° F. Prepare and roll out pastry for Lard-Crust Pastry. Line a 9-inch pie plate with the pastry. Trim pastry and crimp edge as desired.

**2.** For filling, in a large bowl combine eggs, corn syrup, sugar, butter, and salt. Mix well. Stir in the pecan halves.*

**3.** Place the pastry-lined pie plate on the oven rack. Carefully pour the filling into the pastry shell. To prevent over-browning, cover edge of the pie with foil.

**4.** Bake for 25 minutes. Remove foil. Bake for 10 to 15 minutes more or until a knife inserted near the center comes out clean. Cool on a wire rack. Cover and refrigerate within 2 hours. Makes 8 servings.

**LARD-CRUST PASTRY:** In a medium bowl stir together 1 1/4 cups all-purpose flour and 1/2 teaspoon salt. Using a pastry blender, cut in 1/3 cup lard until pieces are pea-size. Sprinkle 1 tablespoon cold water over part of the flour mixture; gently toss with a fork. Push moistened dough to the side of the bowl. Repeat moistening flour mixture, using 1 tablespoon of water at a time, until all the flour mixture is moistened. (You will need about 3 to 4 tablespoons of water.) Form dough into a ball. On a lightly floured surface, use your hands to slightly flatten dough. Roll from center to edges into a circle about 12 inches in diameter.

**\*NOTE:** If desired, prepare egg mixture as above; set aside 2 tablespoon of the mixture. Stir 1 cup of the pecans into the egg mixture and pour into prepared piecrust. Add remaining pecans to the reserved egg mixture; toss to coat. Arrange in a circular pattern on top of the filling. Bake as above.

Each serving: 611 cal., 38 g total fat (10 g sat. fat), 108 mg chol., 423 mg sodium, 67 g carbo., 3 g fiber, 7 g pro. Daily Values: 7% vit. A, 4% calcium, 11% iron.

After expertly rolling out pie dough and draping it into a pan, Bella Hosier, 9, scoops apples into the crust (top photo). Cracking pecans was part of the family tradition when a late uncle used to send boxes from his trees in Texas. Although the kids still have fun with the nut-crackers (above), Joyce admits to using shelled pecans for her pies.

# December

# Fast, Fabulous, No-Fail Holiday Feasting

# Fast
## Fabulous
# No-Fail
## Holiday
# Feasting

**Goat Cheese Pastry Rounds**

SIMPLE RECIPES LET YOU WRAP UP PREP TIME IN NO TIME.

## Goat Cheese Pastry Rounds

**PREP:** 25 minutes **BAKE:** 20 minutes
**STAND:** 15 minutes

½ of a 17.3-oz. pkg. frozen
  puff pastry (1 sheet),
  thawed
3 Tbsp. tomato preserves or
  favorite fruit preserves*

3 2- to 2½-inch diameter
  rounds goat cheese
  (3 to 4 oz. each)
1 egg, beaten
Fresh figs (optional)

**1.** Preheat oven to 400° F. Line a baking sheet with foil; grease foil. Set aside.

**2.** Unfold pastry onto a lightly floured surface; roll into a 12-inch square. Cut pastry into four 6-inch squares. Place 1 tablespoon preserves in the center of 3 of the pastry squares. Place goat cheese on top of preserves. Bring edges of pastry up and over cheese rounds, pleating and pinching edges of pastry to cover and seal; trim excess pastry.

**3.** Invert and place wrapped cheese on prepared baking sheet, smooth side up. Brush pastry with egg. Cut small slits in pastry for steam to escape. Cut remaining pastry square into decorative leaves; place atop brushed pastry and brush with additional egg.

**4.** Bake for 20 to 22 minutes or until pastry is golden brown. Let stand 15 to 20 minutes before serving. If desired, serve with fresh figs. Makes 12 servings.

**\*TEST KITCHEN TIP:** For best results, use thick preserves. If the goat cheese comes in a "log," use damp hands to shape the cheese into a round.

Each serving: 166 cal., 11 g total fat (3 g sat. fat), 27 mg chol., 162 mg sodium, 11 g carbo., 0 g fiber, 5 g pro. Daily Values: 1% vit. C, 3% calcium, 3% iron.

### HOLIDAY APPETIZER PARTY

Goat Cheese Pastry Rounds (above)

Sweet and Salty Nuts (page 240)

Hot Fennel Cheese Dip (page 240)
with vegetable dippers

Assorted fruits, including fresh figs, grapes, and
orange sections

Sparkling wine and sparkling water

# Easy Holiday Foods

Simple, easy-going holidays—you wish for them every year. But just one look at your December "to do" list tells another story. This is probably the most enjoyable time of the year, but it can be a stressful one, too. You feel the scheduling crunch just with your daily routine. Now there are all the holiday add-ons—office parties, children's programs, shopping for gifts, decorating the house, cooking, and baking.

Great decorative holiday food doesn't need to be complicated or stressful, however. Here are all the recipes you need to bring joyous feasting to your holiday gatherings. With few ingredients—many off-the-shelf, little to no measuring, and often no tending—these recipes are so easy, fast, and delicious that you'll make them year after year.

Serve them in festive but low-key fashion. Common items stored in the hall closet or on your kitchen or dining room shelves become fetching flourishes for your table. Pretty wrapping papers used as platter underliners and table runners, ribbons that can be added here and there, and seldom-used serving pieces are all possibilities. Keep it fuss-free.

BY **NANCY BYAL** PHOTOGRAPHS BY **SANG AN** FOOD STYLING BY **ALISON ATTENBOROUGH** PROP STYLING BY **CHRISTINA WRESSELL** PRODUCED BY **JESSICA THOMAS**

## Sweet and Salty Nuts

**PREP:** 10 minutes **BAKE:** 25 minutes **COOL:** 30 minutes

Butter
1  lb. walnut pieces or pecan halves (about 4½ cups)
½  cup granulated sugar
⅓  cup light-colored corn syrup
1  Tbsp. coarse sea salt or kosher salt or 2 tsp. salt
½  tsp. freshly ground black pepper
Coarse raw sugar

**1.** Preheat oven to 325° F. Using about 2 tablespoons butter, generously butter a 15×10×1-inch baking pan; set aside. In a large bowl stir together the nuts, granulated sugar, corn syrup, salt, and pepper until combined; spread in prepared pan.

**2.** Bake for 25 minutes or until golden and bubbly, stirring once or twice. Remove from oven. Sprinkle generously with raw sugar; toss to coat. Transfer mixture to a large piece of foil. Cool completely, about 30 minutes. Break apart to serve.

**3.** Store nuts in an airtight container at room temperature for up to 2 weeks or freeze in freezer container up to 3 months. Makes 20 to 24 (about ¼-cup) servings.

Each serving: 191 cal., 15 g total fat (2 g sat. fat), 1 mg chol., 250 mg sodium, 13 g carbo., 2 g fiber, 3 g pro. Daily Values: 2% calcium, 4% iron.

## Lox or Prosciutto Croustades

*Fast!* **PREP:** 20 minutes **BROIL:** 2 minutes

1  loaf baguette-style French bread
Peel and juice of 1 lemon
¼  cup Champagne vinegar or white wine vinegar
¼  cup olive oil
¼  tsp. sea salt or salt
¼  tsp. cracked black pepper
6  oz. lox (cold-smoked salmon) or prosciutto
1  cup packed fresh watercress or arugula
⅓  cup finely slivered fresh radishes

**1.** Bias-slice enough of the baguette to make twenty-six ¼-inch-thick slices; place on a large baking sheet. Broil baguette slices 3 to 4 inches from heat about 1 minute on each side or until lightly toasted.

**2.** For vinaigrette, in a screw top jar combine lemon peel (2 teaspoons), lemon juice (3 tablespoons), vinegar, olive oil, salt, and pepper. Cover and shake well. Splash some of the vinaigrette over each toasted baguette slice. Place a bit of lox or prosciutto on each baguette slice. Top with watercress and shredded radish. Splash again with the vinaigrette. Makes 26 appetizers.

Healthy Each appetizer: 58 cal., 3 g total fat (0 g sat. fat), 2 mg chol., 214 mg sodium, 6 g carbo., 0 g fiber, 2 g pro. Daily Values: 1% vit. A, 3% vit. C, 1% calcium, 2% iron.

## Hot Fennel Cheese Dip

**PREP:** 25 minutes **COOK:** 10 minutes **BAKE:** 15 minutes

4  slices bacon
3  medium fennel bulbs* (8 oz. each)
2  cloves garlic, minced
1  8-oz. jar mayonnaise
1  8-oz. carton dairy sour cream
1  4-oz. pkg. crumbled blue cheese
20  dried whole black or pink peppercorns, crushed
2  Tbsp. finely shredded Parmesan cheese
2  Tbsp. fine dry bread crumbs
Assorted vegetable dippers, such as sticks of jicama, radishes, and/or Belgian endive leaves

**1.** Preheat oven to 400° F. In a large skillet cook bacon over medium heat until crisp. Remove bacon and drain on paper towels, reserving 1 tablespoon drippings in skillet. Crumble bacon and set aside.

**2.** To prepare fennel, cut off and discard upper stalks of fennel. Remove any wilted outer layers and cut a thin slice from the fennel base. Wash fennel and cut in half lengthwise; remove core. Cut crosswise into very thin slices.

**3.** Add fennel and garlic to drippings in skillet. Cook over medium heat about 10 minutes until fennel is just tender and begins to brown, stirring occasionally. Remove from heat. Add mayonnaise, sour cream, blue cheese, crumbled bacon, and peppercorns to fennel; mix well. Divide mixture between two 16-ounce ovenproof crocks, soufflé dishes, or other ovenproof dishes. In a small bowl combine Parmesan cheese and bread crumbs; top mixture in each crock with Parmesan mixture.

**4.** Bake, uncovered, for 15 minutes or until just heated through and tops are light brown. Do not overbake. Serve with vegetable dippers. Makes 6 to 8 servings.

**\*TEST KITCHEN TIP:** You may substitute 4½ cups shredded cabbage or 3½ cups chopped cauliflower for the fennel. Cook as directed.

Each serving: 553 cal., 51 g total fat (16 g sat. fat), 72 mg chol., 896 mg sodium, 11 g carbo., 3 g fiber, 13 g pro. Daily Values: 9% vit. A, 20% vit. C, 34% calcium, 2% iron.

Sweet and Salty Nuts

Hot Fennel Cheese Dip

Cranberry Beef Stew

## Cranberry Beef Stew

The cranberry juice option produces a sweeter stew.

**PREP:** 30 minutes **BAKE:** 2½ hours

| | |
|---|---|
| 3 | lb. beef stew meat, cut into ¾-inch pieces |
| 8 | oz. cooked country-style ham or boneless ham steak, chopped |
| 2 | Tbsp. cooking oil |
| 2 | red onions, cut into thin wedges |
| 1 | 750-ml bottle Pinot Noir wine or 3¾ cups cranberry juice |
| 1 | 16-oz. can whole cranberry sauce |
| 1 | 14½-oz. can diced tomatoes, undrained |
| 1 | Tbsp. herbes de Provence* |
| ½ | tsp. salt |
| | Fresh thyme sprigs (optional) |

**1.** Preheat oven to 350° F. In a 6- to 8-quart Dutch oven brown stew meat and chopped ham, half at a time, in hot oil. Return all meat to Dutch oven. Add onion, wine, cranberry sauce, tomatoes, herbes de Provence, and salt. Bring to boiling.

**2.** Bake, covered, for 2½ to 3 hours or until meat is tender. If desired, garnish with thyme sprigs. Makes 6 to 8 servings.

**\*HOMEMADE HERBES DE PROVENCE:** In a small bowl combine 1 tablespoon dried marjoram, 1 tablespoon dried thyme, 1 tablespoon dried savory, 1 teaspoon dried basil, 1 teaspoon dried rosemary, ½ teaspoon dried sage, and ½ teaspoon fennel seed. Store remaining herb mixture in a tightly covered container. Makes ¼ cup.

Each serving: 613 cal., 16 g total fat (5 g sat. fat), 156 mg chol., 986 mg sodium, 39 g carbo., 3 g fiber, 56 g pro. Daily Values: 1% vit. A, 21% vit. C, 8% calcium, 40% iron.

## Smoky Mashed Potatoes

**PREP:** 25 minutes **BAKE:** 45 minutes

| | |
|---|---|
| 4 | 20-oz. pkg. refrigerated mashed potatoes or 5 lb. baking potatoes, peeled, cooked, drained, and mashed |
| 8 | oz. smoked Gouda cheese, shredded (2 cups) |
| 1 | 3- to 4-oz. pkg. prosciutto or sliced deli ham, chopped |
| 3 | cloves garlic, minced |
| 2 | chipotle peppers in adobo sauce, very finely chopped* (optional) |

**1.** Preheat oven to 350° F. If preparing homemade mashed potatoes, add milk and butter to desired consistency and season to taste with salt and ground black pepper. In a very large bowl combine mashed potatoes, cheese, prosciutto, garlic, and, if desired, chipotle peppers; mix well. Transfer potato mixture to a 3- to 4-quart casserole.

**2.** Bake, covered, for 45 to 55 minutes or until heated through, stirring once. Makes about 24 (½-cup) servings.

Smoky Mashed Potatoes
Tomato-Crusted Rib Roast

**\*NOTE:** Use caution when handling chile peppers. Wear disposable gloves and wash your hands thoroughly after preparation.

**MAKE AHEAD DIRECTIONS:** Prepare potatoes as at below left, except do not bake. Cover and refrigerate potatoes up to 24 hours. Bake as directed until potatoes are heated through.

Each serving: 110 cal., 4 g total fat (2 g sat. fat), 10 mg chol., 384 mg sodium, 13 g carbo., 1 g fiber, 5 g pro. Daily Values: 27% vit. C, 7% calcium, 3% iron.

## Tomato-Crusted Rib Roast

**PREP:** 15 minutes **ROAST:** 1¾ hours **STAND:** 15 minutes

| | |
|---|---|
| 1 | 5- to 6-lb. boneless beef ribeye roast |
| | Salt and ground black pepper |
| 1 | 6-oz. jar purchased tomato or basil pesto |
| 1 | 4-oz. jar spicy coarse-grained mustard |
| | Finely shredded peel of 1 lemon |
| 2 | to 4 cloves garlic, minced |

**1.** Preheat oven to 350° F. Trim fat from beef, leaving a thin even layer of fat on the top if possible. Season beef with salt and pepper. Place beef, fat side up, on a rack in a shallow roasting pan. Insert an oven-going meat thermometer into center of roast.

**2.** In a small bowl combine pesto, mustard, lemon peel (2 teaspoons), and garlic; set aside.

**3.** For medium rare, roast meat, uncovered, for 1¾ to 2 hours or until meat thermometer registers 135° F. For medium, roast 2 to 2½ hours or until meat thermometer registers 150° F. Spread half of the pesto mixture over top and sides of beef. Continue roasting until desired doneness. Let beef stand, covered, for 15 minutes before carving. Temperature of the beef after standing should be 145° F for medium rare or 160° F for medium. Serve beef with remaining pesto mixture. Makes 15 servings.

Each serving: 289 cal., 15 g total fat (5 g sat. fat), 90 mg chol., 429 mg sodium, 2 g carbo., 1 g fiber, 31 g pro. Daily Values: 2% vit. A, 1% vit. C, 4% calcium, 19% iron.

**Chopped Holiday Salad**

## Chopped Holiday Salad

**PREP:** 30 minutes **CHILL:** 2 hours

| | |
|---|---|
| 1 15- to 19-oz. can cannellini beans (white kidney beans), rinsed and drained | 1/2 of a 16-oz. pkg. radishes, halved or quartered (1 1/2 cups) |
| 2 small green sweet peppers, seeded and cut into bite-size chunks (1 1/2 cups) | 1/4 cup olive oil |
| | 1/4 cup lemon juice |
| | Honey |
| | Coarse salt |
| 1 medium cucumber, cut into bite-size chunks (3 cups) | Cracked black pepper |
| | 8 oz. feta cheese, cubed |
| 1/2 head radicchio or 1/4 head red cabbage, coarsely chopped (2 cups) | Coarsely chopped fresh Italian parsley and/or mint |

**1.** Place beans, sweet peppers, cucumber, radicchio, and radishes in separate self-sealing plastic bags. For dressing, in a screw-top jar combine oil and lemon juice. Cover and shake well. Add honey (about 1 tablespoon), salt (about 1/2 teaspoon), and pepper (about 1/4 teaspoon) to taste; cover and shake well. Pour 1 to 2 tablespoons dressing into each bag. Seal bags. Chill for 2 to 4 hours, turning bags occasionally (beans, sweet peppers, and cucumber may be chilled up to 24 hours).

**2.** To serve, arrange vegetables and dressing along with feta cheese in strips on a serving platter. Sprinkle with parsley. Makes 8 to 10 servings.

Each serving: 191 cal., 13 g total fat (5 g sat. fat), 25 mg chol., 528 mg sodium, 15 g carbo., 4 g fiber, 8 g pro. Daily Values: 6% vit. A, 53% vit. C, 17% calcium, 6% iron.

## Glazed Parsnips and Pears

**PREP:** 25 minutes **COOK:** 30 minutes

| | |
|---|---|
| 2 lb. parsnips (6 to 8) | 1 13-oz. jar sweet onion jam, roasted garlic and onion jam, or orange marmalade (about 1 cup) |
| 1 lb. pears (about 3) | |
| 1/4 cup butter | |
| 2 4-inch sprigs fresh rosemary | Sea salt |
| | Cracked black pepper |
| | 1/2 of a lemon |

**1.** Peel and quarter parsnips lengthwise (if pieces are large at the top, halve larger pieces again lengthwise). In a very large saucepan cook parsnips, covered, in boiling lightly salted water for 5 to 8 minutes or until barely tender; drain. Meanwhile, core pears and cut into thin wedges.

**2.** In a very large cast-iron skillet or nonstick skillet cook parsnips and pears in butter over medium heat for 15 minutes or until the pieces turn golden brown, stirring occasionally. Remove leaves from rosemary sprigs. Stir jam and leaves from rosemary sprigs into mixture in skillet. Bring to boiling; reduce heat to medium-low and cook, uncovered, for 15 minutes or until parsnips are tender and glazed, stirring occasionally. Season to taste with salt and pepper. Transfer to a serving platter. Squeeze lemon over mixture before serving. If desired, garnish serving platter with a bundle of fresh herb sprigs. Makes 6 to 8 servings.

Each serving: 401 cal., 9 g total fat (4 g sat. fat), 22 mg chol., 126 mg sodium, 81 g carbo., 10 g fiber, 2 g pro. Daily Values: 5% vit. A, 48% vit. C, 7% calcium, 7% iron.

### SO-EASY SIDE DISHES

Choosing sides with flashy accents makes your holiday meals merry—no other embellishments required. To make the presentation of the parsnip and pear sauté look as if you fussed, tie up your serving pieces with fresh herb sprigs and a wisp of ribbon. For a glorious red and green salad, place pre-cut and marinated veggies, a can of cannellini beans, and feta cheese crosswise on a large platter to resemble bands of bright ribbon.

In addition, tender and flaky biscuits from the freezer case (page 246) are filled with a quick-to-make blender tapenade of dried cranberries and cherries. And extra-thin apple slices placed on top of spoon bread made from a mix (page 246) add holiday appeal to a homespun favorite.

**Glazed Parsnips and Pears**

**Dried Cherry Tapenade Biscuits**

**\*TEST KITCHEN TIP:** If you do not have a food processor, chop the dried fruit and place in a medium bowl. Stir in syrup, thyme, and, if desired, cayenne pepper.

Each biscuit: 344 cal., 9 g total fat (3 g sat. fat), 0 mg chol., 608 mg sodium, 60 g carbo., 2 g fiber, 5 g pro. Daily Values: 4% calcium, 8% iron.

## Cheese and Apple Spoon Bread

No need to open a large jar of applesauce. Use small individual containers of the fruit.

**PREP:** 25 minutes **BAKE:** 50 minutes **COOL:** 15 minutes

| | |
|---|---|
| 1 large red onion, chopped (1 cup) | 4 oz. shredded sharp cheddar cheese (1 cup) |
| ¼ cup butter | 3 fresh sage leaves, snipped (1 tsp.) |
| 1 8½-oz. pkg. corn muffin mix | Ground black pepper |
| 1 egg | 1 medium red apple, very thinly sliced (optional) |
| ⅓ cup water | Melted butter (optional) |
| 2 4-oz. containers applesauce | Sage leaves (optional) |
| 1 8-oz. carton dairy sour cream | |

**1.** Preheat oven to 375° F. In a medium skillet cook onion in hot butter about 5 minutes or until just tender.

**2.** In a large bowl stir together corn muffin mix, egg, water, applesauce, sour cream, cheddar cheese, snipped sage leaves, and a few dashes pepper. Stir in onion mixture. Pour mixture into a 2-quart square baking dish.

**3.** Bake for 50 to 55 minutes or until golden brown across the top. If desired, brush apple slices with melted butter and arrange apples on spoon bread the last 25 minutes of baking. Let spoon bread cool in baking dish on a wire rack for 15 minutes before serving (the pudding may sink slightly in center while cooling). If desired, garnish with sage leaves before serving. Makes 8 servings.

Each serving: 328 cal., 20 g total fat (10 g sat. fat), 70 mg chol., 367 mg sodium, 29 g carbo., 1 g fiber, 8 g pro. Daily Values: 11% vit. A, 3% vit. C, 15% calcium, 5% iron.

## Dried Cherry Tapenade Biscuits

Cover and refrigerate any leftover fruit mixture and use to prepare additional biscuits. Or thin the fruit mixture with water and serve over cooked turkey or pork or as a pancake topping.

**PREP:** 20 minutes **BAKE:** 25 minutes

| | |
|---|---|
| 1 26-oz. pkg. (12) frozen unbaked biscuits | 2 3-oz. pkg. dried cherries (1⅓ cups) |
| 2 4-inch fresh thyme sprigs | ⅔ cup pure maple syrup |
| 1 6-oz. pkg. dried cranberries (1⅓ cups) | Cayenne pepper (optional) Pure maple syrup |

**1.** Preheat oven to 375° F. Place biscuits on a large baking sheet. Bake for 20 minutes.

**2.** Meanwhile, remove leaves from thyme sprigs, discarding stems (you should have about 1 teaspoon leaves). In a food processor\* combine cranberries, cherries, ⅔ cup maple syrup, and thyme leaves. Cover and process until mixture is a coarse paste. If desired, add cayenne pepper to taste.

**3.** Remove biscuits from oven. Using a fork, carefully split the warm biscuits horizontally. Spread 1 to 2 tablespoons of the fruit mixture onto bottom half of each biscuit. Replace biscuit tops. Brush biscuits with additional maple syrup. Bake for 5 minutes more. Serve warm. Makes 12 biscuits.

Cheese and Apple Spoon Bread

**Figgy Espresso Cake with
Honey Fruit Compote**

## Figgy Espresso Cake

**PREP:** 45 minutes **BAKE:** 45 minutes

- 1 lb. dried figs, stems removed
- 1³/4 cups water
- 1 2-layer-size spice cake mix
- 1 cup walnuts, toasted and chopped
- ¹/2 cup brewed espresso or strong coffee
- Sifted powdered sugar
- 1 recipe Honey Hard Sauce (below)
- 1 recipe Honey Fruit Compote (right)

**1.** Preheat oven to 350° F. Generously grease and flour a 10-inch fluted tube pan. In a medium saucepan combine figs and water. Bring to boiling; remove from heat and let stand, covered, 10 minutes. In a food processor (or half at a time in a blender) process until the figs are chopped.

**2.** Prepare cake mix according to package directions, substituting the fig mixture for the water. Stir in walnuts. Pour into the prepared pan.

**3.** Bake for 45 to 50 minutes or until a wooden toothpick inserted near center comes out clean. Cool in pan on a wire rack 10 minutes.

**4.** Remove cake from pan; set on wire rack placed over a shallow baking pan. Poke holes all over cake with a long-tined fork. Slowly spoon brewed espresso over cake. Cool to room temperature. Wrap in plastic wrap and store at room temperature up to 1 week. Before serving, sprinkle with sifted powdered sugar. Use a serrated knife to slice. Serve with Honey Hard Sauce and Honey Fruit Compote. Makes 16 servings.

**HONEY HARD SAUCE:** In a mixing bowl beat 2 sticks of softened butter (1 cup) and ¹/4 cup honey. Cover and chill.

Each serving: 589 cal., 26 g total fat (9 g sat. fat), 72 mg chol., 317 mg sodium, 85 g carbo., 6 g fiber, 5 g pro. Daily Values: 21% vit. A, 7% vit. C, 14% calcium, 12% iron.

### DASH AND DAZZLE DESSERTS

Nothing says "holiday" quite like a beautiful dessert. A shapely baking pan creates drama for this season's Christmas pudding; a cake mix makes it a winner in the prep department. Constant stirring and attention are not needed for creamy rice pudding (page 251) when a slow cooker does the job for you. A store-bought holiday-red lingonberry sauce adds magic to the pudding.

## Honey Fruit Compote

*Fast!* **PREP:** 30 minutes **CHILL:** up to 2 weeks

- 3¹/2 cups water
- ¹/2 cup sugar
- 2 3-inch sticks cinnamon
- 4 lady apples, halved if desired, or 2 medium cooking apples, cut crosswise and quartered (10 to 12 oz. total)
- 4 Seckel pears, halved if desired, or 2 medium pears, cut crosswise and quartered (11 oz. total)
- 2 cups dried apricot halves
- ¹/2 cup dried cherries or dried cranberries
- ¹/2 cup brandy
- ¹/3 cup honey
- 2 tsp. finely shredded lemon peel

**1.** In a large skillet combine water, sugar, and cinnamon. Bring to boiling, stirring to dissolve sugar. Add apples; return to boiling. Cook, uncovered, 3 minutes. Add the pears and cook 4 to 5 minutes more or until pears are just tender. Drain, reserving liquid and stick cinnamon.

**2.** In two clean 2-quart jars divide apples, pears, apricots, and cherries. Combine reserved liquid, brandy, honey, and lemon peel; pour over fruit in jars. Add 1 reserved stick cinnamon to each jar. Cover and chill in the refrigerator up to 2 weeks, turning jars occasionally. Makes 2 quart jars (16 servings).

Each ¹/2 cup serving: 157 cal., 0 g total fat (0 g sat. fat), 0 mg chol., 4 mg sodium, 36 g carbo., 4 g fiber, 1 g pro. Daily Values: 12% vit A, 6% vit C, 2% calcium, 4% iron.

### CANDLELIGHT DINNER

Tomato-Crusted Rib Roast (page 243)

Smoky Mashed Potatoes (page 243)

Buttered carrots

Chopped Holiday Salad (page 244)

Figgy Espresso Cake (above) with Honey Fruit Compote (above)

Hot coffee or tea

Festive Rice Pudding

## Kid Friendly Festive Rice Pudding

**PREP:** 20 minutes **COOK:** 5 hours on low **STAND:** 15 minutes

| | | | |
|---|---|---|---|
| 1 | qt. whole milk (4 cups) | 1/2 | tsp. salt |
| 1 | qt. half-and-half (4 cups) | 1 | vanilla bean, split |
| 1 | cup sugar | 4 | to 6 whole cloves, tied in |
| 2 1/2 | cups uncooked Arborio | | a 100-percent-cotton |
| | rice (do not use long | | cheesecloth bag |
| | grain rice) | | Purchased lingonberry sauce |

**1.** In a 3 1/2- or 4-quart slow cooker stir together milk, half-and-half, sugar, rice, and salt. Add vanilla bean and cloves. Cook, covered, on low-heat setting for 5 hours. (No need to stir.)

**2.** Remove vanilla bean and cloves. Let stand 15 to 30 minutes before serving. (If pudding gets too thick upon standing, stir in some milk to make desired consistency.) Serve warm or chilled with lingonberry sauce. Makes 16 servings.

Each serving (without lingonberries): 274 cal., 9 g total fat (5 g sat. fat), 28 mg chol., 124 mg sodium, 42 g carbo., 1 g fiber, 6 g pro. Daily Values: 5% vit. A, 1% vit. C, 13% calcium, 8% iron.

## Cookie Wreath

**PREP:** 1 hour **BAKE:** 7 minutes per batch

| | | | |
|---|---|---|---|
| 1 | 18-oz. roll refrigerated | 1/2 | tsp. ground cardamom |
| | sugar cookie dough | 1 | recipe Royal Icing (below) |
| 2 | to 4 Tbsp. all-purpose flour | | Super pearl edible luster dust |

**1.** Preheat oven to 350° F. Place dough in a large mixing bowl; knead in as much flour as necessary and all the cardamom until dough is easy to handle. Roll out dough on a well-floured surface until 1/8 inch thick. Cut out cookies using 3-inch, 2 1/2-inch, and 1 3/4-inch scalloped-edge cookie cutters. Bake on ungreased cookie sheets for 7 to 9 minutes or until edges are firm and bottoms of cookies are lightly browned. Cool on cookie sheet for 1 minute. Transfer to wire rack and cool completely.

**2.** Spoon the Royal Icing over cookies, leaving some cookies without any icing. Let stand until thoroughly dry (2 hours or overnight). To apply the luster dust, use a small soft brush to lightly brush some of the iced cookies and all of the uniced cookies with the powder. To decorate cookies with additional Royal Icing, snip a small piece from one of the corners of the plastic bag. Pipe icing over cookies. Let dry thoroughly. Makes about 36.

**ROYAL ICING:** In a large mixing bowl combine 2 tablespoons meringue powder, 3 tablespoons warm water, 2 1/4 cups sifted powdered sugar, and 1/4 teaspoon cream of tartar. Beat with an electric mixer on low speed until combined. Continue beating on high speed for 7 to 10 minutes or until mixture is stiff. Remove 1/4 cup of the icing; place icing in a small resealable plastic bag. Seal bag and set aside until glazed cookies have dried. Add water to remaining icing, 1 teaspoon at a time, to create an icing that is the consistency of thick paint.

Each cookie: 88 cal., 3 g total fat (1 g sat. fat), 4 mg chol., 60 mg sodium, 15 g carbo., 0 g fiber, 1 g pro. Daily Values: 1% calcium, 1% iron.

Chocolate Spiced Tea
Cookie Wreath

## Chocolate Spiced Tea

**Fast!** **PREP:** 15 minutes **COOK:** 10 minutes

| | | | |
|---|---|---|---|
| 6 | oz. bittersweet or | 3 | 3-inch sticks cinnamon |
| | semisweet chocolate, | 1/2 | tsp. cumin seeds |
| | chopped | | Brandy, cognac, or honey |
| 3 | cups strong brewed tea* | | (optional) |
| 8 | whole allspice | | Cinnamon sticks (optional) |

**1.** In a medium saucepan stir together chocolate and tea. Bring to boiling, whisking constantly to melt chocolate; reduce heat. Add allspice, cinnamon, and cumin seeds. Simmer, uncovered, for 10 minutes, whisking occasionally.

**2.** Pour mixture through a fine-mesh sieve; discard spices. Serve in espresso or demitasse cups. If desired, add a small amount of brandy, cognac, or honey to each and serve with cinnamon stick stirrers. Makes 12 (1/4-cup) servings.

**\*NOTE:** For strong brewed tea, add 6 regular tea bags to 3 1/4 cups boiling water. Let stand 10 minutes. Remove tea bags, pressing gently with a large spoon to remove liquid.

Each serving: 70 cal., 5 g total fat (3 g sat. fat), 0 mg chol., 1 mg sodium, 8 g carbo., 1 g fiber, 1 g pro. Daily Values: 1% calcium, 3% iron.

# Nutty and Good

BY **KEN HAEDRICH** PHOTOGRAPHS BY **COLLEEN DUFFLEY** FOOD STYLING BY **BROOKE LEONARD**

You'd be forgiven if you thought that making candied nuts was a trade secret, the exclusive domain of professional kitchens. Candied nuts can give that impression. Glossy and brittle, they have a polished look and snappy good sweetness that suggests only those with cooking school degrees need apply.

Truth is, they're a breeze to make. Any nut can be candied; in fact, the more varieties the merrier.

## CRUNCHY TIDBITS

Traditionally, candied nut clusters are sprinkled on desserts for a finishing touch. Here are more options for the nutty blend.

■ Break off individual nuts and arrange a row around the outside of any frosted cake or cheesecake. Or break into wedges and stand them on slices of cake or on cupcakes.

■ Stir small clusters of the candied nuts into favorite dips and spreads.

■ Sprinkle the nuts over salads. The sweet nuts taste great with greens topped with goat cheese and balsamic vinaigrette.

## Basic Candied Nut Blend

**Fast!** **START TO FINISH:** 22 minutes

| | |
|---|---|
| ½ cup whole blanched almonds | 1 cup sugar |
| ½ cup pecan halves | 2 Tbsp. butter |
| ½ cup walnut halves | ½ tsp. vanilla |

**1.** Preheat oven to 350° F. Lightly grease a 15×10×1-inch baking pan; set aside on a heatproof surface. Spread almonds, pecans, and walnuts in an ungreased shallow baking pan. Toast nuts in the oven for 7 to 8 minutes or until light golden brown.

**2.** Meanwhile, sprinkle sugar evenly in a 10-inch heavy skillet. Place over medium-high heat, gently shaking skillet occasionally to heat sugar evenly. Do not stir at this point. When sugar begins to melt around edges, reduce heat to medium-low. Carefully add butter and vanilla to skillet. Stir into melting sugar with a long-handled wooden spoon (mixture will bubble up). Continue to cook and stir until a golden brown syrup forms, about 1 to 2 minutes.

**3.** Remove toasted nuts from the oven. Immediately add them to the sugar mixture, stirring until all nuts are coated. Immediately pour mixture onto the greased baking pan; quickly spread nuts out as much as possible with the wooden spoon. Cool thoroughly. Break into clusters. Makes about 14 ounces (16 servings).

Each serving: 135 cal., 9 g total fat (2 g sat. fat), 4 mg chol., 16 mg sodium, 14 g carbo., 1 g fiber, 2 g pro. Daily Values: 1% vit. A, 2% calcium, 2% iron.

## Layered Mocha Mousse

**PREP:** 30 minutes   **CHILL:** 4 hours

BY **DAVID FEDER** PHOTOGRAPH BY **COLLEEN DUFFLEY** FOOD STYLING BY **BROOKE LEONARD**

| | | | |
|---|---|---|---|
| 1 | envelope unflavored gelatin | 1 | Tbsp. instant espresso powder or 2 Tbsp. instant coffee crystals |
| 1/4 | cup water | 1 | Tbsp. water |
| 1 1/4 | cups milk | 1/3 | cup chocolate-flavored syrup |
| 1/4 | cup sugar | | Whipped cream (optional) |
| 1 | egg yolk, beaten | 8 | chocolate-covered coffee beans (optional) |
| 2 | Tbsp. coffee liqueur or strong brewed coffee | | |
| 1 1/2 | cups whipping cream | | |

**1.** In a medium saucepan stir together gelatin and 1/4 cup water. Let stand 5 minutes. Stir in milk and sugar. Cook and stir over low heat until dissolved.

**2.** Slowly stir about half of the gelatin mixture into the beaten yolk. Return yolk mixture to saucepan. Cook and stir 2 minutes. Cool slightly; pour into large bowl. Stir in liqueur. Chill until partially set (about 1 hour), stirring occasionally.

**3.** Beat the 1 1/2 cups whipping cream until soft peaks form. Fold whipped cream into gelatin mixture. Divide mixture in half.

**4.** In a small bowl stir together the espresso powder and 1 tablespoon water until dissolved; stir into one-half of the gelatin mixture. Divide this mixture evenly among eight 5-ounce tumblers. Keep remaining whipped cream-gelatin mixture at room temperature, stirring occasionally.

**5.** Chill for 10 minutes or until partially set. (Surface will be tacky but not quite firm.)

**6.** Gently spoon the remaining whipped cream-gelatin mixture on top of the partially set layer. Cover and chill for 4 to 24 hours or until set. To serve, spoon about 2 teaspoons chocolate-flavored syrup over each portion. If desired, top with whipped cream and chocolate-covered coffee beans. Makes 8 servings.

Each serving: 252 cal., 18 g total fat (11 g sat. fat), 91 mg chol., 52 mg sodium, 18 g carbo., 0 g fiber, 4 g pro. Daily Values: 22% vit. A, 1% vit. C, 8% calcium, 2% iron.

# mocha
## BY THE LAYER

### TIER-BY-TIER TECHNIQUES

Tiered gelatin desserts won't bring you to tears when you use the following tips.

- To keep unflavored gelatin from clumping, dissolve it in a small amount of water before cooking or adding to other liquids.
- Chill each layer until at least partially set before you add the next layer.
- Pour each flavor of the unset mixture into the glass over the back of a spoon to ensure the gelatin will layer evenly.
- Gelatin-based desserts are best when eaten within 1 day after they are prepared.

# Prize.Tested
# Recipes®

OUR MONTHLY RECIPE CONTEST HAS BEEN GOING SINCE 1923.
SEE THE WINNERS FROM 2004.

# CHOCOLATE COOKIES

## Kid Friendly  PB&C Cookie Sandwiches

**PREP:** 45 minutes  **CHILL:** 2 hours  **BAKE:** 7 minutes per batch

| | |
|---|---|
| ½ cup butter, softened | ½ cup unsweetened cocoa |
| ½ cup granulated sugar | powder |
| ½ cup packed brown sugar | 1 11-oz. pkg. peanut butter |
| ½ tsp. baking soda | and milk chocolate pieces |
| ½ tsp. salt | ½ cup purchased chocolate |
| 1 egg | frosting |
| 1 tsp. vanilla | ½ cup peanut butter |
| 1 cup all-purpose flour | |

**1.** In a large mixing bowl beat butter with an electric mixer on medium to high speed for 30 seconds. Add granulated sugar, brown sugar, baking soda, and salt. Beat until combined. Add egg and vanilla. Beat until combined. Beat in as much of the flour as you can with the mixer. Stir in any remaining flour and the cocoa powder. Stir in peanut butter and milk chocolate pieces. Cover; chill dough in refrigerator for 2 to 3 hours or until easy to handle.

**2.** Preheat oven to 375° F. Lightly grease cookie sheets. Roll dough into 1-inch balls. Place 2 inches apart on prepared cookie sheets. Flatten cookies slightly with a glass dipped in sugar. Bake for 7 to 8 minutes or until tops are cracked and look dry. Let cool on cookie sheets for 1 minute. Remove and cool completely on wire racks.

**3.** Stir together frosting and peanut butter; spread a scant 2 teaspoons on bottoms of half of the cookies. Top with remaining cookies, bottom sides together. Makes 24 sandwich cookies.

Each cookie: 217 cal., 12 g total fat (5 g sat. fat), 21 mg chol., 176 mg sodium, 24 g carbo., 1 g fiber, 4 g pro. Daily Values: 3% vit. A, 4% calcium, 6% iron.

## Chocolate-Hazelnut Cookies

**PREP:** 30 minutes  **BAKE:** 10 minutes per batch

| | |
|---|---|
| ¾ cup butter, softened | 1 tsp. ground cinnamon |
| 1 cup granulated sugar | ½ tsp. baking soda |
| 1 cup packed brown sugar | ½ tsp. baking powder |
| 1 13-oz. jar chocolate- | ¼ tsp. salt |
| hazelnut spread | 1 cup semisweet chocolate |
| 1 oz. unsweetened | pieces |
| chocolate, melted | 1 cup coarsely chopped |
| and cooled | hazelnuts, toasted and |
| 1 tsp. vanilla | skinned |
| 2 eggs | 5 oz. white chocolate baking |
| 2½ cups all-purpose flour | squares, melted |

**1.** Preheat oven to 350° F. In a very large mixing bowl beat butter with an electric mixer 30 seconds. Add sugars. Beat until combined, scraping sides of bowl. Add chocolate spread, unsweetened chocolate, and vanilla. Beat until combined. Add eggs, 1 at a time, beating until combined. Combine flour, cinnamon, baking soda, baking powder, and salt. Beat as much of the flour mixture into creamed mixture as you can. Stir in any remaining flour mixture. Stir in chocolate pieces and hazelnuts.

**2.** Drop dough by rounded tablespoons 2 inches apart on ungreased cookie sheets. Bake about 10 minutes or until edges are just set. Cool on cookie sheets 2 minutes. Remove and cool completely on wire racks. Drizzle melted white chocolate over cooled cookies; let stand until set. Makes 48 to 60 cookies.

Each cookie: 180 cal., 9 g total fat (3 g sat. fat), 18 mg chol., 76 mg sodium, 23 g carbo., 1 g fiber, 2 g pro. Daily Values: 3% vit. A, 2% calcium, 4% iron.

## Chocolate-Cherry-Chip Cookies

**PREP:** 40 minutes  **CHILL:** 1 hour
**BAKE:** 10 minutes per batch

12 oz. semisweet chocolate, chopped
4 oz. unsweetened chocolate, chopped
1/3 cup butter
1/2 of an 8-oz. pkg. cream cheese, softened
1 cup sugar
3 eggs
1 Tbsp. brandy or 1 tsp. vanilla
2/3 cup all-purpose flour
1 1/2 tsp. unsweetened cocoa powder
1/2 tsp. baking powder
1/4 tsp. salt
2/3 cup miniature semisweet chocolate pieces
1/2 cup chopped dried cherries or dried cranberries
8 oz. white baking pieces, melted

**1.** In a medium saucepan melt semisweet chocolate, unsweetened chocolate, and butter over low heat until smooth, stirring often. Set aside to cool.

**2.** In a large mixing bowl beat cream cheese and sugar with an electric mixer until well combined. Beat in eggs and brandy. In a small bowl stir together flour, cocoa powder, baking powder, and salt. Add to cream cheese mixture; beat until combined. Stir in melted chocolate mixture, miniature chocolate pieces, and chopped cherries. Cover and chill in the refrigerator 1 hour.

**3.** Preheat oven to 350° F. Lightly grease 2 large cookie sheets. Drop dough by rounded teaspoons 1 inch apart on prepared cookie sheets. Bake about 10 minutes or just until firm. Remove cookies and cool completely on wire racks. Drizzle melted baking pieces over cooled cookies; let stand 5 to 10 minutes or until set. Makes about 60 cookies.

Each cookie: 109 cal., 7 g total fat (4 g sat. fat), 16 mg chol., 37 mg sodium, 12 g carbo., 1 g fiber, 2 g pro. Daily Values: 2% vit. A, 1% calcium, 3% iron.

## Candy-Cheesecake Brownies

**PREP:** 40 minutes  **BAKE:** 40 minutes

1 cup quick-cooking rolled oats
1/2 cup all-purpose flour
1/2 cup packed brown sugar
1/4 tsp. baking soda
6 Tbsp. butter, melted
1 3-oz. pkg. cream cheese, softened
1 egg yolk
1 cup granulated sugar
10 miniature chocolate-coated caramel-topped nougat bars with peanuts, chopped
1/4 cup butter, melted
1 oz. unsweetened chocolate, melted and cooled
1 egg
2/3 cup all-purpose flour
1/4 tsp. baking powder
1/4 cup milk
1/2 tsp. vanilla
1 cup purchased chocolate fudge frosting

**1.** Preheat oven to 325° F. Grease the bottom of a 2-quart rectangular baking dish; set aside. In a mixing bowl combine oats, the 1/2 cup flour, brown sugar, baking soda, and 1/4 teaspoon salt. Stir in the 6 tablespoons melted butter. Pat into prepared dish. Bake for 10 minutes.

**2.** Meanwhile, for cheesecake layer, in a small bowl combine cheese, egg yolk, and 1/4 cup of the granulated sugar; spoon in small dollops on top of the partially baked layer. Sprinkle with chopped candy.

**3.** In a large bowl combine remaining 3/4 cup granulated sugar, the 1/4 cup melted butter, and melted chocolate. Beat in egg. Stir together the 2/3 cup flour, baking powder, and 1/4 teaspoon salt; add to chocolate mixture alternately with a mixture of the milk and vanilla. Carefully spoon on top of cheesecake layer. Bake for 30 minutes or until top springs back when lightly touched. Cool on wire rack. Spread with chocolate frosting. Store, covered, in the refrigerator. Cut into bars. Makes 32.

Each bar: 161 cal., 8 g total fat (4 g sat. fat), 27 mg chol., 130 mg sodium, 22 g carbo., 1 g fiber, 2 g pro. Daily Values: 4% vit. A, 2% calcium, 4% iron.

## Triple-Chocolate Raspberry Fudgies

**PREP:** 40 minutes  **CHILL:** 1 hour
**BAKE:** 8 minutes per batch

1/2 cup shortening
1/4 cup butter, softened
1 1/3 cups granulated sugar
2 eggs
2 oz. unsweetened chocolate, melted and cooled slightly
2 cups all-purpose flour
2 tsp. baking powder
1/4 tsp. salt
1/3 cup seedless raspberry preserves
1/3 cup miniature semisweet chocolate pieces
1/2 cup sifted powdered sugar
1 Tbsp. unsweetened cocoa powder

**1.** In a large mixing bowl beat shortening, butter, and granulated sugar with an electric mixer on medium to high speed until well combined. Beat in eggs and the melted unsweetened chocolate. Stir together flour, baking powder, and salt; add to chocolate mixture alternately with preserves, beating well after each addition. Stir in miniature chocolate pieces. Cover and chill for 1 to 2 hours or until easy to handle.

**2.** Preheat oven to 350° F. Grease cookie sheets; set aside. Sift together powdered sugar and cocoa powder. Roll dough into 1-inch balls. Roll balls in powdered sugar mixture. Place 2 inches apart on prepared cookie sheets.

**3.** Bake for 8 to 10 minutes or until puffed and tops are slightly cracked. Remove cookies and cool completely on wire racks. Makes about 72 cookies.

Each cookie: 61 cal., 3 g total fat (1 g sat. fat), 8 mg chol., 29 mg sodium, 8 g carbo., 0 g fiber, 1 g pro. Daily Values: 1% vit. A, 1% calcium, 1% iron.

# SOUPS AND STEWS

## Curried Spinach Soup

*Fast!* **START TO FINISH:** 30 minutes

| | |
|---|---|
| 1 large potato, peeled and chopped (1 cup) | ¼ cup butter |
| ½ cup sliced green onions (4) | ⅓ cup all-purpose flour |
| 2 Tbsp. butter | 2 tsp. curry powder |
| 1 lb. fresh spinach, washed and stems trimmed (12 cups) | 4 cups chicken broth |
| | 1 Tbsp. lemon juice |
| | 1 8-oz. carton dairy sour cream |
| | Croutons (optional) |

**1.** In a large saucepan cook potato and green onions in 2 tablespoons butter over medium heat about 10 minutes or until potatoes are tender. Slowly add spinach, one-fifth at a time, stirring just until spinach is limp and dark green after each addition. In a food processor or blender process or blend spinach mixture, half at a time, until smooth.

**2.** In the same saucepan melt remaining ¼ cup butter over medium heat. Stir in flour and curry powder; cook and stir for 2 minutes. Slowly add broth, whisking until combined. Stir in spinach mixture and lemon juice. Cook and stir over medium heat until mixture is slightly thickened and bubbly; cook and stir 1 minute more. In a medium bowl stir about 1 cup of the hot mixture into sour cream. Return mixture to saucepan. Heat through but do not boil. If desired, top with croutons. Makes 8 side-dish servings.

Each serving: 192 cal., 15 g total fat (9 g sat. fat), 37 mg chol., 488 mg sodium, 10 g carbo., 6 g fiber, 5 g pro. Daily Values: 72% vit. A, 22% vit. C, 9% calcium, 25% iron.

## Peruvian Chicken Ragout

**PREP:** 20 minutes  **COOK:** 25 minutes

| | |
|---|---|
| 1 lb. skinless, boneless chicken thighs, cut into 1-inch pieces | 1 14-oz. can chicken broth |
| 2 Tbsp. all-purpose flour | 1 medium potato, peeled and diced (½ cup) |
| 1 tsp. chili powder | 1 cup frozen whole kernel corn |
| ½ tsp. salt | ½ cup quinoa |
| ½ tsp. ground black pepper | 2 cups packed fresh spinach leaves |
| 1 medium onion, chopped (½ cup) | Finely shredded lemon peel (set aside) |
| 1 clove garlic, minced | 2 Tbsp. lemon juice |
| 1 Tbsp. cooking oil | |
| 1 28-oz. can diced tomatoes, undrained | |

**1.** Place chicken pieces, flour, chili powder, salt, and pepper in a plastic bag. Seal bag and shake to coat chicken.

**2.** In a 4- to 6-quart Dutch oven cook chicken, onion, and garlic in hot oil over medium heat until browned. Add undrained tomatoes, broth, potato, corn, and quinoa. Bring to boiling; reduce heat. Simmer, covered, for 15 to 20 minutes or until potatoes and quinoa are tender. Stir in spinach and lemon juice; cook just until spinach is wilted. Garnish each serving with shredded lemon peel. Makes 6 servings.

Each serving: 262 cal., 7 g total fat (1 g sat. fat), 63 mg chol., 761 mg sodium, 30 g carbo., 4 g fiber, 20 g pro. Daily Values: 16% vit A, 52% vit. C, 9% calcium, 22% iron.

## Catfish Chowder

Top off chowder servings with crumbled bacon and serve with crisp crackers.

**START TO FINISH:** 40 minutes

2 leeks, chopped ($^2$/3 cup)
2 cloves garlic, minced
2 Tbsp. butter
1 large sweet potato (about 14 oz.), peeled and cut into $^3$/4-inch pieces (1$^2$/3 cups)
2 14-oz. cans chicken broth or vegetable broth
1 cup frozen whole kernel corn
$^1$/2 tsp. ground sage
$^1$/8 tsp. salt
Dash cayenne pepper
1 12-oz. can (1$^1$/2 cups) evaporated milk or 1$^1$/2 cups half-and-half or light cream
3 Tbsp. all-purpose flour
1 lb. skinless catfish fillets, cut into bite-size pieces
Peppered bacon or bacon, crisp-cooked, drained, and crumbled (optional)

**1.** In a large saucepan or 4-quart Dutch oven cook and stir leeks and garlic in hot butter over medium heat until leeks are just tender. Stir in sweet potato. Cook and stir 1 minute. Add chicken broth, corn, sage, salt, and cayenne pepper. Bring to boiling; reduce heat. Simmer, covered, for 10 minutes.

**2.** In a screw-top jar combine evaporated milk and flour; shake vigorously to combine. Stir into soup mixture; cook and stir until slightly thickened and bubbly.

**3.** Add fish; cook, uncovered, 2 to 3 minutes more or until fish flakes easily when tested with a fork, stirring gently. To serve, ladle chowder into bowls. If desired, top with bacon. Makes 6 servings.

Each serving: 325 cal., 16 g total fat (7 g sat. fat), 63 mg chol., 750 mg sodium, 28 g carbo., 2 g fiber, 19 g pro. Daily Values: 179% vit. A, 20% vit. C, 18% calcium, 7% iron.

## Chicken and Artichoke Soup

**PREP:** 30 minutes **COOK:** 1 hour

1 large onion, finely chopped (1 cup)
1 stalk celery, sliced ($^1$/2 cup)
3 Tbsp. butter
2 cloves garlic, minced
3 Tbsp. all-purpose flour
2 14-oz. cans reduced-sodium chicken broth
2 cups water
8 oz. skinless, boneless chicken breast halves, cut into 1-inch pieces
1 large Yukon Gold potato, peeled and chopped (1 cup)
1 medium carrot, peeled and sliced ($^1$/2 cup)
1 14$^1$/2-oz. can diced tomatoes, undrained
1$^1$/2 tsp. snipped fresh rosemary or $^1$/2 tsp. dried rosemary, crushed
1$^1$/2 tsp. snipped fresh thyme or $^1$/2 tsp. dried thyme, crushed
1$^1$/2 tsp. snipped fresh parsley or $^1$/2 tsp. dried parsley
$^1$/2 tsp. salt
$^1$/4 tsp. ground black pepper
$^1$/4 tsp. cayenne pepper
1 14-oz. can artichoke hearts, drained and quartered
2 Tbsp. grated Parmesan cheese

**1.** In a 4-quart Dutch oven cook onion and celery in hot butter over medium heat about 4 minutes or until tender. Add garlic; cook 1 minute more. Stir in flour. Cook and stir about 1 minute or until lightly browned. Stir in broth, water, chicken, potato, carrot, undrained tomatoes, dried herbs (if using), salt, black pepper, and cayenne pepper. Bring to boiling; reduce heat. Simmer, covered, for 55 minutes.

**2.** Stir in artichoke hearts and fresh herbs (if using). Heat through. To serve, ladle soup into bowls. Serve with Parmesan cheese. Makes 5 or 6 servings.

Each serving: 239 cal., 9 g total fat (5 g sat. fat), 48 mg chol., 1,205 mg sodium, 22 g carbo., 5 g fiber, 17 g pro. Daily Values: 79% vit. A, 38% vit. C, 12% calcium, 18% iron.

## Guacamole Soup

If you're a fan of the guacamole appetizer dip, give this creamy soup a try. The heat level depends on the salsa you use.

*Fast!* **START TO FINISH:** 25 minutes

1 head garlic
1 Tbsp. cooking oil
1 Tbsp. butter
1 medium red onion, chopped ($^1$/2 cup)
1 medium yellow onion, chopped ($^1$/2 cup)
3 medium avocados, halved, seeded, peeled, and mashed (1$^3$/4 cups)
1 14-oz. can chicken broth or vegetable broth
1$^1$/2 cups whipping cream
1 cup bottled salsa
2 Tbsp. lime juice
2 Tbsp. lemon juice
1 Tbsp. ground cumin
Desired toppers, such as avocado slices, chopped tomato, tortilla chips, dairy sour cream, and cooked, peeled and deveined shrimp (optional)

**1.** Remove peel from individual cloves of garlic; mince the garlic (should have about 2 tablespoons).

**2.** In a large saucepan heat oil and butter. Cook onions and minced garlic in hot oil-butter mixture over medium heat for 5 minutes or until onion is tender, stirring frequently. Stir in mashed avocados, broth, whipping cream, salsa, lime juice, lemon juice, and cumin. Heat through.

**3.** To serve, ladle soup into bowls. If desired, serve with toppers. Makes 6 to 8 side-dish servings.

Each serving: 353 cal., 34 g total fat (17 g sat. fat), 88 mg chol., 420 mg sodium, 12 g carbo., 3 g fiber, 4 g pro. Daily Values: 27% vit. A, 23% vit. C, 8% calcium, 7% iron.

# OATMEAL RECIPES

## Kid Friendly Buttery Oatmeal Crisps

**PREP:** 35 minutes   **BAKE:** 10 minutes per batch

| | |
|---|---|
| 1¾ cups quick-cooking rolled oats | ¼ cup light-colored corn syrup |
| ¾ cup sugar | ¼ cup whipping cream |
| ¾ cup all-purpose flour | 1½ cups semisweet chocolate pieces |
| ½ tsp. baking powder | |
| ¾ cup butter, melted | 3 Tbsp. shortening |

**1.** Preheat oven to 350° F. Line cookie sheet with foil; set aside.

**2.** In a large bowl combine oats, sugar, flour, and baking powder; set aside. In another bowl combine melted butter, corn syrup, and cream. Add butter mixture to oat mixture and stir until combined. For each cookie, drop dough by rounded teaspoons 3 inches apart onto the prepared cookie sheet.

**3.** Bake for 10 to 12 minutes or until bubbly and golden brown around the edges. Cool cookies on foil. Carefully lift edges of cookies, then peel cookies off foil.

**4.** In a small heavy saucepan heat chocolate pieces and shortening over low heat until melted, stirring occasionally. Dip one half of each cookie into chocolate mixture. Place on waxed paper to cool until chocolate is set. Makes about 60 cookies.

Each cookie: 79 cal., 5 g total fat (3 g sat. fat), 8 mg chol., 31 mg sodium, 9 g carbo., 1 g fiber, 1 g pro. Daily Values: 2% vit. A, 1% calcium, 2% iron.

## Oatmeal Meat Loaf Slices

**PREP:** 45 minutes   **COOL:** 30 minutes
**CHILL:** overnight   **BAKE:** 30 minutes

| | |
|---|---|
| 4½ cups water | ½ cup chopped red sweet pepper |
| ½ tsp. salt | |
| 1½ cups steel-cut oats (10 oz.) (do not use rolled oats) | ¼ cup chopped onion |
| | Nonstick cooking spray |
| 1 lb. bulk pork sausage | 2 Tbsp. cooking oil |

**1.** Line a 9×5×3-inch loaf pan with plastic wrap, allowing plastic wrap to hang over edges of pan; set aside. In a large saucepan bring the water and salt to boiling. Slowly stir in oats. Return to boiling; reduce heat to medium-low. Cover and simmer for 30 minutes or until creamy, stirring occasionally.

**2.** Meanwhile, In a large skillet cook the sausage, sweet pepper, and onion until sausage is no longer pink. Drain off fat. Pat sausage mixture dry with paper towels. Stir cooked sausage mixture into oat mixture. Cool 30 minutes. Spoon mixture into prepared loaf pan. Cover and chill in refrigerator overnight.

**3.** Preheat oven to 450° F. Line a baking sheet with foil; generously coat with cooking spray and set aside. Remove sausage-oat mixture from pan by lifting up on plastic wrap; invert onto a cutting board and remove plastic wrap. Cut loaf crosswise into eight 1-inch-thick slices. Brush both sides of slices with some of the oil. Place slices on prepared baking sheet. Bake for 30 minutes or until lightly browned and heated through, turning slices halfway through baking time. Makes 8 servings.

Each serving: 391 cal., 29 g total fat (9 g sat. fat), 39 mg chol., 528 mg sodium, 22 g carbo., 3 g fiber, 12 g pro. Daily Values: 10% vit. A, 27% vit. C, 1% calcium, 3% iron.

## Maple Oatmeal Bread

**PREP:** 45 minutes **RISE:** 1½ hours
**STAND:** 10 minutes **BAKE:** 30 minutes

5¾ to 6¼ cups all-purpose flour
2 pkg. active dry yeast
1½ cups prepared coffee
1 cup quick-cooking rolled oats
¾ cup pure maple syrup
⅓ cup butter
2 tsp. salt
2 eggs

**1.** In a very large mixing bowl combine 2 cups of the flour and the yeast. In a medium saucepan heat the coffee, oats, maple syrup, butter, and salt just until warm (120° F to 130° F) and butter is almost melted. Add to flour mixture along with eggs. Beat with an electric mixer on low to medium speed for 30 seconds, scraping sides of bowl constantly. Beat on high speed for 3 minutes. Using a wooden spoon, stir in as much of the remaining flour as you can.

**2.** Turn dough out onto a lightly floured surface. Knead in enough remaining flour to make a moderately soft dough that is smooth and elastic (3 to 5 minutes total). Shape dough into a ball. Place in a lightly greased bowl, turning once to grease surface of dough. Cover; let rise in a warm place until double in size (about 1 hour).

**3.** Punch dough down. Turn dough out onto a lightly floured surface. Divide dough in half. Cover; let rest 10 minutes. Meanwhile, lightly grease two 9×5×3-inch loaf pans; set aside.

**4.** Shape dough into 2 loaves by patting or rolling. To shape by patting, gently pat and pinch, tucking edges underneath. To shape by rolling, on a lightly floured surface roll each dough half into a 12×8-inch rectangle. Roll up each rectangle, starting from a short side. Seal seams with your fingertips. Place shaped dough in prepared pans. Cover; let rise in a warm place until nearly double in size (30 to 45 minutes). Preheat oven to 375° F.

**5.** Bake about 30 minutes or until bread sounds hollow when lightly tapped (if necessary, cover loosely with foil the last 10 to 15 minutes of baking to prevent overbrowning). Immediately remove bread from pan. Cool on wire rack. Makes 2 loaves (28 servings).

**Healthy** Each serving: 149 cal., 3 g total fat (2 g sat. fat), 21 mg chol., 196 mg sodium, 26 g carbo., 1 g fiber, 4 g pro. Daily Values: 2% vit. A, 1% calcium, 8% iron.

## Toasted Oat Granola Bars

**Kid Friendly**

**PREP:** 20 minutes **COOL:** 1 hour
**STAND:** 15 minutes

3 cups miniature marshmallows
¼ cup white baking pieces
3 Tbsp. butter
½ tsp. vanilla
2½ cups crisp rice cereal
2½ cups toasted oatmeal cereal flakes
½ cup dried cranberries
½ cup flaked coconut, toasted
½ cup shelled sunflower seeds or chopped peanuts
½ cup white baking pieces
½ tsp. shortening

**1.** Butter a 13×9×2-inch baking pan; set aside.* In a 4-quart Dutch oven heat marshmallows, ¼ cup white baking pieces, and butter over medium-low heat, stirring constantly, until marshmallows are melted. Remove from heat.

**2.** Stir in vanilla and the crisp rice cereal until combined. Stir in oat cereal, dried cranberries, coconut, and sunflower seeds. Turn mixture into prepared pan. Press evenly into pan with the back of a wooden spoon or buttered hands. Cool.

**3.** In a small saucepan combine the ½ cup white baking pieces and shortening; cook and stir over low heat until melted. Drizzle over bars. Let stand 15 minutes or until set. Cut into bars. Makes 24 bars.

**\*TEST KITCHEN TIP:** For easy removal of bars from pan, line pan with foil and butter foil. Continue as above. Lift bars from pan and remove foil before cutting into bars.

Each bar: 127 cal., 6 g total fat (3 g sat. fat), 5 mg chol., 108 mg sodium, 18 g carbo., 1 g fiber, 2 g pro. Daily Values: 2% vit. A, 1% vit. C, 1% calcium, 2% iron.

## Mom's Double Oat Muffins

**PREP:** 45 minutes **BAKE:** 15 minutes
**COOL:** 5 minutes

2 Tbsp. butter
2 cups diced, peeled pears
½ cup chopped pecans
⅓ cup packed brown sugar
2 Tbsp. quick-cooking rolled oats
½ tsp. ground cinnamon
2 cups all-purpose flour
2 cups quick-cooking rolled oats
⅔ cup granulated sugar
4 tsp. baking powder
¾ tsp. salt
2 eggs, beaten
1½ cups milk
½ cup cooking oil
2 Tbsp. granulated sugar
¼ tsp. ground cinnamon

**1.** Preheat oven to 400° F. Line twenty-four 2½-inch muffin cups with paper bake cups; set aside. In a medium saucepan melt the 2 tablespoons butter over medium heat. Stir in pears, pecans, brown sugar, 2 tablespoons oats, and ½ teaspoon cinnamon. Cook and stir 5 to 8 minutes or until pears are tender. Let cool 15 minutes.

**2.** Meanwhile, in a large mixing bowl stir together flour, the 2 cups oats, ⅔ cup granulated sugar, the baking powder, and salt. Make a well in the center. Combine eggs, milk, and oil; add all at once to flour mixture, stirring just until moistened (batter should be lumpy).

**3.** Spoon 1 rounded tablespoon batter into each prepared muffin cup. Spoon about 1 tablespoon pear filling over batter in each cup. Top with remaining batter, filling cups ⅔ full. Combine 2 tablespoons granulated sugar and ¼ teaspoon cinnamon; sprinkle on top of muffins.

**4.** Bake for 15 to 18 minutes or until golden and a wooden toothpick inserted in centers comes out clean. Cool in muffin cups on a wire rack for 5 minutes. Remove from muffin cups. Serve warm. Makes 24.

Each muffin: 186 cal., 8 g total fat (2 g sat. fat), 22 mg chol., 164 mg sodium, 25 g carbo., 2 g fiber, 3 g pro. Daily Values: 2% vit. A, 1% vit. C, 7% calcium, 6% iron.

# BEST-LOVED CASSEROLES

**PRIZE TESTED RECIPES® $400 WINNER**

LINDA MORTEN, KATY, TEXAS

**PRIZE TESTED RECIPES® $200 WINNER**

ABIGAIL KURTZ MIGALA, SPRING VALLEY, CALIF.

## Raspberry Blintz Casserole

**Prep:** 25 minutes **Bake:** 45 minutes **Cool:** 30 minutes

**1.** Preheat oven to 350° F. Grease a 3-quart rectangular baking dish; set aside. For batter, in a blender or food processor combine 6 whole eggs, 2 egg whites, 1½ cups dairy sour cream, 2 teaspoons finely shredded orange peel, ½ cup orange juice, and ¼ cup softened butter. Cover; process until smooth. Add 1 cup all-purpose flour, ½ cup sugar, and 2 teaspoons baking powder. Cover; process until smooth. Transfer to bowl; set aside.

**2.** For filling, in blender or food processor combine one 15-ounce container cottage cheese; one 8-ounce package cream cheese, softened; 2 egg yolks; 2 tablespoons sugar; and 2 teaspoons vanilla. Cover; process until smooth. Set aside. Pour about 2 cups batter into prepared dish. Spoon filling mixture over batter in dish; swirl filling into batter with a knife. Pour remaining batter evenly over mixture in dish. Bake about 45 minutes or until puffed and lightly golden. Cool 30 minutes on a wire rack (edges may fall during cooling). Serve with Raspberry-Orange Sauce. If desired, serve with fresh fruit. Makes 12 to 15 servings.

**RASPBERRY-ORANGE SAUCE:** Thaw one 10-ounce package frozen raspberries in syrup; do not drain. Place in blender or food processor. Cover and blend or process until smooth. Strain through a fine mesh sieve; discard seeds (should have ¾ cup puree). Place puree in small saucepan. Stir in 1 tablespoon cornstarch. Cook and stir over medium heat until thickened and bubbly. Cook and stir 2 minutes more. Stir in ⅓ cup orange juice. Serve warm or at room temperature. Makes 1 cup.

Each serving: 368 cal., 21 g total fat (12 g sat. fat), 189 mg chol., 369 mg sodium, 33 g carbo., 1 g fiber, 12 g pro. Daily Values: 18% vit A, 19% vit. C, 13% calcium, 9% iron.

## Rotini Santorini Bake

**Prep:** 40 minutes **Bake:** 35 minutes **Stand:** 10 minutes

| | | | |
|---|---|---|---|
| 12 | oz. packaged dried rotini pasta | 1 | lb. roma tomatoes, coarsely chopped |
| ½ | cup bottled balsamic vinaigrette | ½ | cup seasoned fine dry bread crumbs |
| 1 | 15-oz. can cannellini or garbanzo beans, rinsed and drained | 1 | 8-oz. carton plain low-fat yogurt |
| 8 | oz. feta cheese, crumbled | ¾ | cup milk |
| 1 | cup coarsely chopped pitted Greek black olives | ⅓ | cup grated Parmesan cheese |
| | | 1 | Tbsp. all-purpose flour |

**1.** Preheat oven to 375° F. Lightly grease a 3-quart rectangular baking dish; set aside. Cook pasta according to package directions. Drain. In a very large bowl combine pasta and vinaigrette; toss to coat. Stir in beans, cheese, olives, and tomatoes.

**2.** Sprinkle ¼ cup of the bread crumbs in prepared dish. Spoon pasta mixture into dish. In a medium bowl stir together yogurt, milk, Parmesan, and flour until smooth. Pour evenly over pasta mixture. Sprinkle top with remaining ¼ cup bread crumbs.

**3.** Bake, covered, for 25 minutes. Uncover and bake 10 to 15 minutes more until heated through and top is lightly browned. Let stand 10 minutes before serving. Makes 8 servings.

Each serving: 425 cal., 15 g total fat (6 g sat. fat), 31 mg chol., 1,045 mg sodium, 57 g carbo., 6 g fiber, 19 g pro. Daily Values: 13% vit. A, 19% vit. C, 31% calcium, 19% iron.

## French Toast Soufflé

Looking for a breakfast casserole that's easy to fix? Make this one up to 24 hours ahead of serving. Accompany with a fruit compote.

**PREP:** 20 minutes  **CHILL:** 4 hours
**BAKE:** 40 minutes  **STAND:** 15 minutes

1   cup packed brown sugar
1/2   cup butter
2   Tbsp. light-colored corn syrup
1   1-lb. loaf unsliced cinnamon bread, sliced 1 inch thick
8   eggs, beaten
3   cups half-and-half or light cream
2   tsp. vanilla
1/2   tsp. salt
1   Tbsp. orange liqueur (optional)

**1.** In a medium saucepan combine brown sugar, butter, and corn syrup; cook and stir until mixture comes to a boil. Boil, uncovered, 1 minute. Pour into a 3-quart rectangular baking dish.

**2.** Arrange bread slices on top of brown sugar mixture. In a bowl combine eggs, half-and-half, vanilla, and salt; pour over bread slices. Cover and chill in the refrigerator for 4 to 24 hours.

**3.** Preheat oven to 350° F. Let baking dish stand at room temperature while oven preheats. Bake, uncovered, for 40 to 45 minutes or until top is browned and puffed and a knife inserted near center comes out clean. Let stand 15 minutes before serving. If desired, drizzle with orange liqueur. Makes 8 servings.

Each serving: 579 cal., 30 g total fat (16 g sat. fat), 279 mg chol., 692 mg sodium, 65 g carbo., 1 g fiber, 14 g pro. Daily Values: 23% vit. A, 1% vit. C, 21% calcium, 17% iron.

## Sausage, Broccoli, and Eggs Brunch Casserole

**PREP:** 40 minutes  **BAKE:** 35 minutes

12   oz. sweet Italian sausage links, sliced 1/2 inch thick
2   cups mushrooms, quartered (crimini, baby portobello, and/or button)
1   medium onion, cut into thin wedges
8   eggs
1/4   cup milk
1 1/2   cups frozen broccoli cuts, thawed
2   Tbsp. butter
2   Tbsp. all-purpose flour
1/4   tsp. ground black pepper
1 1/3   cups milk
1 1/2   cups shredded process Gruyère or Swiss cheese (6 oz.)
2   tsp. honey mustard
3/4   cup soft bread crumbs

**1.** Preheat oven to 350° F. Grease bottom of a 2-quart rectangular baking dish; set aside.

**2.** In a 12-inch skillet cook sausage, mushrooms, and onion until meat is browned and onion is tender. Drain. Combine eggs, the 1/4 cup milk, and 1/4 teaspoon salt; add to skillet along with broccoli. Cook without stirring until mixture begins to set on bottom and around edges. Using a large spatula, lift and fold partially cooked eggs so uncooked portion flows underneath. Continue cooking until eggs are just cooked through. Transfer to bowl; set aside.

**3.** For sauce, in a large saucepan melt butter. Stir in flour and pepper. Add the 1 1/3 cups milk. Cook and stir until mixture is thickened and bubbly. Add 1 cup of the cheese and the mustard; cook and stir just until cheese melts. Remove from heat. Gently fold in egg mixture. Turn into dish.

**4.** Cover and bake for 25 minutes. Combine remaining cheese and bread crumbs. Uncover casserole; sprinkle with crumb mixture. Bake, uncovered, 10 to 15 minutes or until heated through and crumbs are lightly browned. Serves 6.

Each serving: 412 cal., 31 g total fat (12 g sat. fat), 343 mg chol., 721 mg sodium, 12 g carbo., 1 g fiber, 21 g pro. Daily Values: 19% vit. A, 19% vit. C, 14% calcium, 13% iron.

## Italian Polenta Casserole

Use your favorite pasta sauce or select a tomato and basil or a garlic and onion sauce.

**PREP:** 45 minutes  **BAKE:** 20 minutes

2 1/2   cups chicken broth
3   Tbsp. butter
2   cups milk
1 1/2   cups quick-cooking polenta mix
1   3-oz. pkg. cream cheese, cut up
1   cup shredded mozzarella or provolone cheese (4 oz.)
1/2   cup finely shredded or grated Parmesan cheese (2 oz.)
12   oz. sweet or hot bulk Italian sausage
1   cup mushrooms, quartered
1   medium onion, cut into thin wedges
2   cloves garlic, minced
2   cups purchased pasta sauce

**1.** Preheat oven to 400° F. Lightly grease a 3-quart rectangular baking dish; set aside.

**2.** In a large saucepan bring broth and butter to boiling. Meanwhile, stir together the milk and polenta mix. Add polenta mixture to boiling broth. Cook and stir until bubbly; cook and stir for 3 to 5 minutes more or until very thick. Remove from heat. Stir in cream cheese, 3/4 cup of the mozzarella cheese, and 1/4 cup of the Parmesan cheese until well mixed. Spread two-thirds of the polenta mixture in the prepared baking dish; set aside.

**3.** In a large skillet cook sausage, mushrooms, onion, and garlic until meat is browned and onion is tender; drain off fat. Add pasta sauce; heat through. Spoon sausage mixture over polenta in dish, spreading evenly. Dollop remaining polenta on top of sauce and sprinkle with the remaining mozzarella cheese and Parmesan cheese.

**4.** Bake, uncovered, about 20 minutes or until heated through and top is lightly golden. Makes 8 servings.

Each serving: 583 cal., 34 g total fat (18 g sat. fat), 92 mg chol., 1,933 mg sodium, 37 g carbo., 4 g fiber, 31 g pro. Daily Values: 25% vit. A, 26% vit. C, 67% calcium, 24% iron.

# 30-MINUTE PASTA MEALS

## Avocado Basil Pasta

For an interesting appearance, use a combination of the two pastas.

**Fast!** **START TO FINISH:** 30 minutes

| | | | |
|---|---|---|---|
| 8 | oz. dried bow tie and/or wagon wheel pasta | ²/₃ | cup chopped fresh basil |
| 2 | medium avocados, halved, seeded, peeled, and coarsely chopped | 2 | Tbsp. lemon juice |
| | | 1 | Tbsp. olive oil |
| | | 3 | cloves garlic, minced |
| | | ¼ | tsp. ground black pepper |
| 6 | slices bacon, crisp-cooked, drained, and crumbled | ⅛ | tsp. salt |
| | | ½ | cup finely shredded Pecorino Romano cheese |

**1.** Cook pasta according to package directions. Drain.

**2.** Meanwhile, in a large bowl combine the avocados, cooked bacon, basil, lemon juice, olive oil, garlic, pepper, and salt. Add the hot, drained pasta and toss to combine. Transfer to a serving bowl. Sprinkle with cheese. Makes 4 servings.

Each serving: 491 cal., 26 g total fat (6 g sat. fat), 18 mg chol., 358 mg sodium, 50 g carbo., 6 g fiber, 15 g pro. Daily Values: 17% vit. A, 20% vit. C, 14% calcium, 21% iron.

## Shanghai Pasta

**Fast!** **START TO FINISH:** 30 minutes

| | | | |
|---|---|---|---|
| 8 | oz. dried fusilli, linguine, or spaghetti | 12 | oz. frozen peeled and deveined large shrimp without tails, thawed (26 to 30 shrimp per pound count) |
| 3 | Tbsp. soy sauce | | |
| 1 | Tbsp. bottled plum sauce | | |
| 1 | tsp. toasted sesame oil | | |
| ½ | tsp. red chili paste (optional) | 2 | cloves garlic, minced |
| 1 | Tbsp. cooking oil | 1 | tsp. grated fresh ginger |
| 1 | medium red and/or green sweet pepper, cut into bite-size pieces | ¼ | tsp. ground black pepper |
| | | 2 | green onions, bias-sliced into 1-inch pieces |
| 1 | cup fresh green beans, cut into 1-inch pieces, or 1 cup pea pods, trimmed | 2 | tsp. sesame seeds, toasted |

**1.** Cook pasta according to package directions. Drain. Keep warm. For sauce, stir together soy sauce, plum sauce, sesame oil, and chili paste (if using). Set aside.

**2.** Pour cooking oil into wok or large skillet. (If necessary, add more oil during cooking.) Cook and stir sweet pepper and green beans (if using) in hot oil for 5 minutes. Push from center of wok. Add shrimp, garlic, ginger, and black pepper to center of wok. Cook and stir for 2 to 3 minutes or until shrimp are opaque. Stir in sauce and pea pods (if using). Stir in pasta; heat through. Top with green onions and sesame seeds. Makes 4 servings.

Each serving: 387 cal., 8 g total fat (1 g sat. fat), 129 mg chol., 850 mg sodium, 51 g carbo., 3 g fiber, 27 g pro. Daily Values: 39% vit. A, 92% vit. C, 8% calcium, 27% iron.

## Italian Wedding Skillet

**Fast!** **START TO FINISH:** 25 minutes

- 6 oz. dried orzo pasta
- 1/2 cup bottled Italian salad dressing
- 1 16-oz. pkg. frozen cooked meatballs (32), thawed
- 1 6-oz. jar marinated artichoke hearts, drained and chopped
- 1 6-oz. bag baby spinach
- 1/4 cup chopped walnuts, toasted
- Salt and ground black pepper
- Finely shredded Parmesan or Romano cheese (optional)

**1.** Cook pasta according to package directions. Drain.

**2.** Meanwhile, in a 4-quart Dutch oven combine salad dressing and meatballs; cook over medium heat until meatballs are heated through, stirring occasionally. Stir in drained pasta, artichoke hearts, spinach, and walnuts. Heat and stir just until spinach is wilted.

**3.** To serve, season to taste with salt and pepper. If desired, sprinkle with cheese. Makes 4 servings.

Each serving: 730 cal., 52 g total fat (15 g sat. fat), 40 mg chol., 1,383 mg sodium, 48 g carbo., 8 g fiber, 23 g pro. Daily Values: 45% vit. A, 33% vit. C, 11% calcium, 33% iron.

## Cilantro Chicken Pasta with Tomatoes

**Fast!** **START TO FINISH:** 20 minutes

- 8 oz. dried bow tie or penne pasta
- 1 9-oz. pkg. frozen chopped cooked chicken breast, thawed
- 2 medium tomatoes, chopped (1 1/2 cups)
- 1/4 cup sliced green onions (2)
- 1/3 cup snipped fresh cilantro
- 3/4 cup bottled French salad dressing
- 1 Tbsp. balsamic vinegar
- 2 slices packaged ready-to-serve cooked bacon, crumbled
- 1/4 tsp. salt
- 1/4 tsp. freshly cracked black pepper

**1.** Cook pasta according to package directions. Drain. In a large bowl combine drained pasta, cooked chicken, tomatoes, green onions, and cilantro.

**2.** In a small bowl stir together French dressing, balsamic vinegar, crumbled bacon, salt, and pepper. Pour over pasta mixture; toss to coat. Return to pan and heat through. Serve immediately or cover and chill up to 24 hours before serving. Makes 4 servings.

Each serving: 558 cal., 24 g total fat (6 g sat. fat), 57 mg chol., 894 mg sodium, 56 g carbo., 3 g fiber, 29 g pro. Daily Values: 29% vit. A, 28% vit. C, 4% calcium, 17% iron.

## Creamy Seafood Toss

Bay scallops, used in this recipe, are the smaller scallop variety.

**Fast!** **START TO FINISH:** 30 minutes

- 6 oz. dried bow tie pasta
- 1 lb. bay scallops, rinsed and patted dry
- 2 cloves garlic, minced
- 1 Tbsp. butter
- 1 5-oz. container semi-soft cheese with garlic and herb
- 1/4 cup milk
- 1 6- to 6 1/2-oz. can crabmeat, drained, flaked, and cartilage removed
- 1/4 cup chopped bottled roasted red sweet peppers, drained
- 1/2 cup finely shredded Parmesan cheese

**1.** Cook pasta according to package directions. Drain.

**2.** Meanwhile, in a large skillet cook and stir scallops and garlic in hot butter for 1 minute. Add cheese and milk; cook and stir until cheese is melted. Add drained pasta, crabmeat, and sweet peppers; heat through. Sprinkle with Parmesan cheese before serving. Makes 4 servings.

Each serving: 519 cal., 24 g total fat (15 g sat. fat), 110 mg chol., 795 mg sodium, 38 g carbo., 1 g fiber, 39 g pro. Daily Values: 5% vit. A, 48% vit. C, 23% calcium, 12% iron.

## Ricotta and Roasted Red Pepper Pasta

Accompany with a green salad tossed with a vinaigrette dressing and pass crisp hard rolls.

**Fast!** **START TO FINISH:** 25 minutes

- 12 oz. dried bow tie pasta
- 1/4 cup butter
- 1/2 cup ricotta cheese
- 1/4 cup freshly grated Parmesan cheese
- 2 cloves garlic, minced
- 1/4 tsp. crushed red pepper
- 1/4 tsp. salt
- 3/4 cup coarsely chopped fresh basil
- 1 7-ounce jar roasted red sweet peppers, drained and chopped (2/3 cup)

**1.** Cook pasta according to package directions. Drain and return pasta to pan to keep warm.

**2.** Meanwhile, for sauce, in a small saucepan melt butter. Add ricotta cheese, Parmesan cheese, garlic, crushed red pepper, and salt. Cook and stir over medium-low heat just until mixture is heated through. Stir in fresh basil and sweet peppers. Toss sauce with warm pasta until coated. Serve immediately. Makes 4 servings.

Each serving: 511 cal., 19 g total fat (11 g sat. fat), 52 mg chol., 395 mg sodium, 67 g carbo., 3 g fiber, 17 g pro. Daily Values: 19% vit. A, 117% vit. C, 17% calcium, 23% iron.

# FAMILY-FAVORITE CAKES

DENISE HAZEN, CINCINNATI, OHIO

MERRIJO T. DEAN, HARLINGEN, TEXAS

## Graham Cracker Torte

**PREP:** 45 minutes **BAKE:** 25 minutes **COOL:** 1 hour

**1.** Preheat oven to 350° F. Grease a 15×10×1-inch baking pan. Line bottom of pan with waxed paper or parchment paper; grease paper. Beat ½ cup softened butter with electric mixer 30 seconds. Beat in 1½ cups granulated sugar until combined.

**2.** Beat in 5 egg yolks. Finely crush 36 cinnamon graham cracker squares (about 2¾ cups). Combine crumbs, 3 tablespoons all-purpose flour, and 2 teaspoons baking powder; stir in 1¼ cups milk and 1 teaspoon vanilla. Beat into butter mixture, one-third at a time, on low speed just until combined. Stir in 1 cup chopped walnuts; set aside. Wash beaters. In large bowl beat 5 egg whites on medium speed until stiff peaks form. Gently stir half of the whites into graham cracker mixture; fold in remaining whites (batter may appear slightly curdled). Spread in pan.

**3.** Bake for 25 to 30 minutes or until top springs back when lightly touched. Cool in pan 10 minutes. Invert onto large cooling rack; gently peel off paper. Cool completely. Prepare White Frosting. Cut cake crosswise into 3 equal pieces. Place one piece on plate; frost top with one-third of the frosting. Repeat, stacking layers with remaining cake and frosting. Top with chopped crystallized ginger and walnuts. Serve at once or cover and refrigerate up to 8 hours. Makes 10 servings.

**WHITE FROSTING:** In bowl beat ½ cup butter until fluffy. Gradually add 2 cups powdered sugar; beat well. Beat in 3 tablespoons milk and 1 teaspoon vanilla. Beat in 4 cups powdered sugar. Beat in milk (1 to 3 teaspoons), if needed, until spreading consistency.

Each serving: 773 cal., 43 g total fat (21 g sat. fat), 189 mg chol., 586 mg sodium, 91 g carbo., 2 g fiber, 9 g pro. Daily Values: 27% vit. A, 1% vit. C, 15% calcium, 11% iron.

## Almond Cake in a Crust

**PREP:** 45 minutes **BAKE:** 45 minutes **COOL:** 1 hour

**1.** Preheat oven to 350° F. In bowl combine 1½ cups all-purpose flour, 2 tablespoons sugar, and ¼ teaspoon salt. Using pastry blender, cut ½ cup cold butter, cut up, into flour mixture until pieces are pea-size. Stir together 1 egg yolk and 1 tablespoon water. Sprinkle over flour mixture; toss with fork to combine (mixture will be crumbly). Press crumb mixture on bottom and up sides of greased 9×2-inch round cake pan or springform pan.

**2.** Spread ¼ cup peach, strawberry, or raspberry preserves over bottom crust; set aside. For batter, in a large bowl combine 1¼ cups all-purpose flour, ¾ cup sugar, ½ cup finely chopped almonds, 1½ teaspoons baking powder, and ½ teaspoon salt. In small bowl combine 2 egg yolks, ½ cup milk, ⅓ cup cooking oil, and 1 teaspoon vanilla. Add to flour mixture; stir until combined.

**3.** In mixing bowl beat 3 egg whites and ⅛ teaspoon cream of tartar with electric mixer on medium to high speed until stiff peaks form (tips stand straight). Fold egg whites into batter. Pour into crumb-lined pan. Bake about 45 minutes or until cake springs back when lightly touched and wooden toothpick inserted near center comes out clean. Cool on a wire rack 15 minutes. Remove from pan; cool. Place on plate, crust side down. Spread top of cake with ¼ cup peach, strawberry, or raspberry preserves. Arrange 2 cups fresh, frozen, or canned cut-up peaches or strawberries, drained, on top of cake. Heat ¼ cup peach, strawberry, or raspberry preserves over low heat until melted. Drizzle over fruit on cake. Serve with sweetened whipped cream. Makes 8 servings.

Each serving with fruit and whipped cream: 664 cal., 34 g total fat (14 g sat. fat), 134 mg chol., 465 mg sodium, 83 g carbo., 3 g fiber, 10 g pro. Daily Values: 19% vit. A, 25% vit. C, 13% calcium, 17% iron.

### Raisin-Apple Cake

**PREP:** 45 minutes **BAKE:** 35 minutes
**STAND:** 10 minutes **COOL:** 1 hour

1³/₄ cups sugar
1 Tbsp. apple pie spice
1½ tsp. baking powder
½ tsp. baking soda
³/₄ cup butter, softened
3 eggs, slightly beaten
1½ tsp. vanilla
1½ lb. cooking apples (3 or 4), peeled,
    cored, and finely chopped (3½ cups)
1 cup golden raisins
1 Tbsp. finely shredded lemon peel
¼ cup lemon juice
3 cups all-purpose flour
1 recipe Cream Cheese Frosting (below)
1 recipe Apple Topper (below)
¼ cup caramel ice cream topping
2 Tbsp. chopped pecans, toasted
    (optional)

**1.** Preheat oven to 350° F. Grease and flour two 8×1½-inch round cake pans; set aside. Stir together sugar, spice, baking powder, baking soda, and ½ teaspoon salt.

**2.** In very large mixing bowl beat butter with electric mixer for 30 seconds. Add sugar mixture; beat until combined. Add eggs and vanilla; beat until combined. Stir in apples, raisins, lemon peel, and juice. Stir in flour until combined. Spread in pans.

**3.** Bake for 35 to 40 minutes or until a wooden toothpick inserted near centers comes out clean. Cool in pans on wire racks 10 minutes. Remove from pans; cool completely. Split each layer in half horizontally. On serving plate, alternate layers of cake and frosting. Add Apple Topper.

**4.** In a small saucepan heat caramel topping over low heat until warm. If desired, stir in nuts. Drizzle over cake. Serves 12.

**CREAM CHEESE FROSTING:** Beat together one 8-ounce package cream cheese, softened; ½ cup butter, softened; and 2 teaspoons vanilla. Gradually beat in 4 cups sifted powdered sugar until smooth.

**APPLE TOPPER:** Core 2 medium red cooking apples; cut into ³/₄-inch wedges. In large skillet melt 2 tablespoons butter. Stir in ¼ cup packed brown sugar and

apples. Cook over medium heat about 8 minutes or just until tender; stir occasionally. Remove from heat; cool slightly.

Each serving: 754 cal., 31 g total fat (16 g sat. fat), 133 mg chol., 435 mg sodium, 117 g carbo., 4 g fiber, 7 g pro. Daily Values: 21% vit. A, 11% vit. C, 7% calcium, 14% iron.

### Fudgy Tea Cake

**PREP:** 20 minutes **BAKE:** 40 minutes
**COOL:** 1¼ hours

4 tea bags
2 cups all-purpose flour
1 tsp. baking powder
½ tsp. baking soda
³/₄ cup butter, softened
1½ cups granulated sugar
3 Tbsp. unsweetened cocoa powder
2 eggs
1 tsp. vanilla
2 oz. bittersweet or semisweet
    chocolate, coarsely chopped
1 Tbsp. butter
³/₄ cup sifted powdered sugar

**1.** In a small saucepan bring 1³/₄ cups water to boiling; remove from heat. Add tea bags; let stand 5 minutes. Remove tea bags, squeezing gently. Discard tea bags and cool tea to room temperature.

**2.** Preheat oven to 350° F. Grease and lightly flour a 10-inch fluted tube pan; set aside. Stir together flour, baking powder, baking soda, and ½ teaspoon salt.

**3.** In a large mixing bowl beat ³/₄ cup butter with an electric mixer for 30 seconds. Gradually add granulated sugar, beating on medium speed until well combined; scrape sides of bowl occasionally. Add cocoa powder, eggs, and vanilla; beat until combined. Alternately add flour mixture and 1 cup of the cooled tea to butter mixture; beat on low speed after each addition just until combined. Spoon batter into prepared pan.

**4.** Bake about 40 minutes or until a wooden toothpick inserted near center comes out clean. Cool in pan on wire rack 15 minutes. Remove from pan; cool completely. In a small saucepan combine chocolate, 1 tablespoon butter, and 2 tablespoons of the remaining tea. Cook and

stir over medium heat until chocolate and butter are melted. Remove from heat. Stir in powdered sugar. Stir in enough of the remaining tea (2 to 3 teaspoons) until smooth and of a thick glazing consistency. Drizzle over cake. Makes 12 servings.

Each serving: 346 cal., 16 g total fat (9 g sat. fat), 71 mg chol., 328 mg sodium, 48 g carbo., 1 g fiber, 4 g pro. Daily Values: 11% vit. A, 5% calcium, 8% iron.

### Marmalade-Topped Carrot Cake

**PREP:** 30 minutes **BAKE:** 30 minutes
**COOL:** 1¼ hours

½ cup all-purpose flour
½ cup whole wheat flour
½ tsp. baking powder
½ tsp. baking soda
¼ tsp. ground ginger
½ cup olive oil
½ cup granulated sugar
½ cup packed brown sugar
1 tsp. finely shredded lemon peel
1 Tbsp. lemon juice
1 tsp. vanilla
2 eggs
1½ cups finely shredded carrots
¼ cup golden raisins
¹/₃ cup orange marmalade

**1.** Preheat oven to 350° F. Grease and flour one 9×1½-inch round cake pan; set aside. Stir together flours, baking powder, soda, ginger, and ¼ teaspoon salt; set aside.

**2.** In a large mixing bowl beat oil and sugars with electric mixer until combined. Add lemon peel and juice and vanilla. Add eggs, 1 at a time, beating well after each; scrape bowl often. Add flour mixture to oil mixture; beat until combined. Stir in carrots and raisins. Transfer batter to prepared pan.

**3.** Bake for 30 to 35 minutes or until a wooden toothpick inserted near the center comes out clean. Cool in pan on wire rack 15 minutes. Remove from pan; cool completely. Heat marmalade just until melted. Gently spoon over cake. Makes 8 servings.

Each serving: 350 cal., 15 g total fat (2 g sat. fat), 53 mg chol., 214 mg sodium, 52 g carbo., 2 g fiber, 4 g pro. Daily Values: 118% vit. A, 7% vit. C, 5% calcium, 8% iron.

# PEANUT BUTTER TREATS

## Peanut Butter Macaroons

Instead of the usual coconut, these macaroons star honey-roasted peanuts and peanut butter.

**PREP:** 20 minutes **BAKE:** 10 minutes per batch **STAND:** 15 minutes

| | |
|---|---|
| 2 egg whites | 2 cups chocolate-flavored |
| 1/8 tsp. cream of tartar | crisp rice cereal |
| Dash salt | 1/3 cup chopped |
| 1/2 cup sugar | honey-roasted peanuts |
| 1/2 cup creamy peanut butter | |

**1.** Preheat oven to 300° F. Lightly grease 2 cookie sheets or line them with parchment paper; set aside.

**2.** In a medium mixing bowl beat egg whites, cream of tartar, and salt with an electric mixer on high speed until soft peaks form (tips curl). Gradually add sugar, about 1 tablespoon at a time, beating until stiff peaks form (tips stand straight). Gently fold in peanut butter. Fold in cereal. Drop mixture by rounded teaspoons 2 inches apart onto prepared cookie sheets. Sprinkle with chopped peanuts.

**3.** Bake for 10 minutes. Turn oven off and let cookies dry in oven with door closed for 15 minutes. Remove macaroons from cookie sheets to a wire rack; cool completely. Makes about 30 cookies.

**Healthy** Each cookie: 57 cal., 3 g total fat (1 g sat. fat), 0 mg chol., 50 mg sodium, 7 g carbo., 0 g fiber, 2 g pro. Daily Values: 1% vit. A, 2% vit. C, 1% calcium, 3% iron.

## Kid Friendly — Peanut Butter Bars

**PREP:** 30 minutes **BAKE:** 37 minutes

| | |
|---|---|
| 1/2 cup dried cranberries | 2 3-oz. pkg. cream cheese, softened |
| 1/4 cup butter, softened | |
| 1/2 cup chunky peanut butter* | 1/4 cup granulated sugar |
| 1/3 cup packed brown sugar | 1 egg |
| 1 cup all-purpose flour | 2/3 cup chunky peanut butter* |
| 1/2 cup finely chopped peanuts | 1 Tbsp. lemon juice |

**1.** Preheat oven to 350° F. Grease an 8×8×2-inch baking pan; set aside. In a small bowl combine cranberries and 1/4 cup boiling water. Cover and let stand 20 minutes. Drain well.

**2.** In large mixing bowl beat butter and 1/2 cup peanut butter with electric mixer until combined. Beat in brown sugar. Beat in flour on low speed (mixture will be crumbly). Stir in peanuts and cranberries. Reserve 1 cup of the crumb mixture. Press remaining mixture into bottom of prepared pan. Bake for 12 minutes.

**3.** Meanwhile, for filling, in a medium bowl beat the cream cheese and granulated sugar with an electric mixer until smooth. Add the egg, 2/3 cup peanut butter, and lemon juice; beat until well combined. Spread evenly over crust. Sprinkle reserved crumb mixture over top, pressing lightly into filling. Bake about 25 minutes more or until top is lightly browned and edges are puffed. Cool on a wire rack. Cut into bars. Makes 16 bars.

**\*NOTE:** Do not use natural peanut butter in this recipe.

Each bar: 275 cal., 19 g total fat (6 g sat. fat), 33 mg chol., 197 mg sodium, 22 g carbo., 2 g fiber, 8 g pro. Daily Values: 6% vit. A, 1% vit. C, 3% calcium, 6% iron.

## Chicken, Peanut, and Peach Salad

Fast! **START TO FINISH:** 30 minutes

3 medium peaches
1/3 cup creamy peanut butter
1/2 cup peach nectar
3 Tbsp. peanut oil
2 Tbsp. seasoned rice vinegar
1 Tbsp. honey
2 tsp. grated fresh ginger
1 tsp. chili garlic sauce
1 tsp. toasted sesame oil
2/3 cup dry roasted peanuts, finely chopped
1/3 cup fine dry bread crumbs
4 small skinless, boneless chicken breast halves (about 1 lb.)
8 cups torn mixed salad greens or 2 heads butterhead lettuce, torn (8 cups)
1 small cucumber, halved lengthwise and thinly sliced
2 carambola (star fruit), thinly sliced
Peach nectar

**1.** Halve and pit 1 of the peaches. In a blender or food processor combine the peach, peanut butter, 1/2 cup peach nectar, 1 tablespoon of the peanut oil, the vinegar, honey, ginger, chili garlic sauce, and sesame oil. Cover and blend or process until combined. Divide mixture in half. Reserve half of the mixture for a dressing.

**2.** In a shallow bowl combine peanuts and bread crumbs; place remaining half of the dressing in another bowl. Dip chicken first in the dressing and then in the crumb mixture, rolling to coat chicken with crumb mixture. Discard any remaining dressing and crumb mixture.

**3.** In a large nonstick skillet heat the remaining 2 tablespoons peanut oil over medium to medium-low heat. Add chicken; cook for 5 minutes. Turn and cook 5 to 7 minutes more or until no pink remains in chicken (170° F), reducing heat if coating on chicken begins to overbrown.

**4.** Divide greens among 4 individual plates. Add a chicken breast half to each plate. Divide cucumber and carambola slices among plates. Peel, pit, and slice remaining 2 peaches; add to plates. If desired, add additional peach nectar to thin dressing to desired consistency. Drizzle reserved half of dressing over chicken, fruit, and greens. Makes 4 servings.

Each serving: 648 cal., 37 g total fat (6 g sat. fat), 66 mg chol., 638 mg sodium, 45 g carbo., 7 g fiber, 41 g pro. Daily Values: 27% vit. A, 48% vit. C, 8% calcium, 17% iron.

## Nutty Coleslaw

Look for hoisin sauce and toasted sesame oil in the ethnic food aisle of the supermarket. The daikon, a Japanese radish, will be found in the produce section.

**PREP:** 20 minutes **CHILL:** 2 hours

1/4 cup peanut butter
3 Tbsp. mayonnaise or salad dressing
2 Tbsp. bottled hoisin sauce
1 tsp. toasted sesame oil
1 10-oz. pkg. shredded cabbage
1 1/2 cups matchstick-size pieces daikon
1/2 cup matchstick-size pieces red radishes
2 Tbsp. sesame seeds, toasted
3 Tbsp. sliced green onions
2 Tbsp. chopped honey-roasted peanuts

**1.** For dressing, in a small bowl whisk together the peanut butter, mayonnaise, hoisin sauce, and sesame oil; set aside.

**2.** In a large bowl stir together the cabbage, daikon, red radishes, and sesame seeds; add dressing mixture and toss to coat. Cover and chill in the refrigerator for 2 to 3 hours. Sprinkle with green onions and chopped peanuts before serving. Makes 6 servings.

Each serving: 181 cal., 15 g total fat (2 g sat. fat), 3 mg chol., 174 mg sodium, 9 g carbo., 3 g fiber, 5 g pro. Daily Values: 2% vit. A, 40% vit. C, 4% calcium, 5% iron.

## Peanut Butter and Cornmeal Coffee Cake

**PREP:** 25 minutes **BAKE:** 30 minutes

1/2 cup packed brown sugar
1/4 cup all-purpose flour
1/4 cup yellow cornmeal
1/4 cup peanut butter
2 Tbsp. butter, melted
1/2 cup peanut butter
1/4 cup shortening
1 cup packed brown sugar
2 eggs
1 1/2 cups all-purpose flour
1/4 cup yellow cornmeal
2 tsp. baking powder
1/2 tsp. baking soda
1/4 tsp. salt
1 cup buttermilk
1/2 cup golden raisins, dried cherries, or dried cranberries

**1.** Preheat oven to 375° F. Grease a 13×9×2-inch baking pan; set aside.

**2.** In a medium mixing bowl combine the 1/2 cup brown sugar, 1/4 cup flour, 1/4 cup cornmeal, 1/4 cup peanut butter, and melted butter until crumbly. Set aside.

**3.** In a large mixing bowl combine 1/2 cup peanut butter, the shortening, and 1 cup brown sugar; beat with an electric mixer on medium speed until combined. Add eggs, 1 at a time, beating after each addition until combined.

**4.** In another bowl combine 1 1/2 cups flour, 1/4 cup cornmeal, baking powder, baking soda, and salt. Add flour mixture alternately with buttermilk to beaten mixture, beating after each addition until combined. Stir in raisins. Spread in prepared pan. Sprinkle with crumbly mixture.

**5.** Bake for 30 to 35 minutes or until a wooden toothpick inserted off center comes out clean. Cool in pan on wire rack. Makes 16 servings.

Each serving: 289 cal., 12 g total fat (3 g sat. fat), 31 mg chol., 231 mg sodium, 42 g carbo., 2 g fiber, 6 g pro. Daily Values: 2% vit. A, 1% vit. C, 8% calcium, 8% iron.

# LAMB

## Berry-Mustard Crust Lamb

**PREP:** 20 minutes **ROAST:** 35 minutes **STAND:** 10 minutes

| | |
|---|---|
| 2 | 1-lb. or one 1½- to 2-lb. French-style lamb rib roast(s) |
| | Salt and ground black pepper |
| 1 | Tbsp. cooking oil |
| ¼ | cup seedless raspberry jam or preserves |

| | |
|---|---|
| 2 | Tbsp. Dijon-style mustard or stone ground mustard |
| 2 | tsp. chopped fresh garlic |
| ¾ | cup panko (Japanese-style) bread crumbs |
| ½ | cup fresh raspberries |
| 1 | cup beef broth |
| 2 | Tbsp. snipped fresh mint |

**1.** Preheat oven to 375° F. Season lamb generously with salt and pepper. In a very large skillet brown lamb on all sides in hot oil. Set skillet aside. Place lamb, bone side down, in a foil-lined, shallow roasting pan.

**2.** In a small bowl combine jam, mustard, and 1 teaspoon of the garlic; spoon over lamb. Sprinkle evenly with crumbs. Roast, uncovered, for 35 to 40 minutes for smaller roast or 50 to 60 minutes for larger roast until thermometer inserted in thickest portion registers 140° F (medium-rare) to 155° F (medium). Cover with foil; let stand 10 minutes (meat temperature will rise 5° F during standing). Meanwhile, in large skillet cook raspberries and remaining garlic 30 seconds. Add broth; heat to boiling. Boil gently, uncovered, 5 to 8 minutes or until reduced to ⅔ cup. Cool slightly; transfer to blender. Cover; blend until almost smooth. Stir in mint. Season with salt and pepper. To serve, slice lamb between ribs; spoon sauce over lamb. Makes 8 servings.

Each serving: 334 cal., 25 g total fat (10 g sat. fat), 58 mg chol., 284 mg sodium, 12 g carbo., 1 g fiber, 13 g pro. Daily Values: 7% vit. C, 2% calcium, 9% iron.

## Lamb-Stuffed Portobellos

**PREP:** 25 minutes **BAKE:** 40 minutes

| | |
|---|---|
| 6 | portobello mushrooms (3 to 4 inches in diameter), about 12 oz. total |
| 1 | large onion, finely chopped (1 cup) |
| 1 | clove garlic, minced |
| 1 | cup snipped fresh parsley |
| ½ | cup snipped fresh cilantro |
| 1 | tsp. salt |
| 1 | tsp. ground black pepper |

| | |
|---|---|
| 1 | tsp. paprika |
| 1 | tsp. ground cumin |
| ½ | tsp. ground nutmeg |
| ½ | tsp. ground cinnamon |
| ½ | tsp. ground allspice |
| 1 | lb. ground lamb |
| ⅓ | cup crumbled feta cheese (optional) |
| 6 | ¾-inch-thick slices French bread, toasted |

**1.** Preheat oven to 350° F. Wash mushrooms; pat dry. Remove stems and chop (should have about ½ cup). Remove the gills, if desired. Set mushroom caps aside. In a bowl combine chopped mushroom stems, onion, garlic, parsley, cilantro, salt, pepper, paprika, cumin, nutmeg, cinnamon, and allspice; add lamb. Mix well with hands. Shape meat mixture into 6 patties about the same diameter as mushroom caps. Place 1 patty on each mushroom cap. Press patties lightly into caps. Place filled caps on unheated rack of a broiler pan.

**2.** Bake, uncovered, about 40 minutes or until an instant-read thermometer inserted into sides of patties registers 160° F. If desired, top with cheese during last 5 minutes of baking. Serve on toast slices. If desired, season with salt. Makes 6 servings.

Each serving: 254 cal., 12 g total fat (5 g sat. fat), 51 mg chol., 596 mg sodium, 19 g carbo., 3 g fiber, 18 g pro. Daily Values: 22% vit. A, 29% vit. C, 7% calcium, 17% iron.

## Greek Pita Wedges with Tzatziki

**Prep:** 25 minutes  **Chill:** overnight
**Bake:** 10 minutes

½  cup plain yogurt
1  cup finely chopped, seeded, peeled cucumber
1  clove garlic, minced
1  tsp. dried dillweed
Salt and freshly ground black pepper
8  oz. ground lamb
1  medium red onion, chopped (½ cup)
2  cloves garlic, minced
2  Tbsp. snipped fresh Italian parsley
2  Tbsp. tomato paste
½  tsp. paprika
½  tsp. dried oregano, crushed
½  cup coarsely chopped grape tomatoes
½  cup crumbled garlic and herb feta cheese
2  pita bread rounds, split horizontally

**1.** To prepare tzatziki, place 2 coffee filters in a strainer over a medium bowl. Place yogurt in the coffee filters. Cover and chill overnight. Discard liquid. Transfer yogurt to a medium bowl. Stir in cucumber, 1 clove garlic, and dillweed; season to taste with salt and pepper. Cover and refrigerate until ready to serve.

**2.** Preheat oven to 425° F. In a medium skillet cook lamb, onion, and 2 cloves garlic until meat is browned and onion is tender. Drain off fat. Stir in parsley, tomato paste, paprika, and oregano until combined. Transfer to a bowl; stir in tomatoes and feta cheese.

**3.** Place pita bread rounds, rough side up, on baking sheets. Bake for 5 minutes; Spoon lamb mixture evenly over pitas. Return to oven and bake 5 minutes more or until heated through. To serve, cut into wedges. Place a dollop of tzatziki on top of each. Serve warm. Makes 24 appetizers.

Each appetizer: 46 cal., 2 g total fat (1 g sat. fat), 9 mg chol., 86 mg sodium, 4 g carbo., 0 g fiber, 3 g pro. Daily Values: 2% vit. A, 4% vit. C, 3% calcium, 2% iron.

## Southwestern Lamb Shanks

**Prep:** 20 minutes  **Bake:** 3 hours

4  lamb foreshanks (about 6 lb.)
2  Tbsp. olive oil
1  14½-oz. can diced tomatoes and green chile peppers
1  15- to 16-oz. can black beans, rinsed and drained
1  large onion, coarsely chopped (1 cup)
½  cup water
1  4-oz. can diced green chile peppers
2  cloves garlic, minced
½  tsp. ground cumin
½  tsp. salt
½  tsp. ground black pepper
1  recipe Southwestern Polenta (below)
Snipped fresh cilantro (optional)

**1.** Preheat oven to 325° F. In a large Dutch oven brown half of the lamb shanks at a time on all sides in hot oil; remove from pan. Drain off fat. Remove pan from heat and let stand 1 minute. In Dutch oven combine undrained tomatoes, drained black beans, onion, water, undrained chile peppers, garlic, cumin, salt, and black pepper. Return to heat. Return lamb shanks to pan. Bring to boiling.

**2.** Bake, covered, for 3 hours or until meat is very tender. Transfer meat to a serving platter. Skim fat from sauce; discard fat. In Dutch oven bring tomato mixture to boiling over medium-high heat. Simmer, uncovered, about 10 minutes or until thickened. Serve sauce with meat and Southwestern Polenta. If desired, garnish with cilantro. Makes 8 servings.

**SOUTHWESTERN POLENTA:** In a large saucepan cook 1 cup chopped onion and 1 fresh jalapeño chile pepper, seeded and chopped (see page 89), in 2 tablespoons butter until onion is tender. Add 3 cups chicken broth and bring to simmering. In a bowl combine 1 cup yellow cornmeal, 1 cup water, 1 teaspoon ground cumin, ¼ teaspoon salt, and ¼ teaspoon cayenne pepper; gradually stir into simmering broth. Cook and stir until mixture comes to a boil. Reduce heat to low. Cook for 10 to 15 minutes or until mixture is thick, stirring occasionally. Remove from heat.

Stir in 1 cup shredded Monterey Jack cheese or Monterey Jack cheese with jalapeño peppers (4 ounces).

Each serving: 396 cal., 16 g total fat (7 g sat. fat), 116 mg chol., 1,115 mg sodium, 25 g carbo., 5 g fiber, 39 g pro. Daily Values: 11% vit. A, 14% vit. C, 18% calcium, 23% iron.

## Lamb with Fennel, Almonds, and Cherries

**Prep:** 30 minutes  **Cook:** 1 hour

1  Tbsp. olive oil
2  lb. lean boneless lamb shoulder, cut into 1-inch cubes
1  medium onion, cut into thin wedges
1  clove garlic, minced
2  tsp. grated fresh ginger or ½ tsp. ground ginger
½  tsp. fennel seeds, crushed
½  tsp. salt
⅛  to ¼ tsp. cayenne pepper
1¼  cups beef broth
1  medium fennel bulb, trimmed, cored, and thinly sliced
1  8-oz. carton plain yogurt
2  Tbsp. all-purpose flour
½  cup dried tart cherries or raisins
3  cups hot cooked rice
½  cup sliced almonds, toasted

**1.** In a 12-inch skillet heat olive oil over medium-high heat. Add half of the meat and cook until browned. Remove from skillet. Add remaining meat, onion, garlic, ginger, fennel seeds, salt, and cayenne pepper. Cook and stir until meat is browned. Return all meat to skillet. Add broth. Bring to boiling; reduce heat. Cover and simmer for 1 hour or until meat is tender, adding fennel the last 15 minutes.

**2.** In a small bowl stir together the yogurt and flour. Add to skillet. Cook and stir until thickened and bubbly. Cook and stir 1 minute more. Stir in cherries and season to taste with salt and ground black pepper. Serve over hot cooked rice and sprinkle with almonds. Makes 6 servings.

Each serving: 464 cal., 16 g total fat (4 g sat. fat), 98 mg chol., 502 mg sodium, 40 g carbo., 6 g fiber, 38 g pro. Daily Values: 1% vit. A, 5% vit. C, 14% calcium, 24% iron.

# FISH AND SEAFOOD

## Citrus-Glazed Salmon

**Prep:** 20 minutes **Bake:** 4 to 6 minutes per ½-inch thickness

| | |
|---|---|
| 1 2-lb. fresh or frozen salmon fillet, skin removed | 2 tsp. dry white wine |
| Salt | 1 tsp. grated fresh ginger |
| Ground black pepper | 1 tsp. Dijon-style mustard |
| ¾ cup orange marmalade | ¼ tsp. cayenne pepper |
| ¼ cup sliced green onions (2) | ⅛ tsp. five-spice powder |
| 1 clove garlic, minced | 3 Tbsp. sliced almonds, toasted |

**1.** Thaw fish, if frozen. Preheat oven to 450° F. Rinse fish; pat dry with paper towels. Measure thickest portion of fillet; season with salt and pepper. Place in a shallow baking pan; set aside.

**2.** In a small bowl stir together marmalade, green onions, garlic, wine, ginger, mustard, cayenne pepper, and five-spice powder. Spoon mixture over salmon.

**3.** Bake, uncovered, for 4 to 6 minutes per ½-inch thickness or until salmon flakes easily when tested with a fork. Transfer fish and glaze to a serving dish with a lip. Sprinkle with almonds. Makes 8 servings.

**Healthy** Each serving: 227 cal., 6 g total fat (1 g sat. fat), 59 mg chol., 170 mg sodium, 21 g carbo., 1 g fiber, 24 g pro. Daily Values: 3% vit. A, 4% vit. C, 4% calcium, 7% iron.

## Grouper with Tropical Salsa

**Prep:** 20 minutes **Bake:** 12 minutes

| | |
|---|---|
| 4 6- to 8-oz. fresh or frozen grouper or catfish fillets | ¼ cup lemon-flavored olive oil or olive oil |
| ½ cup all-purpose flour | 1 15¼-oz. can tropical fruit salad, drained and coarsely chopped |
| ½ cup finely chopped pistachio nuts or almonds | |
| 1 tsp. ground black pepper | 1 Tbsp. white balsamic vinegar |
| ½ tsp. salt | 1 Tbsp. lime juice |
| ½ tsp. dried tarragon, crushed | 1 Tbsp. snipped fresh cilantro |
| ½ tsp. dried basil, crushed | Lime wedges (optional) |
| ¼ cup milk | |

**1.** Thaw fish, if frozen. Preheat oven to 450° F. Grease a 15×10×1-inch baking pan; set aside. Rinse fish; pat fish dry with paper towels.

**2.** In a shallow dish combine flour, pistachios, pepper, salt, tarragon, and basil. Place milk in another shallow dish. Dip fish in the milk and then coat with the flour mixture, patting flour mixture onto fish, if necessary. Place in an even layer in the prepared pan. Drizzle fish with oil. Bake for 12 to 15 minutes or until fish flakes easily when tested with a fork.

**3.** Meanwhile, for salsa, in a small bowl combine the tropical fruit salad, vinegar, lime juice, and cilantro. Serve salsa with fish. If desired, accompany with lime wedges. Makes 4 servings.

Each serving: 490 cal., 23 g total fat (3 g sat. fat), 64 mg chol., 405 mg sodium, 33 g carbo., 3 g fiber, 39 g pro. Daily Values: 8% vit. A, 48% vit. C, 13% calcium, 21% iron.

## Spiced Salmon over Sautéed Spinach

**PREP:** 20 minutes **BAKE:** 12 minutes

4  6-oz. salmon fillets, about 1 inch thick
1  Tbsp. olive oil
1  tsp. garlic powder
1  tsp. dry mustard
1  tsp. ground cumin
1  tsp. paprika
½  tsp. salt
½  tsp. ground cinnamon
⅛  tsp. cayenne pepper
¼  cup mayonnaise
1  Tbsp. apricot nectar
2  tsp. grated fresh ginger or
   ½ tsp. ground ginger
1  clove garlic, minced
2  Tbsp. olive oil
1  10-oz. bag fresh spinach
Salt
Ground black pepper

**1.** Thaw fish, if frozen. Preheat oven to 425° F. Rinse fish; pat dry with paper towels. Brush fish with 1 tablespoon olive oil. For rub, in a small bowl combine garlic powder, mustard, cumin, paprika, ½ teaspoon salt, cinnamon, and cayenne. Rub mixture over flesh of fish. Place salmon, skin side down, on a baking sheet lined with foil. Bake for 12 to 15 minutes or until fish flakes easily when tested with a fork.

**2.** Meanwhile, in a small bowl whisk together mayonnaise, nectar, and ginger. Cover; chill in refrigerator until serving time.

**3.** In a 12-inch skillet cook the garlic in the 2 tablespoons oil over medium-high heat for 30 seconds. Add the spinach. Using metal tongs, cook and toss for 1 to 2 minutes or until spinach just begins to wilt. Remove from heat. Season spinach to taste with salt and pepper.

**4.** To serve, divide spinach among 4 individual plates. Using a wide metal spatula, slip spatula between skin and flesh of fish and lift fish from skin. Place the fish on top of the spinach mixture. Drizzle with mayonnaise mixture. Makes 4 servings.

Each serving: 520 cal., 40 g total fat (7 g sat. fat), 108 mg chol., 701 mg sodium, 3 g carbo., 7 g fiber, 37 g pro. Daily Values: 83% vit. A, 38% vit. C, 9% calcium, 32% iron.

## Summer Cioppino

**SOAK:** 45 minutes **PREP:** 30 minutes

12  oz. mussels or clams
1  cup salt
½  cup chopped leek
4  cloves garlic, minced
⅛  tsp. crushed red pepper
2  Tbsp. olive oil
1½  cups fish broth or vegetable broth
1  8-oz. can tomato sauce
¼  cup dry white wine
2  tsp. finely shredded lemon peel
   (set aside)
2  Tbsp. lemon juice
8  oz. cod, halibut, or other whitefish
   fillets, cut into 1-inch pieces
12  oz. shrimp, peeled and deveined
2  small zucchini or yellow summer
   squash, halved and sliced ½ inch
   thick
1  cup cherry tomatoes, halved
2  Tbsp. snipped fresh tarragon or
   oregano
Salt
Freshly ground black pepper
6  slices French or Italian bread

**1.** Scrub mussels or clams under cold running water. Pull beards from mussels, if present. In a large pot soak mussels or clams for 15 minutes in water to cover with ⅓ cup of the salt. Drain and rinse. Repeat 2 more times; set aside.

**2.** In a Dutch oven cook leek, garlic, and crushed red pepper in hot oil over medium heat for 4 minutes or until leeks are tender. Carefully stir in broth, tomato sauce, white wine, and lemon juice. Bring to boiling.

**3.** Add mussels or clams, fish, shrimp, squash, and tomatoes. Return just to boiling. Cover and simmer gently for 3 to 6 minutes or until fish flakes when tested with a fork and mussels or clams open. Discard any unopened mussels or clams.

**4.** Stir in tarragon and lemon peel. Season to taste with salt and pepper. Serve in shallow bowls with bread slices. Makes 6 servings.

Each serving: 256 cal., 8 g total fat (1 g sat. fat), 89 mg chol., 636 mg sodium, 21 g carbo., 2 g fiber, 24 g pro. Daily Values: 9% vit. A, 29% vit. C, 7% calcium, 21% iron.

## Spicy Grilled Catfish

**PREP:** 10 minutes **MARINATE:** 20 minutes
**GRILL:** 4 to 6 minutes per ½-inch thickness

4  6-oz. fresh or frozen catfish fillets
2  Tbsp. lime juice
2  Tbsp. red wine vinegar
1  Tbsp. olive oil
1  tsp. dry mustard
1  tsp. ground cumin
1  tsp. chili powder
½  tsp. cayenne pepper
⅛  tsp. salt
1  lime, cut into wedges
2  Tbsp. snipped fresh cilantro

**1.** Thaw fish, if frozen. Rinse fish; pat dry with paper towels. Place in a self-sealing plastic bag set in a shallow bowl. In a small bowl combine the lime juice, red wine vinegar, olive oil, dry mustard, cumin, chili powder, cayenne pepper, and salt. Pour over fish in bag. Close bag and marinate in the refrigerator for 20 minutes. Drain fish; discard marinade.

**2.** For a charcoal grill, grill fish on the greased rack of an uncovered grill directly over medium coals (allow 4 to 6 minutes per ½-inch thickness of fish) until fish flakes easily when tested with a fork, turning once halfway through grilling. (For a gas grill, preheat grill. Reduce heat to medium. Place fish on greased grill rack over heat. Cover and grill as above.) Serve fish with a wedge of lime and sprinkle with cilantro. Makes 4 servings.

Each serving: 274 cal., 17 g total fat (3 g sat. fat), 79 mg chol., 173 mg sodium, 3 g carbo., 1 g fiber, 27 g pro. Daily Values: 11% vit. A, 13% vit. C, 3% calcium, 7% iron.

# RHUBARB RECIPES

**PRIZE TESTED RECIPES® $400 WINNER**

ERIN HILL, KINDRED, N.D.

**PRIZE TESTED RECIPES® $200 WINNER**

ANITA L. DAVY, CAMANO ISLAND, WASH.

## Kid Friendly Rhubarb-Strawberry Ice Cream

**PREP:** 40 minutes **CHILL:** 4 hours **FREEZE:** 25 minutes plus 4 hours

| | |
|---|---|
| 3 cups sliced fresh rhubarb or frozen unsweetened sliced rhubarb (do not thaw frozen rhubarb) | 1 cup sliced fresh strawberries |
| 2 cups sugar | 3 cups miniature marshmallows |
| 2 cups water | 3 Tbsp. lemon juice |
| | 2 cups whipping cream |
| | Red food coloring (optional) |

**1.** In a 4-quart Dutch oven combine rhubarb, sugar, water, and strawberries. Bring to boiling; reduce heat. Simmer, uncovered, for 10 to 15 minutes or until fruit is very tender, stirring occasionally. Reduce heat. Add marshmallows and lemon juice. Cook and stir until marshmallows are melted. Transfer to a very large mixing bowl. Cover and chill in the refrigerator for 4 hours or overnight until completely chilled.

**2.** In a chilled large mixing bowl beat whipping cream with an electric mixer until soft peaks form. Fold whipped cream into chilled fruit mixture. If desired, stir in food coloring to desired color.

**3.** Freeze ice cream mixture in a 4- or 5-quart ice cream freezer according to the manufacturer's directions. Transfer to a freezer container. Cover and freeze about 4 hours or until firm. Makes about 10 cups (twenty 1/2-cup servings).

Each serving: 194 cal., 9 g total fat (6 g sat. fat), 33 mg chol., 20 mg sodium, 29 g carbo., 1 g fiber, 1 g pro. Daily Values: 7% vit. A, 11% vit. C, 3% calcium.

## Rhubarb Conserve

Present this conserve on an appetizer buffet for a sweet choice.

**PREP:** 20 minutes **COOK:** 30 minutes **CHILL:** 2 hours

| | |
|---|---|
| 3 cups sliced fresh rhubarb or frozen unsweetened sliced rhubarb (do not thaw frozen rhubarb) | 2 tsp. finely shredded orange peel |
| 1 cup sugar | 1/4 cup orange juice |
| 1/2 cup golden raisins or raisins | 2 Tbsp. water |
| | 1/8 tsp. salt |
| 2 tsp. finely shredded lemon peel | 1/2 cup chopped walnuts, toasted |
| 1/4 cup lemon juice | Brie or white cheddar cheese wedges |
| | Shortbread cookies |

**1.** In a medium saucepan combine rhubarb, sugar, raisins, lemon peel, lemon juice, orange peel, orange juice, water (omit water if using frozen rhubarb), and salt. Bring to boiling; reduce heat. Boil gently, uncovered, about 30 minutes or until mixture is thickened (should have about 1 3/4 cups). Transfer to a bowl.

**2.** Cover and chill in the refrigerator about 2 hours or until completely cool. Stir in nuts. Serve with cheese and shortbread cookies. Cover and store in refrigerator up to 2 weeks or freeze in freezer container up to 2 months. Makes about 2 cups.

Each tablespoon conserve: 48 cal., 1 g total fat (0 g sat. fat), 0 mg chol., 10 mg sodium, 9 g carbo., 1 g fiber, 0 g pro. Daily Values: 5% vit. C, 1% calcium, 1% iron.

## Rhubarb-Pecan Sticky Rolls

Serve these luscious rolls along with a cup of coffee for a mid-morning break.

**PREP:** 45 minutes **STAND:** 20 minutes
**RISE:** 30 minutes **BAKE:** 35 minutes
**COOL:** 25 minutes

4³/₄ to 5¹/₄ cups all-purpose flour
1 pkg. fast-rising active dry yeast
1¹/₂ cups water
¹/₃ cup granulated sugar
¹/₃ cup butter
1 tsp. salt
1 egg
1 cup packed brown sugar
¹/₂ cup butter, softened
2 cups chopped fresh rhubarb or frozen unsweetened rhubarb, thawed and drained
¹/₂ cup chopped pecans, toasted if desired
¹/₂ cup granulated sugar
1 tsp. ground cinnamon
3 Tbsp. butter, softened

**1.** In a very large mixing bowl stir together 2¹/₄ cups of the flour and the yeast; set aside. In a medium saucepan heat and stir the water, ¹/₃ cup granulated sugar, ¹/₃ cup butter, and the salt just until warm (120° F to 130° F) and butter almost melts. Add to flour mixture along with the egg. Beat with an electric mixer on low to medium speed for 30 seconds, scraping sides of bowl constantly. Beat on high speed for 3 minutes. Using a wooden spoon, stir in as much of the remaining flour as you can.

**2.** Turn dough out onto a lightly floured surface. Knead in enough of the remaining flour to make a soft dough that is smooth and elastic (3 to 5 minutes total). Shape dough into a ball; cover and let dough rest for 20 minutes.

**3.** Grease a 13×9×2-inch baking pan. In a medium bowl stir together brown sugar and ¹/₂ cup butter until combined. Gently stir in the rhubarb and pecans. Spread mixture evenly in prepared pan; set aside.

**4.** In a small bowl stir together ¹/₂ cup granulated sugar and the cinnamon; set aside. On a lightly floured surface roll dough to an 18×12-inch rectangle. Spread dough evenly with the 3 tablespoons butter. Sprinkle evenly with the sugar mixture. Roll up, starting from a long side. Seal seam. Using a sharp knife, cut roll into 16 even slices. Arrange rolls in prepared pan, placing them cut side down over rhubarb mixture.

**5.** Cover; let rise in a warm place until nearly double (about 30 minutes). Preheat oven to 350° F. Bake the rolls about 35 minutes or until golden brown. Cool in pan on a wire rack for 5 minutes. Invert onto serving platter or tray. Cool at least 20 minutes. Serve warm. Makes 16 rolls.

Each roll: 361 cal., 16 g total fat (7 g sat. fat), 46 mg chol., 245 mg sodium, 52 g carbo., 2 g fiber, 5 g pro. Daily Values: 8% vit. A, 2% vit. C, 4% calcium, 12% iron.

## Cheesy Custard Rhubarb Pie

**PREP:** 45 minutes **STAND:** 15 minutes
**BAKE:** 55 minutes **COOL:** 3 hours

²/₃ cup sugar
2 Tbsp. all-purpose flour
¹/₄ tsp. ground mace or nutmeg
¹/₈ tsp. salt
2 cups sliced fresh rhubarb or frozen unsweetened sliced rhubarb, thawed and drained
1 recipe Pastry for Lattice-Top Pie (right)
1 3-oz. pkg. cream cheese, softened
¹/₂ cup sugar
¹/₂ cup half-and-half or light cream
3 eggs, beaten
¹/₃ cup sliced almonds, toasted

**1.** Preheat oven to 375° F. In a large bowl combine ²/₃ cup sugar, flour, mace, and salt. Add rhubarb; toss to coat. Let stand 15 minutes. Meanwhile, prepare and roll out Pastry for Lattice-Top Pie. Line a 9-inch pie plate with half of the pastry.

**2.** In a mixing bowl beat softened cream cheese and ¹/₂ cup sugar until light and fluffy; beat in half-and-half. Gradually stir in eggs until smooth. Spoon rhubarb mixture into pastry-lined pie plate. Pour egg mixture over rhubarb. Top with nuts.

**3.** Top with lattice crust. Cover edge of pie with foil. Bake for 30 minutes. Remove foil; bake for 25 to 30 minutes more or until top is golden and bottom crust is done. Cool. Makes 8 servings.

**PASTRY FOR LATTICE-TOP PIE:** In a medium mixing bowl stir together 2¹/₄ cups all-purpose flour and ³/₄ teaspoon salt. Using a pastry blender, cut in ²/₃ cup shortening until pieces are pea size. Using a total of 8 to 10 tablespoons cold water, sprinkle 1 tablespoon of the water over part of the mixture; gently toss with a fork. Push moistened dough to side of bowl. Repeat, using 1 tablespoon water at a time, until all the dough is moistened. Divide in half. Form each half into a ball.

On a lightly floured surface flatten 1 dough ball. Roll from center to edge into a circle 12 inches in diameter. Transfer pastry to a 9-inch pie plate, being careful to avoid stretching pastry. Trim bottom pastry to ¹/₂ inch beyond edge of pie plate. Roll remaining dough into a circle about 12 inches in diameter. For lattice top, cut pastry into ¹/₂-inch-wide strips. Weave strips over filling in a lattice pattern. Press ends of strips into bottom pastry rim. Fold bottom pastry over strip ends. Seal and crimp edge.

Each serving: 508 cal., 28 g total fat (9 g sat. fat), 97 mg chol., 318 mg sodium, 58 g carbo., 2 g fiber, 9 g pro. Daily Values: 7% vit. A, 4% vit. C, 8% calcium, 13% iron.

# COOKING WITH GINGER

**PRIZE TESTED RECIPES® $400 WINNER**

DIANE HALFERTY, CORPUS CHRISTI, TEXAS

**PRIZE TESTED RECIPES® $200 WINNER**

PAT GREGORY JAMES, FLORENCE, ORE.

## Gingered Lemon Scones

**PREP:** 20 minutes  **BAKE:** 30 minutes  **COOL:** 15 minutes

| | |
|---|---|
| 2 cups all-purpose flour | 3/4 cup buttermilk |
| 1/4 cup granulated sugar | 1 Tbsp. grated fresh ginger |
| 1 Tbsp. baking powder | 1/4 cup lemon curd |
| 1/4 tsp. salt | Coarse sugar or |
| 1/3 cup butter | granulated sugar |

**1.** Preheat oven to 375° F. Lightly grease a baking sheet; set aside. In medium bowl stir together flour, 1/4 cup sugar, baking powder, and salt. Using a pastry blender, cut in butter until mixture resembles coarse crumbs. Make a well in the center of flour mixture; set aside. In a small bowl stir together buttermilk and ginger. Add to flour mixture. Stir with a fork just until moistened.

**2.** Turn dough out onto a lightly floured surface. Knead dough by folding and gently pressing dough for 10 to 12 strokes or until nearly smooth. Divide dough in half. Pat or lightly roll 1 of the dough halves to an 8-inch circle. Place on prepared baking sheet. Spread dough circle with lemon curd to within 1/2 inch of the edges. Pat or roll remaining half of dough to an 8-inch circle. Place on top of dough on baking sheet. Pinch edges to seal. Sprinkle top with coarse or granulated sugar. Using a sharp knife, score top of the dough into 8 wedges, cutting 1/4 inch deep.

**3.** Bake for 30 to 35 minutes or until golden brown. Cool 15 minutes on baking sheet. Remove to a serving plate. Cut into wedges. Serve warm. Makes 8 scones.

Each scone: 245 cal., 9 g total fat (5 g sat. fat), 30 mg chol., 337 mg sodium, 31 g carbo., 2 g fiber, 4 g pro. Daily Values: 6% vit A, 12% calcium, 8% iron.

## Ginger-Spiced Cucumbers

Accompany a grilled or roasted pork loin with this colorful relish.

**PREP:** 15 minutes  **MARINATE:** 30 minutes

| | |
|---|---|
| 1/4 cup seasoned rice vinegar | 1 large English cucumber |
| 1/4 cup mirin (sweet cooking rice wine) | (about 12 oz.), peeled, if desired, and thinly sliced |
| 1/4 cup packed brown sugar | 1/4 cup thinly sliced red onion |
| 2 tsp. grated fresh ginger | |

**1.** In a medium bowl combine rice vinegar, mirin, brown sugar, and ginger. Stir in cucumber and onion slices. Cover and chill in the refrigerator for 30 minutes. Serve with a slotted spoon. Makes 4 to 6 side-dish servings.

Healthy Each serving: 115 cal., 0 g total fat (0 g sat. fat), 0 mg chol., 173 mg sodium, 30 g carbo., 1 g fiber, 1 g pro. Daily Values: 4% vit A, 8% vit. C, 3% calcium, 3% iron.

## Orange-Ginger Fruit Salad

**PREP:** 30 minutes **CHILL:** 1 hour

1/3 cup light mayonnaise dressing
1/3 cup light dairy sour cream
1 Tbsp. white balsamic vinegar
1 tsp. finely shredded orange peel
2 Tbsp. orange juice
3/4 tsp. ground ginger
2 carambola (star fruit), halved and sliced
2 oranges, peeled and sectioned
2 kiwifruit, peeled and chopped
1 large mango or papaya, peeled, seeded, and chopped
1/2 of a small honeydew melon, peeled and cubed
1 recipe Candied Gingered Macadamia Nuts (below)

**1.** For dressing, in a small mixing bowl combine mayonnaise dressing, sour cream, vinegar, orange peel, orange juice, and ginger.

**2.** In a large bowl combine carambola, orange sections, kiwifruit, mango, and honeydew melon; fold in dressing. Cover and chill in the refrigerator for 1 to 2 hours. (Do not chill any longer than 2 hours, as fruit will water out.) Just before serving, sprinkle with Candied Gingered Macadamia Nuts. Makes 12 servings.

**CANDIED GINGERED MACADAMIA NUTS:** Line a small baking sheet with foil. Butter foil; set aside. In a small skillet combine 1/2 cup coarsely chopped macadamia nuts, 3 tablespoons granulated sugar, 1 tablespoon butter, and 1/4 teaspoon ground ginger. Cook over medium-high heat, shaking skillet occasionally, until sugar begins to melt. Do not stir. Reduce heat to low. Continue cooking until sugar is golden brown, stirring occasionally. Remove skillet from heat. Pour nut mixture onto the prepared baking sheet. Cool completely. Break into clusters.

Each serving: 138 cal., 9 g total fat (2 g sat. fat), 7 mg chol., 56 mg sodium, 15 g carbo., 2 g fiber, 1 g pro. Daily Values: 5% vit. A, 54% vit. C, 2% calcium, 2% iron.

## Triple-Ginger Chicken Skillet

*Fast!* **PREP:** 20 minutes **COOK:** 10 minutes

2 Tbsp. all-purpose flour
1/2 tsp. ground ginger
1/2 tsp. salt
1/8 tsp. ground black pepper
4 medium skinless, boneless chicken breast halves (1 1/4 to 1 1/2 lb.)
2 Tbsp. cooking oil
1 Tbsp. butter
1 8-oz. can crushed pineapple (juice pack), undrained
1/2 cup ginger preserves*
Dash salt
1/4 cup sliced almonds, toasted
1 Tbsp. finely chopped crystallized ginger
2 cups hot cooked rice

**1.** In a shallow dish stir together flour, ground ginger, 1/2 teaspoon salt, and pepper. Place a chicken breast half between 2 pieces of plastic wrap. Using the flat side of a meat mallet, pound chicken lightly to about 1/2 inch thick. Remove plastic wrap. Repeat with remaining chicken breast halves. Lightly coat chicken pieces on both sides with flour mixture; shake off excess.

**2.** In a large skillet heat oil and butter over medium-high heat. Add chicken; cook about 6 minutes or until evenly browned, turning once. In a small bowl stir together undrained pineapple, preserves, and dash salt. Carefully add pineapple mixture to skillet. Reduce heat to medium-low. Cook, uncovered, for 4 to 5 minutes more or until pineapple mixture is slightly thickened and chicken is no longer pink, turning chicken pieces once to coat evenly with pineapple mixture.

**3.** Transfer chicken to a serving platter; spoon pineapple mixture from skillet over chicken. Sprinkle with almonds and crystallized ginger. Serve with hot cooked rice. Makes 4 servings.

**\*NOTE:** If you can't locate ginger preserves, substitute 1/2 cup orange marmalade and 1 tablespoon grated fresh ginger.

Each serving: 558 cal., 17 g total fat (4 g sat. fat), 90 mg chol., 439 mg sodium, 63 g carbo., 2 g fiber, 38 g pro. Daily Values: 3% vit. A, 15% vit. C, 6% calcium, 16% iron.

## Pumpkin-Ginger-Raisin Cake

**PREP:** 15 minutes **BAKE:** 30 minutes
**COOL:** 1 hour

2 cups all-purpose flour
1 Tbsp. pumpkin pie spice or apple pie spice
2 tsp. baking powder
1 tsp. salt
1/2 tsp. baking soda
1 cup canned pumpkin
1 cup packed brown sugar
2/3 cup butter, melted
1/2 cup apple cider or apple juice
2 eggs, beaten
1 tsp. vanilla
1/2 tsp. finely shredded orange peel
1/2 cup raisins
2 Tbsp. chopped crystallized ginger
Sifted powdered sugar (optional)

**1.** Preheat oven to 350° F. Grease a 9×9×2-inch baking pan; set aside. In a large bowl combine flour, pumpkin pie spice, baking powder, salt, and baking soda; make a well in the center. Set aside.

**2.** In a medium bowl stir together pumpkin, brown sugar, butter, apple cider, eggs, vanilla, and orange peel. Add the pumpkin mixture all at once to the flour mixture. Stir just until moistened. Stir in raisins and crystallized ginger. Spread batter in prepared pan.

**3.** Bake for 30 to 35 minutes or until a wooden toothpick inserted near center comes out clean. Cool cake in pan on wire rack for 10 minutes. Remove cake from pan. Let cool completely. If desired, sprinkle with powdered sugar before serving. Makes 9 servings.

Each serving: 380 cal., 16 g total fat (8 g sat. fat), 85 mg chol., 514 mg sodium, 56 g carbo., 2 g fiber, 5 g pro. Daily Values: 95% vit. A, 3% vit. C, 7% calcium, 14% iron.

# CALORIE-SAVING RECIPES

PRIZE TESTED RECIPES® $400 WINNER

SYLVIA LAYMON, OAKLAND, CALIF.

PRIZE TESTED RECIPES® $200 WINNER

JUDY DAILEY, QUINCY, CALIF.

## Calorie-Trimmed Potato Salad

**PREP:** 45 minutes **CHILL:** 4 hours

| | |
|---|---|
| 3 lb. round red or Yukon Gold potatoes | 1 cup chopped celery |
| 1 12.3-oz. pkg. soft, silken-style tofu (fresh bean curd) | 1 medium red sweet pepper, chopped |
| 3 Tbsp. lemon juice | 3 hard-cooked eggs, peeled and coarsely chopped |
| 1 Tbsp. yellow mustard | ½ cup sliced green onions (4) |
| 1 clove garlic, minced | ½ cup chopped dill pickles |
| 1 tsp. salt | Salt and ground black pepper |
| 2 Tbsp. olive oil | Milk or pickle juice |

**1.** In a 4-quart Dutch oven place potatoes and enough lightly salted water to cover. Bring to boiling; reduce heat. Simmer, covered, for 20 to 25 minutes or until potatoes are just tender. Drain well; cool slightly. Peel and cube the potatoes.

**2.** Meanwhile, for dressing, in a food processor or blender combine tofu, lemon juice, mustard, garlic, and 1 teaspoon salt. Process or blend until smooth. With the processor or blender running, add oil in a thin, steady stream. When necessary, stop processor or blender and scrape down sides. Set aside.

**3.** In a very large bowl combine cubed potatoes, celery, sweet pepper, eggs, onions, and pickles. Add dressing, tossing lightly to coat. Season with additional salt and pepper. Cover and chill for 4 to 24 hours. Before serving, add milk or pickle juice, 1 tablespoon at a time, to reach desired consistency. Makes 14 servings.

Healthy Each serving: 113 cal., 4 g total fat (1 g sat. fat), 46 mg chol., 286 mg sodium, 16 g carbo., 2 g fiber, 4 g pro. Daily Values: 12% vit. A, 49% vit. C, 3% calcium, 6% iron.

## Savory Stuffed Portobellos

**START TO FINISH:** 50 minutes

| | |
|---|---|
| 1 medium onion, chopped (½ cup) | 1 6-oz. jar marinated artichoke hearts |
| 4 cloves garlic, minced | 6 medium portobello mushroom caps (about 4 inches in diameter) |
| 1 Tbsp. olive oil | |
| 1 6.75- to 8-oz. pkg. rice pilaf with lentil mix | ¼ cup finely shredded Parmesan cheese |

**1.** Preheat oven to 350° F. In a medium saucepan cook onion and garlic in hot oil over medium heat until onion is tender. In the same saucepan with the onion and garlic, prepare rice pilaf mix according to package directions.

**2.** Meanwhile, drain artichoke hearts, reserving marinade. Coarsely chop artichokes; set aside. Cut off mushroom stems even with caps; discard stems. Remove the gills, if desired. Brush mushrooms with some of the reserved marinade; discard any remaining marinade. Place mushroom caps, stemmed sides up, in an ungreased shallow baking pan.

**3.** Bake, uncovered, for 15 to 20 minutes or until mushrooms are tender. Transfer to individual plates, stemmed sides up. Stir artichoke hearts and cheese into rice mixture; spoon into baked mushroom caps. Makes 6 main-dish servings.

Each serving: 288 cal., 14 g total fat (5 g sat. fat), 16 mg chol., 817 mg sodium, 31 g carbo., 4 g fiber, 20 g pro. Daily Values: 19% vit. A, 14% vit. C, 32% calcium, 19% iron.

## Pasta and Soy Bean Salad

**PREP:** 20 minutes **CHILL:** 2 hours

8   oz. dried radiatore pasta
1   12-oz. pkg. frozen shelled sweet
    soybeans (edamame) (2³/4 cups)
1   green sweet pepper, cut into
    bite-size pieces
³/4  cup cherry tomatoes, halved
¹/2  cup sliced green onions (4)
¹/2  cup sliced radishes
³/4  cup bottled reduced-calorie
    cucumber ranch salad dressing
¹/4  cup chopped peanuts or honey-
    roasted peanuts

**1.** Cook pasta according to package directions, adding the soybeans to the boiling water along with the pasta. Drain.

**2.** In a large bowl combine drained pasta mixture, sweet pepper, tomatoes, green onions, and radishes; toss with salad dressing. Cover and chill for 2 to 24 hours. To serve, sprinkle with peanuts. Makes 6 main-dish servings.

Healthy  Each serving: 313 cal., 10 g total fat (1 g sat. fat), 0 mg chol., 477 mg sodium, 41 g carbo., 8 g fiber, 14 g pro. Daily Values: 7% vit. A, 56% vit. C, 8% calcium, 17% iron.

## Wheat Berry-Cabbage Salad

**PREP:** 20 minutes **COOK:** 1 hour
**CHILL:** 2 hours

¹/2  cup wheat berries (soft wheat)
¹/2  cup apple-cranberry juice
3   Tbsp. cooking oil
2   Tbsp. cider vinegar
1   tsp. Dijon-style mustard
¹/4  tsp. salt
¹/4  tsp. ground black pepper
1   10-oz. pkg. shredded cabbage
1   large tart apple, cored, cut into thin
    slices, and slices halved
¹/3  cup thinly sliced green onions
¹/4  cup slivered almonds, toasted

**1.** In a medium saucepan stir together uncooked wheat berries and 2 cups water. Bring to boiling; reduce heat. Cover and simmer for 1 hour. Drain and rinse with cold water. Drain again.

**2.** Meanwhile, for dressing, in a large bowl stir together the apple-cranberry juice, oil, vinegar, mustard, salt, and pepper. Add cooked wheat berries. Cover and chill for 2 to 24 hours.

**3.** Stir cabbage, apple, and green onions into wheat berry mixture. Toss to mix. Sprinkle with almonds. Serve immediately. Makes 8 side-dish servings.

Healthy  Each serving: 136 cal., 8 g total fat (1 g sat. fat), 0 mg chol., 96 mg sodium, 16 g carbo., 3 g fiber, 3 g pro. Daily Values: 1% vit. A, 30% vit. C, 4% calcium, 5% iron.

## Spa Chicken

**PREP:** 30 minutes **COOK:** 20 minutes

4   medium skinless, boneless chicken
    breast halves (1¹/4 to 1¹/2 lb.)
1   Tbsp. butter or olive oil
2   cups mushrooms, sliced (crimini,
    baby portobello, or button)
2   cups sliced leeks
1   shallot, finely chopped (2 Tbsp.)
³/4  cup reduced-sodium chicken broth
2   Tbsp. Worcestershire sauce for
    chicken
1   9-oz. pkg. frozen artichoke hearts,
    thawed
2   Tbsp. fat-free dairy sour cream
4   tsp. all-purpose flour
1   Tbsp. Dijon-style mustard
¹/2  cup chopped roma tomatoes
2   Tbsp. snipped fresh Italian parsley

**1.** Season chicken with salt and ground black pepper. In a large nonstick skillet brown chicken in hot butter over medium heat for 2 minutes on each side. Remove from skillet; add mushrooms, leeks, and shallot. Cook and stir until mushrooms are tender. Return chicken to skillet; add ¹/2 cup of the broth, Worcestershire sauce, and artichoke hearts. Bring to boiling; reduce heat. Simmer, covered, 10 minutes or until no pink remains in chicken (170° F).

**2.** Meanwhile, in a bowl combine sour cream, flour, mustard, and remaining ¹/4 cup chicken broth. Remove chicken and vegetables to serving platter with a slotted spoon; cover and keep warm. Stir sour cream mixture into skillet; cook and stir until thickened and bubbly. Cook and

stir 1 minute more. Spoon sauce over chicken. Sprinkle with tomatoes and parsley. Makes 4 servings.

Each serving: 292 cal., 7 g total fat (3 g sat. fat), 91 mg chol., 586 mg sodium, 20 g carbo., 5 g fiber, 38 g pro. Daily Values: 12% vit. A, 30% vit. C, 10% calcium, 16% iron.

## Pumpkin Spice Muffins

**PREP:** 20 minutes **BAKE:** 18 minutes
**COOL:** 5 minutes

    Nonstick cooking spray
1¹/4 cups all-purpose flour
¹/2  cup whole wheat flour
3   Tbsp. toasted wheat germ
1   Tbsp. pumpkin pie spice or apple pie
    spice
2   tsp. baking powder
³/4  tsp. salt
¹/4  tsp. baking soda
2   eggs, lightly beaten
1   cup canned pumpkin
1   cup buttermilk
¹/3  cup packed brown sugar
¹/4  cup cooking oil
¹/4  cup quick-cooking rolled oats

**1.** Preheat oven to 375° F. Lightly coat twelve 2¹/2-inch muffin cups with cooking spray; set aside.

**2.** In a large bowl combine flours, wheat germ, pumpkin pie spice, baking powder, salt, and baking soda; set aside.

**3.** In another bowl combine eggs, pumpkin, buttermilk, brown sugar, and oil; add pumpkin mixture all at once to flour mixture. Stir just until moistened.

**4.** Divide batter evenly among prepared muffin cups. Sprinkle with oats. Bake for 18 to 20 minutes or until a wooden toothpick inserted near the centers comes out clean. Cool in muffin cups on a wire rack for 5 minutes. Remove from muffin cups; serve warm. Makes 12 muffins.

Each muffin: 167 cal., 6 g total fat (1 g sat. fat), 36 mg chol., 275 mg sodium, 24 g carbo., 2 g fiber, 5 g pro. Daily Values: 91% vit. A, 2% vit. C, 9% calcium, 9% iron.

# RIBS

FRANK HEALEY, WASHINGTON, D.C.

AMY YUDKIN-MERRITT, WOLCOTT, CONN.

## Peachy Pork Spareribs

**PREP:** 15 minutes **CHILL:** overnight **COOK:** 50 minutes **GRILL:** 1½ hours

| | | | |
|---|---|---|---|
| 1 | recipe Five-Spice Rub | ⅓ | cup reduced-sodium soy |
| 6 | lb. meaty pork spareribs | | sauce |
| 3 | cups peach nectar | ¼ | cup rice vinegar |
| 1 | 15-oz. can tomato sauce | 2 | to 3 tsp. bottled hot |
| 1 | cup finely chopped onion | | pepper sauce |

**1.** Prepare rub; sprinkle over surface of ribs. Place ribs on a tray; cover. Refrigerate overnight. For a charcoal grill, arrange medium-hot coals around a drip pan. Test for medium heat above pan. Place ribs, bone side down, on grill rack over drip pan. Cover and grill for 1½ to 1¾ hours; brush with sauce during last 15 minutes of grilling (see Step 2 for sauce). Add coals as necessary to maintain heat. (For a gas grill, preheat grill. Reduce heat to medium. Adjust for indirect cooking. Place ribs on rack in a roasting pan, place on grill, and grill as above. After 1 hour, carefully drain off liquid in pan and discard.)

**2.** Meanwhile, in a large saucepan stir together remaining ingredients. Bring to boiling; reduce heat. Simmer, uncovered, about 50 minutes or until thickened, stirring occasionally (should have about 3 cups). Brush about two-thirds of the sauce over both sides of the ribs during last 15 minutes of grilling. Pass remaining sauce with ribs. Makes 6 to 8 servings.

**FIVE-SPICE RUB:** In bowl combine ½ cup packed brown sugar, 2 tablespoons salt, 1 tablespoon dry mustard, 2 teaspoons five-spice powder, and 1 teaspoon *each* black pepper and garlic powder.

Each serving: 977 cal., 55 g total fat (22 g sat. fat), 228 mg chol., 3,407 mg sodium, 46 g carbo., 1 g fiber, 66 g pro. Daily Values: 4% vit. A, 39% vit. C, 13% calcium, 25% iron.

## Honey 'n' Orange Back Ribs

**PREP:** 40 minutes **COOK:** 1 hour **MARINATE:** 4 hours
**GRILL:** 25 minutes

| | | | |
|---|---|---|---|
| 5 | to 6 lb. pork baby back ribs (loin back ribs), cut into 3- to 4-rib portions | ¼ | cup red wine vinegar |
| | | 2 | tsp. onion powder |
| | | 2 | tsp. finely shredded |
| 1 | 29-oz. can tomato sauce | | orange peel |
| ⅔ | cup honey | 1½ | tsp. garlic powder |
| ½ | cup finely chopped onion | 1½ | tsp. ground ginger |
| ¼ | cup soy sauce | 1 | tsp. barbecue seasoning |

**1.** Place ribs in Dutch oven. Add water to cover. Bring to boiling; reduce heat. Simmer, covered, 1 hour. Drain ribs; cool.

**2.** Meanwhile, for marinade sauce, in a large saucepan combine remaining ingredients. Bring to boiling; reduce heat. Simmer, uncovered, for 10 minutes; stir occasionally. Remove saucepan from heat; cool sauce completely. Place an extra-large self-sealing plastic bag in a large bowl. Place ribs in bag. Pour about 3 cups of the cooled sauce over the ribs; seal bag. Turn ribs in bag to coat. (Cover and refrigerate remaining sauce to serve with ribs.) Refrigerate ribs for 4 to 24 hours, turning bag occasionally.

**3.** To grill ribs, remove ribs from marinade, reserving marinade to brush on during grilling. Place ribs on the rack of an uncovered grill directly over medium coals for 25 to 30 minutes, turning and basting occasionally with some of the reserved marinade. Discard any remaining marinade. In a small saucepan heat the refrigerated sauce and pass with ribs. Makes 6 servings.

Each serving: 1,024 cal., 65 g total fat (25 g sat. fat), 261 mg chol., 1,304 mg sodium, 31 g carbo., 1 g fiber, 74 g pro. Daily Values: 1% vit. A, 3% vit. C, 13% calcium, 25% iron.

## Curried Country-Style Ribs

**PREP:** 20 minutes **BAKE:** 1³/₄ hours

- 3 lb. pork country-style ribs
- 1 large onion, chopped (1 cup)
- 6 cloves garlic, minced
- 1 Tbsp. curry powder
- 2 Tbsp. olive oil
- 1 13½-oz. can unsweetened coconut milk
- 1 14-oz. can chicken broth
- 1 tsp. Louisiana hot sauce
- ¼ tsp. anise seeds, crushed
- 1 Tbsp. honey
- 1 Tbsp. snipped fresh mint

**1.** Preheat oven to 350° F. Place ribs in a shallow roasting pan. Sprinkle lightly with salt and ground black pepper. Bake, uncovered, for 1 hour. Drain off fat.

**2.** In a large skillet cook onion, garlic, and curry powder in hot oil until onion is tender. Stir in coconut milk, broth, hot sauce, anise seeds, and ¼ teaspoon ground black pepper. Bring to boiling; reduce heat. Boil gently, uncovered, 15 to 20 minutes or until reduced to 1³/₄ cups.

**3.** Spoon ½ cup of the sauce over ribs. Bake, covered, 30 minutes. Uncover. Spoon on an additional ½ cup sauce; turn ribs to coat. Bake, uncovered, 15 minutes more or until ribs are tender. Heat remaining sauce; stir in honey and mint. Pass sauce with ribs. Makes 4 servings.

Each serving: 583 cal., 40 g total fat (22 g sat. fat), 121 mg chol., 696 mg sodium, 14 g carbo., 1 g fiber, 40 g pro. Daily Values: 1% vit. A, 10% vit. C, 7% calcium, 22% iron.

## Glazed Loin Back Ribs

**PREP:** 15 minutes **BAKE:** 1³/₄ hours

- 5 lb. pork loin back ribs
- ⅓ cup apricot preserves
- ⅓ cup hibachi grill sauce
- ¼ cup dark beer
- ¼ cup bottled salsa
- ¼ cup full-flavored molasses
- ¼ cup bottled chili sauce
- 2 Tbsp. honey
- 1 tsp. ground ginger
- 1 tsp. garlic powder

**1.** Preheat oven to 350° F. Cut ribs into 2-rib portions. Place ribs, bone side down, in a large roasting pan. Cover and bake for 1¼ hours.

**2.** Meanwhile, in a bowl stir together remaining ingredients; pour over ribs. Bake, uncovered, 30 to 45 minutes more or until ribs are very tender; spoon sauce over ribs occasionally. Makes 6 servings.

Each serving: 528 cal., 16 g total fat (6 g sat. fat), 112 mg chol., 722 mg sodium, 40 g carbo., 1 g fiber, 52 g pro. Daily Values: 2% vit. A, 8% vit. C, 5% calcium, 13% iron.

## Sesame-Molasses Glazed Ribs

**PREP:** 30 minutes **COOK:** 45 minutes

**ROAST:** 20 minutes or **GRILL:** 15 minutes

- 3 lb. meaty pork spareribs
- ⅓ cup finely chopped onion
- 1 clove garlic, minced
- 1 Tbsp. cooking oil
- 1½ tsp. curry powder
- ⅓ cup ketchup
- ¼ cup mild-flavored molasses
- 2 Tbsp. frozen orange juice concentrate, thawed
- 2 Tbsp. Dijon-style mustard
- 1 Tbsp. Worcestershire sauce
- 2 Tbsp. sesame seeds, toasted

**1.** Cut ribs into serving-size pieces. Place ribs in a 4- to 6-quart Dutch oven. Add enough water to cover. Bring to boiling; reduce heat. Simmer, covered, for 45 minutes or until ribs are tender; drain.

**2.** Meanwhile, in a medium saucepan cook onion and garlic in hot oil until onion is tender but not brown. Stir in curry powder; cook and stir for 1 minute. Add ketchup, molasses, orange juice concentrate, mustard, and Worcestershire sauce. Bring to boiling; reduce heat. Simmer, uncovered, for 15 minutes, stirring occasionally. Remove from heat. Stir in 1 tablespoon of the sesame seeds.

**OVEN METHOD:** Preheat oven to 350° F. Place ribs, bone side down, in a shallow roasting pan. Spoon on sauce. Roast, uncovered, for 20 to 30 minutes or until ribs are tender and glazed, spooning sauce over ribs occasionally. Sprinkle with remaining sesame seeds before serving.

**GRILL METHOD:** For a charcoal grill, place ribs on the rack of an uncovered grill directly over medium coals for 15 to 20 minutes, brushing with sauce and turning occasionally, until ribs are tender and glazed. (For a gas grill, preheat grill. Reduce heat to medium. Place ribs on grill rack over heat. Cover and grill as above.) Sprinkle with remaining sesame seeds before serving. Makes 4 servings.

Each serving: 727 cal., 50 g total fat (18 g sat. fat), 159 mg chol., 611 mg sodium, 25 g carbo., 1 g fiber, 38 g pro. Daily Values: 5% vit. A, 29% vit. C, 11% calcium, 20% iron.

## Ribs in Berry Chipotle Sauce

**PREP:** 15 minutes

**COOK:** Low 8 hours; High 4 hours

- 2 medium onions, sliced and separated into rings (1 cup)
- 3 lb. pork country-style ribs
- 1 18-oz. jar seedless raspberry preserves (1½ cups)
- 1 canned chipotle pepper in adobo sauce
- ⅓ cup apple cider or apple juice
- 2 Tbsp. balsamic vinegar

**1.** Place onions in a 4- to 5-quart slow cooker. Top with ribs. In blender combine preserves, chipotle pepper in adobo sauce, cider, and vinegar; cover and process until smooth. Reserve 1¼ cups for sauce; cover and chill until needed. Pour remaining raspberry mixture over ribs in cooker. Cover and cook on low-heat setting for 8 to 10 hours or on high-heat setting for 4 to 5 hours.

**2.** For sauce, in a medium saucepan bring reserved raspberry mixture to boiling; reduce heat. Simmer, uncovered, for 5 minutes. Remove ribs and onions to serving dish; discard cooking liquid. Spoon some of the sauce over ribs and onions. Pass remaining sauce. Serves 4 to 6.

Each serving: 689 cal., 15 g total fat (5 g sat. fat), 121 mg chol., 211 mg sodium, 97 g carbo., 2 g fiber, 38 g pro. Daily Values: 25% vit. C, 8% calcium, 16% iron.

# FROZEN DRINKS

CAROL GILLESPIE, CHAMBERSBURG, PA.

MARY IPPEL, NEW CASTLE, IND.

## Raspberry Cheesecake Shake

**Fast!**   **PREP:** 10 minutes

- 1 12-oz. pkg. frozen unsweetened red raspberries, thawed
- 1 3-oz. pkg. cream cheese, softened
- ¼ tsp. almond extract
- 1 quart vanilla ice cream, softened
- 2 12-oz. cans or bottles cream soda
- Fresh raspberries (optional)

**1.** In a blender combine the raspberries, cream cheese, almond extract, half the ice cream, and ½ cup of the cream soda. Cover and blend until smooth.

**2.** Divide blended mixture among 6 tall 16-ounce chilled glasses. Add a scoop of the remaining ice cream to each drink. Top each drink with remaining cream soda. If desired, garnish with fresh raspberries. Serve immediately. Makes 6 servings.

Each serving: 305 cal., 15 g total fat (9 g sat. fat), 54 mg chol., 130 mg sodium, 36 g carbo., 2 g fiber, 4 g pro. Daily Values: 11% vit. A, 3% vit. C, 12% calcium, 2% iron.

## Apricot Slush

**PREP:** 15 minutes   **FREEZE:** 24 hours   **STAND:** 30 minutes

- 1 46-oz. bottle apricot nectar
- 3 cups pineapple juice
- 1 12-oz. can frozen orange juice concentrate, thawed
- ⅓ cup frozen lemonade concentrate, thawed
- 1 2-liter bottle ginger ale, chilled
- Apricot slices (optional)

**1.** In a 3-quart plastic freezer container combine apricot nectar, pineapple juice, orange juice concentrate, and lemonade concentrate. Seal and freeze at least 24 hours or up to 1 week.

**2.** To serve, let frozen mixture stand at room temperature for 30 minutes. Scrape a large spoon across juice mixture into a slush. For each serving, fill a glass two-thirds full with slush. Carefully add ginger ale, stirring gently to mix. Garnish with apricot slice.

Makes about 24 servings.

Healthy   Each serving: 115 cal., 0 g total fat (0 g sat. fat), 0 mg chol., 9 mg sodium, 29 g carbo., 1 g fiber, 1 g pro. Daily Values: 17% vit. A, 52% vit. C, 2% calcium, 3% iron.

## Chocolate Mousse Shake

 **PREP:** 10 minutes **STAND:** 5 minutes

- 1½ cups milk
- 1 4-serving-size pkg. instant chocolate pudding mix
- 3 Tbsp. unsweetened cocoa powder
- 1 tsp. vanilla
- 3 cups chocolate ice cream
- 1 recipe Sweetened Whipped Cream (below) (optional)

**1.** In a blender combine milk, pudding mix, cocoa powder, and vanilla. Cover and blend 1 minute. Gradually add ice cream, blending until smooth after each addition.

**2.** Divide among four 8-ounce glasses. Let stand 5 minutes to thicken slightly. If desired, top with whipped cream. Serves 4.

**SWEETENED WHIPPED CREAM:** In a small chilled bowl whisk ¼ cup whipping cream, 2 teaspoons sugar, and ¼ teaspoon vanilla until soft peaks form.

Each serving: 368 cal., 14 g total fat (8 g sat. fat), 41 mg chol., 478 mg sodium, 56 g carbo., 2 g fiber, 8 g pro. Daily Values: 11% vit. A, 3% vit. C, 27% calcium, 11% iron.

## Party Fruit Slush Punch

**PREP:** 15 minutes **FREEZE:** overnight

- 2 cups raspberries
- 1 cup orange juice
- ¼ cup sugar
- 1 46-oz. can unsweetened pineapple juice
- ¾ cup cognac or brandy
- Chilled ginger ale or carbonated water

**1.** In a blender combine raspberries and orange juice; cover and blend until combined. Strain through a fine sieve; discard seeds. In a large freezer container combine sieved mixture, sugar, pineapple juice, and cognac. Cover; freeze overnight.

**2.** To serve, scrape large spoon across mixture into a slush; fill tall glasses half full. Carefully add ginger ale to fill glasses. Makes 16 cups slush (32 servings).

Each serving: 91 cal., 0 g total fat (0 g sat. fat), 0 mg chol., 9 mg sodium, 20 g carbo., 0 g fiber, 0 g pro. Daily Values: 1% vit. A, 17% vit. C, 1% calcium, 2% iron.

## Frozen Serpentini

**START TO FINISH:** 10 minutes

- 1 pint lemon sorbet
- ½ cup lemon-flavored vodka
- ¼ cup ginger or orange liqueur
- 4 dashes aromatic bitters (optional)
- 2 to 2½ cups crushed ice
- Lemon peel twists

**1.** In a blender combine sorbet, vodka, liqueur, and, if desired, bitters. Cover and blend until smooth. With blender running, add crushed ice through opening in lid until mixture reaches desired consistency.

**2.** Pour into 4 martini glasses. Garnish with lemon peel twists. Makes 4 servings.

Each serving: 225 cal., 0 g total fat (0 g sat. fat), 0 mg chol., 1 mg sodium, 35 g carbo., 1 g fiber, 0 g pro. Daily Values: 6% vit. C.

## Peach-Raspberry Margaritas

**STAND:** 15 minutes **PREP:** 15 minutes

- 1 10-oz. pkg. frozen red raspberries in syrup
- 2 medium peaches, peeled, pitted, and sliced (about 2 cups)
- ⅓ cup tequila
- ⅓ cup frozen lemonade concentrate
- ¼ cup orange liqueur
- 2 Tbsp. lime juice
- 2 to 2½ cups ice cubes
- 1 thick lemon or lime slice (optional)
- Coarse salt or coarse sugar (optional)

**1.** Let raspberries stand at room temperature 15 minutes. In a blender combine undrained raspberries, peaches, tequila, lemonade concentrate, liqueur, and lime juice. Cover; blend until smooth. With blender running, add ice cubes, about 1 cup at a time, through opening in lid until desired consistency.

**2.** If desired, cut lemon slice in half. Rub around rims of six 6-ounce glasses. Dip rims into a dish of salt or sugar. Pour blended mixture into glasses. Makes 6 servings.

Each serving: 190 cal., 0 g total fat (0 g sat. fat), 0 mg chol., 15 mg sodium, 36 g carbo., 3 g fiber, 1 g pro. Daily Values: 6% vit. A, 20% vit. C, 1% calcium, 4% iron.

## Rum and Mango Slush

**START TO FINISH:** 10 minutes

- 2 fresh mangoes, peeled, seeded, and cubed (do not substitute purchased sliced mangoes)
- ⅓ cup rum
- ¼ cup frozen limeade concentrate
- 2 Tbsp. sugar
- 2½ cups crushed ice
- Kiwifruit, peeled and sliced (optional)

**1.** In a blender combine mangoes, rum, limeade concentrate, and sugar. Cover and blend until smooth. With blender running, add ice through opening in lid. Continue blending until slushy.

**2.** Divide among three 8-ounce glasses. If desired, garnish each glass with a kiwifruit slice. Makes 3 servings.

Each serving: 217 cal., 0 g total fat (0 g sat. fat), 0 mg chol., 5 mg sodium, 41 g carbo., 3 g fiber, 1 g pro. Daily Values: 107% vit. A, 67% vit. C, 2% calcium, 1% iron.

## Banana Cream Pie in a Glass

**PREP:** 15 minutes

- 2 medium bananas, peeled, cut up, and frozen
- ⅔ cup milk
- ¼ cup French vanilla-flavored liquid coffee creamer
- 1½ cups vanilla ice cream
- Pressurized whipped dessert topping
- 3 vanilla wafers

**1.** In a blender combine bananas, milk, and creamer. Cover; blend until smooth. Add about half of the ice cream at a time; blend until smooth after each addition.

**2.** Divide among 3 tall 8-ounce glasses. Top each with dessert topping and a vanilla wafer. Serve with straws and long spoons. Makes 3 servings.

Each serving: 350 cal., 16 g total fat (9 g sat. fat), 78 mg chol., 159 mg sodium, 48 g carbo., 2 g fiber, 6 g pro. Daily Values: 14% vit. A, 13% vit. C, 15% calcium, 2% iron.

# CHICKEN BREASTS

## Cheese-Stuffed Chicken

**PREP:** 25 minutes **BAKE:** 50 minutes

| | |
|---|---|
| 4 | medium chicken breast halves (2 to 2½ lb. total) |
| ¾ | cup shredded mozzarella cheese (3 oz.) |
| ½ | cup crumbled feta cheese |
| ¼ | cup chopped peanuts |

| | |
|---|---|
| 2 | slices bacon, crisp-cooked, drained, and crumbled, or ¼ cup cooked bacon pieces |
| | Salt and ground black pepper |
| | Paprika |
| | Bottled ranch salad dressing (optional) |

**1.** Preheat oven to 350° F. Skin chicken, if desired. Using a sharp knife, make a pocket in each chicken breast by cutting horizontally from side to side, leaving edges intact.

**2.** In a bowl combine mozzarella cheese, feta cheese, peanuts, and bacon. Spoon filling into pockets, packing lightly (pockets will be full). Place chicken, bone side down, in a 3-quart rectangular baking dish. Lightly sprinkle chicken breasts with salt, pepper, and paprika.

**3.** Bake, uncovered, for 50 to 55 minutes or until an instant-read thermometer inserted in the chicken registers 170° F. If desired, drizzle salad dressing over chicken before serving. Makes 4 servings.

Each serving: 457 cal., 29 g total fat (10 g sat. fat), 136 mg chol., 587 mg sodium, 3 g carbo., 1 g fiber, 44 g pro. Daily Values: 7% vit. A, 2% vit. C, 23% calcium, 9% iron.

## Chicken Sandwiches

**PREP:** 25 minutes **CHILL:** up to 24 hours

| | |
|---|---|
| 2 | skinless, boneless chicken breast halves (10 to 12 oz. total), finely chopped |
| 1 | Tbsp. butter |
| 1 | tsp. chili powder |
| ½ | tsp. ground cumin |
| 1 | clove garlic, minced |
| | Dash cayenne pepper |
| 1 | 3-oz. pkg. cream cheese, softened |
| ½ | cup shredded sharp cheddar cheese (2 oz.) |
| ¼ | cup dairy sour cream |

| | |
|---|---|
| 1 | 10-oz. can diced tomatoes and green chile peppers, drained |
| 2 | green onions, thinly sliced |
| 2 | Tbsp. snipped fresh cilantro |
| 12 | slices white sandwich bread, crusts removed, or six 8-inch flour tortillas |
| | Avocado slices, cucumber slices, or tomato slices (optional) |
| 12 | leaves Bibb lettuce |

**1.** In a large skillet cook chicken in hot butter until lightly browned and no pink remains. Stir in chili powder, cumin, garlic, and cayenne; cook for 1 minute more. Cool slightly.

**2.** In a medium bowl beat cheeses and sour cream until combined. Fold in chicken mixture, drained tomatoes and peppers, green onions, and cilantro. Cover and chill up to 24 hours.

**3.** To serve, spread mixture on 6 slices of bread. If desired, top with avocado, cucumber, or tomato slices; add lettuce and remaining 6 slices of bread. (Or spread chicken mixture evenly over tortillas; top with lettuce. If desired, add avocado, cucumber, or tomato slices. Roll up tortillas.) Makes 6 sandwiches.

Each sandwich: 324 cal., 15 g total fat (8 g sat. fat), 62 mg chol., 543 mg sodium, 28 g carbo., 2 g fiber, 20 g pro. Daily Values: 22% vit. A, 11% vit. C, 18% calcium, 14% iron.

## Creamy Tomato Pesto-Filled Chicken Rolls

**PREP:** 40 minutes **BAKE:** 25 minutes

Nonstick cooking spray
6   skinless, boneless chicken breast
    halves (about 2 lb. total)
Salt
Ground black pepper
1/2  of an 8 oz. tub cream cheese with
    chive and onion
1/4  cup purchased dried tomato pesto
2   oz. prosciutto, chopped
1/3  cup seasoned fine dry bread crumbs
2   Tbsp. pine nuts or slivered almonds,
    finely chopped
1   Tbsp. butter, melted
6   cups baby spinach leaves
3   Tbsp. Parmesan Italian salad dressing
    with basil or Italian salad dressing

**1.** Preheat oven to 375° F. Lightly coat a 13×9×2-inch baking pan with cooking spray; set aside.

**2.** Place a chicken breast half between 2 pieces of plastic wrap. Using the flat side of a meat mallet, pound chicken to about 1/8 inch thick. Remove plastic wrap. Repeat with remaining chicken breast halves. Sprinkle lightly with salt and pepper.

**3.** In a small bowl stir together cream cheese, tomato pesto, and prosciutto. Place about 2 tablespoons of cheese mixture in the center of each chicken breast. Fold in bottom and sides and roll up. Secure with wooden toothpick. Combine bread crumbs and pine nuts. Brush chicken rolls with butter and roll in the bread crumb mixture. Place, seam sides down, in prepared pan.

**4.** Bake for 25 to 30 minutes or until chicken is no longer pink (170° F). To serve, toss spinach leaves with the dressing. Divide evenly among 6 plates; top each with a chicken roll. Makes 6 servings.

Each serving: 381 cal., 18 g total fat (8 g sat. fat), 120 mg chol., 883 mg sodium, 10 g carbo., 1 g fiber, 42 g pro. Daily Values: 64% vit. A, 17% vit. C, 11% calcium, 16% iron.

## Lemon-Coconut Chicken

**PREP:** 20 minutes **MARINATE:** 1 hour
**COOK:** 10 minutes

4   skinless, boneless chicken breast
    halves (about 1 1/4 lb. total)
3/4  cup mango or apricot nectar
2   tsp. finely shredded lemon peel
    (set aside)
1/4  cup lemon juice
1/4  tsp. salt
1/8  tsp. cayenne pepper
1/8  tsp. ground allspice
1   cup soft bread crumbs
1/2  cup shredded coconut
1   Tbsp. packed brown sugar
1/4  tsp. salt
1/8  tsp. ground allspice
2   Tbsp. cooking oil
2   tsp. cornstarch
1   tsp. packed brown sugar

**1.** Place a chicken breast half between 2 pieces of plastic wrap. Using the flat side of a meat mallet, pound meat lightly to 1/4 inch thick. Remove plastic wrap. Repeat with remaining chicken breast halves. Place chicken in a large self-sealing plastic bag set in a large bowl. Combine mango nectar, lemon juice, 1/4 teaspoon salt, cayenne pepper, and 1/8 teaspoon allspice; pour over chicken. Seal bag; marinate in the refrigerator for 1 hour, turning occasionally. Drain chicken, reserving marinade.

**2.** In a shallow dish combine bread crumbs, coconut, 1 tablespoon brown sugar, 1/4 teaspoon salt, and 1/8 teaspoon allspice. Coat chicken in crumb mixture. Heat oil in a 12-inch skillet over medium heat. Add chicken; cook 3 to 4 minutes per side or until no pink remains. Transfer to a platter; cover and keep warm.

**3.** Transfer reserved marinade to a small saucepan; stir in cornstarch and 1 teaspoon brown sugar. Cook and stir until thickened and bubbly; cook and stir 2 minutes more. Drizzle the sauce over the chicken; sprinkle with lemon peel. Makes 4 servings.

Each serving: 377 cal., 15 g total fat (7 g sat. fat), 82 mg chol., 514 mg sodium, 26 g carbo., 2 g fiber, 35 g pro. Daily Values: 4% vit. A, 27% vit. C, 6% calcium, 9% iron.

## Spicy Grilled Chicken with Beans and Rice

**PREP:** 25 minutes **COOK:** 28 minutes
**GRILL:** 12 minutes **STAND:** 5 minutes

1   tsp. chili powder
1/2  tsp. ground cumin
1/4  tsp. onion powder
1/4  tsp. cayenne pepper
2   cloves garlic, minced
4   medium skinless, boneless chicken
    breast halves (1 1/4 to 1 1/2 lb. total)
1   32-oz. container chicken broth
2   cups frozen whole kernel corn
1   14 1/2-oz. can Mexican-style stewed
    tomatoes, undrained
1   8-oz. pkg. red beans and rice mix
1   small zucchini, chopped (1 cup)
Shredded Monterey Jack cheese
    (optional)
Avocado slices (optional)

**1.** In a small bowl combine chili powder, cumin, onion powder, cayenne pepper, and garlic. Rub into both sides of chicken breast halves. Set aside.

**2.** In a 4-quart Dutch oven combine chicken broth, corn, undrained tomatoes, and red beans and rice mix. Bring to boiling; reduce heat. Cover and simmer for 25 minutes. Stir in zucchini. Cook, covered, 3 to 5 minutes more or until zucchini is crisp-tender.

**3.** Meanwhile, for a charcoal grill, place chicken breasts on the lightly greased rack of an uncovered grill and grill directly over medium coals for 12 to 15 minutes or until tender and no longer pink (170° F), turning once halfway through grilling. (For a gas grill, preheat grill. Reduce heat to medium. Place chicken on grill rack over heat. Cover and grill as above.)

**4.** Transfer chicken to a cutting board. Slice chicken into bite-size pieces. Add to rice mixture. Let stand for 5 minutes to thicken before serving. If desired, top each serving with Monterey Jack cheese and sliced avocado. Makes 6 servings.

Each serving: 352 cal., 3 g total fat (0 g sat. fat), 56 mg chol., 1,525 mg sodium, 52 g carbo., 7 g fiber, 31 g pro. Daily Values: 11% vit. A, 32% vit. C, 7% calcium, 17% iron.

# CORN

## Corn Smorgasbord

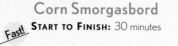 **START TO FINISH:** 30 minutes

| | |
|---|---|
| 1 recipe Mexicali Spice Blend, Italian Spice Blend, and/or Herb Spice Blend | 12 fresh ears of corn |
| | 3/4 cup butter, melted |

**1.** Prepare 1 or more of the spice blends. Place in shaker containers or small bowls. Remove husks and silks from corn; rinse corn. Cook corn, covered, in enough boiling lightly salted water to cover for 5 to 7 minutes or until tender. Drain. To serve, brush corn with some of the butter. Sprinkle with desired spice blend. Drizzle with additional butter. Store any remaining spice blend, covered, at room temperature up to 1 month. Makes 12 servings.

**MEXICALI SPICE BLEND:** Combine 3 tablespoons chili powder; 3 tablespoons grated Parmesan cheese; 1 tablespoon garlic powder; 1 tablespoon ground cumin; 1 tablespoon dried oregano, crushed; and 1/2 teaspoon salt. Makes about 9 tablespoons.

**ITALIAN SPICE BLEND:** Combine 2 tablespoons grated Parmesan cheese; 1 tablespoon ground black pepper; 1 tablespoon fennel seeds, ground; 1 tablespoon dried oregano, crushed; 1 teaspoon garlic powder; and 1/4 teaspoon salt. If desired, to make a powder, grind in coffee grinder. Makes about 6 tablespoons.

**HERB SPICE BLEND:** Combine 3 tablespoons grated Romano or Parmesan cheese; 2 tablespoons dried basil, crushed; 2 teaspoons dried tarragon, crushed; 1 teaspoon garlic powder; and 1/4 teaspoon salt. If desired, to make a powder, grind mixture in a coffee grinder. Makes about 6 tablespoons.

Each serving with 1 tsp. Mexicali Spice Blend: 192 cal., 14 g total fat (8 g sat. fat), 33 mg chol., 200 mg sodium, 18 g carbo., 3 g fiber, 3 g pro. Daily Values: 20% vit. A, 11% vit. C, 2% calcium, 4% iron.

## Curried Corn Pudding

**PREP:** 25 minutes **BAKE:** 25 minutes **STAND:** 10 minutes

| | |
|---|---|
| 4 to 6 fresh ears of corn or 2 cups frozen whole kernel corn, thawed | 3/4 cup milk |
| | 1/2 tsp. salt |
| | 1/4 tsp. ground black pepper |
| 2 Tbsp. finely chopped shallots | 1/4 tsp. ground nutmeg |
| | 2 eggs, slightly beaten |
| 2 Tbsp. butter | 2 Tbsp. packed brown sugar |
| 1 tsp. curry powder | 1/2 cup chopped pecans |

**1.** Preheat oven to 350° F. Lightly grease a 9-inch pie plate; set aside. If using fresh ears of corn, cut kernels from cobs; measure 2 cups kernels. Set aside.

**2.** In a medium saucepan cook the shallots in 1 tablespoon of the butter over medium heat until shallots are tender. Add curry powder; cook and stir for 30 seconds. Stir in milk, salt, pepper, nutmeg, and corn. Remove from heat. Stir in eggs. Pour mixture into the prepared pie plate.

**3.** In a small bowl cut remaining 1 tablespoon butter into the 2 tablespoons brown sugar until crumbly. Stir in pecans. Sprinkle nut mixture evenly over the corn mixture. Bake about 25 minutes or until golden around edges and a knife inserted near center comes out clean. Let stand 10 minutes before serving. Makes 4 to 6 servings.

Each serving: 319 cal., 20 g total fat (6 g sat. fat), 126 mg chol., 424 mg sodium, 30 g carbo., 4 g fiber, 9 g pro. Daily Values: 16% vit. A, 12% vit. C, 9% calcium, 9% iron.

## Crispy Corn Waffles

**PREP:** 20 minutes  **STAND:** 10 minutes
**BAKE:** per waffle baker directions

2 1/4 cups water
1 cup rolled oats
1/2 cup cornmeal
1/2 cup shelled sunflower seeds
1/4 cup all-purpose flour
2 Tbsp. sugar
2 tsp. baking powder
2 tsp. vanilla
1 tsp. salt
3/4 cup frozen whole kernel corn, thawed
1 recipe Tomato-Corn Topping (below)
Dairy sour cream (optional)
Sliced green onions (optional)

**1.** In blender or food processor combine water, oats, cornmeal, sunflower seeds, flour, sugar, baking powder, vanilla, and salt. Cover and blend or process until smooth. Let stand 10 minutes (mixture will thicken). Stir in corn.

**2.** Pour about 1 1/4 to 1 3/4 cups of the batter onto grids of a preheated, well greased waffle baker, spreading almost to edges. Close lid quickly; do not open until done. Bake according to manufacturer's directions (about 9 minutes per batch) or until waffles are golden. When done, use a fork to lift waffle off grid. Repeat with remaining batter.

**3.** Meanwhile, prepare Tomato-Corn Topping; serve topping over waffles. If desired, garnish with sour cream and onions. Makes about 10 (4-inch) waffles.

**TOMATO-CORN TOPPING:** In a small saucepan cook 1 medium onion, quartered and sliced, in 1 tablespoon hot cooking oil until onion is tender. Stir in 1 cup frozen whole kernel corn, thawed, and one 14 1/2-ounce can Mexican-style stewed tomatoes, undrained. Bring mixture to boiling; reduce heat. Simmer, uncovered, about 5 minutes or until thickened.

Each waffle square and topping: 179 cal., 6 g total fat (1 g sat. fat), 0 mg chol., 457 mg sodium, 28 g carbo., 3 g fiber, 5 g pro. Daily Values: 1% vit. A, 14% vit. C, 7% calcium, 7% iron.

## Corn, Apple, and Onion Gratin

**PREP:** 20 minutes  **BAKE:** 50 minutes

2 Tbsp. butter
3 cups fresh corn kernels (6 ears)
2 large onions, halved and thinly sliced (about 3 cups)
2 medium Granny Smith apples, peeled, cored, and chopped
2 Tbsp. all-purpose flour
1/4 tsp. salt
1/4 cup chicken broth
3/4 cup soft bread crumbs
4 slices bacon, crisp-cooked, drained, and crumbled
1/3 cup finely shredded Parmesan cheese

**1.** Preheat oven to 350° F. Lightly grease a 2-quart rectangular baking dish; set aside.

**2.** In a large skillet melt butter over medium heat. Add corn and onions. Cook about 10 minutes or until onions are very tender, stirring occasionally. Add apples, flour, and salt; stir gently to coat. Transfer mixture to the prepared dish. Pour broth over mixture in dish. Cover and bake for 30 minutes.

**3.** Meanwhile, in a medium bowl stir together the bread crumbs, bacon, and cheese. Uncover baking dish. Top corn mixture with bread crumb mixture. Bake, uncovered, for 20 minutes more or until topping is golden. Makes 8 servings.

Each serving: 254 cal., 12 g total fat (7 g sat. fat), 27 mg chol., 606 mg sodium, 26 g carbo., 4 g fiber, 13 g pro. Daily Values: 9% vit. A, 15% vit. C, 29% calcium, 5% iron.

## Pesto-Tomato-Sauced Corn

*Fast!* **START TO FINISH:** 15 minutes

2 cups fresh or frozen whole kernel corn (4 ears)
2 Tbsp. bottled ranch salad dressing
2 Tbsp. chopped oil-packed dried tomatoes
1 Tbsp. purchased basil pesto

**1.** Cook fresh corn, covered, in a small amount of boiling salted water 4 minutes.

(Or cook frozen corn following package directions.) Drain; return corn to saucepan. Stir in salad dressing, tomatoes, and pesto. Heat and stir just until heated through. Do not boil. Makes 4 servings.

**MICROWAVE METHOD:** Place fresh corn in a 1-quart microwave-safe casserole with 2 tablespoons water. Microwave, covered, on 100% power (high) for 5 to 6 minutes; stir once. (Or microwave frozen corn following package directions.) Drain and return corn to casserole. Stir in salad dressing, tomatoes, and pesto. Microwave on high for 30 seconds to heat through.

**Healthy** Each serving: 149 cal., 8 g total fat (1 g sat. fat), 1 mg chol., 112 mg sodium, 19 g carbo., 3 g fiber, 4 g pro. Daily Values: 6% vit. A, 15% vit. C, 3% iron.

## Savory Corn and Barley Stew

**PREP:** 25 minutes  **COOK:** 35 minutes

1 large onion, chopped (1 cup)
4 cloves garlic, minced
2 Tbsp. olive oil
3 14-oz. cans chicken broth
3/4 cup regular barley
1 tsp. dried thyme, crushed
1 tsp. fennel seeds, crushed
1/2 tsp. freshly ground black pepper
1 bay leaf
2 cups fresh or frozen corn
3 medium carrots, chopped (1 1/2 cups)
1 14 1/2-oz. can diced tomatoes, undrained
3 Tbsp. balsamic vinegar
2 cups torn fresh spinach
Shredded Parmesan cheese

**1.** In a Dutch oven cook onion and garlic in hot oil until tender but not brown. Add next 6 ingredients. Bring to boiling; reduce heat. Simmer, covered, 20 minutes.

**2.** Add corn and carrots; return to boiling. Simmer, covered, about 15 minutes more or until carrots are tender. Stir in undrained tomatoes; heat through. Discard bay leaf. Stir in vinegar and spinach. Sprinkle with Parmesan. Serves 6.

Each serving: 281 cal., 9 g total fat (2 g sat. fat), 4 mg chol., 1,067 mg sodium, 42 g carbo., 8 g fiber, 10 g pro. Daily Values: 172% vit. A, 33% vit. C, 14% calcium, 13% iron.

# DUCK, GOOSE, GAME BIRDS

## Duck with Red Cabbage

**Prep:** 30 minutes **Cook:** 1 hour 30 minutes

| | |
|---|---|
| 3 | lb. meaty domestic duck pieces (breast, thighs, and legs) |
| Salt and ground black pepper | |
| 1 | Tbsp. olive oil |
| 4 | slices bacon, cut up |
| 1 | large onion, thinly sliced |
| 2 | medium carrots, peeled and cut into chunks |
| 1 | clove garlic, minced |
| 1 | 14-oz. can beef broth |
| ½ | cup dry red wine or beef broth |
| 1 | Tbsp. grape jelly |
| 1 | tsp. sugar |
| ½ | of a small head red cabbage |
| 2 | Granny Smith apples, cored and sliced |

**1.** Season duck pieces generously with salt and ground black pepper. In a Dutch oven brown duck pieces on all sides in hot oil. Drain off fat. Remove duck; set aside.

**2.** Add bacon to Dutch oven; cook over medium heat until crisp. Drain off fat. Add onion, carrots, garlic, broth, wine, jelly, and sugar. Bring to boiling. Cut cabbage into 4 wedges. Add cabbage and duck to pan. Reduce heat to low. Simmer, covered, 1¼ hours. Add apples. Return to boiling; reduce heat. Simmer, covered, for 15 minutes or until duck is tender.

**3.** Transfer duck to a serving platter. Strain cabbage mixture, reserving juices. Spoon cabbage mixture onto platter with duck. Cover; keep warm. In Dutch oven bring juices to boiling; reduce heat. Simmer until desired consistency. Pour over duck and cabbage. Makes 6 servings.

Each serving: 612 cal., 44 g total fat (15 g sat. fat), 129 mg chol., 669 mg sodium, 19 g carbo., 4 g fiber, 32 g pro. Daily Values: 53% vit. A, 41% vit. C, 7% calcium, 28% iron.

## Grilled Quail Salad

**Prep:** 45 minutes **Marinate:** 2 hours **Grill:** 12 minutes

**1.** Using kitchen shears, cut through backbone of 4 quail. Turn bone side down; gently press to flatten. Arrange in a single layer in a shallow dish. For marinade, combine ¼ cup extra-virgin olive oil, 2 teaspoons snipped fresh sage, ¼ teaspoon each salt and freshly ground black pepper. Pour marinade over quail. Turn once to coat. Cover; marinate in refrigerator for 2 to 24 hours, turning occasionally. Prepare Port Dressing; set aside.

**2.** Cut 2 ounces thinly sliced prosciutto lengthwise into 8 strips. Halve and pit 4 red or purple plums. Wrap prosciutto around plums, securing with wooden toothpicks. Set aside.

**3.** Drain quail; discard marinade. For charcoal grill, arrange medium-hot coals around drip pan. Place quail, bone side down, on rack above drip pan. Cover; grill 12 to 15 minutes or until no longer pink. Place plums over coals the last 4 minutes of grilling, turning once. In a very large bowl toss half of the dressing with 8 ounces torn mixed baby greens. Divide among 4 plates. Top with quail halves and plums. Sprinkle with ³⁄₄ cup crumbled Gorgonzola cheese and ½ cup walnuts, toasted. Season with freshly ground black pepper. Serve with Port Dressing. Serves 4.

**PORT DRESSING:** In a saucepan combine 1 cup port and 2 tablespoons finely chopped shallots. Simmer, uncovered, 20 to 25 minutes or until reduced to ¼ cup. Cool slightly. In a bowl whisk together port mixture, ½ cup extra-virgin olive oil, 3 tablespoons red wine vinegar, 1 tablespoon balsamic vinegar, and ¼ teaspoon salt and ¼ teaspoon black pepper.

Each serving: 998 cal., 71 g total fat (15 g sat. fat), 142 mg chol., 991 mg sodium, 36 g carbo., 5 g fiber, 43 g pro. Daily Values: 29% vit. A, 49% vit. C, 18% calcium, 48% iron.

## Cherry-Chipotle Glazed Duck Breasts

**STAND:** 30 minutes **PREP:** 25 minutes
**BAKE:** 10 minutes **STAND:** 10 minutes
**COOK:** 10 minutes

- ⅓ cup kirsch
- ½ cup dried tart cherries
- ½ of a chipotle pepper in adobo sauce, finely chopped (1 tsp.)
- 4 6½- to 7½-oz. boneless duck breasts
- 1 Tbsp. bottled balsamic glaze
- Salt and ground black pepper
- 2 tsp. cooking oil
- 2 Tbsp. finely chopped shallots
- 2 cloves garlic, minced
- ½ cup chicken broth
- 2 tsp. snipped fresh thyme or ½ teaspoon dried thyme, crushed

**1.** In a small glass bowl combine the kirsch, cherries, and chipotle pepper. Cover and let stand for 30 minutes.

**2.** Preheat oven to 425° F. Score fat side of duck breasts in a diamond pattern at ½-inch intervals. Brush fat side with the balsamic glaze. Season duck with salt and black pepper. In a 12-inch skillet heat oil over medium heat. Add duck, skin side down, and cook about 10 minutes or until browned, turning once. Transfer duck, skin side up, to a foil-lined 13×9×2-inch baking pan, reserving drippings in skillet. Bake for 10 to 15 minutes or until an instant-read thermometer registers 155° F. Cover and let stand for 10 minutes.

**3.** Meanwhile, drain all but 1 tablespoon drippings from skillet. Cook shallots and garlic in the hot drippings for 1 minute. Remove from heat; carefully add broth and cherry mixture. Return skillet to heat. Bring mixture to boiling; reduce heat. Simmer, uncovered, 5 to 10 minutes or until mixture is slightly reduced. Stir in thyme. To serve, thinly slice duck and arrange on serving plates. Spoon cherry mixture over sliced duck. If desired, garnish with additional thyme. Makes 4 servings.

Each serving: 398 cal., 7 g total fat (1 g sat. fat), 272 mg chol., 364 mg sodium, 15 g carbo., 1 g fiber, 53 g pro. Daily Values: 2% vit. A, 13% vit. C, 2% calcium, 48% iron.

## Thai Peanut Pheasant

**PREP:** 45 minutes **BAKE:** 2 hours 20 minutes

- 1 13½-oz. can unsweetened coconut milk
- ¼ cup creamy peanut butter
- ⅓ cup chicken broth
- 2 Tbsp. soy sauce
- 2 Tbsp. rice vinegar
- 1 Tbsp. packed brown sugar
- 1 Tbsp. toasted sesame oil
- 1 tsp. red curry paste
- 1 clove garlic, minced
- 1 tsp. grated fresh ginger
- ⅛ tsp. cayenne pepper
- ⅔ cup all-purpose flour
- ½ tsp. salt
- ½ tsp. ground black pepper
- 2 2¼- to 2½-lb. pheasants, quartered, or two 1- to 1½-lb. Cornish game hens, halved
- 2 Tbsp. cooking oil
- 2 Tbsp. snipped fresh cilantro
- 4 cups hot cooked rice (2 cups if using Cornish game hens)

**1.** In medium saucepan whisk coconut milk and peanut butter until smooth. Add broth, soy sauce, vinegar, brown sugar, sesame oil, curry paste, garlic, ginger, and cayenne pepper. Whisk until smooth. Heat over medium-high heat just until boiling. Reduce heat and simmer, uncovered, 15 minutes, stirring occasionally.

**2.** Preheat oven to 300° F. In a large, sturdy self-sealing plastic bag combine flour, salt, and black pepper. Add pheasant or hen pieces, 1 at a time, to flour mixture; close bag and shake to coat. In a large skillet brown pheasant or hen pieces, 2 to 4 at a time, in hot oil, turning to brown evenly. Arrange browned pieces, meaty side up, in a 13×9×2-inch baking dish.

**3.** Pour peanut butter mixture over pheasant or hen pieces. Cover loosely with a piece of foil large enough to cover top of pan. Bake for 2 hours (1½ hours if using game hens), occasionally spooning sauce over pheasant or hen pieces. Remove foil. Bake, uncovered, 20 to 30 minutes more or until pheasant or hen pieces are very tender.

**4.** To serve, remove pheasant or hen pieces from pan and arrange on a serving platter. Skim fat from sauce in pan. Spoon some of the sauce over pheasant or hen. Sprinkle with cilantro. Serve with remaining sauce and rice. Makes 8 (4 Cornish game hen) servings.

Each serving: 725 cal., 38 g total fat (15 g sat. fat), 155 mg chol., 568 mg sodium, 35 g carbo., 1 g fiber, 56 g pro. Daily Values: 8% vit. A, 17% vit. C, 5% calcium, 25% iron.

## Duck Breast and Mushrooms in Sour Cream Sauce

**START TO FINISH:** 45 minutes

- 2 6½- to 7½-oz. boneless duck breasts
- ½ cup dairy sour cream
- ½ cup chicken broth
- 2 Tbsp. all-purpose flour
- 1 Tbsp. oyster sauce
- ¼ tsp. ground black pepper
- 2 Tbsp. cooking oil
- 8 oz. fresh mushrooms, such as crimini, baby portabello, or button mushrooms, sliced
- 2 shallots, finely chopped
- 2 cloves garlic, minced
- 1½ cups hot cooked wild or brown rice

**1.** Remove and discard skin and fat from duck breasts. Thinly slice duck into bite-size pieces; set aside. In a bowl combine sour cream, chicken broth, flour, oyster sauce, and pepper; set aside.

**2.** In a large nonstick skillet heat 1 tablespoon of the oil; add mushrooms, shallots, and garlic. Cook and stir over medium-high heat until mushrooms are tender. Remove with a slotted spoon. Add remaining oil and the duck to skillet; cook and stir 2 to 3 minutes or until duck is done.

**3.** Stir sour cream mixture and add to the skillet. Cook and stir until thickened and bubbly. Return mushrooms to skillet; heat through. Serve with rice. Makes 2 or 3 servings.

Each serving: 717 cal., 31 g total fat (10 g sat. fat), 294 mg chol., 700 mg sodium, 46 g carbo., 4 g fiber, 66 g pro. Daily Values: 11% vit. A, 15% vit. C, 10% calcium, 59% iron.

# ONE-DISH DINNERS

## Chicken Thighs and Orzo
**PREP:** 20 minutes **COOK:** 25 minutes

| | |
|---|---|
| 1 | 4-oz. pkg. pancetta, chopped, or 4 slices bacon, chopped |
| | Olive oil |
| 6 | chicken thighs (about 2¼ lb.), skinned |
| 2 | 14½-oz. cans diced tomatoes with garlic and onion, undrained |
| 1 | cup water |
| 1 | cup dried orzo |
| 2 | cloves garlic, minced |
| ⅓ | cup pitted kalamata olives |
| ¼ | cup snipped fresh basil |
| 1 | 6-oz. bag prewashed baby spinach leaves |
| 3 | oz. goat cheese with basil and roasted garlic (about ⅓ cup) |

**1.** In a 5- to 6-quart Dutch oven cook pancetta until browned. Remove pancetta, reserving 2 tablespoons drippings in pan (add olive oil, if necessary, to equal 2 tablespoons). Drain pancetta on paper towels; set aside. Cook chicken in drippings about 10 minutes or until light brown, turning to brown evenly; drain off fat. Add undrained tomatoes, water, orzo, and garlic. Bring to boiling; reduce heat.

**2.** Simmer, covered, 25 to 30 minutes or until chicken is no longer pink (180° F) and orzo is tender. If necessary, cook, uncovered, 2 to 3 minutes or until sauce is desired consistency. Stir in pancetta, olives, and basil; heat through. Divide spinach among 6 plates. Top each with a chicken thigh, some of the orzo mixture, and some of the cheese. Makes 6 servings.

Each serving: 395 cal., 18 g total fat (5 g sat. fat), 77 mg chol., 1,229 mg sodium, 32 g carbo., 2 g fiber, 26 g pro. Daily Values: 56% vit. A, 31% vit. C, 8% calcium, 25% iron.

## Kid Friendly Deep-Dish Pizza
**PREP:** 35 minutes **BAKE:** 22 minutes **STAND:** 10 minutes

| | |
|---|---|
| 2 | 13.8-oz. pkg. refrigerated pizza dough |
| 1½ | cups sliced red onion |
| 2 | cloves garlic, minced |
| ¼ | cup olive oil |
| 1 | 10-oz. pkg. frozen chopped spinach, thawed and well drained |
| 1 | cup ricotta cheese |
| 1¼ | cups shredded pizza cheese (4-cheese blend) |
| 2 | Tbsp. snipped fresh parsley |
| ¼ | tsp. crushed red pepper (optional) |
| 4 | roma tomatoes, thinly sliced |

**1.** Preheat oven to 425° F. Lightly coat a 12-inch cast-iron or heavy oven-going skillet with nonstick cooking spray. Unroll 1 package of dough; gently pull into a circle. Place dough in skillet; press into bottom and halfway up sides of skillet. Bake for 5 minutes; remove from oven. Dough will have puffed slightly.

**2.** Meanwhile, in skillet cook onion and garlic in 2 tablespoons of oil until tender. Add spinach and ¼ teaspoon each salt and black pepper. Cook and stir 1 minute. Remove from heat. In bowl combine ricotta, ¼ cup of the pizza cheese, parsley, ¼ teaspoon salt, and red pepper. Spoon spinach mixture over crust.

**3.** Spread ricotta mixture over spinach. Top with tomatoes; drizzle with 1 tablespoon of oil. Sprinkle with ¾ cup pizza cheese. Unroll remaining dough; shape into a 12- to 13-inch circle. Lay dough on layers in skillet. Brush with remaining oil. Bake 15 to 20 minutes or until golden. Top with remaining pizza cheese. Bake 2 to 3 minutes until cheese melts. Let stand 10 minutes. Serves 8.

Each serving: 443 cal., 18 g total fat (7 g sat. fat), 28 mg chol., 882 mg sodium, 52 g carbo., 3 g fiber, 18 g pro. Daily Values: 114% vit. A, 19% vit. C, 22% calcium, 15% iron.

## Pacific Northwest Paella

Use a fresh tomato and either fresh or frozen asparagus for this salmon skillet meal.

**START TO FINISH:** 45 minutes

4   slices apple wood smoked bacon
8   oz. fresh crimini or button
    mushrooms, sliced
1   large onion, chopped (1 cup)
2   cloves garlic, minced
1   cup uncooked long grain white rice
2½  cups chicken broth
2   tsp. snipped fresh thyme or
    ½ tsp. dried thyme, crushed
1¼  lb. skinless salmon fillet, cut 1 inch
    thick
¼   tsp. cracked black pepper
1   lb. fresh asparagus spears or
    one 10-oz. pkg. frozen cut asparagus,
    thawed
1   roma tomato, chopped (⅓ cup)

**1.** In a large deep skillet or paella pan cook the bacon over medium heat until crisp, turning occasionally. Drain bacon on paper towels. Crumble bacon and set aside. Reserve drippings in skillet.

**2.** Add the mushrooms, onion, and garlic to bacon drippings in skillet. Cook and stir about 5 minutes or until the onion is tender. Stir in rice. Add chicken broth and thyme. Bring mixture to boiling; reduce heat. Simmer, covered, for 10 minutes.

**3.** Meanwhile, cut salmon into 1-inch pieces. Toss with pepper and set aside. Snap off and discard woody bases from fresh asparagus. Cut asparagus into 1-inch pieces; set aside. Place the salmon pieces on top of rice mixture. Sprinkle the asparagus over all. Simmer, covered, for 10 to 12 minutes more or until asparagus is crisp-tender and salmon flakes easily when tested with a fork. Sprinkle with tomato and crumbled bacon before serving. Makes 6 servings.

**Healthy** Each serving: 320 cal., 10 g total fat (3 g sat. fat), 56 mg chol., 569 mg sodium, 31 g carbo., 2 g fiber, 27 g pro. Daily Values: 4% vit. A, 24% vit. C, 5% calcium, 16% iron.

## Curried Chicken and Dried Fruit with Dumplings

**PREP:** 20 minutes **COOK:** 45 minutes

1   large onion, cut into wedges
2   cloves garlic, minced
1   Tbsp. cooking oil
2   tsp. curry powder
3   lb. meaty chicken pieces (breast
    halves, thighs, and drumsticks),
    skinned
1   14-oz. can chicken broth
½   cup water
¼   tsp. salt
¼   tsp. ground black pepper
⅓   cup dried apricots, quartered
⅓   cup pitted dried plums, halved
⅓   cup dried apples, cut into 1-inch
    pieces
1   recipe Dumplings (below)
2   Tbsp. apricot jam or preserves
1   Tbsp. cornstarch

**1.** In a 4-quart Dutch oven cook onion and garlic in hot oil over medium heat for 2 minutes. Add curry powder; cook 1 minute. Add chicken, chicken broth, water, ¼ teaspoon salt, and pepper to Dutch oven. Bring to boiling; reduce heat. Simmer, covered, for 25 minutes.

**2.** Add dried apricots, plums, and apples. Return mixture to boiling; reduce heat. Simmer, covered, for 10 minutes.

**3.** Meanwhile, prepare Dumplings.

**4.** Combine apricot jam and cornstarch; stir into Dutch oven. Return mixture to boiling. Drop Dumplings in 4 to 6 mounds on the chicken. Simmer, covered, for 10 to 12 minutes or until a wooden toothpick inserted into dumpling comes out clean (do not uncover before 10 minutes). Makes 4 to 6 servings.

**DUMPLINGS:** In a medium mixing bowl combine ⅔ cup all-purpose flour, 2 tablespoons snipped fresh parsley, 1 teaspoon baking powder, ¼ teaspoon salt, and ¼ teaspoon curry powder. Combine

¼ cup milk and 2 tablespoons cooking oil; pour into flour mixture. Stir with a fork until combined.

Each serving: 599 cal., 22 g total fat (5 g sat. fat), 140 mg chol., 903 mg sodium, 50 g carbo., 4 g fiber, 49 g pro. Daily Values: 17% vit. A, 12% vit. C, 10% calcium, 23% iron.

## Picadillo Chili

Raisins add a surprise and a hint of sweetness to this mildly flavored chili.

**PREP:** 20 minutes **COOK:** 45 minutes

1   lb. uncooked ground turkey
1   large onion, chopped (1 cup)
2   cloves garlic, minced
1½  tsp. chili powder
½   tsp. ground cumin
¼   tsp. ground cinnamon
⅛   tsp. cayenne pepper
1   28-oz. can diced tomatoes,
    undrained
1   15-oz. can tomato sauce
1   15-oz. can black beans, rinsed and
    drained
1   4-oz. can diced green chile peppers
½   cup golden raisins
½   cup sliced pimiento-stuffed green
    olives
½   cup slivered almonds, toasted
⅓   cup sliced green onions

**1.** In a 4-quart Dutch oven cook turkey and onion until turkey is browned, stirring to break up ground turkey. Drain off fat. Add garlic, chili powder, cumin, cinnamon, and cayenne pepper; cook 2 minutes more. Stir in undrained tomatoes, tomato sauce, black beans, chile peppers, and raisins. Bring to boiling; reduce heat. Simmer, covered, for 45 minutes.

**2.** Stir in olives, almonds, and green onions. Ladle into bowls. Makes 6 servings.

Each serving: 349 cal., 14 g total fat (2 g sat. fat), 60 mg chol., 1,086 mg sodium, 37 g carbo., 8 g fiber, 23 g pro. Daily Values: 8% vit. A, 46% vit. C, 17% calcium, 22% iron.

# ETHNIC FLAVORS

## Lingonberry Cheesecake

**PREP:** 30 minutes **BAKE:** 40 minutes **COOL:** 2 hours **CHILL:** 4 hours

| | |
|---|---|
| 1¼ cups graham cracker crumbs | ¾ cup sugar |
| ½ cup finely chopped hazelnuts (filberts) | ½ tsp. ground cardamom |
| | 1½ tsp. vanilla |
| ⅓ cup butter, melted | 3 eggs, slightly beaten |
| 3 8-oz. pkg. cream cheese, softened | 1 14- to 14½-oz. jar lingonberries or one 16-oz. can whole cranberry sauce |

**1.** Preheat oven to 350° F. For crust, in bowl combine crumbs, nuts, and butter. Press into bottom of 9-inch springform pan. Bake for 10 minutes. Cool on wire rack. For filling, in large bowl beat cheese, sugar, cardamom, and vanilla until smooth. Stir in eggs.

**2.** In a small saucepan heat berries over low heat until melted or completely softened; stir occasionally. Strain syrup from berries. (Cranberries have less syrup, so if using them, add enough cranberry mixture to drained syrup to make ¾ cup.) Cover; chill syrup until serving time. Reserve berries. Stir strained berries into cheese mixture. Pour cheese mixture over crust. Place springform pan in shallow baking pan. Bake 40 to 45 minutes or until a 2½-inch area around outside edge appears set when gently shaken.

**3.** Cool in springform pan on wire rack for 15 minutes. Using a small sharp knife, loosen crust from sides of pan. Cool 30 minutes more. Remove sides of pan; cool cheesecake completely. Cover; chill at least 4 hours before serving. Stir reserved syrup; spoon over servings of cheesecake. Makes 12 servings.

Each serving: 445 cal., 31 g total fat (16 g sat. fat), 129 mg chol., 276 mg sodium, 37 g carbo., 2 g fiber, 7 g pro. Daily Values: 20% vit. A, 1% vit. C, 6% calcium, 9% iron.

## Cuban Burgers

**PREP:** 25 minutes **GRILL:** 14 minutes **COOK:** 5 minutes

| | |
|---|---|
| 1 lb. ground beef | 4 rolls or buns, split and toasted |
| 1 tsp. garlic powder | |
| ½ tsp. ground cumin | 2 whole dill pickles, cut into 8 slices |
| 4 thin slices cooked ham (about 3 oz.) | |
| | 4 slices red onion |
| 4 slices fontina or provolone cheese | 4 slices tomato |
| | 1 recipe Mojo Sauce (below) |

**1.** In a bowl combine beef, garlic powder, cumin, and ½ teaspoon *each* salt and ground black pepper. Shape into four ¾-inch-thick patties. For a charcoal grill, place patties on rack of uncovered grill directly over medium coals for 14 to 18 minutes or until meat is done (160° F), turning once halfway through grilling. Top each with a slice of ham and cheese. Cover; grill 30 seconds more or just until cheese begins to melt. Serve on rolls with pickle, onion, and tomato. Drizzle with some of the Mojo Sauce sauce; pass remaining sauce. Makes 4 servings.

**MOJO SAUCE:** In a skillet cook 6 minced cloves garlic in 2 tablespoons olive oil over medium heat until just starting to brown. Remove from heat. Carefully add ⅓ cup orange juice, ⅓ cup lemon juice, 1 teaspoon ground cumin, and ½ teaspoon each salt and ground black pepper. Bring to boiling; reduce heat. Simmer, uncovered, about 5 minutes or until slightly reduced. Remove from heat; cool. Whisk before serving.

Each serving: 558 cal., 31 g total fat (12 g sat. fat), 108 mg chol., 1,716 mg sodium, 32 g carbo., 3 g fiber, 36 g pro. Daily Values: 11% vit. A, 44% vit. C, 22% calcium, 24% iron.

## Fennel-Leek Moussaka

**PREP:** 20 minutes **BAKE:** 30 minutes
**STAND:** 5 minutes

1  10-oz. pkg. frozen chopped spinach, thawed and well drained
2  medium fennel bulbs
2  large leeks, thinly sliced
1/2  tsp. salt
1/4  tsp. ground black pepper
2  Tbsp. olive oil
1  cup crumbled feta cheese (4 oz.)
3  Tbsp. butter
3  Tbsp. all-purpose flour
1/2  tsp. salt
1/2  tsp. fennel seeds, crushed
1/8  tsp. ground nutmeg
1/8  tsp. ground black pepper
1 3/4  cups milk
2  eggs, beaten
2  roma tomatoes, coarsely chopped

**1.** Preheat oven to 350° F. Grease a 2-quart square baking dish. Spread spinach in dish; set aside. Reserve the leafy fennel tops. Slice remaining fennel (should have about 4 cups). In a medium skillet cook fennel, leeks, the 1/2 teaspoon salt, and 1/4 teaspoon pepper in hot oil over medium-high heat until tender.

**2.** Spoon fennel mixture on top of spinach in dish. Sprinkle feta cheese over fennel mixture.

**3.** In a medium saucepan melt butter; stir in flour, 1/2 teaspoon salt, fennel seeds, ground nutmeg, and 1/8 teaspoon pepper. Add milk all at once; cook and stir until thickened and bubbly. Stir half of the hot mixture into the eggs; return all to the saucepan. Pour hot sauce on top of feta cheese in baking dish.

**4.** Bake, uncovered, 30 to 35 minutes or until set. Finely snip 1 tablespoon of the reserved leafy fennel tops. Top moussaka with tomatoes and snipped fennel tops. Let stand 5 minutes before serving. Makes 6 main-dish or 8 to 10 side-dish servings.

Each main-dish serving: 252 cal., 18 g total fat (8 g sat. fat), 109 mg chol., 781 mg sodium, 14 g carbo., 9 g fiber, 10 g pro. Daily Values: 156% vit. A, 21% vit. C, 25% calcium, 8% iron.

## Italian Spice Cookies

**PREP:** 35 minutes **BAKE:** 8 minutes per batch
**STAND:** 30 minutes

2  cups all-purpose flour
1/2  cup unsweetened cocoa powder
1  Tbsp. baking powder
1/2  tsp. salt
1/2  tsp. ground cinnamon
1/4  tsp. ground allspice
1/4  tsp. ground black pepper (optional)
1/8  tsp. ground cloves
1/2  cup shortening
3/4  cup granulated sugar
2/3  cup strong brewed coffee, cooled
1/2  cup chopped walnuts, toasted
1/2  cup raisins
1  recipe Powdered Sugar Glaze (below)
Colored sugar (optional)

**1.** Preheat oven to 350° F. In a medium bowl combine flour, cocoa powder, baking powder, salt, cinnamon, allspice, pepper (if desired), and cloves; set aside.

**2.** In a large mixing bowl beat shortening with an electric mixer on medium to high speed for 30 seconds. Beat in sugar until combined. Alternately add flour mixture and coffee to shortening mixture, beating on low speed after each addition until combined. If necessary, stir in the last portion of flour with a wooden spoon. Stir in walnuts and raisins.

**3.** Shape dough into 1-inch balls. Place balls about 2 inches apart on ungreased cookie sheets. Bake for 8 minutes or until puffed and set (do not overbake). Remove cookies and cool completely on wire racks.

**4.** Prepare Powdered Sugar Glaze. Dip tops of cooled cookies in the glaze; allow excess glaze to run off. Place on wire racks set over waxed paper. If desired, before glaze sets, sprinkle glazed cookies with colored sugar. Allow to stand about 30 minutes or until glaze sets. Makes about 48 cookies.

**POWDERED SUGAR GLAZE:** In a small mixing bowl whisk together 1 cup sifted powdered sugar and 2 tablespoons warm water until smooth (glaze will be thin). Makes about 1/3 cup glaze.

Each cookie: 73 cal., 3 g total fat (1 g sat. fat), 0 mg chol., 40 mg sodium, 11 g carbo., 0 g fiber, 1 g pro. Daily Values: 2% calcium, 2% iron.

## Fragrant Lentil Rice

**PREP:** 20 minutes **COOK:** 23 minutes
**STAND:** 5 minutes

2  Tbsp. olive oil
1  small onion, chopped (1/3 cup)
2  cloves garlic, minced
1  tsp. cumin seeds, crushed
1  tsp. garam masala
1  tsp. salt
1/8  tsp. cayenne pepper
1  cup uncooked basmati or long grain rice
3  cups chicken broth
2/3  cup frozen peas, thawed
1/2  cup dry red lentils, rinsed
1/4  cup snipped fresh mint
2  Tbsp. snipped fresh cilantro
1  recipe Yogurt Raita (below)

**1.** In a large saucepan heat olive oil over medium heat. Add onion, garlic, cumin seeds, garam masala, salt, and cayenne pepper. Cook and stir for 2 minutes. Add rice; cook and stir for 1 minute more. Carefully add broth; bring to boiling. Reduce heat and simmer, covered, for 15 minutes.

**2.** Stir in peas and lentils; cover and cook 5 to 8 minutes more or until lentils are just tender. Remove from heat; stir in mint and cilantro. Let stand, covered, 5 minutes before serving. Serve with Yogurt Raita. Makes 8 to 10 side-dish servings.

**YOGURT RAITA:** In a medium bowl combine one 8-ounce carton plain yogurt; 1 small cucumber, seeded and chopped; 1 tomato, seeded and chopped; 1 tablespoon snipped fresh mint; and 1 tablespoon snipped fresh cilantro. Season to taste with salt and freshly ground black pepper.

Each serving: 198 cal., 4 g total fat (1 g sat. fat), 3 mg chol., 736 mg sodium, 32 g carbo., 3 g fiber, 8 g pro. Daily Values: 11% vit. A, 13% vit. C, 9% calcium, 16% iron.

# GREAT POTATOES

**PRIZE TESTED RECIPES® $400 WINNER**

ELAINE SWEET, DALLAS, TEXAS

**PRIZE TESTED RECIPES® $200 WINNER**

SHER BIRD GARFIELD, BELLEVUE, WASH.

## Pecan Potato Salad

**PREP:** 40 minutes  **COOK:** 15 minutes

- 2 lb. medium round red potatoes, cut into wedges
- ½ cup finely chopped shallots
- ¼ tsp. ground coriander
- ⅔ cup olive oil
- 1 to 2 tsp. bottled hot pepper sauce
- ⅔ cup milk
- ⅓ cup chopped pecans, toasted
- 3 Tbsp. finely crushed stone-ground wheat crackers
- 2 tsp. lemon juice
- 8 red lettuce leaves
- 4 oz. feta cheese, crumbled
- ½ cup pitted kalamata olives
- ⅓ cup fresh Italian parsley leaves
- ¼ cup pecan halves, toasted
- 2 hard-cooked eggs, cut into wedges

**1.** In a 4-quart Dutch oven cook potatoes and 1 teaspoon salt, covered, in enough boiling water to cover about 15 minutes or until tender; drain. Cool. For dressing, in small skillet cook shallots and coriander in 2 tablespoons of oil over medium heat 3 minutes; stir frequently. Stir in hot pepper sauce; cook and stir 1 minute. Remove from heat; cool slightly. In blender or food processor combine shallot mixture, milk, ⅓ cup pecans, crackers, and lemon juice. Cover; process until nearly smooth. With blender or processor running, slowly add remaining oil in a steady stream (mixture will thicken). Season with salt and pepper.

**2.** Arrange lettuce on platter. Top with potatoes. Drizzle with some dressing. Sprinkle with cheese, olives, parsley, and pecans. Garnish with eggs. Pass remaining dressing. Makes 6 to 8 servings.

Each serving: 500 cal., 40 g total fat (8 g sat. fat), 89 mg chol., 646 mg sodium, 28 g carbo., 4 g fiber, 10 g pro. Daily Values: 33% vit. A, 43% vit. C, 17% calcium, 16% iron.

## Smashed Potatoes Olé

*Fast!*  **PREP:** 15 minutes  **COOK:** 15 minutes

- 2 to 3 fresh ears of corn or 1 cup frozen whole kernel corn
- 1 lb. medium yellow potatoes, peeled and cut up (3 medium)
- 1 lb. medium round red potatoes, peeled and cut up (3 medium)
- 3 medium carrots, peeled and sliced
- 2 medium fresh jalapeño chile peppers, halved, seeded, and sliced*
- 4 cloves garlic, minced
- ¼ cup butter
- ¼ cup dairy sour cream
- 1 cup shredded sharp cheddar cheese
- Salt
- Ground black pepper

**1.** Cut corn kernels from cobs (you should have about 1 cup). In a large saucepan cook corn, potatoes, carrots, jalapeño peppers, and garlic, covered, in enough boiling water to cover for 15 to 20 minutes or until vegetables are tender. Drain.

**2.** Add butter to vegetables. Coarsely mash vegetables with potato masher. Stir in sour cream and ¾ cup of the cheese. Season to taste with salt and pepper. Top with remaining cheese. Makes 6 servings.

***NOTE:** Use caution when handling chile peppers. Wear disposable gloves and wash your hands thoroughly after preparation.

Each serving: 320 cal., 17 g total fat (9 g sat. fat), 45 mg chol., 311 mg sodium, 35 g carbo., 4 g fiber, 10 g pro. Daily Values: 78% vit. A, 47% vit. C, 18% calcium, 14% iron.

## Mashed Potatoes Alfredo

**PREP:** 15 minutes **COOK:** 20 minutes

- 2 lb. round red or round white potatoes, peeled and cut up
- 1 large onion, chopped (1 cup)
- 2 Tbsp. cooking oil
- 2 Tbsp. butter
- 1 10-oz. container refrigerated light Alfredo pasta sauce
- Salt and ground black pepper

**1.** In a large saucepan place potatoes and enough lightly salted water to cover. Bring to boiling; reduce heat. Simmer, covered, about 20 minutes or until potatoes are tender.

**2.** Meanwhile, in a large skillet cook and stir onion in hot oil over medium heat about 10 minutes or until very tender and golden. Drain potatoes thoroughly. Return to saucepan. Mash potatoes with the butter. Stir in onion mixture and Alfredo pasta sauce. Heat through, if necessary. Season to taste with salt and pepper. Makes 8 servings.

Each serving: 179 cal., 10 g total fat (4 g sat. fat), 23 mg chol., 319 mg sodium, 19 g carbo., 2 g fiber, 3 g pro. Daily Values: 4% vit. A, 22% vit. C, 6% calcium, 4% iron.

## Mashed Sweets with Sage and Cranberries

**PREP:** 25 minutes **COOK:** 20 minutes

- 2½ to 3 lb. sweet potatoes, peeled and cut into eighths
- 1 medium onion, finely chopped (½ cup)
- ¼ cup butter
- 1 Tbsp. snipped fresh sage or 1 tsp. ground sage
- ½ tsp. salt
- ½ tsp. ground black pepper
- ½ cup dried cranberries
- ¼ cup half-and-half or light cream

**1.** In a Dutch oven place potatoes and enough lightly salted water to cover. Bring to boiling; reduce heat. Simmer, covered, for 20 to 25 minutes or until tender.

**2.** Meanwhile, in a large skillet cook onion in butter over medium heat until tender. Add sage, salt, and pepper. Cook 1 minute. Stir in cranberries. Remove skillet from the heat.

**3.** Drain potatoes. Return to Dutch oven. Add half-and-half; mash with a potato masher or beat with an electric mixer on low speed until smooth. Stir in onion-sage mixture. Makes 6 servings.

Each serving: 225 cal., 9 g total fat (5 g sat. fat), 25 mg chol., 274 mg sodium, 34 g carbo., 5 g fiber, 3 g pro. Daily Values: 342% vit. A, 40% vit. C, 6% calcium, 5% iron.

## Potatoes with an Asian Flair

**Fast!** **START TO FINISH:** 27 minutes

- 3 lb. potatoes, scrubbed and cut into bite-size pieces
- 2 cups fresh snow pea pods, strings and tips removed
- ⅓ cup teriyaki sauce
- 2 Tbsp. hoisin sauce or oyster sauce
- 2 Tbsp. cooking oil
- 1 Tbsp. rice vinegar
- 1 Tbsp. minced fresh ginger
- ⅛ to ¼ tsp. cayenne pepper
- ½ cup sliced green onions (4)
- ¼ cup snipped fresh Thai basil or basil leaves

**1.** In a Dutch oven place potatoes and enough water to cover. Bring to boiling; reduce heat. Simmer, covered, 10 minutes. Add pea pods; return to boiling. Cook 2 minutes more or until potatoes are tender; drain well.

**2.** In a small saucepan combine teriyaki sauce, hoisin sauce, oil, vinegar, ginger, and cayenne. Cook and stir over medium heat until mixture just comes to boiling.

**3.** In a large bowl combine potato-pea pod mixture, green onions, and teriyaki mixture. Toss to coat. Top with fresh basil. Serve warm. Makes 12 servings.

**Healthy** Each serving: 105 cal., 2 g total fat (0 g sat. fat), 0 mg chol., 311 mg sodium, 17 g carbo., 2 g fiber, 3 g pro. Daily Values: 3% vit. A, 24% vit. C, 3% calcium, 8% iron.

## Potato Sauté with Herbed Tomato Topping

**START TO FINISH:** 45 minutes

- 1 recipe Herbed Tomato Topping (below)
- 2 lb. red potatoes, peeled and coarsely chopped (6 medium)
- 3 slices bacon, coarsely chopped
- 1 medium onion, chopped (½ cup)
- ¼ cup whipping cream
- 1½ tsp. coarse-grain Dijon-style mustard or Dijon-style mustard
- Salt and ground black pepper
- 2 oz. Asiago or Parmesan cheese, shaved
- Fresh basil sprigs (optional)

**1.** Prepare Herbed Tomato Topping. Cover and let stand at room temperature while preparing potatoes.

**2.** In a large saucepan place potatoes and enough lightly salted water to cover. Bring to boiling; reduce heat. Simmer, covered, for 8 to 10 minutes or until potatoes are just tender. Drain well.

**3.** In a large skillet cook bacon until crisp; remove with a slotted spoon. Reserve 2 tablespoons bacon drippings in skillet. Add onion; cook and stir until onion is tender. Add potatoes and bacon to skillet; cover and cook over medium-low heat for 5 to 8 minutes or until heated through, turning mixture occasionally.

**4.** Combine whipping cream and mustard; add to potato mixture. Cook, uncovered, 1 to 2 minutes, turning potatoes to coat with sauce. Season to taste with salt and pepper. Transfer to a large serving bowl; top with Herbed Tomato Topping and cheese. If desired, garnish with fresh basil sprigs. Makes 8 servings.

**HERBED TOMATO TOPPING:** In a large bowl combine 3 roma tomatoes, seeded and chopped; ½ cup bottled roasted red sweet peppers, drained and chopped; 2 tablespoons extra-virgin olive oil; 2 tablespoons snipped fresh basil; and 1 tablespoon balsamic vinegar.

Each serving: 213 cal., 14 g total fat (6 g sat. fat), 23 mg chol., 232 mg sodium, 18 g carbo., 2 g fiber, 5 g pro. Daily Values: 8% vit. A, 71% vit. C, 8% calcium, 8% iron.

# FIVE-INGREDIENT DINNERS

**PRIZE TESTED RECIPES® $400 WINNER**

JAN OLIVER, GOLDEN, COLO.

**PRIZE TESTED RECIPES® $200 WINNER**

KAY KRAUSE, SIOUX FALLS, S.D.

## Polenta and Black Beans

*Fast!* **START TO FINISH:** 20 minutes

| | |
|---|---|
| 3 cups water | 1 14½-oz. can diced |
| 1 cup yellow cornmeal | tomatoes, undrained |
| 1 cup water | 1 cup bottled salsa with |
| ½ tsp. salt | cilantro or other salsa |
| 1 15-oz. can black beans, | ¾ cup shredded Mexican |
| rinsed and drained | cheese blend (3 oz.) |

**1.** For polenta,* in a large saucepan bring the 3 cups water to boiling. In a medium bowl combine cornmeal, the 1 cup water, and ½ teaspoon salt. Stir cornmeal mixture slowly into the boiling water. Cook and stir until mixture comes to boiling. Reduce heat to low. Cook for 5 to 10 minutes or until mixture is thick, stirring occasionally. (If mixture is too thick, stir in additional water.)

**2.** Meanwhile, in a large skillet combine the beans, undrained tomatoes, and salsa. Bring mixture to boiling; reduce heat. Simmer, uncovered, for 10 minutes, stirring frequently. Stir ½ cup of the cheese into the polenta. Divide polenta among 4 shallow bowls. Top with the bean mixture and sprinkle with the remaining cheese. Makes 4 servings.

***NOTE:** Polenta can be made from a variety of cornmeal products. In this recipe, yellow cornmeal produced the best results.

Each serving: 311 cal., 8 g total fat (4 g sat. fat), 19 mg chol., 751 mg sodium, 49 g carbo., 8 g fiber, 15 g pro. Daily Values: 6% vit. A, 28% vit. C, 21% calcium, 13% iron.

## Curried Apple Pork Chops

**PREP:** 15 minutes **COOK:** 36 minutes

| | |
|---|---|
| 4 boneless pork loin chops, | 1 21-oz. can apple or peach |
| cut ¾ inch thick | pie filling |
| (about 1½ lb.) | 2 tsp. curry powder |
| Salt and ground black pepper | 1 8-oz. pkg. frozen sugar |
| 1 Tbsp. olive oil | snap peas |
| 2 large sweet potatoes, | |
| peeled and thinly sliced | |
| (about 1¼ lb.) | |

**1.** Season pork chops with salt and pepper. In a 12-inch skillet brown pork on both sides in hot oil. Add sweet potatoes. Cover and cook over medium heat for 15 minutes.

**2.** Meanwhile, combine pie filling and curry powder; spoon over sweet potatoes. Cover and cook 15 minutes more or until potatoes are nearly tender. Add sugar snap peas. Cover and cook 6 to 8 minutes more or until the peas are crisp-tender. Makes 4 servings.

Each serving: 539 cal., 13 g total fat (4 g sat. fat), 92 mg chol., 301 mg sodium, 63 g carbo., 6 g fiber, 41 g pro. Daily Values: 253% vit. A, 50% vit. C, 9% calcium, 17% iron.

## Chicken Caesar

**PREP:** 10 minutes **BAKE:** 40 minutes
**STAND:** 10 minutes

4   medium skinless, boneless chicken
    breast halves (1¼ to 1½ lb. total)
1½  cups water
¾   cup bottled creamy Caesar salad
    dressing
½   tsp. salt
¼   tsp. ground black pepper
2   cups uncooked instant white rice
2   to 2½ cups frozen broccoli cuts,
    thawed
½   cup finely shredded Parmesan
    cheese

**1.** Preheat oven to 375° F. Cut each chicken breast half into thirds. In a 2-quart rectangular baking dish arrange chicken pieces in a single layer. In a medium bowl whisk together water, salad dressing, salt, and pepper; pour over chicken.

**2.** Bake, covered, for 20 minutes. Remove from oven. Add rice and broccoli around the chicken; stir gently to combine. Return to oven and bake, covered, 15 minutes more. Top with Parmesan cheese. Bake, uncovered, 5 minutes more. Let stand 10 minutes before serving. Makes 4 to 6 servings.

Each serving: 867 cal., 46 g total fat (16 g sat. fat), 131 mg chol., 1,998 mg sodium, 45 g carbo., 2 g fiber, 63 g pro. Daily Values: 19% vit. A, 30% vit. C, 88% calcium, 21% iron.

## Coconut Curry Chicken

*Fast!* **PREP:** 15 minutes **COOK:** 15 minutes

6   skinless, boneless chicken breast
    halves (about 2 lb. total)
1½  tsp. red curry paste
½   tsp. salt
¼   tsp. ground black pepper
1   Tbsp. cooking oil
½   cup unsweetened coconut milk
2   9-oz. pkg. frozen peas and potatoes
    with cream sauce, thawed
¼   cup coconut, toasted

**1.** Rub chicken with a mixture of ½ teaspoon of the curry paste, the salt, and the pepper. In a 12-inch skillet brown chicken on both sides in hot oil; remove from skillet.

**2.** In a small mixing bowl whisk coconut milk and remaining curry paste together until combined. In the skillet combine thawed peas and potatoes with cream sauce and coconut milk mixture. Bring to boiling, stirring occasionally. Top with chicken pieces.

**3.** Cover and simmer 15 to 20 minutes or until chicken is tender and no longer pink (170° F). Sprinkle with coconut before serving. Makes 6 servings.

Each serving: 314 cal., 12 g total fat (7 g sat. fat), 94 mg chol., 571 mg sodium, 12 g carbo., 1 g fiber, 39 g pro. Daily Values: 3% vit. A, 7% vit. C, 6% calcium, 8% iron.

## Italian Chicken Skillet

*Fast!* **START TO FINISH:** 25 minutes

1½  lb. skinless, boneless chicken breast
    halves, cut into thin bite-size strips
2   Tbsp. olive oil
¼   tsp. salt
⅛   tsp. ground black pepper
1   14½-oz. can diced tomatoes with
    basil, garlic, and oregano, drained
2   Tbsp. snipped fresh basil
1   10-oz. pkg. prewashed fresh spinach
1   cup shredded mozzarella cheese
    (4 oz.)

**1.** In a 12-inch skillet cook chicken, half at a time, in hot oil over medium-high heat until no longer pink; drain off fat. Return chicken to skillet. Sprinkle chicken with the salt and pepper.

**2.** Add drained tomatoes and fresh basil to skillet. Bring to boiling. Gradually add spinach to skillet, tossing with tongs just until spinach is wilted. Remove from heat. Sprinkle with mozzarella cheese. Let stand 3 to 5 minutes until cheese melts. Makes 4 servings.

Each serving: 380 cal., 14 g total fat (4 g sat. fat), 116 mg chol., 998 mg sodium, 12 g carbo., 2 g fiber, 50 g pro. Daily Values: 150% vit. A, 46% vit. C, 38% calcium, 26% iron.

## Quick Thai Chicken Salad

*Fast!* **START TO FINISH:** 20 minutes

1   2- to 2¼-lb. purchased whole
    roasted chicken
1   5-oz. pkg. mixed baby salad greens
⅓   cup mayonnaise
⅓   cup bottled peanut sauce
1   cup chow mein noodles, ¾ cup dry
    roasted peanuts, ½ cup snipped
    fresh cilantro or mint, or ½ cup
    coconut, toasted

**1.** Remove skin from chicken and discard. Remove meat from bones; discard bones. Cut chicken into bite-size pieces.

**2.** Divide greens among 4 serving plates; top with chicken. In a small bowl combine mayonnaise and peanut sauce; drizzle over chicken. To serve, sprinkle with chow mein noodles, peanuts, cilantro, mint, or coconut. Makes 4 servings.

Each serving: 548 cal., 37 g total fat (8 g sat. fat), 113 mg chol., 642 mg sodium, 16 g carbo., 2 g fiber, 35 g pro. Daily Values: 11% vit. A, 7% vit. C, 4% calcium, 13% iron.

## Beef Tips on Toast

*Fast!* **START TO FINISH:** 25 minutes

2   small zucchini and/or yellow summer
    squash, thinly sliced (about 2 cups)
½   of a medium red onion, cut into thin
    wedges (about ¾ cup)
1   Tbsp. olive oil or cooking oil
1   17-oz. pkg. refrigerated cooked beef
    tips with gravy
4   1-inch-thick slices white or wheat
    bread, toasted
½   cup crumbled feta cheese (2 oz.)

**1.** In a large skillet cook zucchini and onion in hot oil just until tender. Add beef tips with gravy; heat through, breaking up meat with a spoon.

**2.** To serve, spoon beef mixture over toast slices. Sprinkle each serving with feta cheese. Makes 4 servings.

Each serving: 354 cal., 14 g total fat (5 g sat. fat), 60 mg chol., 1,157 mg sodium, 34 g carbo., 3 g fiber, 24 g pro. Daily Values: 3% vit. A, 13% vit. C, 19% calcium, 21% iron.

# CRANBERRIES

## Double Cranberry Crostini

**PREP:** 45 minutes **BAKE:** 6 minutes **COOL:** 1 hour

**1.** Prepare Cranberry-Ginger Chutney; set aside to cool.

**2.** Preheat oven to 375° F. Place 1/3 cup dried cranberries in a small bowl; add enough boiling water to cover. Cover; let stand 15 minutes. Drain well. In a medium mixing bowl beat two 3-ounce packages softened cream cheese until smooth. Beat in drained cranberries; 2 tablespoons chopped pecans, toasted; 1 teaspoon finely chopped, peeled fresh ginger; and 1 teaspoon lime juice. Set aside.

**3.** Slice one 16-ounce loaf baguette-style French bread diagonally into 1/2-inch slices. Place on a large baking sheet (use 2 sheets if necessary to fit all slices in 1 layer). Bake for 6 to 8 minutes or until edges just start to brown. Cool slightly.

**4.** Cut 4 ounces thinly sliced smoked turkey or ham into about 30 pieces to fit on bread slices. Spread bread with cranberry-cheese mixture. Top each with a piece of turkey. Dollop with Cranberry-Ginger Chutney. Makes about 30 appetizers.

**CRANBERRY-GINGER CHUTNEY:** In saucepan combine 1 1/2 cups cranberries; 3/4 cup packed brown sugar; 1/3 cup dried apricot halves, chopped; 1/3 cup golden raisins; 2 tablespoons finely chopped, peeled fresh ginger; 2 tablespoons cranberry juice; 3/4 teaspoon ground cardamom; and 1/4 teaspoon cayenne pepper. Cook over medium heat, stirring constantly, until sugar is dissolved. Cook, uncovered, 3 to 4 minutes more or until cranberries pop, stirring occasionally. Transfer to bowl; let stand about 1 hour or until completely cool. Cover and chill up to 1 week.

Each appetizer: 107 cal., 3 g total fat (1 g sat. fat), 8 mg chol., 150 mg sodium, 18 g carbo., 1 g fiber, 3 g pro. Daily Values: 3% vit. A, 2% vit. C, 2% calcium, 4% iron.

## Cranberry Cake

**PREP:** 20 minutes **BAKE:** 40 minutes **COOL:** 30 minutes

| | | |
|---|---|---|
| 3 | cups fresh cranberries | 1/2 cup butter, melted |
| 1 | cup chopped pecans | 2 Tbsp. milk |
| 2 | cups sugar | Sweetened whipped cream |
| 2 | eggs | (optional) |
| 1 | cup all-purpose flour | |

**1.** Preheat oven to 350° F. Generously grease a 2-quart rectangular baking dish. Spread cranberries and pecans over bottom of the dish. Sprinkle with 1 cup of the sugar.

**2.** In a mixing bowl beat eggs with an electric mixer on high speed until foamy. Add remaining 1 cup sugar, the flour, melted butter, and milk; beat on low speed just until combined (batter will be thick). Carefully spread batter over cranberries and nuts.

**3.** Bake for 40 to 45 minutes or until top is brown and a wooden toothpick inserted near the center comes out clean. Cool on wire rack at least 30 minutes. To serve, spoon warm cake into dessert dishes, cranberry side up. If desired, top with sweetened whipped cream. Makes 12 servings.

Each serving: 319 cal., 16 g total fat (5 g sat. fat), 57 mg chol., 71 mg sodium, 44 g carbo., 2 g fiber, 3 g pro. Daily Values: 6% vit. A, 6% vit. C, 2% calcium, 5% iron.

## Cranberry Chutney

Serve this relish either warm or cool over roast pork, ham, or poultry.

**PREP:** 20 minutes **COOK:** 20 minutes
**COOL:** 15 minutes

1 tsp. cardamom seeds
1/2 cup finely chopped green onions (4)
1 Tbsp. butter or margarine
2 cups fresh or frozen cranberries
1 12-oz. jar red currant jelly (1 cup)
1/4 cup sugar
2 tsp. pomegranate vinegar or balsamic vinegar

**1.** Heat a medium saucepan over medium heat. Add cardamom seeds and heat for 30 seconds or until fragrant. Transfer seeds to a spice grinder; cover and process until finely crushed, or finely crush with a mortar and pestle.

**2.** In the same saucepan cook green onions in hot butter until just tender. Add cranberries, jelly, sugar, vinegar, and the toasted cardamom seeds. Heat to boiling; reduce heat. Simmer, covered, for 20 minutes. Cool 15 minutes. Makes about 2 cups (eight 1/4-cup servings).

Each serving: 155 cal., 2 g total fat (1 g sat. fat), 4 mg chol., 24 mg sodium, 37 g carbo., 2 g fiber, 0 g pro. Daily Values: 3% vit. A, 9% vit. C, 1% calcium, 1% iron.

## French Orchid

*Fast!* **START TO FINISH:** 5 minutes

Ice cubes
1/2 cup rosé wine or pink sparkling wine, chilled
1/2 cup cranberry juice, chilled
2 Tbsp. orange liqueur
Orange slice

**1.** Fill a 12-ounce glass about one-third full with ice cubes. Add wine, cranberry juice, and orange liqueur. Garnish with a fresh orange slice. Makes 1 serving.

Each serving: 230 cal., 0 g total fat (0 g sat. fat), 0 mg chol., 18 mg sodium, 28 g carbo., 0 g fiber, 0 g pro. Daily Values: 50% vit. C.

## Cranberry-Pumpkin Mini Loaves

These festive-looking loaves make tasty holiday gifts.

**PREP:** 45 minutes **BAKE:** 35 minutes
**COOL:** 2 hours

2 cups all-purpose flour
1/2 cup granulated sugar
1/2 cup packed brown sugar
2 1/2 tsp. baking powder
1 tsp. ground cinnamon
1 tsp. finely shredded orange peel
1/2 tsp. baking soda
1/2 tsp. salt
1/4 tsp. ground ginger
1 cup canned pumpkin
1/3 cup cooking oil
1/3 cup milk
2 eggs, beaten
1/2 cup chopped pecans
1/2 cup fresh cranberries, coarsely chopped
1 recipe Cranberry Streusel Topping (above right)

**1.** Preheat oven to 350° F. Grease and flour the bottom and half way up sides of six 4 1/2×2 1/2×1 1/2-inch loaf pans; set aside. In a large bowl stir together the flour, granulated sugar, brown sugar, baking powder, cinnamon, orange peel, baking soda, salt, and ginger. Make a well in center of the flour mixture; set aside.

**2.** In a medium bowl combine pumpkin, oil, milk, and eggs. Add the pumpkin mixture all at once to the flour mixture. Stir just until moistened. Fold in pecans and cranberries. Spoon the batter into the prepared pans. Sprinkle Cranberry Streusel Topping over batter.

**3.** Bake for 35 to 40 minutes or until a wooden toothpick inserted in centers comes out clean. Cool in pans on wire racks for 10 minutes. Carefully remove from pans, trying not to disturb topping. Cool completely on wire racks. Wrap and store overnight before serving. Makes 6 small loaves (12 servings).

**CRANBERRY STREUSEL TOPPING:** In a medium bowl combine 3/4 cup coarsely chopped fresh cranberries, 1/2 cup coarsely chopped pecans, 1/4 cup packed brown sugar, 1/4 teaspoon ground cinnamon, and 1/4 teaspoon ground ginger. Stir to mix.

Each serving: 300 cal., 14 g total fat (2 g sat. fat), 36 mg chol., 222 mg sodium, 42 g carbo., 3 g fiber, 4 g pro. Daily Values: 65% vit. A, 5% vit. C, 6% calcium, 11% iron.

## Holiday Cranberry Salsa

**PREP:** 25 minutes **CHILL:** 4 hours

2 cups fresh cranberries, coarsely chopped
1 or 2 fresh jalapeño chile peppers, seeded and finely chopped*
1 tsp. finely shredded orange peel
1 large orange, peeled, sectioned, and cut up (1/2 cup)
1/2 cup chopped cucumber
1/4 cup chopped yellow sweet pepper
1/4 cup chopped celery
1/4 cup chopped red onion
1 Tbsp. snipped fresh cilantro
3 Tbsp. honey
2 Tbsp. lime juice
2 tsp. olive oil
1/4 tsp. salt

**1.** In a large bowl combine cranberries, jalapeño pepper, orange peel, orange pieces, cucumber, sweet pepper, celery, onion, and cilantro.

**2.** In a small bowl combine honey, lime juice, olive oil, and salt. Add to cranberry mixture, tossing gently to coat. Cover and chill 4 to 24 hours before serving. Makes about 4 cups (sixteen 1/4-cup servings).

**\*NOTE:** Use caution when handling chile peppers. Wear disposable gloves and wash your hands thoroughly after preparation.

*Healthy* Each serving: 30 cal., 1 g total fat (0 g sat. fat), 0 mg chol., 39 mg sodium, 7 g carbo., 1 g fiber, 0 g pro. Daily Values: 1% vit. A, 22% vit. C, 1% calcium, 1% iron.

# DESSERTS FOR ENTERTAINING

## Pear-Almond Tart

**PREP:** 25 minutes  **BAKE:** 45 minutes

Nonstick cooking spray
1 cup unblanched whole almonds, toasted
2/3 cup sugar
1/2 cup milk
5 Tbsp. butter, melted
1/4 cup all-purpose flour
3 eggs
1 tsp. vanilla
1/2 tsp. ground cinnamon
1/4 tsp. salt
1/4 tsp. ground nutmeg
2 ripe medium pears
2 Tbsp. sugar
Ice cream or whipped cream (optional)

**1.** Preheat oven to 375° F. Lightly coat a 10-inch quiche dish with cooking spray; set aside. In a food processor combine almonds and the 2/3 cup sugar; cover and process until nuts are ground. Add milk, butter, flour, eggs, vanilla, cinnamon, salt, and nutmeg. Cover and process with several on-off turns until combined. Pour mixture into prepared dish. Set aside.

**2.** Core and quarter pears. Place pears, skin side up, on a cutting board. Slice thinly, cutting from bottom end almost to, but not through, stem end; do not separate slices. Arrange pears in nut mixture, fanning slices slightly. Sprinkle with remaining sugar.

**3.** Bake for 45 to 50 minutes or until surface is puffed and browned. If edges brown faster than center, cover edges with foil the last 10 minutes to prevent overbrowning. Loosen edges; serve warm or cool. If desired, add ice cream. Makes 10 servings.

Each serving: 248 cal., 15 g total fat (4 g sat. fat), 81 mg chol., 129 mg sodium, 26 g carbo., 3 g fiber, 6 g pro. Daily Values: 6% vit. A, 2% vit. C, 6% calcium, 6% iron.

## Creamy Apple Pie

**PREP:** 1 hour  **BAKE:** 10 minutes  **COOL:** 15 minutes  **CHILL:** 4 hours

Nonstick cooking spray
2 cups finely crushed crunchy oat and honey granola bars (12 bars)
1 cup flaked coconut
1/4 cup butter, melted
2 Tbsp. butter
1/2 cup packed brown sugar
1 Tbsp. lemon juice
1 tsp. ground cinnamon
7 large cooking apples, peeled, cored, and cut into thick slices (about 3 1/2 lb.)
1 8-oz. carton mascarpone cheese or one 8-oz. pkg. cream cheese, softened
1/4 cup granulated sugar
2 Tbsp. amaretto or 1/2 tsp. almond extract
1 cup whipping cream

**1.** Preheat oven to 350° F. Coat a 9-inch pie plate with cooking spray. Combine crushed granola bars, coconut, and 1/4 cup butter. Press on bottom and up sides of pie plate. Bake 10 minutes. Cool. In very large skillet melt 2 tablespoons butter over medium heat. Stir in brown sugar, lemon juice, and cinnamon. Stir in apples. Cook, uncovered, over medium heat for 25 minutes or until very tender; stir occasionally. Cool 15 minutes.

**2.** In large bowl beat cheese, granulated sugar, and amaretto with electric mixer on medium speed for 30 seconds or until fluffy. In bowl beat cream on medium speed until soft peaks form. Beat whipped cream into mascarpone mixture on low speed until combined. Layer half of the apple mixture in crust. Spread half of the cheese mixture over apples. Repeat layers. Cover loosely and chill at least 4 hours or up to 24 hours. Makes 8 to 10 servings.

Each serving: 698 cal., 43 g total fat (24 g sat. fat), 101 mg chol., 265 mg sodium, 77 g carbo., 7 g fiber, 11 g pro. Daily Values: 16% vit. A, 13% vit. C, 5% calcium, 8% iron.

## Mango Cheesecake

The coconut adds a chewiness to this cheesecake's crust.

**PREP:** 30 minutes **BAKE:** 55 minutes
**COOL:** 1³/4 hours **CHILL:** 4 hours

1 cup regular rolled oats
1 cup sliced almonds
1 cup shredded or flaked coconut
¹/₃ cup sugar
¹/₄ cup butter, melted
¹/₄ tsp. vanilla
¹/₄ tsp. almond extract
2 medium mangoes
3 8-oz. pkg. cream cheese, softened
1 cup sugar
2 Tbsp. all-purpose flour
2 tsp. vanilla
2 eggs, slightly beaten
2 tsp. finely shredded lemon peel

**1.** Preheat oven to 350° F. For crust, in a food processor or blender place rolled oats. Cover and process or blend until oats are finely chopped. Transfer to a medium bowl. Repeat to finely chop the almonds; transfer to the bowl. Repeat to finely chop the coconut; transfer to the bowl. Add the ¹/₃ cup sugar to the bowl. Combine melted butter, ¹/₄ teaspoon vanilla, and the almond extract; add to oat mixture. Stir to combine. Press mixture onto the bottom and ¹/₂ inch up the sides of a 9-inch springform pan. Bake for 10 minutes.

**2.** Seed, peel, and slice mangoes.* In the food processor or blender puree enough mango to equal ¹/₂ cup. Wrap remaining mango slices and chill.

**3.** For filling, in a large bowl beat cream cheese, 1 cup sugar, the flour, and 2 teaspoons vanilla until combined. Beat in pureed mango until smooth. Stir in eggs and lemon peel. Pour into baked crust.

**4.** Bake for 45 to 50 minutes or until a 2¹/₂-inch area around the outside edge appears set when gently shaken. Cool in pan on a wire rack for 15 minutes. Using a sharp small knife, loosen the crust from sides of pan; cool 30 minutes more. Remove sides of the pan; cool cheesecake completely on the rack. Cover and chill at least 4 hours or up to 24 hours before serving. Top with reserved mango slices before serving. Makes 12 servings.

**\*NOTE:** To prepare each mango, slide a sharp knife next to the seed along 1 side, cutting through the fruit. Repeat on the other side of the seed, dividing the mango into 2 large pieces. Cut away the fruit that remains around the seed. Remove the peel and slice all the fruit.

Each serving: 501 cal., 34 g total fat (19 g sat. fat), 108 mg chol., 239 mg sodium, 42 g carbo., 4 g fiber, 10 g pro. Daily Values: 24% vit. A, 17% vit. C, 9% calcium, 10% iron.

## Tiramisu Brownie Trifle

**PREP:** 45 minutes **BAKE:** 25 minutes
**CHILL:** 2 hours

1 recipe Fudgy Coffee Brownies (right)
¹/₃ cup water
¹/₄ cup granulated sugar
2 Tbsp. instant espresso coffee powder or instant coffee crystals
1 3-oz. pkg. ladyfingers, split
1 8-oz. pkg. cream cheese, softened
¹/₂ of an 8-oz. carton dairy sour cream
¹/₄ cup coffee liqueur or 1 tsp. instant espresso coffee powder or instant coffee crystals dissolved in ¹/₄ cup warm water
¹/₂ cup sifted powdered sugar
1 tsp. vanilla
1 cup whipping cream
1 recipe Coffee Whipped Cream (right)

**1.** Prepare Fudgy Coffee Brownies and cool completely. For coffee syrup, in a small saucepan combine ¹/₃ cup water, granulated sugar, and 2 tablespoons espresso powder. Cook over medium heat until boiling. Boil, uncovered, 1 minute. Remove from heat and cool.

**2.** Brush flat sides of ladyfingers with cooled coffee syrup; drizzle any remaining syrup over brownies. Arrange ladyfingers, rounded side out, around outside and over the bottom of a 3-quart clear soufflé dish or trifle bowl.

**3.** In a large mixing bowl beat cream cheese with an electric mixer until light and fluffy. Beat in sour cream, coffee liqueur, powdered sugar, and vanilla until combined. Gradually add whipping cream to cream cheese mixture, beating on medium to high speed until thickened. Spoon half of the whipping cream mixture into center of ladyfinger-lined dish.

**4.** Coarsely crumble brownies. Layer half of the crumbled brownies over the whipping cream layer. Repeat layers. Cover and chill for 2 to 24 hours. To serve, drop Coffee Whipped Cream by spoonfuls over the brownie layer. Makes 12 servings.

**FUDGY COFFEE BROWNIES:** Preheat oven to 350° F. Grease a 9×9×2-inch baking pan; set aside. In medium saucepan melt ¹/₂ cup butter and 3 ounces unsweetened chocolate, coarsely chopped. Remove from heat. Stir in 1 tablespoon instant espresso coffee powder or instant coffee crystals; cool 15 minutes. Stir in 1 cup granulated sugar and 2 eggs, beating well with a wooden spoon. Combine ²/₃ cup flour and ¹/₄ teaspoon baking soda; stir into chocolate mixture. Spread in prepared pan. Bake for 25 minutes.

**COFFEE WHIPPED CREAM:** Chill a medium mixing bowl and the beaters of an electric mixer. In the chilled bowl combine 1 cup whipping cream, 2 tablespoons granulated sugar, and 2 tablespoons coffee liqueur or cooled brewed espresso coffee. Beat on medium speed until soft peaks form.

Each serving: 524 cal., 37 g total fat (21 g sat. fat), 162 mg chol., 183 mg sodium, 43 g carbo., 1 g fiber, 6 g pro. Daily Values: 25% vit. A, 1% vit. C, 7% calcium, 10% iron.

# PARTY SNACK MIXES

## Kid Friendly Tropical Snack Mix

**PREP:** 20 minutes  **BAKE:** 45 minutes

| | |
|---|---|
| 12 | cups popped popcorn (about ½ cup unpopped) |
| 1 | cup chopped macadamia nuts |
| 1 | 7-oz. pkg. tropical blend mixed dried fruit bits |
| ½ | cup dried cranberries |
| ½ | cup butter |
| 1 | cup raw or granulated sugar |
| 1 | tsp. finely shredded lime peel |
| 1 | tsp. finely shredded orange peel |
| ½ | tsp. ground ginger |

**1.** Preheat oven to 300° F. Remove all unpopped kernels from popped popcorn. In a large roasting pan combine the popcorn, nuts, fruit bits, and cranberries; set aside.

**2.** In a small saucepan combine butter, sugar, lime peel, orange peel, and ginger. Cook and stir over medium heat until butter is melted and mixture is nearly smooth (the sugar will not completely dissolve). Pour mixture over popcorn mixture; stir gently to coat.

**3.** Bake for 45 minutes, stirring every 15 minutes. Remove from oven. Spread mixture on a large piece of foil to cool. Store in an airtight container up to 1 week. Makes about 15 cups (15 servings).

Each serving: 254 cal., 14 g total fat (5 g sat. fat), 17 mg chol., 87 mg sodium, 33 g carbo., 3 g fiber, 2 g pro. Daily Values: 6% vit. A, 1% vit. C, 2% calcium, 3% iron.

## Crunchy Munchies

**PREP:** 20 minutes  **BAKE:** 15 minutes

| | |
|---|---|
| ¼ | cup jalapeño pepper jelly |
| 2 | Tbsp. butter |
| ¼ | tsp. five-spice powder |
| ¼ | tsp. salt |
| ¼ | tsp. bottled hot pepper sauce |
| 2 | cups whole cashews or dry-roasted peanuts |
| 1 | cup dried banana chips |
| 1 | cup dried pineapple chunks, cut up |
| 1 | cup chopped dates |
| 1 | cup chow mein noodles |

**1.** Preheat oven to 325° F. In a large saucepan combine jelly, butter, five-spice powder, salt, and hot pepper sauce. Heat over low heat until jelly is melted. Stir in nuts, banana chips, pineapple, dates, and chow mein noodles until well coated. Pour mixture into a large roasting pan.

**2.** Bake for 15 to 20 minutes or until cashews are lightly browned, stirring once. Remove from oven. Spread mixture on a large piece of foil to cool. Store in an airtight container up to 3 days. Makes about 6 cups (16 servings).

Each serving: 232 cal., 13 g total fat (4 g sat. fat), 4 mg chol., 131 mg sodium, 29 g carbo., 2 g fiber, 4 g pro. Daily Values: 1% vit. A, 1% vit. C, 2% calcium, 7% iron.

## Double Chocolate Spiced Snack Mix

**Kid Friendly**

**PREP:** 15 minutes **BAKE:** 30 minutes

- 1 12-oz. box crispy corn and rice cereal (about 10 cups)
- 1½ cups mixed nuts
- ½ cup packed brown sugar
- ½ cup light-colored corn syrup
- ½ cup butter
- 1 tsp. ground cinnamon
- ½ tsp. ground ginger
- 1½ cups chocolate-covered raisins or chocolate-covered peanuts
- 1½ cups semisweet or milk chocolate pieces

**1.** Preheat oven to 300° F. In a large roasting pan combine cereal and nuts; set aside. In a small saucepan combine sugar, corn syrup, butter, cinnamon, and ginger. Cook and stir over medium heat until butter is melted and mixture is smooth. Pour over cereal mixture; stir gently to coat.

**2.** Bake for 30 minutes, stirring twice. Remove from oven. Spread mixture on a large piece of buttered foil to cool. Break into pieces and place in a bowl. Stir in chocolate-covered raisins and chocolate pieces. Store in an airtight container up to 1 week. Makes 16 cups (32 servings).

Each serving: 216 cal., 10 g total fat (5 g sat. fat), 10 mg chol., 129 mg sodium, 30 g carbo., 1 g fiber, 2 g pro. Daily Values: 6% vit. A, 4% vit. C, 1% calcium, 19% iron.

## Haystack Snack

**Kid Friendly**

**PREP:** 25 minutes **BAKE:** 20 minutes

- 12 cups popped popcorn (about ½ cup unpopped)
- 2 1¾-oz. cans shoestring potatoes
- 2 cups sesame sticks
- ⅓ cup butter, melted
- 1 Tbsp. dried dillweed
- 1 Tbsp. Worcestershire sauce
- ½ to 1 tsp. garlic salt
- ½ tsp. onion powder

**1.** Preheat oven to 350° F. Remove all unpopped kernels from popped popcorn. In a large roasting pan combine popcorn, shoestring potatoes, and sesame sticks; set aside. In a small bowl combine melted butter, dillweed, Worcestershire sauce, garlic salt, and onion powder. Drizzle over popcorn mixture in pan; stir gently to coat.

**2.** Bake for 20 minutes, stirring once. Remove from oven. Spread mixture on a large piece of foil to cool. Store in an airtight container up to 4 days. Makes about 13 cups (12 to 16 servings).

Each serving: 174 cal., 12 g total fat (4 g sat. fat), 14 mg chol., 119 mg sodium, 15 g carbo., 2 g fiber, 3 g pro. Daily Values: 4% vit. A, 7% vit. C, 2% calcium, 4% iron.

## Sweet Party Snack Mix

**PREP:** 20 minutes **BAKE:** 30 minutes

- 6 cups bite-size square rice cereal
- 3 cups round toasted oat cereal
- ½ cup slivered almonds or chopped pecans
- ½ cup butter
- ⅓ cup granulated sugar
- ⅓ cup packed brown sugar
- 1 tsp. ground cinnamon
- 1 tsp. vanilla
- ½ cup golden raisins
- ½ cup raisins
- ½ cup dried cranberries
- ½ cup dried tart red cherries

**1.** Preheat oven to 300° F. In a large roasting pan stir together the cereals and almonds; set aside. In a medium saucepan cook butter, granulated sugar, and brown sugar over medium heat until butter is melted. Remove from heat; stir in cinnamon and vanilla. Pour over cereal mixture in pan; toss to coat.

**2.** Bake for 30 minutes, stirring twice. Remove from oven. Stir in raisins, cranberries, and cherries. Cool mixture in pan on a wire rack. Transfer to a covered storage container and store at room temperature up to 1 week. Makes about 12 cups (24 servings).

**Healthy** Each serving: 148 cal., 6 g total fat (2 g sat. fat), 11 mg chol., 124 mg sodium, 24 g carbo., 1 g fiber, 2 g pro. Daily Values: 6% vit. A, 4% vit. C, 5% calcium, 18% iron.

## Spicy Lime Snack Mix

**PREP:** 20 minutes **BAKE:** 20 minutes

- 4 cups bite-size shredded wheat biscuits
- 1½ cups chow mein noodles or pretzel sticks
- 1 cup peanuts
- 1 cup cashews
- 1 cup whole almonds
- ¼ cup finely chopped shallots
- ¼ cup butter, melted
- 1 Tbsp. finely shredded lime peel
- 2 Tbsp. fresh lime juice
- 1 serrano chile pepper, seeded and finely chopped*, or ½ teaspoon crushed red pepper
- 1 Tbsp. dried cilantro, crushed
- 1 tsp. garlic salt
- ½ tsp. onion salt
- ½ tsp. ground ancho chile pepper or chili powder

**1.** Preheat oven to 300° F. Line a 15×10×1-inch baking pan with foil; set aside.

**2.** In a large mixing bowl combine shredded wheat biscuits, chow mein noodles, peanuts, cashews, and almonds; set aside.

**3.** In a small saucepan cook shallots in hot butter until tender. Stir in lime peel, lime juice, serrano chile pepper, dried cilantro, garlic salt, onion salt, and ground ancho chile pepper; cook and stir 1 minute. Pour over cereal-nut mixture; toss to coat. Pour into prepared pan.

**4.** Bake for 20 minutes, stirring twice. Remove from oven. Spread mixture on a large piece of buttered foil to cool. Store in an airtight container for up to 3 days. Makes about 8 cups (16 servings).

***NOTE:** Use caution when handling chile peppers. Wear disposable gloves and wash your hands thoroughly after preparation.

Each serving: 242 cal., 18 g total fat (4 g sat. fat), 8 mg chol., 229 mg sodium, 16 g carbo., 3 g fiber, 7 g pro. Daily Values: 4% vit. A, 3% vit. C, 4% calcium, 9% iron.

# Menus

LOOKING FOR SOME ADDITIONAL MENU IDEAS? GIVE THESE MENUS STARRING THE PRIZEWINNING RECIPES A TRY.

# Menus for Family and Friends

While you'll find a menu based on each month's recipes throughout the book, the menus in this chapter are planned around the 2004 Prize Tested Recipes® from *Better Homes and Gardens®* magazine. Use the menus as they are, or pick and choose the recipes you want to prepare and add your own favorites to round out the meal.

# seasonal celebrations

WHAT BETTER WAY TO CELEBRATE EACH OF THE FOUR SEASONS OF THE YEAR THAN WITH A DINNER OR LUNCHEON PREPARED FOR FAMILY AND FRIENDS.

## SPRING SENSATIONS
Quick Thai Chicken Salad (page 297)
Gingered Lemon Scones (page 276)
Assorted fresh fruit platter
Chocolate-Cherry-Chip Cookies (page 257)
Sweetened iced tea or iced coffee

## SUMMER SUNSHINE
Spicy Grilled Catfish (page 273)
Avocado Basil Pasta (page 264)
Purchased focaccia bread
Rhubarb-Strawberry Ice Cream (page 274)
Lemonade with lemon and/or lime wedges

## AUTUMN HARVEST
Curried Apple Pork Chops (page 296)
Biscuits served with herbed butter
Mixed greens salad with vinaigrette dressing
Relish tray
Graham Cracker Torte (page 266)
Hot apple cider or flavored coffee

## HOME FOR THE HOLIDAYS
Holiday Cranberry Salsa (page 299) served with
toasted pita chips or assorted crackers
Roast turkey or baked ham
Twice-baked potatoes
Curried Corn Pudding (page 286)
Dinner rolls served with butter
Lingonberry Cheesecake (page 292)
Hot coffee or hot chocolate

**Curried Apple Pork Chops**
(page 296)

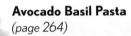

**Avocado Basil Pasta**
(page 264)

**Curried Corn Pudding**
(page 286)

# good ol' fashioned favorites

BRING BACK MEMORIES OF THOSE LUSCIOUS MEALS THAT MOM OR GRANDMA USED TO SERVE THE FAMILY AT EVERYDAY MEALS OR ON SPECIAL OCCASIONS.

## SUNDAY DINNER
Beef pot roast with carrots
Potato Sauté with Herbed Tomato Topping (page 295)
Steamed green beans
Crescent dinner rolls served with jam
Raisin-Apple Cake (page 267)
Iced tea, hot coffee, or hot tea

## ALL-AMERICAN CELEBRATION
Crunchy Munchies (page 302)
Honey 'n' Orange Back Ribs (page 280)
Scalloped potatoes or potato salad
Baked beans
Creamy Apple Pie (page 300)
Root beer

## COMFORTS OF THE COUNTRYSIDE
Oatmeal Meat Loaf Slices (page 260)
Corn, Apple, and Onion Gratin (page 287)
Cranberry-Pumpkin Mini Loaves (page 299) served with maple butter
Assorted fresh berries
Chocolate cake with chocolate frosting
Fruit-flavored iced tea

## BED-AND-BREAKFAST
Assorted cut-up fruit served with fruit dip
Rhubarb-Pecan Sticky Rolls (page 275)
Assorted mini muffins served with whipped butter and/or assorted jams
Sausage, Broccoli, and Eggs Brunch Casserole (page 263)
Skillet-cooked ham slices or crisp-cooked bacon strips
Fruit juice, milk, hot coffee, and/or hot tea

**Honey 'n' Orange Back Ribs**
*(page 280)*

**Oatmeal Meat Loaf Slices**
*(page 260)*

# outdoor adventures

EATING IN THE GREAT OUTDOORS—WHETHER IT'S IN THE BACKYARD, AT A NEARBY PARK, OR TAILGATING AT THE FOOTBALL STADIUM—IS AN ADVENTURE FOR BOTH THE YOUNG AND THE YOUNG AT HEART.

## PICNIC IN THE PARK
Cuban Burgers (page 292)
Calorie-Trimmed Potato Salad (page 278)
Fresh strawberries
Toasted Oat Granola Bars (page 261)
Lemonade and/or assorted soft drinks

## GAME-DAY TAILGATE
Picadillo Chili (page 291) served with shredded cheese
Grilled bratwurst and/or foot-long hot dogs served with sauerkraut
Purchased bakery buns
Corn chips and/or potato chips
Nutty Coleslaw (page 269)
Fudge brownies
Party Fruit Slush Punch (page 283)
Favorite nonalcohol beverages

## BACKYARD COOKOUT
Grilled steaks, hamburgers, and/or chicken breasts
Condiments
Purchased bakery bread or buns
Sliced tomatoes
Corn Smorgasbord (page 286)
Peanut Butter Bars (page 268)
Strawberry-lemonade or iced tea

## BUTTERFLY GARDEN BRUNCH
Double Cranberry Crostini (page 298)
French Toast Soufflé (page 263)
Chicken Sandwiches (page 284)
Fresh fruit kabobs or fresh fruit salad
Purchased shortbread and/or butter cookies
Hot or iced coffee, hot or iced tea

**Calorie-Trimmed Potato Salad**
*(page 278)*

**Corn Smorgasbord**
*(page 286)*

**Chicken Sandwiches**
*(page 284)*

# around the world

THERE'S NO NEED TO LEAVE THE COMFORTS OF HOME TO ENJOY SOME INTERNATIONAL FLAVORS. PREPARE ONE OF THESE MENUS IN YOUR KITCHEN FOR A GLOBAL TREAT.

## FIESTA OF FLAVORS
Guacamole Soup (page 259)
Spicy Grilled Chicken with Beans and Rice (page 285)
Corn bread squares
Tortilla chips with purchased fruit salsa
Peach-Raspberry Margaritas (page 283)

## ITALIAN ESCAPE
Deep-Dish Pizza (page 290)
Mixed greens salad with purchased Italian salad dressing
Fresh fruit and cheese
Italian Spice Cookies (page 293)
Dry red wine
Espresso or cappuccino

## TASTE OF THE TROPICS
Citrus-Glazed Salmon (page 272)
Steamed green beans
Orange-Ginger Fruit Salad (page 277)
Purchased bakery sweet bread
Coconut ice cream
Rum and Mango Slush (page 283)
Sparkling water

## GLORIOUSLY GREEK
Lamb-Stuffed Portobellos (page 270)
Tabbouleh salad or pasta salad
Toasted pita bread
Purchased baklava
Iced or hot tea

**Lamb-Stuffed Portobellos**
*(page 270)*

**Citrus-Glazed Salmon**
*(page 272)*

# especially
## sweet
## celebrations

WHEN IT'S TIME TO CELEBRATE A SPECIAL EVENT, SUCH AS A BIRTHDAY, ANNIVERSARY, BABY SHOWER, OR THE LAST DAY OF SCHOOL, INVITE GUESTS TO SHARE IN THE OCCASION.

## VERY BEST BIRTHDAY DINNER
Rhubarb Conserve (page 274) served with cheese and crackers
Cheese-Stuffed Chicken (page 284)
Steamed rice
Buttered asparagus spears
Birthday cake
Homemade or purchased ice cream
Coffee or milk

## SENTIMENTAL SHOWER
Assorted mixed nuts
Raspberry Blintz Casserole (page 262)
Pumpkin Spice Muffins (page 279) served with flavored cream cheese
Buttery Oatmeal Crisps (page 260)
Apricot Slush (page 282)
Hot or iced coffee

## ANNIVERSARY DINNER
Cherry-Chipotle Glazed Duck Breasts (page 289)
Ricotta and Roasted Red Pepper Pasta (page 265)
Mixed greens salad with purchased vinaigrette dressing
Sliced sourdough bread served with butter
Almond Cake in a Crust (page 266)
Wine or champagne

## JUST FOR KIDS
Tropical Snack Mix (page 302)
Grilled ham and cheese sandwiches
Carrot sticks, celery sticks, and sweet pepper strips served with bottled ranch dressing or vegetable dip
PB&C Cookie Sandwiches (page 256)
Chocolate milk

**PB&C Cookie Sandwiches**
*(page 256)*

**Almond Cake in a Crust**
*(page 266)*

**Apricot Slush**
*(page 282)*

# ANNUAL Recipes INDEX

# B

# D–E

# G

# H–I

# J–L

# T-Z

# Nutrition information.

With each recipe, we give important nutrition information you easily can apply to your own needs. You'll find the calorie count of each serving and the amount, in grams, of fat, saturated fat, cholesterol, sodium, carbohydrates, fiber, and protein to help you keep tabs on what you eat. You can check the levels of each recipe serving for vitamin A, vitamin C, calcium, and iron, if they are present. These are noted in percentages of the Daily Values. The Daily Values are dietary standards determined by the Food and Drug Administration (FDA). To stay in line with the nutrition breakdown of each recipe, follow the suggested number of servings.

# How we analyze.

The *Better Homes and Gardens*® Test Kitchen computer analyzes each recipe for the nutritional value of a single serving.

- The analysis does not include optional ingredients.
- We use the first serving size listed when a range is given. For example: If we say a recipe "Makes 4 to 6 servings," the nutrition information is based on 4 servings.
- When ingredient choices (such as butter or margarine) appear in a recipe, we use the first one mentioned for analysis. The ingredient order does not mean we prefer one ingredient over another.
- When milk and eggs are recipe ingredients, the analysis is calculated using 2 percent (reduced-fat) milk and large eggs.

# What you need.

The dietary guidelines below suggest nutrient levels that moderately active adults should strive to eat each day. There is no real harm in going over or under these guidelines in any single day, but it is a good idea to aim for a balanced diet over time.

Calories: About 2,000
Total fat: Less than 65 grams
Saturated fat: Less than 20 grams
Cholesterol: Less than 300 milligrams
Carbohydrates: About 300 grams
Sodium: Less than 2,400 milligrams
Dietary fiber: 20 to 30 grams